# Contents

*Spark plug condition and bodywork repair colour pages between pages 32 and 33*

**Lada Samara SL 5-door**

**Lada Samara Van**

# About this manual

## Its aim

The aim of this manual is to help you get the best value from your vehicle. It can do so in several ways. It can help you decide what work must be done (even should you choose to get it done by a garage), provide information on routine maintenance and servicing, and give a logical course of action and diagnosis when random faults occur. However, it is hoped that you will use the manual by tackling the work yourself. On simpler jobs it may even be quicker than booking the car into a garage and going there twice, to leave and collect it. Perhaps most important, a lot of money can be saved by avoiding the costs a garage must charge to cover its labour and overheads.

The manual has drawings and descriptions to show the function of the various components so that their layout can be understood. Then the tasks are described and photographed in a step-by-step sequence so that even a novice can do the work.

## Its arrangement

The manual is divided into eleven Chapters, each covering a logical sub-division of the vehicle. The Chapters are each divided into Sections, numbered with single figures, eg 5; and the Sections into paragraphs (or sub-sections), with decimal numbers following on from the Section they are in, eg 5.1, 5.2, 5.3 etc.

It is freely illustrated, especially in those parts where there is a detailed sequence of operations to be carried out. There are two forms of illustration: figures and photographs. The figures are numbered in sequence with decimal numbers, according to their position in the Chapter – eg Fig. 6.4 is the fourth drawing /illustration in Chapter 6. Photographs carry the same number (either individually or in related groups) as the Section or sub-section to which they relate.

There is an alphabetical index at the back of the manual as well as a contents list at the front. Each Chapter is also preceded by its own individual contents list.

References to the 'left' or 'right' of the vehicle are in the sense of a person in the driver's seat facing forwards.

Unless otherwise stated, nuts and bolts are removed by turning anti-clockwise, and tightened by turning clockwise.

Vehicle manufacturers continually make changes to specifications and recommendations, and these, when notified, are incorporated into our manuals at the earliest opportunity.

**Whilst every care is taken to ensure that the information in this manual is correct, no liability can be accepted by the authors or publishers for loss, damage or injury caused by any errors in, or omissions from, the information given.**

## Project vehicles

The project vehicle used in the preparation of this manual and appearing in the photographic sequences was a 1989 Lada Samara 1500SLX.

# Introduction to the Lada Samara

The VAZ (Volga Auto Works) factory at Togliatti, situated by the River Volga 600 miles east of Moscow, was opened in 1970. It is the largest car plant in Europe with 25 million square feet of space and produces 750,000 Lada vehicles each year.

Named after a tributary of the Volga, the Samara is the first Lada with front-wheel-drive and rack and pinion steering. It features UK-designed components (principally from AP) in its drive train and braking system and follows current conventions in European car design but is otherwise USSR-designed and built. During development, the Samara was tested in conditions ranging from Siberian winters to the Kara-Kum desert.

On import to the UK the vehicles are given a thorough check at Lada Cars' site at Carnaby, near Bridlington. On the higher-specification versions, certain UK-built items of trim are fitted.

The Samara is a conventional three or five-door Hatchback with an overhead camshaft engine (of 1100, 1300 or 1500 cc capacity) and five-speed transmission mounted transversely at the front of the vehicle. It features fully-independent MacPherson strut front suspension and semi-independent torsion beam axle rear suspension, rack and pinion steering and vacuum servo-assisted braking system (discs front, drums rear). The interior trim and equipment level is well up to the standards of the vehicle's class.

# General dimensions, weights and capacities

## Dimensions

| | |
|---|---|
| Overall length | 4006 mm (157.7 in) |
| Overall width | 1880 mm (74.0 in) |
| Overall height: | |
|     Early L models, Van | 1335 mm (52.6 in) |
|     Later L models, SL, SLX | 1315 mm (51.8 in) |
| Wheelbase | 2460 mm (96.9 in) |
| Front track | 1400 mm (55.1 in) |
| Rear track | 1370 mm (53.9 in) |
| Ground clearance | 152 mm (6.0 in) |
| Turning circle | 10.0 m (32.8 ft) |

## Weights

| | |
|---|---|
| Kerb weight (vehicle unladen, but with coolant and all fluids, full fuel tank, spare wheel and tool kit): | |
|     3-door, Van | 900 kg (1984 lb/17.7 cwt) |
|     5-door | 915 kg (2017 lb/18.0 cwt) |
| Maximum gross vehicle weight: | |
|     3-door, Van | 1325 kg (2921 lb/26.1 cwt) |
|     5-door | 1340 kg (2954 lb/26.4 cwt) |
| Maximum towing weight (braked trailer): | |
|     1100 | 843 kg (1859 lb/16.6 cwt) |
|     1300 (including Van) | 894 kg (1971 lb/17.6 cwt) |
|     1500 (including Van) | 945 kg (2083 lb/18.6 cwt) |
| Maximum towing hitch downward load | 50 kg (110 lb) |
| Payload (including driver) | 425 kg (937 lb/8.4 cwt) |

## Capacities

| | |
|---|---|
| Engine oil (including filter) | 3.5 litres (6.2 Imp pints) |
| Cooling system | 7.8 litres (13.7 Imp pints) |
| Fuel tank | 43 litres (9.5 Imp gallons) |
| Transmission oil | 3.0 litres (5.3 Imp pints) |

# Jacking, towing and wheel changing

## Jacking and wheel changing

With the vehicle parked on firm, level ground, apply the handbrake firmly and select first or reverse gear. Ask any passengers to get out of the vehicle and stay clear, then remove the jack, tools and spare roadwheel from the luggage compartment.

Remove the roadwheel trim (where fitted) and slacken the roadwheel bolts through half to one turn each, working in a diagonal sequence. Using chalk or similar, mark the relationship of the roadwheel to the hub.

Place chocks at the front and rear of the roadwheel diagonally opposite the one to be removed, then engage the jack arm in the jacking point (photo) nearest the roadwheel to be removed, ensure that the jack base rests on a firm surface, and jack up the vehicle.

Unscrew the roadwheel bolts and remove the wheel. Check that the threads and wheel-to-hub mating surfaces are clean and undamaged. The threads may be cleaned with a brass wire brush if rusty. Apply a thin smear of anti-seize compound (Holts Copaslip) to the threads (and also to the roadwheel/hub mating surfaces) to prevent the formation of corrosion. Clean the inside of the roadwheel.

On refitting, align the marks made on removal (if the same roadwheel is being refitted) and locate the roadwheel on its guide pins, insert the bolts and tighten them as much as possible by hand.

Lower the vehicle to the ground, remove the jack and tighten the bolts, working in progressive stages and in a diagonal sequence, to the specified torque wrench setting (photo). If a torque wrench is not available, have the tightness of the nuts checked as soon as possible. Check the tyre pressure.

Refit the roadwheel trim (where fitted), remove the chocks and stow the jack and tools. If a new roadwheel has been fitted have it balanced as soon as possible.

## Servicing

**Note**: *Never work under a vehicle that is supported only by the car jack supplied, which is intended only for changing roadwheels at the roadside (see above). The vehicle must **always** be supported by axle stands at least during servicing work.*

When raising the vehicle for servicing work, preferably use a trolley or hydraulic jack with a wooden block as an insulator to prevent damage to the underbody. Place the jack under a flat and reinforced part of the underbody, either a chassis box-section or next to a suspension mounting point. **Do not** jack up the vehicle by a suspension component or on the engine/transmission. It may be necessary to raise the vehicle in stages, jacking one side at a time and then supporting it while the opposite side is raised.

It is preferable that the vehicle is placed over an inspection pit or raised on a lift. When such equipment is not available, use ramps or jack up the vehicle, but **always** supplement the lifting device with axle stands.

## Towing

Towing hooks are provided at front and rear of the vehicle (photos). The rear towing hook should be used only for emergency towing of another vehicle. For trailer towing a properly fitted towing bracket is required.

If the vehicle is to be towed, arrange it so that the front roadwheels are clear of the ground and check that the handbrake is released. If the vehicle must be towed with the rear roadwheels clear of the ground, use a towing dolly to keep the front roadwheels clear of the ground as well.

If the vehicle must be towed with all four roadwheels on the ground, insert the ignition key and switch on to ensure that the steering is unlocked and that the lamps, direction indicators and horn can be used. Expect to apply greater than usual pressure to the brake pedal as vacuum servo assistance will not be available.

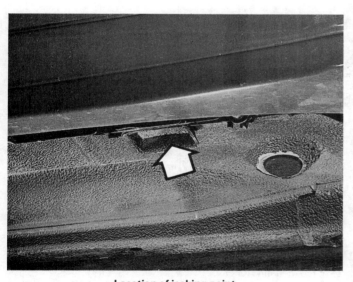

**Location of jacking point**

**Roadwheel nuts should be tightened to specified torque setting**

**Front towing hook**

**Rear towing hook**

# Buying spare parts and vehicle identification numbers

## Buying spare parts

Spare parts are available from many sources, for example: Lada garages, other garages and accessory shops, and motor factors. Our advice regarding spare part sources is as follows.

*Officially appointed Lada garages* – This is the best source for parts which are peculiar to your car, and are not generally available (eg complete cylinder heads, internal gearbox components, badges, interior trim etc). It is also the only place at which you should buy parts if the vehicle is still under warranty. To be sure of obtaining the correct parts, it will always be necessary to give the storeman your car's vehicle identification number, and if possible, take the old parts along for positive identification. Many parts are available under a factory exchange scheme, but any parts returned should always be clean. It obviously makes good sense to go straight to the specialists on your car for this type of part, as they are best equipped to supply you.

*Other garages and accessory shops* – These are often very good places to buy materials and components needed for the maintenance of your car (eg oil filters, spark plugs, bulbs, drivebelts, oils and greases, touch-up paint, filler paste etc). They also sell general accessories, usually have convenient opening hours, charge lower prices and can often be found not far from home.

*Motor factors* – Good factors will stock all of the more important components which wear out relatively quickly (eg exhaust systems. brake pads, seals and hydraulic parts, clutch components, bearing shells, pistons, valves etc). Motor factors will often provide new or reconditioned components on a part exchange basis – this can save a considerable amount of money.

## Vehicle identification numbers

Modifications are a continuing and unpublicised process in vehicle manufacture, quite apart from major model changes. Spare parts manuals and lists are compiled upon a numerical basis, the individual vehicle numbers being essential to correct identification of the component concerned.

When ordering spare parts, always give as much information as possible. Quote the car model, year of manufacture, body and engine numbers as appropriate.

The vehicle identification number is stamped on a plate riveted to the right-hand side of the engine compartment bulkhead (photo).

The body number is stamped on the front suspension right-hand strut top mounting (photo).

The engine number is stamped into the cylinder block/crankcase, just above the bellhousing (photo).

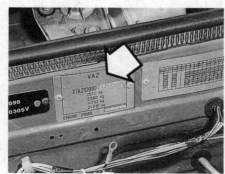
**Location of vehicle identification plate**

**Location of body number**

**Location of engine number**

# General repair procedures

Whenever servicing, repair or overhaul work is carried out on the car or its components, it is necessary to observe the following procedures and instructions. This will assist in carrying out the operation efficiently and to a professional standard of workmanship.

### Joint mating faces and gaskets

Where a gasket is used between the mating faces of two components, ensure that it is renewed on reassembly, and fit it dry unless otherwise stated in the repair procedure. Make sure that the mating faces are clean and dry with all traces of old gasket removed. When cleaning a joint face, use a tool which is not likely to score or damage the face, and remove any burrs or nicks with an oilstone or fine file.

Make sure that tapped holes are cleaned with a pipe cleaner, and keep them free of jointing compound if this is being used unless specifically instructed otherwise.

Ensure that all orifices, channels or pipes are clear and blow through them, preferably using compressed air.

### Oil seals

Whenever an oil seal is removed from its working location, either individually or as part of an assembly, it should be renewed.

The very fine sealing lip of the seal is easily damaged and will not seal if the surface it contacts is not completely clean and free from scratches, nicks or grooves. If the original sealing surface of the component cannot be restored, the component should be renewed.

Protect the lips of the seal from any surface which may damage them in the course of fitting. Use tape or a conical sleeve where possible. Lubricate the seal lips with oil before fitting and, on dual lipped seals, fill the space between the lips with grease.

Unless otherwise stated, oil seals must be fitted with their sealing lips toward the lubricant to be sealed.

Use a tubular drift or block of wood of the appropriate size to install the seal and, if the seal housing is shouldered, drive the seal down to the shoulder. If the seal housing is unshouldered, the seal should be fitted with its face flush with the housing top face.

### Screw threads and fastenings

Always ensure that a blind tapped hole is completely free from oil, grease, water or other fluid before installing the bolt or stud. Failure to do this could cause the housing to crack due to the hydraulic action of the bolt or stud as it is screwed in.

When tightening a castellated nut to accept a split pin, tighten the nut to the specified torque, where applicable, and then tighten further to the next split pin hole. Never slacken the nut to align a split pin hole unless stated in the repair procedure.

When checking or retightening a nut or bolt to a specified torque setting, slacken the nut or bolt by a quarter of a turn, and then retighten to the specified setting.

### Locknuts, locktabs and washers

Any fastening which will rotate against a component or housing in the course of tightening should always have a washer between it and the relevant component or housing.

Spring or split washers should always be renewed when they are used to lock a critical component such as a big-end bearing retaining nut or bolt.

Locktabs which are folded over to retain a nut or bolt should always be renewed.

Self-locking nuts can be reused in non-critical areas, providing resistance can be felt when the locking portion passes over the bolt or stud thread.

Split pins must always be replaced with new ones of the correct size for the hole.

### Special tools

Some repair procedures in this manual entail the use of special tools such as a press, two or three-legged pullers, spring compressors etc. Wherever possible, suitable readily available alternatives to the manufacturer's special tools are described, and are shown in use. In some instances, where no alternative is possible, it has been necessary to resort to the use of a manufacturer's tool and this has been done for reasons of safety as well as the efficient completion of the repair operation. Unless you are highly skilled and have a thorough understanding of the procedure described, never attempt to bypass the use of any special tool when the procedure described specifies its use. Not only is there a very great risk of personal injury, but expensive damage could be caused to the components involved.

# Tools and working facilities

## Introduction

A selection of good tools is a fundamental requirement for anyone contemplating the maintenance and repair of a motor vehicle. For the owner who does not possess any, their purchase will prove a considerable expense, offsetting some of the savings made by doing-it-yourself. However, provided that the tools purchased meet the relevant national safety standards and are of good quality, they will last for many years and prove an extremely worthwhile investment.

To help the average owner to decide which tools are needed to carry out the various tasks detailed in this manual, we have compiled three lists of tools under the following headings: *Maintenance and minor repair, Repair and overhaul,* and *Special.* The newcomer to practical mechanics should start off with the *Maintenance and minor repair* tool kit and confine himself to the simpler jobs around the vehicle. Then, as his confidence and experience grow, he can undertake more difficult tasks, buying extra tools as, and when, they are needed. In this way, a *Maintenance and minor repair* tool kit can be built-up into a *Repair and overhaul* tool kit over a considerable period of time without any major cash outlays. The experienced do-it-yourselfer will have a tool kit good enough for most repair and overhaul procedures and will add tools from the *Special* category when he feels the expense is justified by the amount of use to which these tools will be put.

It is obviously not possible to cover the subject of tools fully here. For those who wish to learn more about tools and their use there is a book entitled *How to Choose and Use Car Tools* available from the publishers of this manual.

## Maintenance and minor repair tool kit

The tools given in this list should be considered as a minimum requirement if routine maintenance, servicing and minor repair operations are to be undertaken. We recommend the purchase of combination spanners (ring one end, open-ended the other); although more expensive than open-ended ones, they do give the advantages of both types of spanner.

*Combination spanners – 10, 11, 12, 13, 14 & 17 mm*
*Adjustable spanner – 9 inch*
*Spark plug spanner (with rubber insert)*
*Spark plug gap adjustment tool*
*Set of feeler gauges*
*Brake bleed nipple spanner*
*Screwdriver – 4 in long x ¼ in dia (flat blade)*
*Screwdriver – 4 in long x ¼ in dia (cross blade)*
*Combination pliers – 6 inch*
*Hacksaw (junior)*
*Tyre pump*
*Tyre pressure gauge*
*Oil can*
*Oil filter removal tool*
*Fine emery cloth (1 sheet)*
*Wire brush (small)*
*Funnel (medium size)*

## Repair and overhaul tool kit

These tools are virtually essential for anyone undertaking any major repairs to a motor vehicle, and are additional to those given in the *Maintenance and minor repair* list. Included in this list is a comprehensive set of sockets. Although these are expensive they will be found invaluable as they are so versatile – particularly if various drives are included in the set. We recommend the $\frac{1}{2}$ in square-drive type, as this can be used with most proprietary torque wrenches. If you cannot afford a socket set, even bought piecemeal, then inexpensive tubular box spanners are a useful alternative.

The tools in this list will occasionally need to be supplemented by tools from the *Special* list.

*Sockets (or box spanners) to cover range in previous list*
*Reversible ratchet drive (for use with sockets)*
*Extension piece, 10 inch (for use with sockets)*
*Universal joint (for use with sockets)*
*Torque wrench (for use with sockets)*
*Self-locking grips*
*Ball pein hammer*
*Soft-faced hammer, plastic or rubber*
*Screwdriver – 6 in long x $\frac{5}{16}$ in dia (flat blade)*
*Screwdriver – 2 in long x $\frac{5}{16}$ in square (flat blade)*
*Screwdriver – 1½ in long x ¼ in dia (cross blade)*
*Screwdriver – 3 in long x $\frac{1}{8}$ in dia (electricians)*
*Pliers – electricians side cutters*
*Pliers – needle nosed*
*Pliers – circlip (internal and external)*
*Cold chisel – ½ inch*
*Scriber*
*Scraper*
*Centre punch*
*Pin punch*
*Hacksaw*
*Steel rule/straight-edge*
*Allen keys (inc. splined/Torx type if necessary)*
*Selection of files*
*Wire brush (large)*
*Axle-stands*
*Jack (strong trolley or hydraulic type)*
*Light with extension lead*

## Special tools

The tools in this list are those which are not used regularly, are expensive to buy, or which need to be used in accordance with their manufacturers' instructions. Unless relatively difficult mechanical jobs are undertaken frequently, it will not be economic to buy many of these tools. Where this is the case, you could consider clubbing together with friends (or joining a motorists' club) to make a joint purchase, or borrowing the tools against a deposit from a local garage or tool hire specialist.

The following list contains only those tools and instruments freely available to the public, and not those special tools produced by the vehicle manufacturer specifically for its dealer network. You will find occasional references to these manufacturers' special tools in the text of this manual. Generally, an alternative method of doing the job without the vehicle manufacturers' special tool is given. However, sometimes, there is no alternative to using them. Where this is the case and the relevant tool cannot be bought or borrowed, you will have to entrust the work to a franchised garage.

Valve spring compressor (where applicable)
Coil spring compressors
Piston ring compressor
Balljoint separator
Universal hub/bearing puller
Impact screwdriver
Micrometer and/or vernier gauge
Dial gauge
Stroboscopic timing light
Tachometer
Universal electrical multi-meter
Cylinder compression gauge
Lifting tackle
Trolley jack

## Buying tools

For practically all tools, a tool factor is the best source since he will have a very comprehensive range compared with the average garage or accessory shop. Having said that, accessory shops often offer excellent quality tools at discount prices, so it pays to shop around.

There are plenty of good tools around at reasonable prices, but always aim to purchase items which meet the relevant national safety standards. If in doubt, ask the proprietor or manager of the shop for advice before making a purchase.

## Care and maintenance of tools

Having purchased a reasonable tool kit, it is necessary to keep the tools in a clean serviceable condition. After use, always wipe off any dirt, grease and metal particles using a clean, dry cloth, before putting the tools away. Never leave them lying around after they have been used. A simple tool rack on the garage or workshop wall, for items such as screwdrivers and pliers is a good idea. Store all normal wrenches and sockets in a metal box. Any measuring instruments, gauges, meters, etc, must be carefully stored where they cannot be damaged or become rusty.

Take a little care when tools are used. Hammer heads inevitably become marked and screwdrivers lose the keen edge on their blades from time to time. A little timely attention with emery cloth or a file will soon restore items like this to a good serviceable finish.

## Working facilities

Not to be forgotten when discussing tools, is the workshop itself. If anything more than routine maintenance is to be carried out, some form of suitable working area becomes essential.

It is appreciated that many an owner mechanic is forced by circumstances to remove an engine or similar item, without the benefit of a garage or workshop. Having done this, any repairs should always be done under the cover of a roof.

Wherever possible, any dismantling should be done on a clean, flat workbench or table at a suitable working height.

Any workbench needs a vice: one with a jaw opening of 4 in (100 mm) is suitable for most jobs. As mentioned previously, some clean dry storage space is also required for tools, as well as for lubricants, cleaning fluids, touch-up paints and so on, which become necessary.

Another item which may be required, and which has a much more general usage, is an electric drill with a chuck capacity of at least $\frac{5}{16}$ in (8 mm). This, together with a good range of twist drills, is virtually essential for fitting accessories such as mirrors and reversing lights.

Last, but not least, always keep a supply of old newspapers and clean, lint-free rags available, and try to keep any working area as clean as possible.

## Spanner jaw gap comparison table

| Jaw gap (in) | Spanner size |
|---|---|
| 0.250 | $\frac{1}{4}$ in AF |
| 0.276 | 7 mm |
| 0.313 | $\frac{5}{16}$ in AF |
| 0.315 | 8 mm |
| 0.344 | $\frac{11}{32}$ in AF; $\frac{1}{8}$ in Whitworth |
| 0.354 | 9 mm |
| 0.375 | $\frac{3}{8}$ in AF |
| 0.394 | 10 mm |
| 0.433 | 11 mm |
| 0.438 | $\frac{7}{16}$ in AF |
| 0.445 | $\frac{3}{16}$ in Whitworth; $\frac{1}{4}$ in BSF |
| 0.472 | 12 mm |
| 0.500 | $\frac{1}{2}$ in AF |
| 0.512 | 13 mm |
| 0.525 | $\frac{1}{4}$ in Whitworth; $\frac{5}{16}$ in BSF |
| 0.551 | 14 mm |
| 0.563 | $\frac{9}{16}$ in AF |
| 0.591 | 15 mm |
| 0.600 | $\frac{5}{16}$ in Whitworth; $\frac{3}{8}$ in BSF |
| 0.625 | $\frac{5}{8}$ in AF |
| 0.630 | 16 mm |
| 0.669 | 17 mm |
| 0.686 | $\frac{11}{16}$ in AF |
| 0.709 | 18 mm |
| 0.710 | $\frac{3}{8}$ in Whitworth; $\frac{7}{16}$ in BSF |
| 0.748 | 19 mm |
| 0.750 | $\frac{3}{4}$ in AF |
| 0.813 | $\frac{13}{16}$ in AF |
| 0.820 | $\frac{7}{16}$ in Whitworth; $\frac{1}{2}$ in BSF |
| 0.866 | 22 mm |
| 0.875 | $\frac{7}{8}$ in AF |
| 0.920 | $\frac{1}{2}$ in Whitworth; $\frac{9}{16}$ in BSF |
| 0.938 | $\frac{15}{16}$ in AF |
| 0.945 | 24 mm |
| 1.000 | 1 in AF |
| 1.010 | $\frac{9}{16}$ in Whitworth; $\frac{5}{8}$ in BSF |
| 1.024 | 26 mm |
| 1.063 | $1\frac{1}{16}$ in AF; 27 mm |
| 1.100 | $\frac{5}{8}$ in Whitworth; $\frac{11}{16}$ in BSF |
| 1.125 | $1\frac{1}{8}$ in AF |
| 1.181 | 30 mm |
| 1.200 | $\frac{11}{16}$ in Whitworth; $\frac{3}{4}$ in BSF |
| 1.250 | $1\frac{1}{4}$ in AF |
| 1.260 | 32 mm |
| 1.300 | $\frac{3}{4}$ in Whitworth; $\frac{7}{8}$ in BSF |
| 1.313 | $1\frac{5}{16}$ in AF |
| 1.390 | $\frac{13}{16}$ in Whitworth; $\frac{15}{16}$ in BSF |
| 1.417 | 36 mm |
| 1.438 | $1\frac{7}{16}$ in AF |
| 1.480 | $\frac{7}{8}$ in Whitworth; 1 in BSF |
| 1.500 | $1\frac{1}{2}$ in AF |
| 1.575 | 40 mm; $\frac{15}{16}$ in Whitworth |
| 1.614 | 41 mm |
| 1.625 | $1\frac{5}{8}$ in AF |
| 1.670 | 1 in Whitworth; $1\frac{1}{8}$ in BSF |
| 1.688 | $1\frac{11}{16}$ in AF |
| 1.811 | 46 mm |
| 1.813 | $1\frac{13}{16}$ in AF |
| 1.860 | $1\frac{1}{8}$ in Whitworth; $1\frac{1}{4}$ in BSF |
| 1.875 | $1\frac{7}{8}$ in AF |
| 1.969 | 50 mm |
| 2.000 | 2 in AF |
| 2.050 | $1\frac{1}{4}$ in Whitworth; $1\frac{3}{8}$ in BSF |
| 2.165 | 55 mm |
| 2.362 | 60 mm |

# Safety first!

Professional motor mechanics are trained in safe working procedures. However enthusiastic you may be about getting on with the job in hand, do take the time to ensure that your safety is not put at risk. A moment's lack of attention can result in an accident, as can failure to observe certain elementary precautions.

There will always be new ways of having accidents, and the following points do not pretend to be a comprehensive list of all dangers; they are intended rather to make you aware of the risks and to encourage a safety-conscious approach to all work you carry out on your vehicle.

## Essential DOs and DON'Ts

**DON'T** rely on a single jack when working underneath the vehicle. Always use reliable additional means of support, such as axle stands, securely placed under a part of the vehicle that you know will not give way.

**DON'T** attempt to loosen or tighten high-torque nuts (e.g. wheel hub nuts) while the vehicle is on a jack; it may be pulled off.

**DON'T** start the engine without first ascertaining that the transmission is in neutral (or 'Park' where applicable) and the parking brake applied.

**DON'T** suddenly remove the filler cap from a hot cooling system – cover it with a cloth and release the pressure gradually first, or you may get scalded by escaping coolant.

**DON'T** attempt to drain oil until you are sure it has cooled sufficiently to avoid scalding you.

**DON'T** grasp any part of the engine, exhaust or catalytic converter without first ascertaining that it is sufficiently cool to avoid burning you.

**DON'T** allow brake fluid or antifreeze to contact vehicle paintwork.

**DON'T** syphon toxic liquids such as fuel, brake fluid or antifreeze by mouth, or allow them to remain on your skin.

**DON'T** inhale dust – it may be injurious to health (see *Asbestos* below).

**DON'T** allow any spilt oil or grease to remain on the floor – wipe it up straight away, before someone slips on it.

**DON'T** use ill-fitting spanners or other tools which may slip and cause injury.

**DON'T** attempt to lift a heavy component which may be beyond your capability – get assistance.

**DON'T** rush to finish a job, or take unverified short cuts.

**DON'T** allow children or animals in or around an unattended vehicle.

**DO** wear eye protection when using power tools such as drill, sander, bench grinder etc, and when working under the vehicle.

**DO** use a barrier cream on your hands prior to undertaking dirty jobs – it will protect your skin from infection as well as making the dirt easier to remove afterwards; but make sure your hands aren't left slippery. Note that long-term contact with used engine oil can be a health hazard.

**DO** keep loose clothing (cuffs, tie etc) and long hair well out of the way of moving mechanical parts.

**DO** remove rings, wristwatch etc, before working on the vehicle – especially the electrical system.

**DO** ensure that any lifting tackle used has a safe working load rating adequate for the job.

**DO** keep your work area tidy – it is only too easy to fall over articles left lying around.

**DO** get someone to check periodically that all is well, when working alone on the vehicle.

**DO** carry out work in a logical sequence and check that everything is correctly assembled and tightened afterwards.

**DO** remember that your vehicle's safety affects that of yourself and others. If in doubt on any point, get specialist advice.

**IF,** in spite of following these precautions, you are unfortunate enough to injure yourself, seek medical attention as soon as possible.

## Asbestos

Certain friction, insulating, sealing, and other products – such as brake linings, brake bands, clutch linings, torque converters, gaskets, etc – contain asbestos. *Extreme care must be taken to avoid inhalation of dust from such products since it is hazardous to health.* If in doubt, assume that they *do* contain asbestos.

## Fire

Remember at all times that petrol (gasoline) is highly flammable. Never smoke, or have any kind of naked flame around, when working on the vehicle. But the risk does not end there – a spark caused by an electrical short-circuit, by two metal surfaces contacting each other, by careless use of tools, or even by static electricity built up in your body under certain conditions, can ignite petrol vapour, which in a confined space is highly explosive.

Always disconnect the battery earth (ground) terminal before working on any part of the fuel or electrical system, and never risk spilling fuel on to a hot engine or exhaust.

It is recommended that a fire extinguisher of a type suitable for fuel and electrical fires is kept handy in the garage or workplace at all times. Never try to extinguish a fuel or electrical fire with water.

**Note:** *Any reference to a 'torch' appearing in this manual should always be taken to mean a hand-held battery-operated electric lamp or flashlight. It does NOT mean a welding/gas torch or blowlamp.*

## Fumes

Certain fumes are highly toxic and can quickly cause unconsciousness and even death if inhaled to any extent. Petrol (gasoline) vapour comes into this category, as do the vapours from certain solvents such as trichloroethylene. Any draining or pouring of such volatile fluids should be done in a well ventilated area.

When using cleaning fluids and solvents, read the instructions carefully. Never use materials from unmarked containers – they may give off poisonous vapours.

Never run the engine of a motor vehicle in an enclosed space such as a garage. Exhaust fumes contain carbon monoxide which is extremely poisonous; if you need to run the engine, always do so in the open air or at least have the rear of the vehicle outside the workplace.

If you are fortunate enough to have the use of an inspection pit, never drain or pour petrol, and never run the engine, while the vehicle is standing over it; the fumes, being heavier than air, will concentrate in the pit with possibly lethal results.

## The battery

Never cause a spark, or allow a naked light, near the vehicle's battery. It will normally be giving off a certain amount of hydrogen gas, which is highly explosive.

Always disconnect the battery earth (ground) terminal before working on the fuel or electrical systems.

If possible, loosen the filler plugs or cover when charging the battery from an external source. Do not charge at an excessive rate or the battery may burst.

Take care when topping up and when carrying the battery. The acid electrolyte, even when diluted, is very corrosive and should not be allowed to contact the eyes or skin.

If you ever need to prepare electrolyte yourself, always add the acid slowly to the water, and never the other way round. Protect against splashes by wearing rubber gloves and goggles.

When jump starting a car using a booster battery, for negative earth (ground) vehicles, connect the jump leads in the following sequence: First connect one jump lead between the positive (+) terminals of the two batteries. Then connect the other jump lead first to the negative (–) terminal of the booster battery, and then to a good earthing (ground) point on the vehicle to be started, at least 18 in (45 cm) from the battery if possible. Ensure that hands and jump leads are clear of any moving parts, and that the two vehicles do not touch. Disconnect the leads in the reverse order.

## Mains electricity and electrical equipment

When using an electric power tool, inspection light etc, always ensure that the appliance is correctly connected to its plug and that, where necessary, it is properly earthed (grounded). Do not use such appliances in damp conditions and, again, beware of creating a spark or applying excessive heat in the vicinity of fuel or fuel vapour. Also ensure that the appliances meet the relevant national safety standards.

## Ignition HT voltage

A severe electric shock can result from touching certain parts of the ignition system, such as the HT leads, when the engine is running or being cranked, particularly if components are damp or the insulation is defective. Where an electronic ignition system is fitted, the HT voltage is much higher and could prove fatal.

# Routine maintenance

Maintenance is essential for ensuring safety, and desirable for the purpose of getting the best in terms of performance and economy from your vehicle. Over the years, the need for periodic lubrication has been greatly reduced, if not totally eliminated. This has unfortunately tended to lead some owners to think that because no such action is required, the items either no longer exist, or will last forever. This is certainly not the case; it is essential to carry out regular visual examination as comprehensively as possible, in order to spot any potential defects at an early stage before they develop into major expensive repairs.

The following service schedules are a list of the maintenance requirements, and the intervals at which they should be carried out, as recommended by the manufacturers. Where applicable, these procedures are covered in greater detail near the beginning of each relevant Chapter.

**Daily**

Check the operation of all controls, gauges and lamps (interior and exterior)

**Every 300 miles (500 km) or weekly – whichever occurs first**

## Engine, cooling system, steering and brakes
Check the engine oil level and top up if necessary
Check the coolant level and top up if necessary
Check the brake fluid level and top up if necessary

## Lamps and wipers
Check the operation of all lamps, wipers and washers
Check the windscreen and tailgate glass washer/wiper system
Check and if necessary top up the battery electrolyte level

## Tyres
Check the tyre pressures (including the spare)
Visually examine the tyres for wear or damage – make a careful check at monthly intervals

## Bodywork
Wash and polish (especially in winter) – at monthly intervals check for damage to the paintwork and touch up or repair where necessary

**Every 9000 miles (15 000 km) or 12 months – whichever occurs first**

## Engine (Chapter 1)
Change the engine oil and filter
Check the timing belt tension and condition

## Cooling system (Chapter 2)
Check the coolant level
Check for leaks all radiator and heater hoses
Have the coolant specific gravity checked

## Fuel and exhaust systems (Chapter 3)
Renew the air cleaner filter element
Renew the fuel filter

Clean the carburettor and fuel pump filters
Check the tightness of the manifold and carburettor mounting nuts and carburettor top mounting screws
Lubricate the accelerator and choke cables and carburettor linkage
Check and adjust the idle speed and mixture
Check the exhaust system
Clean the crankcase emission control system

## Ignition system (Chapter 4)
Check the spark plugs
Check the ignition timing

## Clutch (Chapter 5)
Lubricate the clutch cable
Check and adjust the clutch pedal travel

## Transmission (Chapter 6)
Check for oil leaks
Check the transmission oil level

## Driveshafts (Chapter 7)
Check the driveshafts and joints

## Braking system (Chapter 8)
Check the brake hydraulic fluid level
Check the adjustment of the brake pedal and stop-lamp switch
Check the operation of the vacuum servo unit
Check the metal hydraulic pipes and flexible hoses
Check the brake pads and the caliper operation
Check the brake shoes and the wheel cylinder condition
Check the pressure regulator operation and condition
Check the handbrake operation and adjustment

## Suspension and steering (Chapter 9)
Check the steering gear and linkage
Check the suspension, roadwheels and tyres

## Bodywork (Chapter 10)
Check the hinges, locks and door catches
Check the seat belts

## Electrical system (Chapter 11)
Check the alternator drivebelt
Check the battery electrolyte level and terminals
Check the charging rate
Check the operation of all instruments, lights and controls
Check the headlamp beam alignment

**Every 18 000 miles (30 000 km) or 24 months – whichever occurs first**

In addition to the items in the 12-monthly service, carry out the following:

## Engine (Chapter 1)
Check the valve clearances

## Ignition system (Chapter 4)
Renew the spark plugs

**Engine and underbonnet component locations (air cleaner removed)**

1 Vehicle identification plate
2 Windscreen wiper motor
3 Heater fan motor
4 Fuse and relay unit
5 Inspection lamp socket
6 Cooling system expansion tank
7 Battery negative terminal
8 Battery positive terminal
9 Bonnet release cable
10 Engine oil filler cap
11 Engine oil level dipstick
12 Alternator
13 Windscreen/tailgate glass washer system solenoid valves

14 Headlamp beam alignment knob
15 Windscreen/tailgate glass washer system fluid reservoir
16 Body number
17 Front suspension strut top mounting
18 Carburettor
19 Fuel return one-way valve
20 Fuel pump
21 Braking system master cylinder fluid reservoir
22 Starter motor auxiliary relay
23 Diagnostic socket
24 Fuel cut-off system control module
25 Ignition amplifier module
26 Ignition HT coil
27 Spark plug HT leads

**Front underbody view (engine compartment undershields removed)**

1  Front bumper end mounting
2  Front towing hook
3  Front suspension tie-bar
4  Reversing lamp switch
5  Starter motor
6  Radiator electric cooling fan
7  Engine/transmission front
   mounting
8  Alternator
9  Front brake caliper
10 Front suspension lower arm
   balljoint

11 Front suspension lower arm
12 Anti-roll bar
13 Oil filter
14 Sump drain plug
15 Right-hand driveshaft
16 Exhaust system downpipe
17 Gearchange control rod
18 Transmission oil drain plug
19 Left-hand driveshaft
20 Engine/transmission rear
   mounting

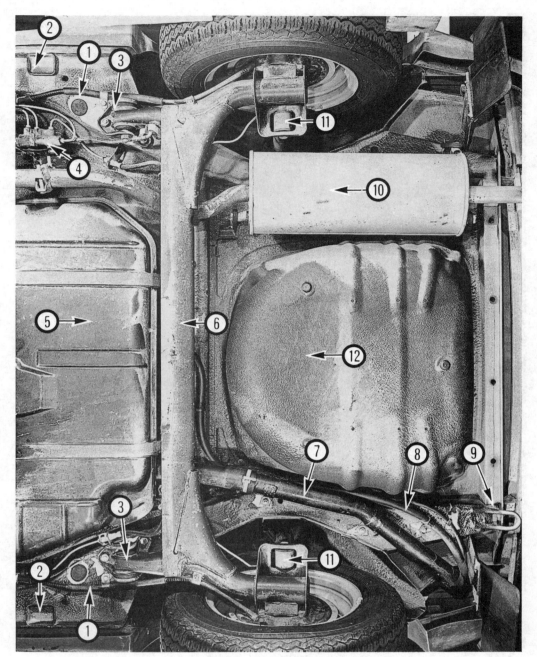

**Rear underbody view**

1  Handbrake cable
2  Jacking point
3  Rear suspension pivot
4  Braking system pressure
   regulator
5  Fuel tank
6  Rear suspension torsion
   beam axle
7  Fuel tank filler tube

8  Fuel tank and separator
   breather hoses
9  Rear towing hook
10 Exhaust system tailpipe
   and main silencer
11 Rear suspension unit
   bottom mounting
12 Spare wheel well

**Every 27 000 miles (45 000 km) or 36 months – whichever occurs first**

In addition to all the items in the previous services, carry out the following:

## Fuel and exhaust system (Chapter 3)
Check and adjust the carburettor fuel level

## Electrical system (Chapter 11)
Check and lubricate the starter motor

**Every 45 000 miles (75 000 km) or 60 months – whichever occurs first**

In addition to all the items in the previous services, carry out the following:

## Transmission (Chapter 6)
Change the transmission oil

## Additional maintenance items

In addition to the work in the regular service schedule, the following items must be renewed at the interval specified, regardless of their apparent condition.

## Engine (Chapter 1)
Renew the timing belt every 24 months or 27 000 miles/45 000 km, whichever occurs first

## Cooling system (Chapter 2)
Drain, flush and refill the cooling system, renewing the coolant every 36 months or 36 000 miles/60 000 km, whichever occurs first

## Braking system (Chapter 8)
Renew the brake hydraulic fluid every 24 months or 45 000 miles/75 000 km, whichever occurs first
Renew the brake flexible hoses every 60 months or 75 000 miles/125 000 km, whichever occurs first

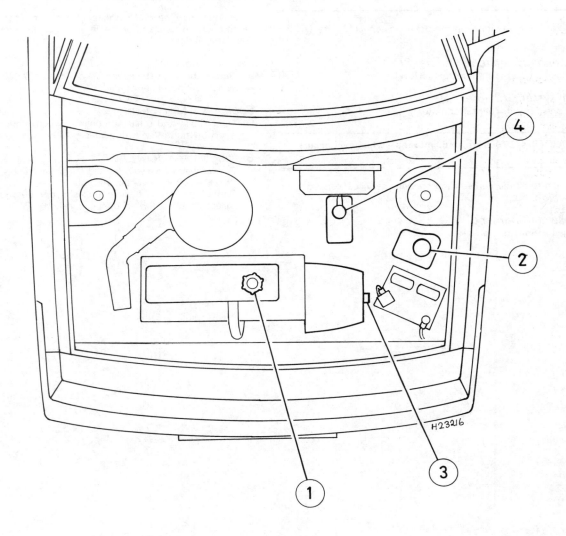

# Recommended lubricants and fluids

| Component or system | Lubricant type/specification | Duckhams recommendation |
| --- | --- | --- |
| Engine (1) | Multigrade engine oil, viscosity SAE 10W/40 to 15W/40, to API SF or better | Duckhams QXR, Hypergrade, or 10W/40 Motor Oil |
| Cooling system (2) | Ethylene glycol based antifreeze with corrosion inhibitors | Duckhams Universal Antifreeze and Summer Coolant |
| Transmission (3) | Multigrade engine oil, viscosity SAE 10W/40 to 15W/40, to API SF or better | Duckhams QXR Hypergrade, or 10W/40 Motor Oil |
| Brake hydraulic system (4) | Hydraulic fluid to SAE J1703 or DOT 4 | Duckhams Universal Brake and Clutch Fluid |
| General greasing | Multi-purpose lithium-based grease | Duckhams LB 10 or LBM 10 |

# Conversion factors

## Length (distance)
| | | | | |
|---|---|---|---|---|
| Inches (in) | X 25.4 | = Millimetres (mm) | X 0.0394 | = Inches (in) |
| Feet (ft) | X 0.305 | = Metres (m) | X 3.281 | = Feet (ft) |
| Miles | X 1.609 | = Kilometres (km) | X 0.621 | = Miles |

## Volume (capacity)
| | | | | |
|---|---|---|---|---|
| Cubic inches (cu in; in³) | X 16.387 | = Cubic centimetres (cc; cm³) | X 0.061 | = Cubic inches (cu in; in³) |
| Imperial pints (Imp pt) | X 0.568 | = Litres (l) | X 1.76 | = Imperial pints (Imp pt) |
| Imperial quarts (Imp qt) | X 1.137 | = Litres (l) | X 0.88 | = Imperial quarts (Imp qt) |
| Imperial quarts (Imp qt) | X 1.201 | = US quarts (US qt) | X 0.833 | = Imperial quarts (Imp qt) |
| US quarts (US qt) | X 0.946 | = Litres (l) | X 1.057 | = US quarts (US qt) |
| Imperial gallons (Imp gal) | X 4.546 | = Litres (l) | X 0.22 | = Imperial gallons (Imp gal) |
| Imperial gallons (Imp gal) | X 1.201 | = US gallons (US gal) | X 0.833 | = Imperial gallons (Imp gal) |
| US gallons (US gal) | X 3.785 | = Litres (l) | X 0.264 | = US gallons (US gal) |

## Mass (weight)
| | | | | |
|---|---|---|---|---|
| Ounces (oz) | X 28.35 | = Grams (g) | X 0.035 | = Ounces (oz) |
| Pounds (lb) | X 0.454 | = Kilograms (kg) | X 2.205 | = Pounds (lb) |

## Force
| | | | | |
|---|---|---|---|---|
| Ounces-force (ozf; oz) | X 0.278 | = Newtons (N) | X 3.6 | = Ounces-force (ozf; oz) |
| Pounds-force (lbf; lb) | X 4.448 | = Newtons (N) | X 0.225 | = Pounds-force (lbf; lb) |
| Newtons (N) | X 0.1 | = Kilograms-force (kgf; kg) | X 9.81 | = Newtons (N) |

## Pressure
| | | | | |
|---|---|---|---|---|
| Pounds-force per square inch (psi; lbf/in²; lb/in²) | X 0.070 | = Kilograms-force per square centimetre (kgf/cm²; kg/cm²) | X 14.223 | = Pounds-force per square inch (psi; lbf/in²; lb/in²) |
| Pounds-force per square inch (psi; lbf/in²; lb/in²) | X 0.068 | = Atmospheres (atm) | X 14.696 | = Pounds-force per square inch (psi; lbf/in²; lb/in²) |
| Pounds-force per square inch (psi; lbf/in²; lb/in²) | X 0.069 | = Bars | X 14.5 | = Pounds-force per square inch (psi; lbf/in²; lb/in²) |
| Pounds-force per square inch (psi; lbf/in²; lb/in²) | X 6.895 | = Kilopascals (kPa) | X 0.145 | = Pounds-force per square inch (psi; lbf/in²; lb/in²) |
| Kilopascals (kPa) | X 0.01 | = Kilograms-force per square centimetre (kgf/cm²; kg/cm²) | X 98.1 | = Kilopascals (kPa) |
| Millibar (mbar) | X 100 | = Pascals (Pa) | X 0.01 | = Millibar (mbar) |
| Millibar (mbar) | X 0.0145 | = Pounds-force per square inch (psi; lbf/in²; lb/in²) | X 68.947 | = Millibar (mbar) |
| Millibar (mbar) | X 0.75 | = Millimetres of mercury (mmHg) | X 1.333 | = Millibar (mbar) |
| Millibar (mbar) | X 0.401 | = Inches of water (inH₂O) | X 2.491 | = Millibar (mbar) |
| Millimetres of mercury (mmHg) | X 0.535 | = Inches of water (inH₂O) | X 1.868 | = Millimetres of mercury (mmHg) |
| Inches of water (inH₂O) | X 0.036 | = Pounds-force per square inch (psi; lbf/in²; lb/in²) | X 27.68 | = Inches of water (inH₂O) |

## Torque (moment of force)
| | | | | |
|---|---|---|---|---|
| Pounds-force inches (lbf in; lb in) | X 1.152 | = Kilograms-force centimetre (kgf cm; kg cm) | X 0.868 | = Pounds-force inches (lbf in; lb in) |
| Pounds-force inches (lbf in; lb in) | X 0.113 | = Newton metres (Nm) | X 8.85 | = Pounds-force inches (lbf in; lb in) |
| Pounds-force inches (lbf in; lb in) | X 0.083 | = Pounds-force feet (lbf ft; lb ft) | X 12 | = Pounds-force inches (lbf in; lb in) |
| Pounds-force feet (lbf ft; lb ft) | X 0.138 | = Kilograms-force metres (kgf m; kg m) | X 7.233 | = Pounds-force feet (lbf ft; lb ft) |
| Pounds-force feet (lbf ft; lb ft) | X 1.356 | = Newton metres (Nm) | X 0.738 | = Pounds-force feet (lbf ft; lb ft) |
| Newton metres (Nm) | X 0.102 | = Kilograms-force metres (kgf m; kg m) | X 9.804 | = Newton metres (Nm) |

## Power
| | | | | |
|---|---|---|---|---|
| Horsepower (hp) | X 745.7 | = Watts (W) | X 0.0013 | = Horsepower (hp) |

## Velocity (speed)
| | | | | |
|---|---|---|---|---|
| Miles per hour (miles/hr; mph) | X 1.609 | = Kilometres per hour (km/hr; kph) | X 0.621 | = Miles per hour (miles/hr; mph) |

## Fuel consumption*
| | | | | |
|---|---|---|---|---|
| Miles per gallon, Imperial (mpg) | X 0.354 | = Kilometres per litre (km/l) | X 2.825 | = Miles per gallon, Imperial (mpg) |
| Miles per gallon, US (mpg) | X 0.425 | = Kilometres per litre (km/l) | X 2.352 | = Miles per gallon, US (mpg) |

## Temperature
Degrees Fahrenheit = (°C x 1.8) + 32

Degrees Celsius (Degrees Centigrade; °C) = (°F - 32) x 0.56

*It is common practice to convert from miles per gallon (mpg) to litres/100 kilometres (l/100km), where mpg (Imperial) x l/100 km = 282 and mpg (US) x l/100 km = 235

# Fault diagnosis

## Introduction

The vehicle owner who does his or her own maintenance according to the recommended schedules should not have to use this section of the manual very often. Modern component reliability is such that, provided those items subject to wear or deterioration are inspected or renewed at the specified intervals, sudden failure is comparatively rare. Faults do not usually just happen as a result of sudden failure, but develop over a period of time. Major mechanical failures in particular are usually preceded by characteristic symptoms over hundreds or even thousands of miles. Those components which do occasionally fail without warning are often small and easily carried in the vehicle.

With any fault finding, the first step is to decide where to begin investigations. Sometimes this is obvious, but on other occasions a little detective work will be necessary. The owner who makes half a dozen haphazard adjustments or replacements may be successful in curing a fault (or its symptoms), but he will be none the wiser if the fault recurs and he may well have spent more time and money than was necessary. A calm and logical approach will be found to be more satisfactory in the long run. Always take into account any warning signs or abnormalities that may have been noticed in the period preceding the fault – power loss, high or low gauge readings, unusual noises or smells, etc – and remember that failure of components such as fuses or spark plugs may only be pointers to some underlying fault.

The pages which follow here are intended to help in cases of failure to start or breakdown on the road. There is also a Fault Diagnosis Section at the end of each Chapter which should be consulted if the preliminary checks prove unfruitful. Whatever the fault, certain basic principles apply. These are as follows:

**Verify the fault.** This is simply a matter of being sure that you know what the symptoms are before starting work. This is particularly important if you are investigating a fault for someone else who may not have described it very accurately.

**Don't overlook the obvious.** For example, if the vehicle won't start, is there petrol in the tank? (Don't take anyone else's word on this particular point, and don't trust the fuel gauge either!) If an electrical fault is indicated, look for loose or broken wires before digging out the test gear.

**Cure the disease, not the symptom.** Substituting a flat battery with a fully charged one will get you off the hard shoulder, but if the underlying cause is not attended to, the new battery will go the same way. Similarly, changing oil-fouled spark plugs for a new set will get you moving again, but remember that the reason for the fouling (if it wasn't simply an incorrect grade of plug) will have to be established and corrected.

**Don't take anything for granted.** Particularly, don't forget that a 'new' component may itself be defective (especially if it's been rattling round in the boot for months), and don't leave components out of a fault diagnosis sequence just because they are new or recently fitted. When you do finally diagnose a difficult fault, you'll probably realise that all the evidence was there from the start.

## Electrical faults

Electrical faults can be more puzzling than straightforward mechanical failures, but they are no less susceptible to logical analysis if the basic principles of operation are understood. Vehicle electrical wiring exists in extremely unfavourable conditions – heat, vibration and chemical attack – and the first things to look for are loose or corroded connections and broken or chafed wires, especially where the wires pass through holes in the bodywork or are subject to vibration.

All metal-bodied vehicles in current production have one pole of the battery 'earthed', ie connected to the vehicle bodywork, and in nearly all modern vehicles it is the negative (–) terminal. The various electrical components – motors, bulb holders etc – are also connected to earth, either by means of a lead or directly by their mountings. Electric current flows through the component and then back to the battery via the bodywork. If the component mounting is loose or corroded, or if a good path back to the battery is not available, the circuit will be incomplete and malfunction will result. The engine and/or gearbox are also earthed by means of flexible metal straps to the body or subframe; if these straps are loose or missing, starter motor, generator and ignition trouble may result.

Assuming the earth return to be satisfactory, electrical faults will be due either to component malfunction or to defects in the current supply. Individual components are dealt with in Chapter 11. If supply wires are broken or cracked internally this results in an open-circuit, and the easiest way to check for this is to bypass the suspect wire temporarily with a length of wire having a crocodile clip or suitable connector at each end. Alternatively, a 12V test lamp can be used to verify the presence of supply voltage at various points along the wire and the break can be thus isolated.

If a bare portion of a live wire touches the bodywork or other earthed metal part, the electricity will take the low-resistance path thus formed back to the battery: this is known as a short-circuit. Hopefully a short-circuit will blow a fuse, but otherwise it may cause burning of the insulation (and possibly further short-circuits) or even a fire. This is why it is inadvisable to bypass persistently blowing fuses with silver foil or wire.

## Spares and tool kit

Most vehicles are supplied only with sufficient tools for wheel changing; the *Maintenance and minor repair* tool kit detailed in *Tools and working facilities,* with the addition of a hammer, is probably sufficient for those repairs that most motorists would consider attempting at the roadside. In addition a few items which can be fitted without too much trouble in the event of a breakdown should be carried. Experience and available space will modify the list below, but the following may save having to call on professional assistance:

*Spark plugs, clean and correctly gapped*
*HT lead and plug cap – long enough to reach the plug furthest from the distributor*
*Distributor rotor, condenser and contact breaker points*
*Drivebelt(s) – emergency type may suffice*
*Spare fuses*
*Set of principal light bulbs*
*Tin of radiator sealer and hose bandage*
*Exhaust bandage*
*Roll of insulating tape*
*Length of soft iron wire*
*Length of electrical flex*
*Torch or inspection lamp (can double as test lamp)*
*Battery jump leads*
*Tow-rope*
*Ignition water dispersant aerosol*
*Litre of engine oil*
*Sealed can of hydraulic fluid*
*Emergency windscreen*
*Worm drive clips*

If spare fuel is carried, a can designed for the purpose should be used to minimise risks of leakage and collision damage. A first aid kit and a warning triangle, whilst not at present compulsory in the UK, are obviously sensible items to carry in addition to the above.

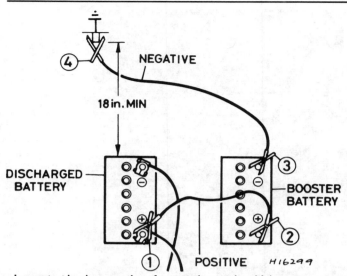

**Jump start lead connections for negative earth vehicles – connect leads in order shown**

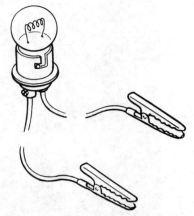

**A simple test lamp for tracing electrical faults**

When touring abroad it may be advisable to carry additional spares which, even if you cannot fit them yourself, could save having to wait while parts are obtained. The items below may be worth considering:

*Clutch and throttle cables*
*Cylinder head gasket*
*Alternator brushes*
*Tyre valve core*

One of the motoring organisations will be able to advise on availability of fuel etc in foreign countries.

### Engine will not start

#### Engine fails to turn when starter operated
Flat battery (recharge, use jump leads, or push start)
Battery terminals loose or corroded
Battery earth to body defective
Engine earth strap loose or broken
Starter motor (or solenoid) wiring loose or broken
Automatic transmission selector in wrong position, or inhibitor faulty
Ignition/starter switch faulty
Major mechanical failure (seizure)
Starter or solenoid internal fault (see Chapter 11)

#### Starter motor turns engine slowly
Partially discharged battery (recharge, use jump leads, or push start)
Battery terminals loose or corroded
Battery earth to body defective
Engine earth strap loose
Starter motor (or solenoid) wiring loose
Starter motor internal fault (see Chapter 11)

#### Starter motor spins without turning engine
Flat battery
Starter motor pinion sticking on sleeve
Flywheel gear teeth damaged or worn
Starter motor mounting bolts loose

#### Engine turns normally but fails to start
Damp or dirty HT leads and distributor cap (crank engine and check for spark)
No fuel in tank (check for delivery at carburettor)
Excessive choke (hot engine) or insufficient choke (cold engine)

Fouled or incorrectly gapped spark plugs (remove, renew and regap)
Other ignition system fault (see Chapter 4)
Other fuel system fault (see Chapter 3)
Poor compression (see Chapter 1)
Major mechanical failure (eg camshaft drive)

#### Engine fires but will not run
Insufficient choke (cold engine)
Air leaks at carburettor or inlet manifold
Fuel starvation (see Chapter 3)
Ballast resistor defective, or other ignition fault (see Chapter 4)
Other fuel system fault (see Chapter 3)

### Engine cuts out and will not restart

#### Engine cuts out suddenly – ignition fault
Loose or disconnected LT wires
Wet HT leads or distributor cap (after traversing water splash)
Coil or condenser failure (check for spark)
Other ignition fault (see Chapter 4)

#### Engine misfires before cutting out – fuel fault
Fuel tank empty
Fuel pump defective or filter blocked (check for delivery)
Fuel tank filler vent blocked (suction will be evident on releasing cap)

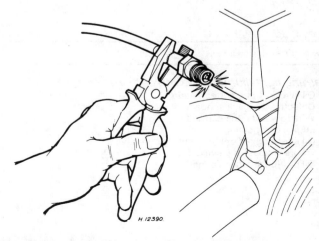

**Crank engine and check for spark. Note use of insulated tool to hold plug lead**

**Carrying a few spares may save a long walk!**

Carburettor needle valve sticking
Carburettor jets blocked (fuel contaminated)
Other fuel system fault (see Chapter 3)

## Engine cuts out – other causes
Serious overheating
Major mechanical failure (eg camshaft drive)

---

### Engine overheats

## Ignition warning light not illuminated
Coolant loss due to internal or external leakage (see Chapter 2)
Thermostat defective
Low oil level
Brakes binding
Radiator clogged externally or internally
Electric cooling fan not operating correctly
Engine waterways clogged
Ignition timing incorrect or automatic advance malfunctioning
Mixture too weak
**Note:** *Do not add cold water to an overheated engine or damage may result*

---

### Low engine oil pressure

## Warning light illuminated with engine running
Oil level low or incorrect grade
Defective gauge or sender unit
Wire to sender unit earthed
Engine overheating
Oil filter clogged or bypass valve defective
Oil pressure relief valve defective
Oil pick-up strainer clogged

Oil pump worn or mountings loose
Worn main or big-end bearings
**Note:** *Low oil pressure in a high-mileage engine at tickover is not necessarily a cause for concern. Sudden pressure loss at speed is far more significant. In any event, check the pressure switch before condemning the engine.*

---

### Engine noises

## Pre-ignition (pinking) on acceleration
Incorrect grade of fuel
Ignition timing incorrect
Distributor faulty or worn
Worn or maladjusted carburettor
Excessive carbon build-up in engine

## Whistling or wheezing noises
Leaking vacuum hose
Leaking carburettor or manifold gasket
Blowing head gasket

## Tapping or rattling
Incorrect valve clearances
Worn valve gear
Worn timing chain or belt
Broken piston ring (ticking noise)

## Knocking or thumping
Unintentional mechanical contact (eg fan blades)
Worn drivebelt
Peripheral component fault (alternator, water pump etc)
Worn big-end bearings (regular heavy knocking, perhaps less under load)
Worn main bearings (rumbling and knocking, perhaps worsening under load)
Piston slap (most noticeable when cold)

# Chapter 1 Engine

## Contents

## Specifications

### General

| Type | Four-cylinder, in-line, sohc | | |
|---|---|---|---|
| | **1100** | **1300** | **1500** |
| Designation | 21081 | 2108 | 21083 |
| Bore | 76 mm | 76 mm | 82 mm |
| Stroke | 60.6 mm | 71 mm | 71 mm |
| Capacity | 1099 cc | 1288 cc | 1499 cc |
| Compression ratio | 9.0:1 | 9.9:1 | 9.9:1 |
| Firing order | 1–3–4–2 (No 1 cylinder at timing belt end) | | |
| Direction of crankshaft rotation | Clockwise (seen from right-hand side of vehicle) | | |
| Minimum compression pressure | 10.0 bar | | |

### Cylinder block

| Material | Cast iron | |
|---|---|---|
| Cylinder bore diameter: | **1100, 1300** | **1500** |
| Standard grade A | 76.00 to 76.01 mm | 82.00 to 82.01 mm |
| Standard grade B | 76.01 to 76.02 mm | 82.01 to 82.02 mm |
| Standard grade C | 76.02 to 76.03 mm | 82.02 to 82.03 mm |
| Standard grade D | 76.03 to 76.04 mm | 82.03 to 82.04 mm |
| Standard grade E | 76.04 to 76.05 mm | 82.04 to 82.05 mm |
| 1st oversize (0.4 mm) | 76.40 to 76.41 mm | 82.40 to 82.41 mm |
| 2nd oversize (0.8 mm) | 76.80 to 76.81 mm | 82.80 to 82.81 mm |
| Maximum cylinder bore ovality | 0.15 mm | |
| Maximum cylinder bore taper | 0.15 mm | |
| Height – from cylinder head to sump gasket faces: | | |
| 1100 | 242.0 to 242.2 mm | |
| 1300, 1500 | 247.6 to 247.8 mm | |
| Maximum gasket face distortion – at cylinder head face | 0.10 mm | |

## Crankshaft

Number of main bearings.................................................................... 5
Main bearing journal diameter:
    Standard................................................................................... 50.799 to 50.819 mm
    1st undersize (0.25 mm)......................................................... 50.549 to 50.569 mm
    2nd undersize (0.50 mm)........................................................ 50.299 to 50.319 mm
    3rd undersize (0.75 mm)......................................................... 50.049 to 50.069 mm
    4th undersize (1.00 mm)......................................................... 49.799 to 49.819 mm
Main bearing journal running clearance:
    Standard................................................................................... 0.026 to 0.073 mm
    Maximum.................................................................................. 0.150 mm
Crankpin journal diameter:
    Standard................................................................................... 47.830 to 47.850 mm
    1st undersize (0.25 mm)......................................................... 47.580 to 47.600 mm
    2nd undersize (0.50 mm)........................................................ 47.330 to 47.350 mm
    3rd undersize (0.75 mm)......................................................... 47.080 to 47.100 mm
    4th undersize (1.00 mm)......................................................... 46.830 to 46.850 mm
Crankpin journal running clearance:
    Standard................................................................................... 0.020 to 0.070 mm
    Maximum.................................................................................. 0.100 mm
Crankshaft endfloat:
    Standard................................................................................... 0.055 to 0.265 mm
    Maximum.................................................................................. 0.350 mm
Thrustwasher thickness:
    Standard................................................................................... 2.310 to 2.360 mm
    Oversize .................................................................................. 2.437 to 2.487 mm

## Pistons and piston rings

| | 1100, 1300 | 1500 |
|---|---|---|
| Piston diameter: | | |
|   Standard grade A | 75.965 to 75.975 mm | 81.965 to 81.975 mm |
|   Standard grade B | 75.975 to 75.985 mm | 81.975 to 81.985 mm |
|   Standard grade C | 75.985 to 75.995 mm | 81.985 to 81.995 mm |
|   Standard grade D | 75.995 to 76.005 mm | 81.995 to 82.005 mm |
|   Standard grade E | 76.005 to 76.015 mm | 82.005 to 82.015 mm |
|   1st oversize | 76.365 to 76.375 mm | 82.365 to 82.375 mm |
|   2nd oversize | 76.765 to 76.775 mm | 82.765 to 82.775 mm |

Piston-to-bore clearance:
    Standard................................................................................... 0.025 to 0.045 mm
    Maximum.................................................................................. 0.150 mm
Piston ring end gaps (fitted in bore):
    Top and second compression rings........................................ 0.250 to 0.450 mm
    Oil control ring ....................................................................... 0.250 to 0.500 mm
Piston ring-to-groove clearance:
    Top compression ring (nominal)............................................. 0.040 to 0.075 mm
    Second compression ring (nominal) ....................................... 0.030 to 0.065 mm
    Oil control ring (nominal)........................................................ 0.020 to 0.055 mm
    Maximum clearance (all)......................................................... 0.150 mm
Gudgeon pin bore diameter:
    Class 1..................................................................................... 21.982 to 21.986 mm
    Class 2..................................................................................... 21.986 to 21.990 mm
    Class 3..................................................................................... 21.990 to 21.994 mm

## Gudgeon pins

Diameter:
    Class 1 (Blue)......................................................................... 21.970 to 21.974 mm
    Class 2 (Green) ...................................................................... 21.974 to 21.978 mm
    Class 3 (Red) ......................................................................... 21.978 to 21.982 mm

## Connecting rods

Small-end bore diameter....................................................................... 21.940 to 21.960 mm
Big-end bore diameter .......................................................................... 51.330 to 51.346 mm

## Cylinder head

Material ................................................................................................. Aluminium alloy
Valve seat angle................................................................................... 45° ± 5′
Seat cutter correction angle:
    Upper (inlet only).................................................................... 30°
    Lower ...................................................................................... 45° ± 5′
Camshaft bearing bore diameter........................................................... 25.000 to 25.025 mm
Cam follower bore diameter................................................................... 35.320 to 35.345 mm

## Camshaft

| | |
|---|---|
| Drive | Toothed belt |
| Number of bearings | 5 |
| Bearing journal diameter | 24.915 to 24.931 mm |
| Bearing journal running clearance: | |
|    Standard | 0.069 to 0.110 mm |
|    Maximum | 0.200 mm |

## Valve clearances (cold)

| | |
|---|---|
| Inlet | 0.20 ± 0.05 mm (0.008 ± 0.002 in) |
| Exhaust | 0.35 ± 0.05 mm (0.014 ± 0.002 in) |

## Valves

| | |
|---|---|
| Operation | Direct from camshaft lobes, via inverted cam followers (buckets), clearance adjusted by shims |
| Seat angle | 45° 30′ ± 5′ |
| Head diameter: | |
|    Inlet (1100, 1300) | 35.0 mm |
|    Inlet (1500) | 37.0 mm |
|    Exhaust | 31.5 mm |
| Stem diameter | 7.985 to 8.000 mm |
| Stem-to-guide clearance: | |
|    Inlet | 0.022 to 0.055 mm |
|    Exhaust | 0.029 to 0.062 mm |
| Valve spring free length: | |
|    Inner | 44.7 mm |
|    Outer | 35.2 mm |
| Valve guide internal diameter: | |
|    Inlet | 8.022 to 8.040 mm |
|    Exhaust | 8.029 to 8.047 mm |
| Cam follower diameter | 35.295 to 35.275 mm |

## Lubrication system

| | |
|---|---|
| System pressure – minimum: | |
|    @ idle speed | 0.8 bar (12 psi) |
|    @ 5600 rpm | 4.5 bar (65 psi) |
| Engine oil type/specification | Multigrade engine oil, viscosity SAE 10W/40 to 15W/50, to API SF or better (Duckhams QXR, Hypergrade, or 10W/40 Motor Oil) |
| Engine oil capacity (including filter) | 3.50 litres (6.2 Imp pints) |
| Difference between MAX and MIN marks on dipstick | 0.56 litres (1.0 Imp pint) |
| Oil filter | Champion C107 |
| Oil pump type | Trochoidal gear and crescent |
| Oil pump clearances: | |
|    Outer gear maximum endfloat | 0.150 mm |
|    Inner gear maximum endfloat | 0.120 mm |
| Pressure relief valve spring free length | 46.5 mm |

## Torque wrench settings

| | Nm | lbf ft |
|---|---|---|
| Camshaft toothed pulley bolt | 67.5 to 83.5 | 50 to 61.5 |
| Camshaft upper bearing nuts: | | |
|    1st stage | Tighten until bearing touches cylinder head | |
|    2nd stage | 18.5 to 22.5 | 13.5 to 16.5 |
| Distributor/fuel pump drive extension Allen screw | 6.5 to 8 | 5 to 6 |
| Cylinder head bolts: | | |
|    1st stage | 20 | 15 |
|    2nd stage | 69.5 to 85.5 | 51 to 63 |
|    3rd stage | + 90° | + 90° |
|    4th stage | + (further) 90° | + (further) 90° |
| Timing belt tensioning roller locknut | 33 to 41 | 24.5 to 30 |
| Alternator drive pulley bolt | 98 to 109 | 72 to 80 |
| Sump bolt | 5 to 8 | 4 to 6 |
| Oil pump bolt | 8.5 to 10.5 | 6 to 7.5 |
| Oil pump inner-to-outer cover bolts | 7 to 9 | 5 to 7 |
| Oil pump pick-up pipe-to-pump retaining bolt | 7 to 8 | 5 to 6 |
| Oil pump pick-up pipe-to-main bearing cap retaining bolts | 8.5 to 10.5 | 6 to 7.5 |
| Pressure relief valve threaded plug | 45.5 to 73.5 | 33.5 to 54 |
| Oil filter element mounting stub | 70.5 to 87 | 52 to 64 |
| Big-end cap nuts | 43.5 to 53.5 | 32 to 39.5 |
| Main bearing cap bolts | 68.5 to 84.5 | 50.5 to 62 |
| Flywheel bolts | 61 to 87.5 | 45 to 64.5 |
| Engine/transmission front mounting: | | |
|    Through-bolt retaining nut | 41.5 to 52.5 | 30.5 to 38.5 |
|    Mounting bracket-to-cylinder block/crankcase bolts | N/av | N/av |

## Torque wrench settings (continued)

| | Nm | lbf ft |
|---|---|---|
| Engine/transmission left-hand mounting: | | |
|    Through-bolt retaining nut | 41.5 to 52.5 | 30.5 to 38.5 |
|    Mounting bracket-to-transmission casing nuts | 29 to 34 | 21 to 25 |
| Engine/transmission rear mounting: | | |
|    Bracket-to-transmission retaining nuts | 66.5 to 84 | 49 to 62 |
|    Mounting-to-body nuts or bolts | 27.5 to 34 | 20 to 25 |

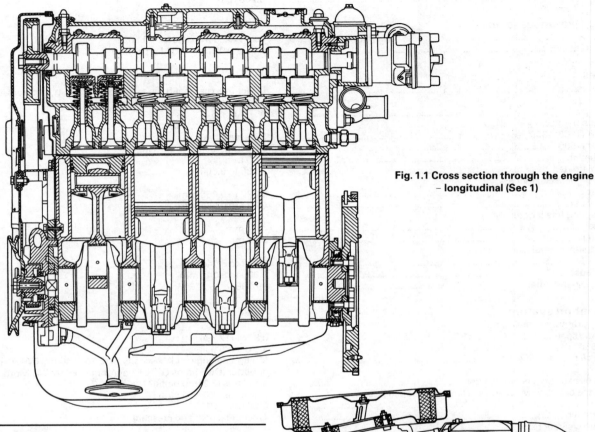

Fig. 1.1 Cross section through the engine
– longitudinal (Sec 1)

## 1   General description

The engine is of four-cylinder, in-line, single overhead camshaft type, mounted transversely at the front of the vehicle with the clutch and transmission on its left-hand end. Variations in capacity are achieved by altering the bore and stroke dimensions.

The crankshaft runs in five main bearings. Thrustwashers are fitted to the centre main bearing to control crankshaft endfloat.

The connecting rods rotate on horizontally-split bearing shells at their big-ends. The pistons are attached to the connecting rods by gudgeon pins which are an interference fit in the connecting rod small-end eyes. The aluminium alloy pistons are fitted with three piston rings, two compression rings and an oil control ring.

The camshaft is driven by a toothed timing belt and operates the valves via inverted cam followers (buckets), the clearance being adjusted by shims. The cylinder head follower bores are lined with cermet (a compound of sintered ceramics and metals). The camshaft rotates in five bearings that are machined direct in the cylinder head, and the bolted-on upper bearings. This means that the upper bearings are not available separately from the cylinder head and must not be interchanged with others from another engine.

The distributor and fuel pump are driven from the camshaft left-hand end, and the water pump is driven by the timing belt.

The inlet and exhaust valves are each closed by double coil-type valve springs and operate in guides pressed into the cylinder head.

Lubrication is by means of a trochoidal gear and crescent-type pump which is mounted on the crankshaft right-hand end and draws oil through a strainer located in the sump. It then forces the oil through an externally-mounted full-flow cartridge-type filter into oil galleries from where it is distributed to the crankshaft and camshaft. The big-end

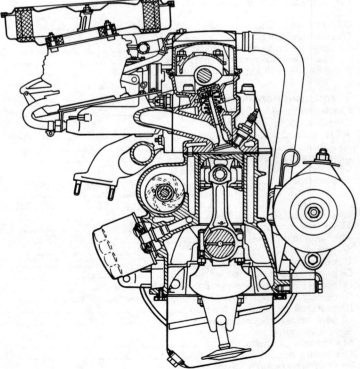

Fig. 1.2 Cross-section through the engine – lateral (Sec 1)

lobes, cam followers and valves are lubricated by splash, as are all other engine components.

## 2  Routine maintenance

1    Carry out the following procedures at the intervals given in *'Routine maintenance'* at the beginning of this manual.

### Check the engine oil level

2    With the engine at normal operating temperature, park the vehicle on level ground.
3    Switch off the ignition. If the engine has just been run, wait for a few minutes to allow the oil to drain down into the sump.
4    Withdraw the oil level dipstick from the front of the cylinder block/crankcase, wipe it clean and re-insert it fully.
5    Withdraw the dipstick again and check the oil level, which should be between the 'MAX' and 'MIN' marks (photo). Do not run the engine with the oil level below the 'MIN' mark or above the 'MAX' mark; either condition can cause damage.
6    If topping-up is necessary, add only good quality oil of the specified type through the cylinder head cover oil filler aperture (photo).
7    The quantity of oil required to raise the level from 'MIN' to 'MAX' on the dipstick is approximately 0.56 litres (1.0 Imp pint); do not overfill.
8    Ensure the oil filler cap and dipstick are securely refitted.

### Change the engine oil and filter

9    The oil should be drained when the engine is hot, immediately after a run.
10    Park the vehicle on level ground and position a container of suitable capacity under the sump.
11    Remove the oil filler cap from the cylinder head cover, withdraw the dipstick, then unscrew the sump drain plug (photo). The oil will be hot, so take precautions against scalding. Allow all the oil to drain.
12    When the oil has finished draining, clean the drain plug threads and the mating face of the sump, then refit and tighten the drain plug.
13    Place a suitable container under the oil filter, and remove the filter. It can be reached from above (once the air cleaner assembly has been removed), but is easier to remove and refit from below (photos). If necessary use a strap wrench to slacken the filter, then unscrew it by hand. If a strap wrench is not available, drive a large screwdriver through the filter and use the screwdriver as a lever to unscrew the filter. Be prepared for the spillage of hot oil.
14    Wipe clean the filter mounting face on the cylinder block and smear a little clean engine oil on the sealing ring of the new filter, then screw the filter on to its mounting stub.
15    If there are no specific instructions included with the new filter, tighten it until the sealing ring seats firmly on the cylinder block/crankcase, then tighten, by hand only, no more than a further three-quarters of a turn.
16    Refill the engine with the correct grade and quantity of oil. Ensure that the filler cap and the dipstick are refitted on completion.
17    When the engine is started, there may be a delay in the extinguishing of the oil pressure warning lamp while the new filter fills with oil. Run the engine and check for leaks from the filter and drain plug, then stop

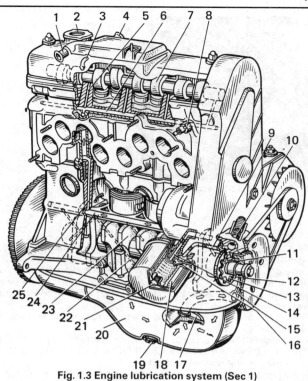

**Fig. 1.3 Engine lubrication system (Sec 1)**

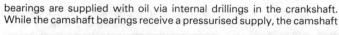

| | |
|---|---|
| 1 Breather hose union – cylinder head cover-to-air cleaner | 13 Oil pump crescent |
| 2 Oil filler cap | 14 Oil gallery – filter-to-main gallery |
| 3 Breather hose union – cylinder head cover-to-carburettor | 15 Oil pump feed gallery |
| | 16 Oil filter anti-drain valve |
| 4 Breather hose union – cylinder head cover-to-cylinder block/crankcase | 17 Oil pump pick-up pipe and strainer |
| | 18 Oil filter |
| 5 Oil feed gallery to camshaft bearings | 19 Sump drain plug |
| | 20 Sump |
| 6 Cylinder head main oil gallery | 21 Oil filter bypass valve |
| 7 Camshaft | 22 Crankshaft oilway – main bearing-to-crankpin |
| 8 Oil pressure switch | 23 Crankshaft oilway – main bearing supply |
| 9 Oil gallery – pump-to-filter | 24 Cylinder block/crankcase main oil gallery |
| 10 Oil pressure relief valve | 25 Oil gallery – main gallery-to-cylinder head main oil gallery |
| 11 Oil pump inner gear | |
| 12 Oil pump outer gear | |

bearings are supplied with oil via internal drillings in the crankshaft. While the camshaft bearings receive a pressurised supply, the camshaft

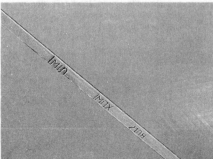

2.5 Engine oil level must be maintained between dipstick markings

2.6 Add only good quality oil of specified type when topping-up engine oil

2.11 Unscrewing sump drain plug

2.13A Oil filter can be seen from above (air cleaner removed) ...

2.13B ... but is easiest to reach from below

the engine and check the oil level (see above). Top up the level if necessary.

18    Dispose safely of the old engine oil. **Do not** pour it down a drain – this is illegal and causes pollution. Your dealer or Local Authority may be able to dispose of it safely.

### Check the valve clearances
19    Refer to Section 5.

### Check the timing belt tension and condition
20    Refer to Section 8.

### Renew the timing belt
21    Refer to Section 7.

---

### 3   Major operations possible with the engine in the vehicle

The following operations can be carried out without removing the engine from the vehicle:

(a)  *Valve clearances – adjustment*
(b)  *Timing belt, tensioner, belt covers and toothed pulleys – removal and refitting*
(c)  *Timing belt – checking and adjustment*
(d)  *Camshaft – removal and refitting*
(e)  *Cylinder head – removal, refitting and overhaul*
(f)  *Sump – removal and refitting*
(g)  *Crankshaft right-hand oil seal – renewal*
(h)  *Oil pump – removal and refitting*
(i)  *Pistons and connecting rods – removal and refitting*
(j)  *Flywheel – removal and refitting*
(k)  *Crankshaft left-hand oil seal – renewal*
(l)  *Engine/transmission mountings – removal and refitting*

---

### 4   Compression test – description and interpretation

1    When engine performance is down, or if misfiring occurs which cannot be attributed to the ignition or fuel systems, a compression test can provide diagnostic clues as to the engine's condition. If the test is performed regularly it can give warning of trouble before any other symptoms become apparent.
2    The engine must be fully warmed up to normal operating temperature, the battery must be fully charged and the spark plugs must be removed. The aid of an assistant will be required also.
3    Disable the ignition system by disconnecting the distributor wiring at its connector plug and the ignition HT coil lead from the distributor cap.

4    Fit a compression tester to the number 1 cylinder spark plug hole – the type of tester which screws into the plug thread is to be preferred.
5    Have the assistant hold the throttle wide open and crank the engine on the starter motor. After a few revolutions the compression pressure should build up to a maximum figure and then stabilise. Record the highest reading obtained.
6    Repeat the test on the remaining cylinders, recording the pressure developed in each.
7    All cylinders should produce very similar pressures (as a general rule, within 1.0 bar/14.5 psi of each other). Any significant variation indicates the possible existence of a fault.
8    If the pressure in any cylinder is reduced to the specified minimum or less, introduce a teaspoonful of clean oil into the cylinder through the spark plug hole and repeat the test.
9    If the addition of oil temporarily improves the compression pressure, this indicates that bore or piston wear is responsible for the pressure loss. No improvement suggests that leaking or burnt valves, or a blown head gasket may be to blame.
10    A low reading from two adjacent cylinders is almost certainly due to the head gasket having blown between them.
11    On completion of the test, refit the spark plugs and reconnect the ignition system.

---

### 5   Valve clearances – checking and adjustment

**Note:** *While the valve clearances can be checked with only a few tools and the minimum of experience, adjusting them is a different matter. Due to the infrequent service interval, the number of special tools required and the fact that access is required to a range of shims, owners are advised to check the clearances at the specified intervals, but leave adjustment to a Lada dealer. It is essential however, that the clearances are correctly set at all times. If the engine is run for long periods with incorrect clearances, its performance and economy will suffer, pollution will increase and ultimately there is a high risk of severe engine damage.*

### Checking
1    The valve clearances must be checked with the engine **cold**.
2    Remove the air cleaner and warm air intake hose, then either disconnect the accelerator and choke cables or secure them clear of the cylinder head cover (Chapter 3).
3    Remove the spark plugs (Chapter 4) and cover their holes with rag to prevent the entry of dirt.
4    Remove the cylinder head cover (Sec 10).
5    Using the rule of 9, measure and record carefully all valve clearances. That is, rotate the crankshaft clockwise by means of a spanner applied to the alternator drive pulley bolt until any valve is fully open (camshaft lobe pressing it fully down), then measure the clearance of the fully-closed (lobe pointing away from the valve) valve whose

5.6 Measuring valve clearance

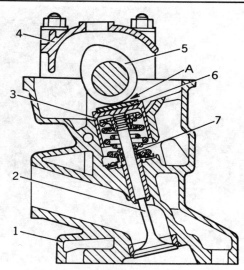

**Fig. 1.4 Cross-section through valvegear (Sec 5)**

| | | | |
|---|---|---|---|
| 1 | Cylinder head | 5 | Cam lobe |
| 2 | Valve | 6 | Shim |
| 3 | Cam follower | 7 | Valve stem oil seal |
| 4 | Camshaft upper bearing | A | Valve clearance |

number (counted from the timing belt end) added to that of the open valve, adds up to 9, as follows:

| Valve fully open | Valve to check |
|---|---|
| Number 1 | Number 8 (No. 4 cyl. Exhaust) |
| Number 2 | Number 7 (No. 4 cyl. Inlet) |
| Number 3 | Number 6 (No. 3 cyl. Inlet) |
| Number 4 | Number 5 (No. 3 cyl. Exhaust) |
| Number 5 | Number 4 (No. 2 cyl. Exhaust) |
| Number 6 | Number 3 (No. 2 cyl. Inlet) |
| Number 7 | Number 2 (No. 1 cyl. Inlet) |
| Number 8 | Number 1 (No. 1 cyl. Exhaust) |

6    Measure the clearance by inserting feeler gauge blades of various thicknesses between the cam lobe (base circle) and the shim (photo). When a firm sliding fit is obtained, note and record the total thickness of blade.

7    Enter all the measured clearances on a chart. None should be more than 0.05 mm (0.002 in) above or below the specified clearance, and if any is, adjustment (ie, a shim of different thickness) is required.

8    If all clearances are correct, refit the disturbed components (paragraph 15), and keep the recorded clearances for future reference.

*Adjustment*

9    Three special tools are required: a cam follower-depressing tool (Lada service tool 67.7800.9503) which is secured by two nuts to the cylinder head cover mountings, a cam follower-locking tool (Lada service tool 67.7800.9504) to hold down the follower once it is depressed, and a magnetic lifting tool (Lada service tool 67.7800.9505) to extract the shim.

10    While these tools are only available through Lada dealers, their purchase is not a worthwhile proposition for the ordinary owner due to the factors outlined above.

11    The usual alternative to these tools requires a great deal of care if serious engine damage is to be avoided (note that it is of course possible to remove the camshaft, but this requires a great deal of extra work). Position the camshaft so that its lobe is pointing away from the valve being adjusted, and rotate the follower so that the cut-out in its rim is pointing outwards. Then use a C-spanner or screwdriver to depress the cam follower, ensuring that it bears only on the follower's rim. Flick out the shim using an electrical screwdriver and extract it (photo). **Do not** rotate the camshaft when any shim is removed as the lobe may stick in the follower or damage it.

12    Each shim's thickness is marked (in mm) on one face. Check and record the thickness on removal, always check the thickness before refitting and always refit shims with their marked faces downwards so that the number cannot be polished off by the cam lobe. If the number has been erased, use a micrometer to check the shim's thickness (photos).

13    Shims are available in a range of thicknesses from 3.00 to 4.25 mm, in 0.05 mm increments. It is helpful for future adjustments to keep full

5.11 Extracting a shim using a screwdriver and a magnetic lifting tool

5.12A Shim thickness is marked on lower face (3.85 mm) ...

5.12B ... but can be checked using a micrometer

6.2 Location of timing belt outer cover mounting bolts (arrowed)

the air cleaner and warm air intake hose, then disconnect the accelerator and choke cables or secure them clear of the cover (Chapter 3).
2    Remove the three bolts, noting their washers and rubber grommets (photo), then withdraw the cover from behind the alternator drive pulley.
3    On refitting, ensure that the cover seats properly on its seal.

### Left-hand (inner) cover

4    Remove the timing belt outer cover, the belt and its tensioner assembly and the camshaft toothed pulley (Sec 7).
5    Unscrew the water pump mounting bolts (photo).
6    Unscrew the bolt and nut securing the cover and withdraw it (photos).
7    If the water pump joint is disturbed on removing the cover, the gasket must be renewed (Chapter 2), otherwise **do not** disturb the pump unless necessary.
8    Refitting is the reverse of the removal procedure.

records of the clearances measured and the shim thicknesses used, both before and after adjustment, so that an accurate picture can be built up of the state of the valvegear and so that the shims required can be purchased in advance.
14    If the measured clearance was larger than the specified value a thicker shim must be fitted; if smaller, a thinner shim is required.
15    For example – the specified clearance for an inlet valve is 0.20 mm. Supposing the clearance of an inlet valve is measured at 0.30 mm, the clearance is 0.10 mm too large, therefore a shim 0.10 mm thicker is required. If the shim removed is 3.55 mm thick, the new shim required is 3.65 mm.
16    Whenever a new shim is installed, rotate the follower through one full turn to ensure that the shim is correctly seated. When all shims have been replaced as required, rotate the crankshaft through several full turns to settle the shims, then recheck the clearances.
17    When all valve clearances are correct, fill the cylinder head wells around the cam followers with clean engine oil and refit the cylinder head cover (Sec 10), the spark plugs (Chapter 4) and the control cables and air cleaner (Chapter 3). Run the engine to check that the valvegear sounds quiet and that there are no oil leaks.

### 7   Timing belt, tensioner and toothed pulleys – removal and refitting

1    Remove the air cleaner and warm air intake hose, then disconnect the accelerator and choke cables or secure them clear of the timing belt outer cover (Chapter 3).
2    Remove the spark plugs (Chapter 4) and cover their holes with rag to prevent the entry of dirt.
3    Rotate the crankshaft clockwise by means of a spanner applied to the alternator drive pulley bolt until the pulley timing mark aligns with the timing belt cover (longer) TDC mark.
4    Unbolt and remove the timing belt outer cover (Sec 6).
5    Check that the camshaft toothed pulley timing mark aligns with the bracket on the belt's left-hand (inner) cover (at the 9 o'clock position from the pulley bolt).
6    Remove the alternator drive pulley and drivebelt. To prevent crankshaft rotation while the pulley bolt is unscrewed, select top gear and have an assistant apply the brakes hard. If the engine has been removed from the vehicle, use either the tool shown in photo 7.13 to hold the pulley or lock the flywheel using the arrangement shown (photos).
7    Check that the crankshaft toothed pulley timing mark aligns with the oil pump cover mark (at the 12 o'clock position from the crankshaft centre).
8    Slacken the timing belt tension by slackening its locknut and rotating the tensioning roller adjuster clockwise (photo).
9    Remove the belt – it has rounded teeth so there is no need to mark the direction of rotation (photo).
10    With the belt removed, unscrew its locknut and withdraw the tensioning roller and its adjuster, noting the nut's washer and the spacer behind the roller (photos).
11    With the belt removed, the crankshaft toothed pulley can be pulled off the crankshaft end, noting the locating Woodruff key (photos).
12    Unscrew its bolt and remove the camshaft pulley. To prevent crankshaft rotation while the pulley bolt is unscrewed, a suitable tool

### 6   Timing belt covers – removal and refitting

#### Outer cover

1    If the cover is being removed with the engine in the vehicle, remove

6.5 Unscrewing water pump mounting bolts (two arrowed)

6.6A Timing belt left-hand (inner) cover mounting bolt and nut (arrowed)

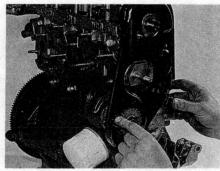

6.6B Removing timing belt left-hand (inner) cover

7.6A Locking flywheel using engine/transmission bolt, washers and metal sprag

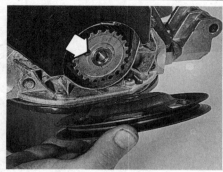

7.6B Removing alternator drive pulley – note locating roll pin (arrowed)

7.8 Slackening timing belt by rotating adjuster

7.9 Removing timing belt

7.10A Timing belt tensioning roller secured by nut and washer

7.10B Note spacer behind tensioning roller and adjuster

7.11A Removing crankshaft toothed pulley ...

7.11B ... noting Woodruff key

7.12A Remove camshaft toothed pulley bolt and washer ...

7.12B ... and withdraw pulley, noting Woodruff key

7.13 Use tool shown to hold pulley while bolt is tightened

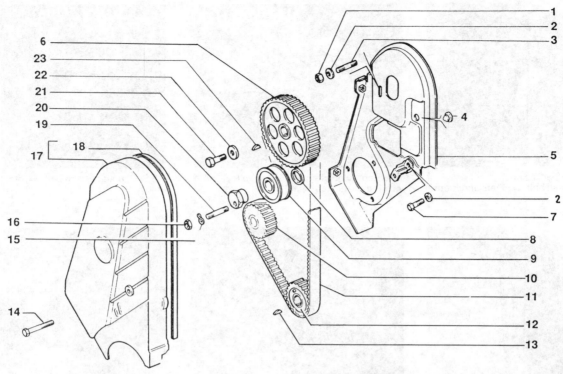

**Fig. 1.5 Timing belt and covers (Secs 6, 7, and 8)**

| | | | |
|---|---|---|---|
| 1   Nut | 7   Bolt | 13  Woodruff key | 19  Stud |
| 2   Washer | 8   Spacer | 14  Bolt | 20  Tensioning roller adjuster |
| 3   Stud | 9   Tensioning roller | 15  Washer | 21  Bolt |
| 4   Rubber plug | 10  Water pump toothed pulley | 16  Nut | 22  Washer |
| 5   Left-hand (inner) cover | 11  Timing belt | 17  Outer cover | 23  Woodruff key |
| 6   Camshaft toothed pulley | 12  Crankshaft toothed pulley | 18  Seal | |

can be made up as shown in photo 7.13, using two lengths of steel strip joined together by a pivot bolt, with suitable bolts at the ends to engage with the pulley holes. Again, note the locating Woodruff key (photos).

13    On refitting, note that while the camshaft pulley can be physically fitted either way round, the valve timing marks are on one side only and the pulley will foul the timing belt left-hand cover mounting stud if wrongly installed. Ensure that both pulleys are aligned correctly on their Woodruff keys and tighten the camshaft pulley bolt to the specified torque setting (photo). Check that the tensioning roller is free to rotate on its adjuster.

14    Check that the camshaft and crankshaft toothed pulley timing marks are aligned as described in paragraphs 5 and 7 above (photos). It is most important that these marks are aligned exactly as this sets the valve timing.

15    Fit the timing belt over the camshaft and crankshaft toothed

pulleys, ensuring that the belt front run is taut (ie, all slack is at the tensioning roller), then over the water pump pulley and tensioning roller. Do not twist the belt sharply while refitting it, and ensure that the belt teeth are correctly seated in the pulleys and that the timing marks remain in alignment.

16    Rotate the tensioning roller anti-clockwise and tighten its locknut to tension the belt, then rotate the crankshaft through two full turns to settle the belt, and check that the timing marks are still aligned exactly.

17    Refit the alternator drive pulley and drivebelt, ensuring that the pulley engages with the toothed pulley locating roll pin and tighten the pulley bolt to the specified torque wrench setting (photo), then adjust the drivebelt's tension (Chapter 11).

18    Adjust the timing belt's tension (Sec 8).

19    Refit the timing belt outer cover (Sec 6), the spark plugs (Chapter 4) and the control cables and air cleaner (Chapter 3).

7.14A Camshaft toothed pulley and left-hand (inner) cover valve timing marks (arrowed)

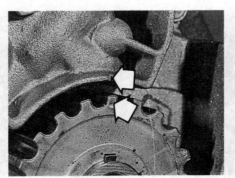

7.14B Crankshaft toothed pulley and oil pump cover valve timing marks (arrowed)

7.17 Locate alternator drive pulley on roll pin before tightening bolt

# Are your plugs trying to tell you something?

**Normal.**
Grey-brown deposits, lightly coated core nose. Plugs ideally suited to engine, and engine in good condition.

**Heavy Deposits.**
A build up of crusty deposits, light-grey sandy colour in appearance.
Fault: Often caused by worn valve guides, excessive use of upper cylinder lubricant, or idling for long periods.

**Lead Glazing.**
Plug insulator firing tip appears yellow or green/yellow and shiny in appearance.
Fault: Often caused by incorrect carburation, excessive idling followed by sharp acceleration. Also check ignition timing.

**Carbon fouling.**
Dry, black, sooty deposits.
Fault: over-rich fuel mixture.
Check: carburettor mixture settings, float level, choke operation, air filter.

**Oil fouling.**
Wet, oily deposits. Fault: worn bores/piston rings or valve guides; sometimes occurs (temporarily) during running-in period.

**Overheating.**
Electrodes have glazed appearance, core nose very white – few deposits. Fault: plug overheating. Check: plug value, ignition timing, fuel octane rating (too low) and fuel mixture (too weak).

**Electrode damage.**
Electrodes burned away; core nose has burned, glazed appearance. Fault: pre-ignition. Check: for correct heat range and as for 'overheating'.

**Split core nose.**
(May appear initially as a crack). Fault: detonation or wrong gap-setting technique.
Check: ignition timing, cooling system, fuel mixture (too weak).

# WHY DOUBLE COPPER IS BETTER FOR YOUR ENGINE.

Unique Trapezoidal Copper Cored Earth Electrode — 50% Larger Spark Area — Copper Cored Centre Electrode

Champion Double Copper plugs are the first in the world to have copper core in both centre <u>and</u> earth electrode. This innovative design means that they run cooler by up to 100°C – giving greater efficiency and longer life. These double copper cores transfer heat away from the tip of the plug faster and more efficiently. Therefore, Double Copper runs at cooler temperatures than conventional plugs giving improved acceleration response and high speed performance with no fear of pre-ignition.

Champion Double Copper plugs also feature a unique trapezoidal earth electrode giving a 50% increase in spark area. This, together with the double copper cores, offers greatly reduced electrode wear, so the spark stays stronger for longer.

 **FASTER COLD STARTING**

 **FOR UNLEADED OR LEADED FUEL**

 **ELECTRODES UP TO 100°C COOLER**

 **BETTER ACCELERATION RESPONSE**

 **LOWER EMISSIONS**

 **50% BIGGER SPARK AREA**

 **THE LONGER LIFE PLUG**

**Plug Tips/Hot and Cold.**
Spark plugs must operate within well-defined temperature limits to avoid cold fouling at one extreme and overheating at the other.
Champion and the car manufacturers work out the best plugs for an engine to give optimum performance under all conditions, from freezing cold starts to sustained high speed motorway cruising.
Plugs are often referred to as hot or cold. With Champion, the higher the number on its body, the hotter the plug, and the lower the number the cooler the plug.

**Plug Cleaning**
Modern plug design and materials mean that Champion no longer recommends periodic plug cleaning. Certainly don't clean your plugs with a wire brush as this can cause metal conductive paths across the nose of the insulator so impairing its performance and resulting in loss of acceleration and reduced m.p.g.
However, if plugs are removed, always carefully clean the area where the plug seats in the cylinder head as grit and dirt can sometimes cause gas leakage.
Also wipe any traces of oil or grease from plug leads as this may lead to arcing.

DOUBLE ◄◄ COPPER

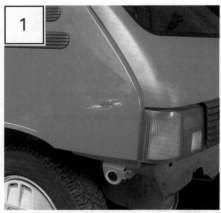

This photographic sequence shows the steps taken to repair the dent and paintwork damage shown above. In general, the procedure for repairing a hole will be similar; where there are substantial differences, the procedure is clearly described and shown in a separate photograph.

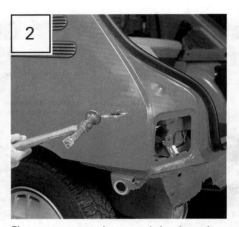

First remove any trim around the dent, then hammer out the dent where access is possible. This will minimise filling. Here, after the large dent has been hammered out, the damaged area is being made slightly concave.

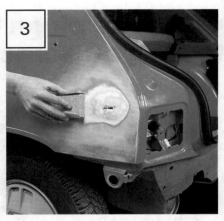

Next, remove all paint from the damaged area by rubbing with coarse abrasive paper or using a power drill fitted with a wire brush or abrasive pad. 'Feather' the edge of the boundary with good paintwork using a finer grade of abrasive paper.

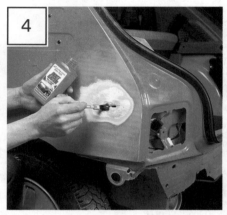

Where there are holes or other damage, the sheet metal should be cut away before proceeding further. The damaged area and any signs of rust should be treated with Turtle Wax Hi-Tech Rust Eater, which will also inhibit further rust formation.

*For a large dent or hole* mix Holts Body Plus Resin and Hardener according to the manufacturer's instructions and apply around the edge of the repair. Press Glass Fibre Matting over the repair area and leave for 20-30 minutes to harden. Then ...

... brush more Holts Body Plus Resin and Hardener onto the matting and leave to harden. Repeat the sequence with two or three layers of matting, checking that the final layer is lower than the surrounding area. Apply Holts Body Plus Filler Paste as shown in Step 5B.

*For a medium dent*, mix Holts Body Plus Filler Paste and Hardener according to the manufacturer's instructions and apply it with a flexible applicator. Apply thin layers of filler at 20-minute intervals, until the filler surface is slightly proud of the surrounding bodywork.

*For small dents and scratches* use Holts No Mix Filler Paste straight from the tube. Apply it according to the instructions in thin layers, using the spatula provided. It will harden in minutes if applied outdoors and may then be used as its own knifing putty.

Use a plane or file for initial shaping. Then, using progressively finer grades of wet-and-dry paper, wrapped round a sanding block, and copious amounts of clean water, rub down the filler until glass smooth. 'Feather' the edges of adjoining paintwork.

**7**

Protect adjoining areas before spraying the whole repair area and at least one inch of the surrounding sound paintwork with Holts Dupli-Color primer.

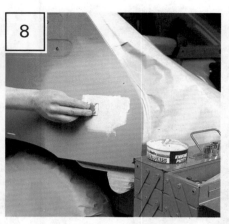

**8**

Fill any imperfections in the filler surface with a small amount of Holts Body Plus Knifing Putty. Using plenty of clean water, rub down the surface with a fine grade wet-and-dry paper – 400 grade is recommended – until it is really smooth.

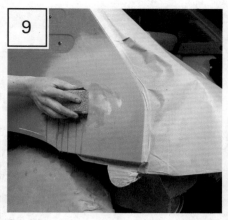

**9**

Carefully fill any remaining imperfections with knifing putty before applying the last coat of primer. Then rub down the surface with Holts Body Plus Rubbing Compound to ensure a really smooth surface.

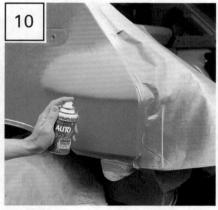

**10**

Protect surrounding areas from overspray before applying the topcoat in several thin layers. Agitate Holts Dupli-Color aerosol thoroughly. Start at the repair centre, spraying outwards with a side-to-side motion.

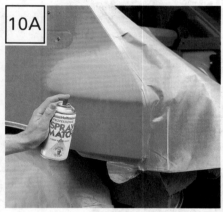

**10A**

If the exact colour is not available off the shelf, local Holts Professional Spraymatch Centres will custom fill an aerosol to match perfectly.

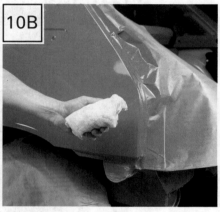

**10B**

To identify whether a lacquer finish is required, rub a painted unrepaired part of the body with wax and a clean cloth.

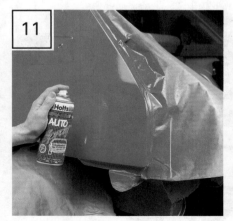

**11**

If *no* traces of paint appear on the cloth, spray Holts Dupli-Color clear lacquer over the repaired area to achieve the correct gloss level.

**12**

**13**

The paint will take about two weeks to harden fully. After this time it can be 'cut' with a mild cutting compound such as Turtle Wax Minute Cut prior to polishing with a final coating of Turtle Wax Extra.

**14**

When carrying out bodywork repairs, remember that the quality of the finished job is proportional to the time and effort expended.

# HAYNES No1 for DIY

Haynes publish a wide variety of books besides the world famous range of **Haynes Owners Workshop Manuals**. They cover all sorts of DIY jobs. Specialist books such as the **Improve and Modify** series and the **Purchase and DIY Restoration Guides** give you all the information you require to carry out everything from minor modifications to complete restoration on a number of popular cars. In addition there are the publications dealing with specific tasks, such as the **Car Bodywork Repair Manual** and the **In-Car Entertainment Manual**. The **Household DIY** series gives clear step-by-step instructions on how to repair everyday household objects ranging from toasters to washing machines.

Whether it is under the bonnet or around the home there is a Haynes Manual that can help you save money. Available from motor accessory stores and bookshops or direct from the publisher.

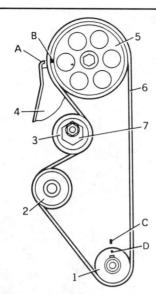

**Fig. 1.6 Timing belt and valve timing marks (Sec 7)**

| | | | |
|---|---|---|---|
| 1 | Crankshaft toothed pulley | A | Left-hand (inner) cover |
| 2 | Water pump toothed | | bracket |
| | pulley | B | Camshaft toothed pulley |
| 3 | Tensioning roller | | timing mark |
| 4 | Left-hand (inner) cover | C | Oil pump cover timing |
| 5 | Camshaft toothed pulley | | mark |
| 6 | Timing belt | D | Crankshaft toothed pulley |
| 7 | Tensioning roller adjuster | | timing mark |

## 8 Timing belt – checking and adjustment

**Note:** *Never run the engine with the timing belt outer cover removed.*

1 Unbolt and remove the timing belt outer cover (Sec 6).
2 Check the timing belt carefully, looking for signs of oil contamination, of cracks or wear on its back and sides, or for excessive wear, cracks or missing teeth on the toothed surface. If any such signs are found the belt must be renewed. For safety's sake the belt must be renewed as a matter of course at the specified service interval.
3 To check the timing belt's tension, first use a spanner applied to the alternator drive pulley bolt to rotate the crankshaft two full turns clockwise to take up any slack in the belt.
4 Use the thumb and forefinger to apply a moderate force (between 15 and 20 N/3.4 and 4.5 lbf) to try to twist the timing belt through 90°, testing midway between the camshaft and crankshaft toothed pulleys, on the belt's front run (photo). If the belt can be twisted through more than 90° (or if it cannot be twisted at all), adjustment is required.
5 To adjust the timing belt, slacken its locknut and rotate the tensioning roller adjuster as necessary (anti-clockwise to tighten the belt, clockwise to slacken it) until the belt can just be twisted through 90°.

Hold the adjuster and tighten the locknut securely, to the specified torque wrench setting if possible (photos).
6 Rotate the crankshaft through two further full turns to settle the timing belt and recheck the tension. **Do not** overtighten the belt, as this will considerably reduce its life expectancy.
7 Refit the timing belt outer cover (Sec 6) and the control cables and air cleaner (Chapter 3).

## 9 Camshaft right-hand oil seal – renewal

1 Remove the timing belt and the camshaft toothed pulley (Sec 7).
2 Punch or drill two small holes opposite each other in the seal. Screw a self-tapping screw into each and pull on the screws with pliers to extract the seal.
3 Clean the seal housing and polish off any burrs or raised edges which may have caused the seal to fail in the first place.
4 Lubricate the lips of the new seal with clean engine oil and drive it into position until it seats on its locating shoulder, using a suitable socket or tube. Take care not to damage the seal lips during fitting. Note that the seal lips should face inwards.
5 Refit the camshaft toothed pulley and the timing belt (Sec 7).

## 10 Camshaft and followers – removal and refitting

1 Remove the air cleaner and warm air intake hose, then either disconnect the accelerator and choke cables or secure them clear of the cylinder head cover (Chapter 3).
2 Remove the spark plugs (Chapter 4) and cover their holes with rag to prevent the entry of dirt.
3 Disconnect the two breather hoses from the cylinder head cover (photo).
4 Unscrew the two retaining nuts, noting the dished washer and rubber grommet under each, then remove the cylinder head cover (photos). While the cover is off, clean its underside and the separator (Chapter 3), removing all traces of sludge and dirt. Check the gasket and rubber grommets for signs of wear, damage or distortion and renew them if necessary.
5 Remove the fuel pump (Chapter 3).
6 Remove the distributor (Chapter 4).
7 Unscrew the single Allen screw and remove the extension from the cylinder head left-hand end, noting its sealing O-ring (photos).
8 Remove the timing belt left-hand (inner) cover (Sec 6).
9 Working in the sequence shown (photo) unscrew slowly and by one turn at a time the camshaft upper bearing nuts. Work only as described to release the pressure of the valve springs on the upper bearing castings gradually and evenly.
10 Withdraw the upper bearings, lift out the camshaft and remove the oil seal. Note the locating dowels fitted around four of the front (spark plug side) upper bearing mounting studs.
11 Obtain eight small, clean containers and number them 1 to 8. Using a rubber sucker, withdraw each cam follower in turn and place it in its respective container, with its shim. **Do not** interchange the cam follow-

8.4 Checking tension of timing belt

8.5A Adjusting timing belt tension – engine in vehicle ...

8.5B ... rotate adjuster until belt is correctly tensioned, then tighten locknut

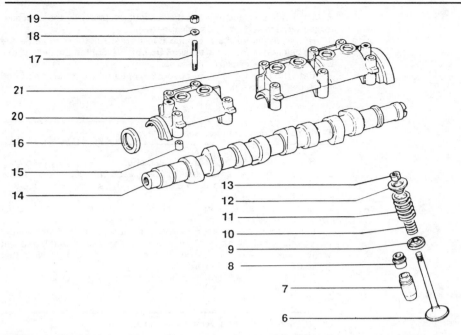

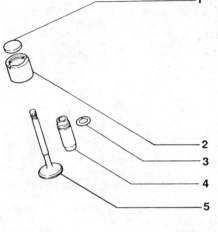

**Fig. 1.7 Camshaft and valves (Sec 10)**

| | | | | | | | |
|---|---|---|---|---|---|---|---|
| 1 | Shim | 7 | Inlet valve guide | 13 | Split collets | 19 | Nut |
| 2 | Cam follower | 8 | Valve stem oil seal (all valves) | 14 | Camshaft | 20 | Camshaft upper bearing* |
| 3 | Circlip (all valves) | 9 | Spring seat | 15 | Dowel | 21 | Camshaft upper bearing* |
| 4 | Exhaust valve guide | 10 | Inner valve spring | 16 | Oil seal | | |
| 5 | Exhaust valve | 11 | Outer valve spring | 17 | Stud | | |
| 6 | Inlet valve | 12 | Spring retainer | 18 | Washer | | |

*Note: camshaft upper bearings shown for reference only – not available separately from cylinder head

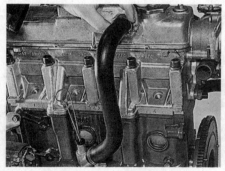

10.3 Disconnecting crankcase breather hose from cylinder head cover

10.4A Unscrew retaining nuts, noting dished washers ...

10.4B ... and rubber grommets under each ...

10.4C ... then lift off cylinder head cover

10.7A Unscrewing cylinder head extension retaining Allen screw

10.7B Removing extension from cylinder head

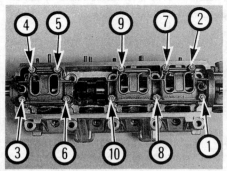

10.9 Camshaft upper bearing nut slackening sequence

10.12 Lubricate cam followers on refitting

10.13A Refitting camshaft – note upper bearing locating dowels (arrowed)

10.13B Install camshaft so that Number 1 cylinder lobes point away from valves

10.14A Refitting camshaft right-hand upper bearing – note location of sealant

10.14B Refitting camshaft left-hand upper bearing – note location of sealant

10.15 Tighten camshaft upper bearing nuts to specified torque wrench settings

10.17 Installing camshaft right-hand oil seal

10.18 Renew O-ring whenever extension is removed

ers or their shims, or the rate of wear will be much increased and all the valve clearances will have to be rechecked on reassembly.

12    On reassembly, liberally oil the cylinder head cam follower bores then carefully refit the cam followers to the cylinder head, ensuring that each follower is refitted to its original bore, with its original shim (photo). Remember that each shim's marked surface must face downwards. Some care will be required to enter the cam followers squarely into their relevant bores.

13    Liberally oil the camshaft bearings and lobes then refit the camshaft, rotating it so that Number 1 cylinder lobes are pointing away from their valves, as shown (photos).

14    Ensure that the locating dowels are pressed firmly into their recesses and apply a thin smear of suitable sealant (Lada recommend Super Three Bond No. 50) to the cylinder head mating surface with each upper bearing, **only** at the extreme ends (photos). Refit the upper bearings.

15    Working in the sequence shown in Fig. 1.8, tighten slowly and by one turn at a time the camshaft upper bearing nuts until the bearings

touch the cylinder head evenly, then go round again, in the same sequence, tightening the nuts to the specified torque wrench setting (photo). Work only as described to impose the pressure of the valve springs on the upper bearing castings gradually and evenly.

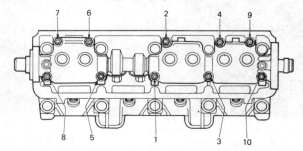

Fig. 1.8 Camshaft upper bearing nut tightening sequence (Sec 10)

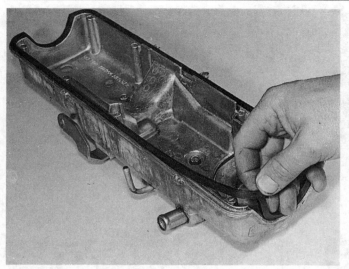

10.24 Ensure cylinder head cover gasket is seated in cover groove

16   Wipe off all surplus sealant so that none is left to find its way into any oilways. Follow the sealant manufacturer's instructions as to the time needed for curing. Usually, at least an hour must be allowed between application of the sealant and starting the engine.
17   Lubricate the lips of the new right-hand oil seal with clean engine oil and drive it into position until it seats on its locating shoulder, using a suitable socket or tube (photo). Take care not to damage the seal lips during fitting. Note that the seal lips should face inwards.
18   Using a soft-faced mallet, tap the camshaft fully to the right and refit the extension to the cylinder head left-hand end, using a new sealing O-ring (photo). Note that the extension's inner boss controls camshaft endfloat. Tighten the Allen screw to the specified torque wrench setting.
19   Refit the timing belt covers, the timing belt, its tensioner and the camshaft toothed pulley and adjust the belt's tension (Secs 6, 7 and 8).
20   Check, and if necessary, adjust, the valve clearances (Sec 5).
21   Refit the distributor (Chapter 4).
22   Refit the fuel pump (Chapter 3).
23   Fill the cylinder head wells around the cam followers with clean engine oil.
24   Ensuring that the cylinder head cover gasket is correctly seated in its groove (photo) and that the oil separator is cleaned, refit the cover, then insert the rubber grommets into their locations around the studs. Refit the dished washers and the nuts and tighten the nuts evenly until the washers seat on the stud shoulders. **Do not** overtighten the nuts in an attempt to cure oil leaks; this will merely make matters worse and risk shearing the studs. If the cover leaks oil, check the gasket and rubber grommets and renew them if necessary.
25   Reconnect the breather hoses to the cylinder head cover.

26   Refit the spark plugs (Chapter 4) and the control cables and air cleaner (Chapter 3).

**11   Cylinder head – removal and refitting**

1   If the engine is still in the vehicle, carry out the following preliminary dismantling operations.

(a)   *Remove the air cleaner and warm air intake hose, then discon-nect the accelerator and choke cables (Chapter 3)*
(b)   *Drain the cooling system, then disconnect the thermostat as-sembly and cooling system hoses from the cylinder head return union and the carburettor (Chapter 2)*
(c)   *Disconnect the battery negative lead*
(d)   *Remove the spark plugs, then either remove the distributor or disconnect its wiring so that it can be removed with the cylinder head (Chapter 4)*
(e)   *Disconnect the vacuum servo unit vacuum hose and the econometer hose from the inlet manifold*
(f)   *Disconnect the wires from the coolant temperature gauge sender unit, the carburettor and the oil pressure switch (photo)*
(g)   *Disconnect the fuel feed hose from the pump and the return hose from the carburettor (Chapter 3)*
(h)   *Disconnect the exhaust system downpipe from the manifold, then unbolt its bracket from the cylinder block/crankcase (Chap-ter 3)*
(i)   *Unbolt the inlet manifold-to-coolant feed pipe bracket (Chap-ter 3)*
(j)   **Note**: *The cylinder head can be removed complete with the manifolds and carburettor, or the manifolds can be detached from the cylinder head before removal (Chapter 3)*

2   Remove the timing belt left-hand (inner) cover (Sec 6).
3   Remove the cylinder head cover (Sec 10).
4   Working in the reverse of the sequence shown in Fig. 1.10, slacken progressively and by one turn at a time the ten cylinder head bolts.
5   Remove the cylinder head bolts and recover the washers. Measure the length of each bolt (less washer) from under its head to its tip (photo). If any bolt has stretched to more than the maximum permiss-ible length of 135.5 ± 0.8 mm, it must be renewed. Owners are advised to renew all the bolts as a set if any is found to be over-stretched.
6   Lift the cylinder head from the cylinder block/crankcase. If necess-ary, tap the cylinder head gently with a soft-faced mallet to free it from the block, but do not lever at the joint surfaces. Note that the cylinder head is located on dowels.
7   Recover the cylinder head gasket and discard it.
8   Clean the cylinder head and cylinder block/crankcase mating sur-faces by careful scraping. Take care not to damage the cylinder head, which is made from light alloy, and is easily scored. Cover the coolant passages and other openings with masking tape or rag to prevent dirt and carbon falling in. Mop out all the oil from the bolt holes; if oil is left in the holes, hydraulic pressure could crack the cylinder block/crankcase when the bolts are refitted.

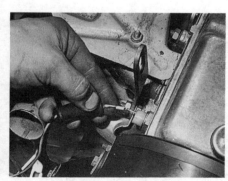

11.1 Disconnecting oil pressure switch

11.5 Measuring length of cylinder head bolts – renew if stretched

11.10A Fit locating dowels to cylinder block/crankcase recesses

11.10B Cylinder head gasket will fit only correct way on dowels

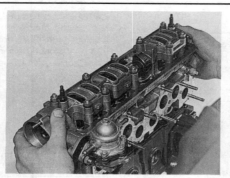

11.11 Refitting cylinder head

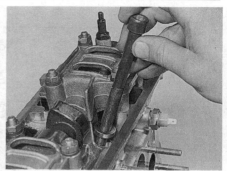

11.12 Lightly oil threads and do not forget washers when refitting cylinder head bolts

11.13A Tighten bolts in specified stages to torque wrench setting ...

11.13B ... then to angles specified, using angular torque gauge

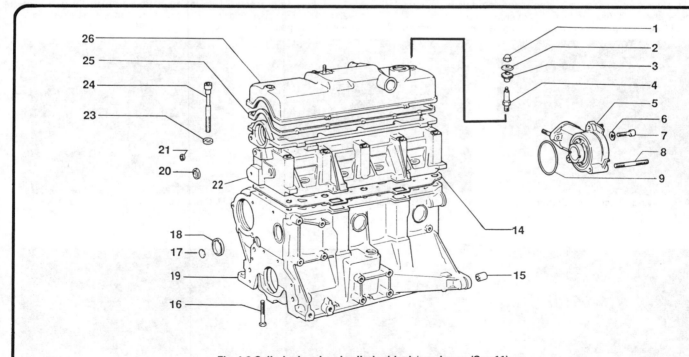

Fig. 1.9 Cylinder head and cylinder block/crankcase (Sec 11)

| | | | |
|---|---|---|---|
| 1 Nut | 7 Allen screw | 13 Cylinder head cover | 19 Cylinder block/crankcase |
| 2 Dished washer | 8 Stud | 14 Cylinder head gasket | 20 Ring |
| 3 Rubber grommet | 9 O-ring | 15 Dowel | 21 Blanking plug |
| 4 Stud | 10 Washer | 16 Main bearing cap bolt | 22 Cylinder head |
| 5 Cylinder head extension | 11 Cylinder head bolt | 17 Blanking plug | |
| 6 Washer | 12 Gasket | 18 Core plug | |

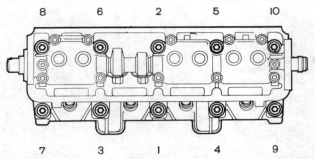

Fig. 1.10 Cylinder head bolt tightening sequence (Sec 11)

9    If desired, the cylinder head can be dismantled and inspected (Secs 12, 13 and 27).
10   On reassembly, ensure that the mating surfaces are scrupulously clean, press the two locating dowels into their recesses and place a new cylinder head gasket on the cylinder block/crankcase (photos). Note that if the dowels are in place, the gasket will only fit the correct way. Take care to avoid any oil or grease coming into contact with the gasket.
11   Check that Number 1 cylinder piston is at TDC and that Number 1 cylinder valves are closed. Refit the cylinder head, locating it on the dowels (photo).
12   Lightly oil their threads and refit the cylinder head bolts, ensuring that the washers are in place under their heads (photo). Screw the bolts in by hand as far as possible.
13   Tighten the cylinder head bolts working in the sequence shown in Fig. 1.10. Tighten the bolts in the four stages given in the Specifications, using a torque wrench for Stages 1 and 2, and an angular torque gauge (or a protractor and cardboard template) for Stages 3 and 4 (photos).
14   If the specified bolt-tightening procedure is followed exactly, there is no need to check-tighten the bolts after the engine has first been run, or as a regular maintenance operation at any time.
15   Check, and if necessary adjust, the valve clearances (Sec 5).
16   Fill the cylinder head wells around the cam followers with clean engine oil, then refit the cylinder head cover (Sec 10).
17   Refit the timing belt covers, the timing belt, its tensioner and the

camshaft toothed pulley and adjust the belt's tension (Secs 6, 7 and 8).
18   If the cylinder head was removed with the engine still in the vehicle, refit all removed components, following the reverse of the removal procedure and working as described in the relevant Sections of this Chapter, as well as in Chapters 2, 3 and 4.

## 12   Cylinder head – dismantling and reassembly

1    Remove the cylinder head (Sec 11).
2    Remove the inlet and exhaust manifolds (Chapter 3) and the coolant return hose union (Chapter 2).
3    Unscrew the coolant temperature gauge sender unit and the oil pressure switch from the cylinder head (photos).
4    Remove the camshaft and followers (Sec 10).
5    Obtain eight small, clean containers and number them 1 to 8.
6    Using a valve spring compressor with a long reach, compress the springs of the first valve (each valve has double valve springs, one inside the other) until the split collets can be removed from the groove in the valve stem (photo). If the retainer is difficult to release, do not tighten the compressor further, but gently tap the top of the tool with a hammer. Always make sure that the compressor is firmly located on the retainer.
7    Release the compressor and remove the spring retainer and springs, noting which way up the springs are fitted (photos).
8    Withdraw the valve (photo).
9    Prise the oil seal from the valve stem and discard it, then remove the spring seat (photos).
10   Keep all components of each valve assembly together in their respective container, so that there is no chance of any component being interchanged with that from another valve assembly.
11   Repeat the procedure given in paragraphs 6 to 10 for the remaining valves, keeping separate all components so that they can be refitted in their original positions.

12.3A Removing coolant temperature gauge sender unit ...

12.3B ... and oil pressure switch from cylinder head

12.6 Compress valve springs and remove split collets ...

12.7A ... then remove spring retainer ...

12.7B ... note how valve springs are fitted before removing ...

12.8 ... then withdraw valve

12.9A Valve stem oil seals must be removed ...

12.9B ... to allow removal of spring seat

12.12 Using a socket and extension to fit valve stem oil seals

12   On reassembly, ensure that all components are refitted in their original locations. Fit the spring seat, then use a suitable socket and extension to press a new oil seal on to the valve stem (photo).

13   Use fine abrasive paper to check that the valve stem is free from burrs or sharp edges which might damage a new stem oil seal, then oil the valve stem before refitting it.

14   Refit the springs, ensuring that they are the correct way up and are seated correctly, followed by the retainer. Compress the springs and locate the split collets in the stem groove, using grease to stick them in place.

15   Release the compressor, ensuring that the collets are not displaced, then tap the stem end with a soft-faced mallet to settle the components.

16   Refit the cam followers and camshaft (Sec 10).

17   Refit the oil pressure switch and the coolant temperature gauge sender unit, applying a smear of sealant to their threads, and tightening them securely.

18   Refit the coolant return hose union (Chapter 2) and the inlet and exhaust manifolds (Chapter 3).

19   Refit the cylinder head (Sec 11).

## 13   Cylinder head and pistons – decarbonising

1   Remove and dismantle the cylinder head (Sec 12).

2   This operation will normally only be required at comparatively high mileages. However, if persistent pre-ignition ('pinking') occurs and performance has deteriorated even though the engine adjustments are correct, decarbonising and valve grinding may be required.

3   Bearing in mind that the cylinder head is of light alloy construction and is easily damaged, use a blunt scraper or rotary wire brush to clean all traces of carbon deposits from the combustion chambers and the ports. The valve stems and the valve guides should also be freed from any carbon deposits. Wash the combustion chambers and ports down with paraffin, and scrape the cylinder head surface free of any foreign matter with the side of a steel rule, or similar. Remove all traces of gasket from the cylinder head lower surface, then wash it thoroughly with paraffin.

4   If the engine is still in the vehicle, clean the piston crowns and cylinder bore upper edges. If the pistons are still in the cylinder block, then it is essential that great care is taken to ensure that no carbon gets into the cylinder bores, as this could scratch the cylinder walls or cause damage to the pistons and rings. To ensure that this does not happen, first turn the crankshaft so that two of the pistons are at the top of their bores. Push rag into the other two bores or seal them off with paper and masking tape. The coolant passages should also be covered with small pieces of masking tape, to prevent particles of carbon entering the cooling system and damaging the water pump.

5   Press a little grease into the gap between the cylinder walls and the two pistons which are to be worked on. With a blunt, rounded-off scraper and wire wool, carefully remove the carbon from the piston crown, taking great care not to scratch the aluminium. Also scrape away the carbon from the surrounding lip of the cylinder wall. When all carbon has been removed, scrape away the grease which will now be contaminated with carbon particles, taking care not to press any into the bores. To assist prevention of carbon build-up, the piston crowns can be polished with metal polish. Remove the rags or masking tape from the other two cylinders, and turn the crankshaft so that the two pistons which were at the bottom are now at the top. Place a rag or masking tape in the cylinders, which have been decarbonised, and proceed as just described.

6   Examine the heads of the valves for pitting and burning, especially the heads of the exhaust valves. The valve seats should be examined at the same time. If the pitting on the valve and seat is very slight, the marks can be removed by grinding the seats and valves together with coarse, and then fine valve grinding paste.

7   Where excessive pitting has occurred to the valve seats, it will be necessary to recut them and fit new valves. This latter job should be entrusted to a local dealer, or suitably-equipped engineering works. In practice it is very seldom that the seats are so badly worn. Normally it is the valve that is too badly worn for refitting, and the owner can easily purchase a new set of valves and match them to the seats by valve grinding.

8   Valve grinding is carried out as follows. Place the cylinder head upsidedown on blocks of wood on a bench. Smear a trace of coarse carborundum paste on the valve seat face and press a suction grinding tool onto the valve head (photo). With a semi-rotary action, grind the valve head to its seat, lifting the valve occasionally to redistribute the grinding paste. When a dull matt even surface is produced on the mating surfaces of both the valve seat and the valve, wipe off the paste and repeat the process with fine carborundum paste as before. A light spring placed under the valve head will greatly ease this operation.

13.8 Grinding in a valve

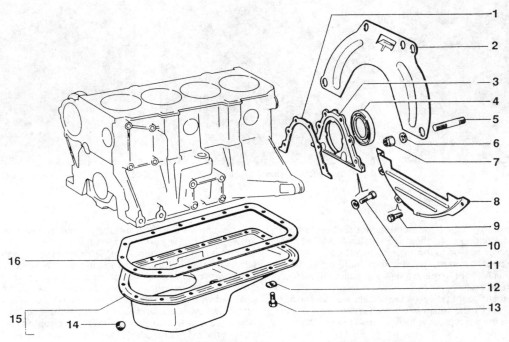

**Fig. 1.11 Sump and crankshaft left-hand oil seal (Sec 14)**

| | | | |
|---|---|---|---|
| 1 | Gasket | 5 | Stud | 9 | Bolt | 13 | Bolt |
| 2 | Engine/transmission | 6 | Washer | 10 | Bolt | 14 | Sump drain plug |
| | adaptor plate | 7 | Nut | 11 | Washer | 15 | Sump |
| 3 | Oil seal holder | 8 | Bellhousing dust cover | 12 | Washer | 16 | Gasket |
| 4 | Oil seal | | | | | | |

When a smooth unbroken ring of light grey matt finish is produced on the mating surfaces of both the valve and seat, the grinding operation is complete.

9    Carefully clean away every trace of grinding compound, taking great care to leave none in the ports or in the valve guides. Clean the valves and valve seats with a paraffin-soaked rag, then with a clean rag, and finally if an air line is available, blow clean the valves, valve guides and ports.

10    If the valve guides are worn (evident from perceptible side-to-side rock of a valve in its guide), new guides will have to be fitted. This is a job for a dealer, as a special tool is required to remove and refit the guides without risk of damage and the guides must be reamed to the correct internal diameter once installed.

11    Check that all valve springs are intact. If any one is broken, all the springs should be renewed. Check the free height of the springs against new ones. If any one spring appears short, indicating wear, all should be renewed. Do not renew individual springs. Springs suffer from fatigue and it is a good idea to renew them after a high mileage, even if they look serviceable.

12    The cylinder head can be checked for warping either by placing it on a piece of plate glass or using a straight-edge and feeler blades. If there is any doubt or if the cylinder block/crankcase mating surface is corroded, check with a local dealer to see if it is possible to have the cylinder head refaced. If not, renewal is the only course of action possible.

## 14   Sump – removal and refitting

1    If the engine is still in the vehicle, carry out the following preliminary dismantling operations:

(a)   Drain the engine oil and remove the filter (Sec 2)
(b)   If better access is required, remove the engine compartment right-hand undershield (Chapter 10)
(c)   Unbolt the bellhousing dust cover (photo)

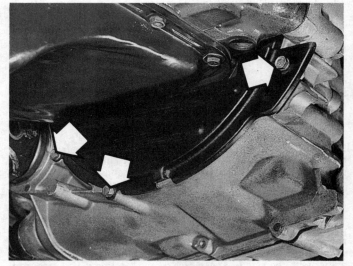

14.1 Bellhousing dust cover mountings (arrowed)

2    Progressively unscrew the sump bolts, noting the washers.

3    Withdraw the sump and discard the gasket.

4    Clean all traces of old gasket and sealant from the mating faces of the cylinder block/crankcase, oil seal/pump housings and sump.

5    On reassembly, use heavy grease to stick a new sump gasket on the cylinder block/crankcase, then refit the sump and the bolts (with their washers) and progressively tighten the bolts to the specified torque wrench setting (photos). Sealant should not be used unless the mating surfaces are damaged or distorted. **Do not** overtighten the sump bolts in an attempt to cure oil leaks; this will merely make matters worse.

6    If the engine is in the vehicle, further refitting is the reverse of the removal procedure. Fit a new filter and refill the engine with oil (Sec 2).

14.5A Use grease to stick new sump gasket in place ...

14.5B ... then refit sump ...

14.5C ... and tighten bolts evenly to specified torque setting

## 15 Crankshaft right-hand oil seal – renewal

1 If the engine is still in the vehicle, remove the engine compartment right-hand undershield (Chapter 10).
2 Remove the alternator drive pulley and drivebelt, the timing belt outer cover, the timing belt and tensioner and the crankshaft toothed pulley (Sec 7).
3 Punch or drill two small holes opposite each other in the seal. Screw a self-tapping screw into each and pull on the screws with pliers to extract the seal.
4 Clean the seal housing and polish off any burrs or raised edges which may have caused the seal to fail in the first place.
5 Lubricate the lips of the new seal with clean engine oil and drive it

into position until it seats on its locating shoulder, using a suitable socket or tube. Take care not to damage the seal lips during fitting. Note that the seal lips should face inwards.
6 Refit the crankshaft toothed pulley and the timing belt and all other removed components (Sec 7).

## 16 Oil pump – removal and refitting

1 Remove the sump (Sec 14).
2 Remove the alternator drive pulley and drivebelt, the timing belt outer cover, the timing belt and tensioner and the crankshaft toothed pulley (Sec 7).

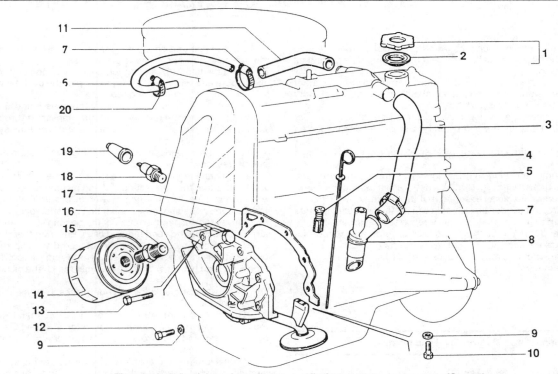

**Fig. 1.12 Lubrication and crankcase ventilation system components (Sec 16)**

| | | | | | |
|---|---|---|---|---|---|
| 1 | Oil filler cap | 5 | Dipstick seal | 10 | Bolt | 15 | Mounting stub |
| 2 | Gasket | 6 | Breather hose – cylinder head cover-to-carburettor | 11 | Breather hose – cylinder head cover-to-air cleaner | 16 | Oil pump assembly |
| 3 | Breather hose – cylinder block/crankcase-to-cylinder head cover | 7 | Clamp | 12 | Bolt | 17 | Gasket |
| | | 8 | Breather hose union | 13 | Bolt | 18 | Oil pressure switch |
| 4 | Engine oil level dipstick | 9 | Washer | 14 | Oil filter | 19 | Rubber cover |
| | | | | | | 20 | Clamp |

16.3A Oil pump pick-up pipe and strainer mountings (arrowed)

16.3B Note sealing O-ring on pick-up pipe end (arrowed)

16.7A Use grease to stick new gasket in place ...

16.7B Oil pump locating dowels and recesses (arrowed)

16.7C Tighten pump mounting bolts to specified torque wrench setting

3    Unbolt the oil pump pick-up pipe from the crankshaft main bearing cap and from the oil pump itself. Withdraw the pick-up pipe, noting its sealing O-ring (photos).
4    Unscrew the bolts securing the oil pump to the cylinder block/crankcase, noting their varying lengths, then carefully withdraw the oil pump. Recover and discard the gasket.
5    Thoroughly clean the mating faces of the oil pump and cylinder block/crankcase. If desired the pump can be dismantled and inspected (Sec 27).
6    On reassembly, prime the pump by injecting oil into it and turning it by hand.
7    Refit the pump, ensuring that its inner gear engages fully on the crankshaft flats, then use grease to stick a new gasket behind the pump and push the pump into place, ensuring that its locating dowels fit into their recesses in the cylinder block/crankcase. Refit the retaining bolts and tighten them to the specified torque wrench setting (photos).
8    Using a new O-ring, refit the pump pick-up pipe and tighten its mounting bolts to the specified torque wrench settings.
9    Refit all components removed in paragraph 2 (Sec 7).
10    Refit the sump (Sec 14).

## 17   Pistons/connecting rods – removal and refitting

1    Remove the cylinder head (Sec 11).
2    Remove the sump (Sec 14).
3    Unbolt and remove the oil pump pick-up pipe (Sec 16).
4    Note that the connecting rod and big-end cap are marked with the number of the cylinder they belong to stamped into them on the rear (oil filter) side, Number 1 cylinder being at the timing belt end. If no marks are present, use a centre-punch to identify the caps and connecting rods.
5    Turn the crankshaft so that Number 1 crankpin is at its lowest point, then unscrew the nuts and tap off the big-end cap. Keep the bearing

shells in the cap and connecting rod if they are to be re-used, taping them in position if necessary to avoid loss.
6    Using the handle of a hammer, push the piston and connecting rod up the bore and withdraw it from the top of the cylinder block. Loosely refit the cap to the connecting rod.
7    Repeat the procedure given in paragraphs 5 and 6 on Number 4 piston and connecting rod, then turn the crankshaft through half a turn and repeat the procedure on Numbers 2 and 3 pistons and connecting rods.
8    The pistons, connecting rods and big-end bearings can be examined as described in Section 27.
9    If the connecting rod bolts are to be renewed, they must be tapped out. Ensure that the connecting rod and piston are correctly supported while this is done. When fitting new bolts, ensure that the head shaped end fits correctly against the connecting rod shoulder (photos).
10    On refitting, clean the backs of the bearing shells and the recesses in the connecting rods and big-end caps. Ensuring that the shells are of the correct size, fit them to the connecting rod and cap so that the shell locating tabs engage with the slot in the cap or rod. Note that the connecting rod has an oilway which must match the oil hole in the shell (photo).
11    Lubricate the crankpins, cylinder bores, pistons and piston rings with engine oil.
12    Fit a ring compressor to Number 1 piston, then insert the piston and connecting rod into Number 1 cylinder, ensuring that the connecting rod oilway and the arrow on the piston crown both point towards the timing belt end.
13    With Number 1 crankpin at its lowest point, drive the piston carefully into the cylinder with the wooden handle of a hammer. Guide the connecting rod into position on the crankpin (photo).
14    Fit the big-end cap (with bearing shell), ensuring that the identifying numbers or markings are on the same (oil filter) side. Tighten the big-end cap nuts to the specified torque wrench setting (photos).
15    Check that the crankshaft turns freely.
16    Repeat on the remaining piston and connecting rod assemblies the procedure given in paragraphs 10 to 15 above.
17    Refit the oil pump pick-up pipe (Sec 16), the sump (Sec 14) and the cylinder head (Sec 11).

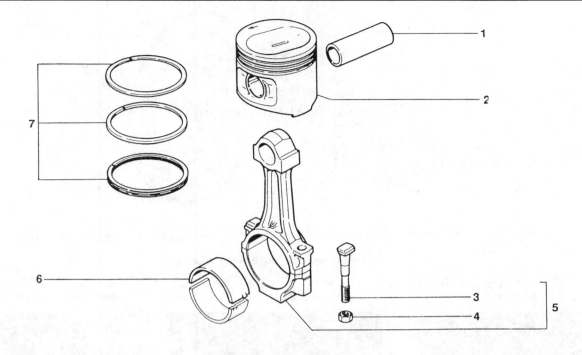

**Fig. 1.13 Piston and connecting rod (Sec 17)**

| | | | |
|---|---|---|---|
| 1 Gudgeon pin | 3 Bolt | 5 Connecting rod and cap assembly | 6 Big-end bearing shells |
| 2 Piston | 4 Nut | | 7 Piston rings |

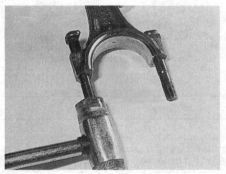

17.9A Removing a connecting rod cap bolt

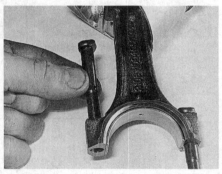

17.9B When refitting bolt, ensure head fits against rod shoulder

17.10 Big-end bearing shell tab must engage with recess in rod or cap

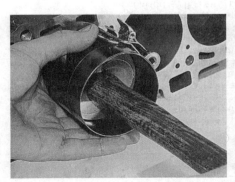

17.13 Driving piston into cylinder bore

17.14A Ensure marks are on same side when refitting big-end cap

17.14B Tighten big-end cap nuts to specified torque wrench setting

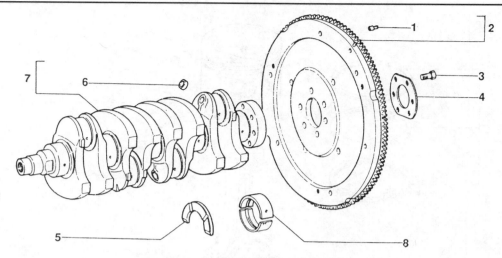

**Fig. 1.14 Crankshaft and flywheel (Sec 18)**

1  Clutch locating dowel pin (3 off)   3  Bolt   5  Thrustwasher   7  Crankshaft
2  Flywheel                            4  Washer plate   6  Blanking plug   8  Main bearing shells

18.3 Unscrew flywheel securing bolts and remove washer plate ...

18.4 ... then note flywheel/crankshaft alignment marks (arrowed)

18.6 Conical hollow in flywheel must align with No 4 cylinder crankpin (arrowed)

18.7 Crankshaft must be locked while flywheel bolts are tightened

## 18  Flywheel – removal and refitting

1   If the engine is still in the vehicle, remove the clutch (Chapter 5).
2   Prevent the flywheel from turning by locking the ring gear teeth (see photo 7.6a), or by bolting a strap between the flywheel and the cylinder block. If the sump has been removed, wedge a clean block of wood between the wall of the cylinder block/crankcase and the crankshaft.
3   Unscrew the securing bolts and remove the washer plate (photo).
4   Note the alignment punch marks on the flywheel and the end of the crankshaft (photo). If none can be found, make your own so that the flywheel can be refitted in its original position.
5   Withdraw the flywheel. Do not drop it, it is very heavy.
6   On reassembly, ensure that the mating faces are clean, then refit the flywheel to the crankshaft, aligning their punch marks. As an additional aid to correct location, the conical hollow machined in the outer edge of the flywheel's left-hand surface (just inside the ring gear) should be aligned with the Number 4 cylinder crankpin (photo).
7   Fit the washer plate and the bolts, lock the flywheel by the method used on dismantling, then tighten the bolts to the specified torque setting progressively and in a diagonal sequence (photo).
8   Refit the clutch and transmission (Chapters 5 and 6).

## 19  Crankshaft left-hand oil seal – renewal

1   Remove the flywheel (Sec 18).
2   Unbolt the oil seal holder from the cylinder block/crankcase and discard the gasket (photo).

19.2 Unbolting left-hand oil seal holder from cylinder block/crankcase

3    Using a hammer and punch applied to the slot in the holder, drive out the seal from the holder right-hand side (photo).
4    Clean the seal housing and polish off any burrs or raised edges which may have caused the seal to fail in the first place.
5    Lubricate the new seal with clean engine oil and drive it into position until it seats on its locating shoulder, using a suitable (clean) block of wood (photos).
6    Use grease to stick a new gasket in position on the cylinder block/crankcase and grease the seal lips and crankshaft flange, then carefully refit the holder using the fingers only to guide the oil seal lips over the crankshaft end (photos). Note that this is difficult as the holder's three locating projections fit too closely around the crankshaft to allow

room to manoeuvre, so be very careful not to damage the seal lips during fitting.
7    When the new seal is located correctly on the crankshaft, check that the gasket is properly aligned and refit the holder bolts. Using a straight-edge to ensure that the holder and cylinder block/crankcase mating surfaces are aligned **exactly** (or oil will leak at this point), tighten the bolts evenly and securely (photo).
8    Refit the flywheel (Sec 18).

## 20   Engine/transmission mountings – removal and refitting

1    The engine/transmission assembly is supported on three mountings, two of which are attached to the transmission and one to the engine.

### Front mounting
2    Apply the handbrake, jack up the front of the vehicle and support it securely on axle stands.
3    Remove the engine compartment right-hand undershield (Chapter 10).
4    Suitable lifting equipment must now be used to support the engine/transmission as the mounting is removed. The best would be either an engine hoist or an adjustable crosspiece (Chapter 6, Fig. 6.3). The support must be adjustable as it may be necessary to raise or lower the assembly. Attach the equipment to the lifting eye on one of the exhaust manifold mounting studs, then just take the weight of the assembly.
5    Working under the vehicle, unbolt the engine mounting from the cylinder block/crankcase, then unscrew the through-bolt retaining nut, tap out the bolt and withdraw the mounting (photos).
6    Refitting is the reverse of the removal procedure. Tighten the nut to its specified torque wrench setting when the mounting is reassembled.
7    Disconnect the lifting equipment from the engine, refit the undershield and lower the vehicle to the ground.

19.3 Driving out oil seal

19.5A Lubricate new seal on installation ...

19.5B ... and tap into place as shown

19.6A Use grease to stick new gasket in place ...

19.6B ... then guide seal lips over crankshaft flange while refitting holder

19.7 Use straight-edge to align exactly seal holder with sump surface when tightening bolts

20.5A Engine/transmission front mounting seen from below

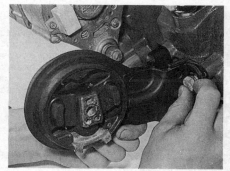

20.5B Unbolting front mounting from cylinder block/crankcase

20.11A Note location of lifting eye on left-hand mounting

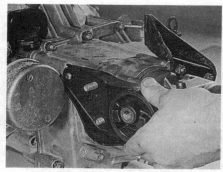

20.11B Removing left-hand mounting from transmission

20.16A Engine/transmission rear mounting nuts (arrowed)

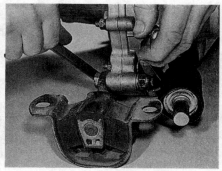

20.16B Unbolting rear mounting from transmission

### Left-hand mounting

8    Apply the handbrake, jack up the front of the vehicle and support it securely on axle stands.

9    Remove the engine compartment left-hand undershield (Chapter 10).

10   Suitable lifting equipment must now be used to support the engine/transmission as the mounting is removed. The best would be either an engine hoist or an adjustable crosspiece (Chapter 6, Fig. 6.3). The support must be adjustable as it may be necessary to raise or lower the assembly. Attach the equipment to a lifting eye bolted to the exhaust manifold left-hand mounting stud, then just take the weight of the assembly.

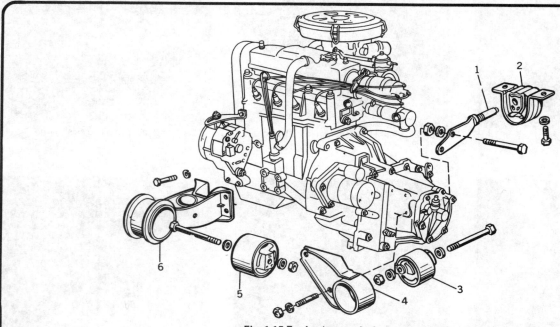

**Fig. 1.15 Engine/transmission mounting (Sec 20)**

| | | |
|---|---|---|
| 1   Rear mounting bracket | 3   Left-hand mounting rubber | 5   Front mounting rubber | 6   Front mounting bracket |
| 2   Rear mounting | 4   Left-hand mounting bracket | | |

11  Working under the vehicle, unscrew the nuts securing the mounting to the transmission (noting the lifting eye), then unscrew the through-bolt retaining nut, tap out the bolt and withdraw the mounting (photos).
12  Refitting is the reverse of the removal procedure. Assemble the mounting, then tighten the various nuts to their specified torque wrench settings.
13  Disconnect the lifting equipment from the engine, refit the undershield and lower the vehicle to the ground.

*Rear mounting*
14  Apply the handbrake, jack up the front of the vehicle and support it securely on axle stands.
15  Support the weight of the engine/transmission using a trolley jack and wooden spacer, or similar.
16  Unscrew the nuts securing the mounting to the vehicle's body, then unbolt the mounting from the transmission (photos).
17  Refitting is the reverse of the removal procedure. Assemble the mounting, then tighten the various nuts to their specified torque wrench settings.
18  Remove the lifting equipment from the transmission and lower the vehicle to the ground.

---

### 21  Major operations requiring engine removal

The following operations can be carried out only after removing the engine from the vehicle:

(a)  *Removal of the crankshaft main bearings*
(b)  *Removal of the crankshaft*

---

### 22  Engine – method of removal

The engine must be removed complete with the transmission by raising the front of the vehicle (approximately 0.76 m/30 in), lowering the engine/transmission assembly to the ground and then withdrawing it. The items of equipment required to achieve this are a strong trolley jack, axle stands (capable of supporting the vehicle at a height of approximately 0.5 m/21 in), chocks, an engine hoist and lifting tackle. An engine dolly would be very useful to save strain and prevent the risk of damage when moving the engine/transmission, out of the vehicle.

---

### 23  Engine and transmission – removal and separation

1  Park the vehicle on firm, level ground, apply the handbrake and remove the bonnet and engine compartment undershields (Chapter 10).
2  Jack up the front of the vehicle and support it securely on axle stands, then remove the roadwheels (see '*Jacking, towing and wheel changing*').

3  If the engine is to be dismantled, drain its oil and remove the oil filter (Sec 2).
4  Drain the transmission oil (Chapter 6).
5  Drain the cooling system (Chapter 2).
6  Disconnect the battery negative terminal (Chapter 11).
7  Remove the air cleaner and warm air intake hose, then disconnect the accelerator and choke cables (Chapter 3).
8  Disconnect the alternator and starter motor wiring (Chapter 11).
9  Disconnect the wires from the coolant temperature gauge sender unit, the carburettor and the oil pressure switch.
10  Disconnect the distributor wiring, including the ignition HT coil lead (Chapter 4).
11  Removing its single retaining screw, withdraw the TDC sensor from the bellhousing.
12  Disconnect the clutch cable (Chapter 5).
13  Disconnect the speedometer drive cable (Chapter 11).
14  Disconnect the vacuum servo unit vacuum hose and the econometer hose from the inlet manifold.
15  Disconnect the fuel feed hose from the pump and the return hose from the carburettor (Chapter 3).
16  Disconnect the expansion tank, radiator and heater hoses from the thermostat assembly and coolant feed pipe (Chapter 2).
17  Working underneath the vehicle, disconnect the engine/transmission earth lead from the transmission.
18  Disconnect the gearchange linkage control rod from the transmission (Chapter 6).
19  Disconnect the reversing lamp switch wires (Chapter 6).
20  Either disconnect the exhaust downpipe from the system at the downpipe-to-mid-section joint so that the downpipe is removed with the engine/transmission, or remove the downpipe completely (Chapter 3).
21  Working as described in Chapter 9, slacken the front suspension tie-bar rear nuts, unbolt the tie-bar front mountings and swing the tie-bars clear of the engine/transmission.
22  At the bottom of each hub carrier, unscrew the two bolts to separate the hub carrier from its suspension lower arm balljoint, then slacken by one or two turns only the three top mounting nuts of each suspension strut.
23  Remove both driveshafts from the transmission and support the differential sun gears (Chapter 7, Section 3, paragraphs 9 and 10), then secure the driveshafts (complete with each suspension strut, hub carrier and brake caliper) clear of the transmission. Take care not to stretch or kink the brake hoses.
24  The engine/transmission assembly should now be retained only by the three mountings. Check that all components have been removed or disconnected that might prevent the removal of the assembly.
25  Using an engine hoist or similar attached to the lifting eyes fitted to the inlet manifold and to the engine/transmission left-hand mounting, take the weight of the engine/transmission assembly and unfasten the mountings from the vehicle's body.
26  Lower the engine/transmission assembly to the ground and remove it from under the vehicle (photos).
27  Remove the starter motor (Chapter 11).
28  Unbolt the mountings from the engine and transmission (Sec 20).
29  Unbolt the bellhousing dust cover (Sec 14).
30  Unscrew the bolts and the nut securing the transmission to the cylinder block/crankcase. Check that all components that might prevent

23.26A Using engine hoist to lower engine/transmission to ground

23.26B Front of vehicle must be raised to allow removal of engine/transmission

24.0 Removing thermostat assembly and coolant feed pipe

25.14 Removing cylinder head (less manifolds)

the removal of the transmission have been removed or disconnected.
31    Prise the transmission off the locating dowels and move it squarely away from the engine, ensuring that the clutch components are not damaged. Collect the engine/transmission adaptor plate.
32    Remove the clutch. Do not forget to overhaul the clutch components before the engine and transmission are reconnected (Chapter 5).

## 24   Ancillary components – removal and refitting

Before dismantling the main engine components, the following externally-mounted ancillary components can be removed, with reference to the relevant Chapters where applicable:

*Exhaust system downpipe (Chapter 3)*
*Inlet manifold, carburettor and exhaust manifold (Chapter 3)*
*Dipstick and crankcase breather hose union and hoses (Chapter 3)*
*Alternator and mountings (Chapter 11)*
*Distributor, HT leads and spark plugs (Chapter 4)*
*Oil pressure switch*
*Coolant temperature gauge sender unit*
*Fuel pump (Chapter 3)*
*Thermostat assembly and coolant feed pipe (photo) (Chapter 2)*
*Oil filter, if not already removed (Sec 2)*

## 25   Engine dismantling – general

### General

1    It is preferable to mount the engine on a dismantling stand, but if this is not possible, stand the engine on a strong bench at a comfortable working height. Failing this, it will have to be stripped down on the floor.
2    Cleanliness is most important, and if the engine is dirty, it should first be cleaned with paraffin.
3    Avoid working with the engine directly on a concrete floor, as grit presents a real source of trouble.
4    If the engine oil appears extremely dirty or contaminated, avoid inverting the engine until the sump has been removed. This will prevent any sludge from entering the oilways.
5    As components are removed, clean them in a paraffin bath. However, do not immerse components with internal oilways in paraffin,

as it is difficult to remove, usually requiring a high pressure hose. Clean oilways with nylon pipe cleaners.
6    It is advisable to have suitable containers available to hold small items according to their use, as this will help when reassembling the engine and will also prevent possible losses.
7    Always obtain a complete set of new gaskets for use during engine reassembly, but retain the old gaskets with a view to using them as a pattern to make replacements if a suitable new one is not available.
8    Where possible, refit securing nuts, bolts and washers to their locations after removing the relevant components. This will help to protect the threads and will also prevent possible losses.
9    Retain unserviceable components in order to compare them with the new components supplied.
10    Read through the relevant Section of this Chapter carefully before commencing work, to ensure that any special tools which may be required are available. Many components (particularly gaskets and oil seals) must be renewed on reassembly. Where applicable, obtain the required new components before starting work.

### Dismantling

11    With the engine removed from the vehicle and separated from the transmission (Sec 23), remove all ancillary components (Sec 24).
12    Remove the timing belt with its covers, tensioner and toothed pulleys (Secs 6 and 7).
13    Remove the water pump (Chapter 2).
14    Remove the cylinder head (Sec 11). If required, it can be dismantled as described in Section 12 (photo).
15    Turn the engine over and rest it on a clean wooden surface so that the cylinder head mating surface is not damaged.
16    Remove the sump (Sec 14).
17    Remove the oil pump (Sec 16).
18    Remove the flywheel (Sec 18).
19    Remove the pistons and connecting rods (Sec 17).
20    Remove the crankshaft and main bearings (Sec 26).

## 26   Crankshaft and main bearings – removal and refitting

1    With the engine removed from the vehicle, remove the oil pump (Sec 16).
2    Remove the flywheel (Sec 18) and the crankshaft left-hand oil seal (Sec 19).

26.4 Crankshaft main bearing cap identification marks (arrowed)

26.7 Removing crankshaft from cylinder block/crankcase

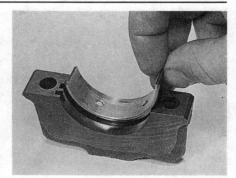

26.10A Main bearing shell tab must engage with recess in cap

26.10B Grooved shells must be refitted in original locations

26.11 Lubricate bearing surfaces ...

3    Remove the pistons and connecting rods (Sec 17). If no work is to be done on the pistons and connecting rods, there is no need to push the pistons out of the cylinder bores.

4    Check the main bearing caps for identification marks and if necessary use a centre-punch to identify them. Normally the caps have identifying notches cut into them as shown in Fig. 1.16, though those on the project vehicle were found to be slightly different (photo). The main difference was that Number 5 cap had only two notches. Note that all caps are numbered from the timing belt end and their marks are on the front (alternator) side.

5    Before removing the crankshaft, check that the endfloat is within the specified limits (Sec 27). If the endfloat is outside the specified limits, new thrustwashers will be required.

6    Unscrew the bolts and tap off the main bearing caps complete with bearing shells. If the bearing shells are to be re-used, tape them to their respective caps.

7    Lift the crankshaft from the cylinder block/crankcase (photo).

8    Extract the bearing shells from the crankcase, keeping them with their respective caps if they are to be re-used and recover the thrustwashers from the Number 3 main bearing location. Note that some of the shells may have oil grooves in them. Note carefully which these are and ensure that they are correctly refitted. If new shells are to be fitted

which do not have these grooves, seek the advice of the supplying dealer as to how the shells are to be installed.

9    On refitting, ensure that the cylinder block/crankcase and crankshaft are thoroughly clean and that the oilways are clear. If possible, blow through the oilways with compressed air and inject clean engine oil into them. Wipe clean the backs of the bearing shells and the recesses in the cylinder block/crankcase main bearing locations and the caps.

10    Ensuring that the shells are of the correct size, fit them to the cylinder block/crankcase recesses and caps so that each shell's locating tab engages with the slot in the cap or recess. Ensure that any grooved shells (see paragraph 8) are refitted in their original locations (photos).

11    Lubricate the shells and main bearing journals with engine oil (photo).

12    Use heavy grease to stick the thrustwashers on each side of the Number 3 main bearing shell location, with the grooved side of each washer facing outwards from the cylinder block/crankcase (ie towards the crankshaft thrust face) (photo).

13    Carefully refit the crankshaft to the cylinder block/crankcase. If necessary, seat the crankshaft using light taps with a soft-faced mallet on the crankshaft webs.

14    Lubricate the crankshaft main bearing journals again, then fit the main bearing caps, ensuring that they are refitted on their original journals with the largest number of notches on the front (alternator) side. Fit the cap bolts and lightly tighten them by hand (photos).

15    Working in the cap order 3-4-2-5-1, tighten each main bearing cap's bolts; first tighten them evenly until the cap touches the cylinder block/crankcase, then tighten them to the specified torque wrench setting (photo).

16    After each main bearing cap is tightened, check that the crankshaft is free to rotate. Some stiffness is to be expected with new components, but there should be no tight spots or binding.

17    Check that the crankshaft endfloat is within the specified limits (Sec 27).

18    Refit the pistons and connecting rods (Sec 17).

19    Refit the crankshaft left-hand oil seal (Sec 19).

20    Refit the flywheel (Sec 18).

21    Refit the oil pump (Sec 16).

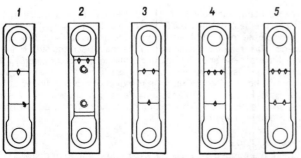

Fig. 1.16 Crankshaft main bearing cap identifying notches (Sec 26)

26.12 ... and use grease to stick thrustwashers in place

26.14A Refit crankshaft main bearing caps (and shells) ...

26.14B ... so that notches are on alternator side ...

26.14C ... then refit cap bolts

26.15 Tighten main bearing cap bolts to specified torque wrench setting

## 27   Engine components – examination and renovation

### General

1   With the engine completely stripped, clean all the components and examine them for wear. Each part should be checked and where necessary renewed or renovated as described in the relevant Sections of this Chapter. Renew main and big-end bearing shells as a matter of course, unless it is known that they have had little wear and are in perfect condition.

2   If in doubt as to whether to renew a component which is still just serviceable, consider the time and effort which will be incurred should the component fail at an early date. Obviously the age and expected life of the vehicle must influence the standards applied.

### Crankshaft

3   The checking of crankshaft endfloat requires a dial gauge (photo), but alternatively feeler gauges can be used as follows. Push the crankshaft as far as possible towards the timing belt end of the engine and using a feeler gauge, measure the gap between the crankshaft thrust face and the thrustwasher. Now push the crankshaft as far as possible in the opposite direction and take the same measurement again. The difference between the two measurements is the crankshaft endfloat. If it is outside the specified limits, new or oversized thrustwashers will be required. These are usually supplied together with the main and big-end bearing shells on a reground crankshaft.

4   Examine the crankpin and main journal surfaces for signs of scoring or scratches, and check the ovality of the crankpins and main journals using micrometer. If wear is excessive, or if the bearing surface ovality is outside the specified limits, the crankpins and/or main journals will have to be reground, and undersize bearing shells fitted.

5   Big-end and crankpin wear is accompanied by distinct metallic knocking, particularly noticeable when the engine is pulling from low revs, and some loss of oil pressure.

6   Main bearing and main journal wear is accompanied by severe engine vibration rumble, getting progressively worse as engine revs increase, and again by loss of oil pressure.

7   Crankshaft regrinding should be carried out by a suitable engineering works, who will normally supply the matching undersize bearing shells.

8   Note that undersize bearing shells may already have been fitted, either in production or by a previous repairer. Check the markings on the backs of the old bearing shells, and if in doubt take them along when buying new ones.

### Main and big-end bearings

9   Unless they are virtually new, the original bearing shells should be renewed. Not to do so is a false economy.

10   Inspect the big-end and main bearing shells for signs of general wear, scoring, pitting and scratches. The bearings should be matt grey in colour. With lead-indium bearings, should a trace of copper colour be noticed, the bearings are badly worn, as the lead bearing material has worn away to expose the indium underlay. Renew the bearings if they are in this condition, or if there are any signs of scoring or pitting. You are strongly advised to renew the bearings regardless of their condition at the time of major overhaul.

11   The undersizes available are designed to correspond with crankshaft regrind sizes. The bearings are in fact, slightly more than the stated undersize, as running clearances have to be allowed for during their manufacture.

12   Main and big-end bearing shells can be identified as to size by the marking on the back of the shell. Refer to paragraph 8.

13   An accurate method of determining bearing wear is by the use of Plastigage. The crankshaft is located in the main bearings (and big-end bearings if necessary) and the Plastigage filament is located across the journal, which must be dry. The cap is then fitted and the bolts/nuts tightened to the specified torque. On removal of the cap, the width of the filaments is checked against a scale which shows the bearing running clearance (photo). This clearance is then compared with that given in the Specifications.

### Connecting rods

14   Check the connecting rods for wear and damage. If distortion of the connecting rods is suspected, have them checked by a dealer or

27.3 Measuring crankshaft endfloat

27.13 Checking bearing clearance using Plastigage

27.16 Cylinder bore standard size grade code letter in sump mating surface

engine reconditioning specialist. The pistons cannot be removed and refitted from the connecting rods by the ordinary owner.

### Cylinder block/crankcase

15    The cylinder bores must be examined for taper, ovality, scoring and scratches. Start by examining the top of the bores. If these are worn, a slight ridge will be found on the thrust side, which marks the top of the piston ring travel. If the wear is excessive, the engine will have a high oil consumption rate accompanied by blue smoke from the exhaust.

16    If available, use an internal micrometer, or a dial gauge to measure the bore diameter just below the ridge and compare it with the diameter at the bottom of the bore, which is not subject to wear. The size grade of standard bores is shown by the code letter stamped in the cylinder block/crankcase sump mating surface (photo). If no measuring instruments are available, use a piston from which the rings have been removed, and measure the gap between it and the cylinder wall with a feeler gauge. If the difference in bore diameter is more than the specified amount, the cylinders will normally require reboring in order to fit new oversize pistons.

17    It may be possible to obtain proprietary oil control rings for fitting to the existing pistons if it is felt that the degree of wear does not justify a rebore. However, any improvement brought about by such rings may be shortlived.

18    Whenever new piston rings are being installed, the glaze on the original cylinder bores should be removed using either abrasive paper or a glaze-removing tool in an electric drill. If abrasive paper is used, use strokes at 60° to the bore centre-line, to create a cross-hatching effect.

19    Check the cylinder bores for signs of wear ridges towards the top of the bores. If wear ridges are evident, and new piston rings are being fitted, the top ring must be stepped in order to clear the wear ridge, or the bore must be de-ridged using a suitable scraper.

20    Thoroughly examine the cylinder block/crankcase for cracks and damage and use a piece of wire to probe all oilways and waterways to ensure that they are all unobstructed.

21    Use a straight-edge and feeler gauge to check that the cylinder head gasket face of the cylinder block/crankcase is not distorted. If the distortion exceeds the specified limit, it may be possible to have the block refaced by a suitably-equipped engineering works, otherwise it must be renewed.

22    Take the opportunity to check the engine core plugs while they are easily accessible. To renew them, knock out the old plugs with a hammer and chisel or punch. Clean the plug seats, smear the new plugs with sealant and tap them squarely into position.

### Pistons and piston rings

23    Examine the pistons for ovality, scoring and scratches.

24    The gudgeon pins are an interference fit in the connecting rod small-end eyes, and separation of the pistons from the connecting rods and refitting is therefore a job for a dealer or engine reconditioning specialist.

25    The pistons should be fitted to the connecting rods so that the arrow on the piston crown points to the same side as the connecting rod oilway (see Fig. 1.17).

26    New pistons are normally supplied complete with rings. If new rings are being fitted to the existing pistons, expand the old rings over the top of the pistons. The use of two or three old feeler gauges will be

helpful in preventing the rings dropping into empty grooves. Note that the oil control ring is in two sections and note which way up each ring is fitted for use when reassembling (photos).

27    Before fitting the new rings to the pistons, insert them into the cylinder bore and use a feeler gauge to check that the end gaps are within the specified limits. Check the end gaps at the upper and lower limits of the piston travel in the bores. Adjustment of the gap can be made by careful grinding to bring it within the specified tolerance, but this is best carried out by a suitably-equipped specialist. Also check the piston ring-to-groove clearances, again using a feeler gauge. If the ring grooves in the pistons are worn, new pistons may be required (photos).

28    Clean out the piston ring grooves using a piece of old piston ring as a scraper. Be careful not to scratch the surface of the pistons. Protect your fingers, as piston ring edges are sharp. Also probe the groove oil return holes in the pistons, and the oil holes in the connecting rod big-ends.

29    Prepare the cylinder block/crankcase as described in paragraphs 18 and 19 above, if applicable.

30    The top compression rings should be fitted with the word 'TOP' facing uppermost, or if no marks are visible, as noted during removal (photo). If a stepped top compression ring is being fitted, fit the ring with the smaller diameter of the step uppermost. The standard second compression ring is fitted with its step downwards. The oil control ring expander spring has a narrower section at one point, which must be

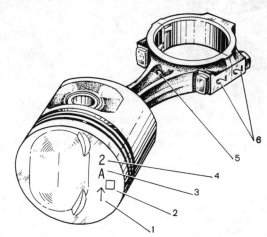
Fig. 1.17 Piston and connecting rod markings (Sec 27)

1   Arrow indicating orientation of piston in cylinder – points to timing belt end of engine
2   Repair size mark:
    No mark – standard size
    Triangle – first oversize
    Square – second oversize
3   Piston diameter grading code letter

4   Gudgeon pin bore grading code number
5   Connecting rod oilway – points to timing belt end of engine
6   Cylinder number – rod and cap numbers should always match and be aligned together

27.26A Using feeler gauge blade to remove piston ring

27.26B Note oil control ring expander spring's narrow section – must be fitted next to end gap

27.27A Measuring piston ring end gap

27.27B Measuring piston ring-to-groove clearance

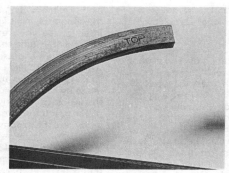

27.30 'TOP' marking indicates top compressing ring top surface

27.33 Lifting off oil pump outer cover

27.34A Unscrew threaded plug, noting sealing washer ...

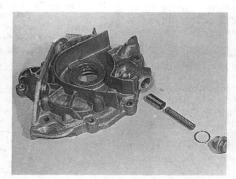

27.34B ... to release pressure relief valve components

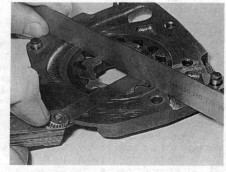

27.37A Measuring oil pump inner gear endfloat

fitted next to the ring end gap. The ring end gaps should be offset 120° from each other. Use two or three old feeler gauges to assist fitting, as during removal. Note that the compression rings are brittle, and will snap if expanded too far.

31   If new pistons are to be fitted, they must be selected from the grades available, after measuring the cylinder bores, and fitted by a dealer or engine reconditioning specialist. Normally, the appropriate oversize pistons are supplied by the dealer when the block is rebored.

### Oil pump – dismantling, inspection and reassembly

32   If oil pump wear is suspected, check the cost and availability of new parts and the cost of a new pump. Examine the pump as described in this Section and then decide whether renewal or repair is the best course of action.

33   Unscrew the Allen bolts and remove the outer cover (photo). Note

that the gears will be left in the inner cover.

34   Unscrew the threaded plug and recover the oil pressure relief valve spring and plunger (photos).

35   The gears can now be removed from the pump inner cover.

36   Inspect the gears for obvious signs of wear or damage, and renew if necessary.

37   Using a straight-edge placed across the top of the pump inner cover and the gears and a feeler gauge, check that the gear endfloat is within the specified limits (photos).

38   If either gear's endfloat is outside the specified limits, both gears should be renewed.

39   On reassembly, lubricate the gears with clean engine oil and refit them to the inner cover.

40   Renew the crankshaft right-hand oil seal (Sec 15) whenever the pump is removed (photo).

41   Reassembly is the reverse of the removal procedure but tighten

27.37B Measuring oil pump outer gear endfloat

27.40 Installing crankshaft right-hand oil seal

27.41 Tighten oil pump inner-to-outer cover Allen bolts to specified torque wrench setting

the pump inner-to-outer cover bolts to the specified torque wrench setting (photo).

### Cylinder head and valves
42   Refer to Section 13.

### Camshaft and followers
43   With the camshaft removed, examine the camshaft bearings and the cam follower bores for signs of obvious wear or pitting. If evident, a new cylinder head will probably be required.
44   The camshaft itself should show no signs of marks or scoring on the journals or cam lobe surfaces. If evident, renew the camshaft.
45   Examine the cam followers for signs of obvious wear and for ovality, and renew if necessary.

### Timing belt, tensioner and toothed pulleys
46   Refer to Section 8.

### Flywheel
47   With the flywheel removed, the ring gear can be examined for wear and damage.
48   If the ring gear is badly worn or has missing teeth the flywheel must be renewed.
49   If the flywheel's clutch mating surface is deeply scored, cracked or

otherwise damaged, the flywheel must be renewed, unless it is possible to have it surface ground; seek the advice of a dealer or engine reconditioning specialist.

### Oil seals and gaskets
50   Gaskets, oil seals and O-rings must all be renewed as a matter of routine.

---

### 28   Engine reassembly – general

### General
1   To ensure maximum life with minimum trouble from a rebuilt engine, not only must everything be correctly assembled, but it must also be spotlessly clean. All oilways must be clear, and all washers must be fitted in their original positions. Oil all bearings and other working surfaces thoroughly with clean engine oil during reassembly.
2   Before assembly begins, renew any bolts or studs which have damaged threads.
3   Gather together a torque wrench, an angular torque gauge, suitable sockets and bits, an oil can, clean lint-free rag and a full set of engine gaskets and oil seals, together with a new oil filter.

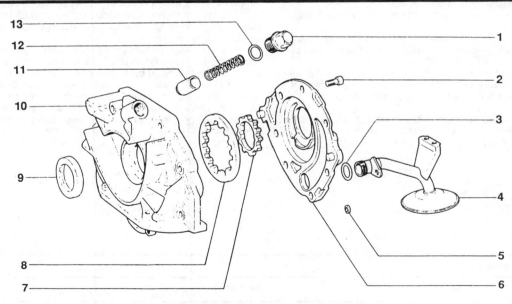

**Fig. 1.18 Oil pump components (Sec 27)**

| | | | |
|---|---|---|---|
| 1 | Threaded plug | 5 | Washer |
| 2 | Allen bolt | 6 | Inner cover |
| 3 | O-ring | 7 | Inner gear |
| 4 | Oil pump pick-up pipe and strainer | | |

| | | | |
|---|---|---|---|
| 8 | Outer gear | 11 | Pressure relief valve plunger |
| 9 | Crankshaft right-hand oil seal | 12 | Pressure relief valve spring |
| 10 | Outer cover | 13 | Sealing washer |

29.3A Locate engine/transmission adaptor plate on dowels

29.3B Refitting transmission to engine

29.3C Tighten engine/transmission fasteners to specified torque wrench settings

4    After reassembling the engine, refit the ancillary components (Sec 24), referring to the Chapters indicated where necessary.

## Reassembly

5    Working in the reverse of the sequence given in Section 25, paragraphs 11 to 20, reassemble the engine following the instructions given in the relevant Sections of this Chapter and Chapter 2.

## 29  Engine and transmission – reconnection and refitting

1    Refitting is the reverse of the removal procedure, noting the following points.
2    Refit the clutch as described in Chapter 5.
3    Reconnect the transmission to the engine as described in Chapter 6, Section 7, paragraphs 24 to 29 (photos).
4    Refit the bellhousing dust cover (Sec 14) and the starter motor (Chapter 11).
5    Push the engine/transmission assembly back under the vehicle, lift it into place and refasten the mountings (Sec 20).
6    Refit the driveshafts as described in Chapter 7, Section 3, paragraphs 11 to 15.
7    Working as described in the relevant Sections of Chapter 9, reassemble the front suspension lower arm balljoints and tighten the front suspension strut top mountings, then refit the tie-bars.
8    The remainder of the refitting procedure is a straightforward reversal of the removal sequence given in Section 23, following the instructions given in the relevant Sections of this Chapter and Chapters 2, 3, 4, 5, 6, 10 and 11.
9    When reassembly is complete and the bonnet and the engine compartment undershields have been refitted, lower the vehicle to the ground, check that the battery is fully charged and reconnect it, then

check carefully the engine oil, transmission oil and cooling system levels before attempting to start the engine.

## 30  Engine – initial start-up after overhaul

1    Make a final check to ensure that everything has been reconnected to the engine and that no tools or rags have been left in the engine compartment.
2    Check that oil and coolant levels are correct.
3    Start the engine. This may take a little longer than usual as fuel is pumped to the engine.
4    Check that the oil pressure warning lamp goes out when the engine starts. This too may take a little longer than usual as the oil filter fills with oil. If the warning lamp does not extinguish after a few seconds, stop the engine immediately and investigate the cause.
5    Run the engine at a fast tickover only (no faster) and check for leaks of oil, fuel, coolant or exhaust. Some smoke and odd smells may be experienced as assembly lubricant burns off the hot components.
6    Bring the engine to normal operating temperature, then check the ignition timing (Chapter 4) and the idle speed and mixture (Chapter 3).
7    When the engine has completely cooled, recheck the oil and coolant levels. Check again for signs of oil or coolant leaks which should be cured immediately.
8    If new bearings, pistons etc have been fitted, the engine should be run-in at reduced speeds and loads for the first 500 miles (800 km) or so. It is beneficial to change the engine oil and filter after this mileage.
9    If the specified procedure was followed exactly (Sec 11), there is no need to check-tighten the cylinder head bolts after the engine has first been run. Similarly, there is no need to check the valve clearances as a matter of routine (unless, of course excessive engine noise is heard from the valve gear or uneven running indicates the need to check the clearances on other grounds).

## 31  Fault diagnosis – engine

| Symptom | Reason(s) |
| --- | --- |
| Engine fails to turn over when starter operated | Discharged or defective battery<br>Dirty or loose battery leads<br>Defective starter solenoid or switch<br>Engine/transmission earth lead disconnected<br>Defective starter motor |

| Symptom | Reason(s) |
|---------|-----------|
| Engine turns over but will not start | Ignition system components damp or wet<br>HT leads loose or disconnected<br>Shorted or disconnected LT leads<br>Coil LT leads connected wrong way round<br>Defective ignition switch<br>Faulty ignition HT coil<br>No fuel in tank<br>Vapour lock in fuel line (in hot conditions or at high altitude)<br>Blocked carburettor float chamber needle valve<br>Faulty fuel pump<br>Fuel filter blocked<br>Blocked carburettor jets |
| Engine stalls and will not start | Ignition failure (in severe rain or after traversing water splash)<br>No fuel in tank!<br>Fuel tank breather choked<br>Sudden obstruction in carburettor<br>Water in fuel system |
| Engine misfires or idles unevenly | Ignition leads loose<br>Battery leads loose on terminals<br>Battery earth strap loose on body attachment point<br>Engine/transmission earth lead loose<br>Dirty or incorrectly gapped spark plugs<br>Tracking across distributor cap (oily or cracked cap)<br>Ignition timing incorrect<br>Faulty ignition HT coil<br>Fuel mixture too weak<br>Sticking inlet or exhaust valve<br>Incorrect valve clearance(s)<br>Air leak at carburettor<br>Air leak at inlet manifold-to-cylinder head or inlet manifold-to-carburettor joint<br>Weak or broken valve spring(s)<br>Worn valve guides or stems<br>Worn pistons or piston rings<br>Incorrect spark plug gap(s) |
| Lack of power and poor compression | Burnt exhaust valve(s)<br>Sticking or leaking valve(s)<br>Worn valve guides and stems<br>Weak or broken valve spring(s)<br>Blown cylinder head gasket (accompanied by increase in noise)<br>Worn pistons or piston rings<br>Worn or scored cylinder bores<br>Ignition timing incorrect<br>Valve clearances incorrect<br>Incorrect fuel mixture<br>Fuel filter partially blocked<br>Distributor advance mechanism faulty<br>Faulty fuel pump |
| Excessive oil consumption | Badly worn or missing valve stem oil seals<br>Excessively worn valve stems and valve guides<br>Worn piston rings<br>Worn pistons and cylinder bores |
| Oil being lost due to leaks | Leaking oil filter seal<br>Leaking cylinder head cover gasket<br>Leaking camshaft or crankshaft oil seal(s)<br>Leaking sump gasket |
| Unusual noises from engine | Worn valvegear (noisy tapping from cylinder head cover)<br>Worn big-end bearings (regular heavy knocking)<br>Worn main bearings (rumbling and vibration)<br>Worn crankshaft (knocking, rumbling and vibration) |
| Engine runs on after switching off | Faulty fuel cut-off system solenoid valve<br>Excessive carbon build-up in combustion chambers |

**Note:** *This Section is not intended to be an exhaustive guide to fault diagnosis but summarises the more common faults which may be encountered during a vehicle's life. Consult a dealer for more specific advice.*

# Chapter 2 Cooling system

**Contents**

**Specifications**

**System type** ............................................................ Pressurised, pump-assisted thermo-syphon with front-mounted radiator and thermostatically-controlled electric cooling fan

**System capacity** .................................................... 7.8 litres (13.7 Imp pints)

**Thermostat**
Type ........................................................................... Wax
Start to open temperature ......................................... 87 ± 2°C
Fully open temperature ............................................. 102°C
Minimum lift height ................................................... 8 mm

**Expansion tank filler cap**
Pressure relief valve opens at ................................... 1.1 bar
Vacuum relief valve opens at .................................... 0.03 to 0.13 bar

**Cooling fan operating temperature**
Switches on at ........................................................... 99 ± 3°C
Switches off at ........................................................... 94 ± 3°C

**Coolant mixture**
Mixture ratio ............................................................. 50% antifreeze (by volume)

| **Antifreeze** | **Water** |
|---|---|
| 3.9 litres (6.9 Imp pints) | 3.9 litres (6.9 Imp pints) |

Quantities (system refill) .........................................
Antifreeze type ......................................................... Ethylene glycol based antifreeze with corrosion inhibitors (Duckhams Universal Antifreeze and Summer Coolant)
Water type ................................................................. Clean, soft water (distilled water, soft tap water or clean rain water)
Coolant specific gravity ............................................ 1.078 to 1.095 gm/cc @ 20°C

**Torque wrench settings**

| | Nm | lbf ft |
|---|---|---|
| Coolant return hose union-to-cylinder head nuts | 16 to 22.5 | 12 to 16.5 |
| Coolant feed pipe-to-cylinder block bolts | 4 to 5 | 3 to 4 |
| Water pump mounting bolts | 7.5 to 8 | 5.5 to 6 |

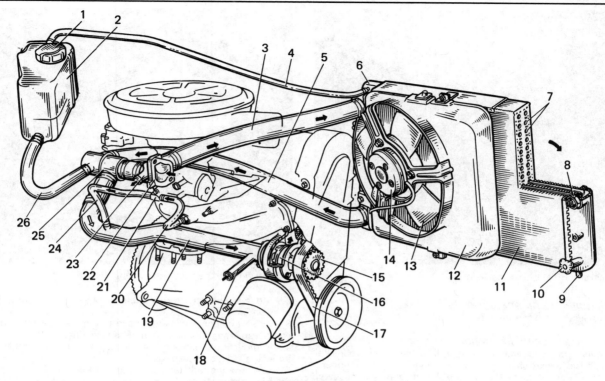

**Fig. 2.1 Layout of cooling system (Sec 1)**

| | | | |
|---|---|---|---|
| 1 | *Expansion tank filler cap* | 8 | *Electric cooling fan* |
| 2 | *Expansion tank* | | *thermostatic switch* |
| 3 | *Radiator top hose* | 9 | *Radiator bottom mounting* |
| 4 | *Expansion tank/radiator* | | *peg* |
| | *hose* | 10 | *Radiator drain plug* |
| 5 | *Radiator bottom hose* | 11 | *Radiator core* |
| 6 | *Radiator left-hand header* | 12 | *Cooling fan shroud* |
| | *tank* | 13 | *Cooling fan* |
| 7 | *Radiator coolant passages* | | |

| | |
|---|---|
| 14 | *Cooling fan electric motor* |
| 15 | *Water pump toothed pulley* |
| 16 | *Water pump* |
| 17 | *Timing belt* |
| 18 | *Heater return union* |
| 19 | *Coolant feed pipe* |
| 20 | *Carburettor heater feed* |
| | *hose* |

| | |
|---|---|
| 21 | *Carburettor heater* |
| 22 | *Coolant return hose union* |
| 23 | *Heater feed union* |
| 24 | *Carburettor heater return* |
| | *hose* |
| 25 | *Thermostat assembly* |
| 26 | *Expansion tank/thermostat* |
| | *hose* |

## 1   General description

The cooling system is of the pressurised, pump-assisted thermo-syphon type. It consists of the front-mounted aluminium radiator with a transparent expansion tank mounted on the left-hand inner wing, a thermostatically-controlled four-bladed electric cooling fan mounted on the back of the radiator, a thermostat and a centrifugal water pump as well as the connecting hoses. The water pump is driven by the engine's timing belt.

The location of the system's components and the direction of coolant flow are shown in Fig. 2.1.

**Warning:** *DO NOT attempt to remove the expansion tank filler cap or to disturb any part of the cooling system while it or the engine is hot, as there is a very great risk of scalding. If the expansion tank filler cap* **must** *be removed before the engine and radiator have fully cooled down (even though this is not recommended) the pressure in the cooling system must first be released. Cover the cap with a thick layer of cloth, to avoid scalding, and slowly unscrew the filler cap until a hissing sound can be heard. When the hissing has stopped, showing that pressure is released, slowly unscrew further the filler cap until it can be removed. If more hissing sounds are heard, wait until they have stopped before unscrewing the cap completely. At all times keep well away from the filler opening.*

**Warning:** *Do not allow antifreeze to come in contact with your skin or painted surfaces of the vehicle. Rinse off spills immediately with plenty of water. Never leave antifreeze lying around in an open container or in a puddle in the driveway or on the garage floor. Children and pets are attracted by its sweet smell but antifreeze is fatal if ingested.*

**Warning:** *If the engine is hot, the electric cooling fan may start rotating*

*even if the engine is not running, so be careful to keep hands, hair and loose clothing well clear when working in the engine compartment.*

## 2   Routine maintenance

**Note:** *Refer to the warnings given in Section 1 of this Chapter before starting work.*

1   Carry out the following procedures at the intervals given in *'Routine maintenance'* at the beginning of this manual.

### Check the coolant level

2   Check the coolant level when the engine and radiator are **cold**.

3   Check the level at the expansion tank. With the engine and radiator cold and the system fully filled, the coolant level should be between 30 and 40 mm (1.2 and 1.6 in) above the expansion tank 'Min' level line (photo).

4   If topping-up is required, add only the specified coolant mixture via the expansion tank filler cap opening (photo).

5   With a sealed-type cooling system, topping-up should be necessary only at very infrequent intervals. If frequent topping-up is required, then it is likely that there is a leak in the system or that the engine is overheating. Check all hoses and joint faces for any staining or actual wetness and rectify as necessary. If no leaks can be found it is advisable to have the system pressure-tested as the leak could possibly be internal. In such circumstances it is a good idea to keep a careful watch on the engine oil level as a serious internal coolant leak can often cause the sump level to rise, which will help to confirm your suspicions.

2.3 Maintain coolant at the correct level ...

2.4 ... using only the specified coolant mixture

### Check all radiator and heater hoses for leaks
6    Refer to Section 7 of this Chapter.

### Have the coolant specific gravity checked
7    Once every year, usually in preparation for winter, have your local Lada dealer check the specific gravity of the coolant using an antifreeze hydrometer or tester. If the test shows the specific gravity to be lower than the range specified, add neat antifreeze until it is correct. If the specific gravity should be too high, add only distilled water until it is correct.

### Drain, flush and refill the cooling system, renewing the coolant
8    Refer to Sections 3, 4, 5 and 6 of this Chapter.

2    Move the heater temperature control lever to the maximum 'Hot' position.
3    If the additional working space is required, remove the engine compartment right-hand front undershield (Chapter 10).
4    Remove the expansion tank filler cap and place a suitable container under the radiator drain plug.
5    Unscrew the radiator drain plug (photo) and allow the coolant to drain into the container. Release the expansion tank and ensure that it is fully emptied.
6    The above procedure will suffice for most normal draining operations, but note that the coolant remaining in the engine can be drained, if required, by unscrewing the drain plug found at the front of the cylinder block next to No 4 cylinder (photo). On refitting this plug, apply a suitable sealant to its threads and tighten it securely.
7    Once the coolant has fully drained, flush the system (Sec 4) and refill it (Secs 5 and 6).

### 3   Cooling system – draining

**Note:** *Refer to the warnings given in Section 1 of this Chapter before starting work.*

1    Drain the coolant only when the engine and radiator are **cold** (Sec 1).

### 4   Cooling system – flushing

**Note:** *Refer to the warnings given in Section 1 of this Chapter before starting work.*

1    With time the cooling system may gradually lose its efficiency, as the radiator core becomes choked with rust, scale deposits from the

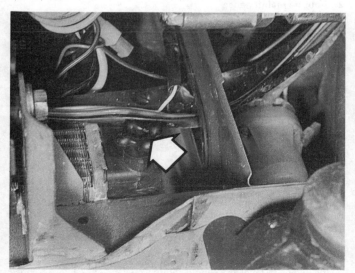

3.5 Location of radiator drain plug (arrowed) – undershield removed

3.6 Unscrewing cylinder block drain plug

water and other sediment. To minimise this, Lada recommend that as well as using only good quality antifreeze and clean soft water, the system is flushed whenever the coolant is renewed. Proceed as follows.

2  With the coolant drained (Sec 3) tighten the drain plugs securely and refill the system with fresh water. Refit the expansion tank filler cap, start the engine and warm it up to normal operating temperature, then stop it and (after allowing it to cool down completely) drain the system again. Repeat as necessary until only clean water can be seen to emerge, then refill finally with the specified coolant mixture (Sec 5).

3  If the specified coolant mixture has been used and has been renewed at the specific intervals, the above procedure will be sufficient to keep the system clean for a considerable length of time. If, however, the system has been neglected a more thorough operation will be required, as follows.

4  To flush the system thoroughly, first drain the coolant (Sec 3).

5  Disconnect the radiator top hose at the coolant return hose union on the cylinder head and the bottom hose at the radiator union.

6  Insert a garden hose into the top hose and allow water to circulate through the radiator until it runs clear from the bottom outlet.

7  To flush the engine, disconnect the coolant feed pipe coupling hose from the thermostat, insert the garden hose into the feed pipe and allow water to circulate until it runs clear from the return hose union.

8  In severe cases of contamination, reverse-flushing of the radiator may be necessary. To do this, remove the radiator (Sec 8), invert it and insert the garden hose into the bottom outlet. Continue flushing until clear water runs from the top hose outlet. If, after a reasonable period the water still does not run clear the radiator can be flushed with a good proprietary cleaning agent such as Holts Radflush or Holts Speedflush. A similar procedure can be used to flush the heater matrix, though in this case the use of chemical cleaners should be avoided if possible.

## 5  Cooling system – refilling

**Note:** *Refer to the warnings given in Section 1 of this Chapter before starting work.*

1  With the cooling system drained and flushed (Secs 3 and 4), refit the drain plugs and (if removed) the undershield, then ensure that all disturbed hose unions are correctly secured.

2  Prepare a sufficient quantity of the specified coolant mixture (Sec 6). Allow for a surplus so as to have a reserve supply for topping-up.

3  Disconnect at the carburettor its heater feed hose (item 20, Fig. 2.1). This being the highest accessible point in the cooling system, its removal will allow the escape of air trapped during refilling, thus preventing the formation of air-locks.

4  Fill the system slowly through the expansion tank. When coolant can be seen emerging from both sides of the disconnected union, reconnect it and top the expansion tank up to the correct level (Sec 2). Refit the filler cap.

5  Start the engine and run it at no more than idle speed until it has warmed up to normal operating temperature, watching the temperature gauge to checks for signs of overheating.

6  Stop the engine and allow it to cool down **completely**, then remove the expansion tank filler cap and top up the tank to the correct level. Refit the filler cap and wash off any spilt coolant.

7  After refilling, always check carefully all components of the system (but especially any unions disturbed during draining and flushing) for signs of coolant leaks. Fresh antifreeze has a searching action which will rapidly expose any weak points in the system.

8  Note that if, after draining and refilling the system, symptoms of overheating are found which did not occur previously, then the fault is almost certainly due to trapped air at some point in the system causing an air-lock and restricting the flow of coolant. Usually the air is trapped because the system was refilled too quickly. In some cases air-locks can be released by tapping or squeezing the various hoses. If the problem persists, stop the engine and allow it to cool down completely before disconnecting the carburettor feed hose (paragraph 3 above) to bleed out the trapped air.

## 6  Coolant mixture

**Note:** *Refer to the warnings given in Section 1 of this Chapter before starting work.*

1  The antifreeze in the coolant should be renewed at regular intervals (see *Routine maintenance*). This is necessary not only to maintain the antifreeze properties but also to prevent corrosion which would otherwise occur as the corrosion inhibitors become progressively less effective.

2  Always use a good quality ethylene glycol-based antifreeze with non-phosphate corrosion inhibitors, containing **no** methanol and which is suitable for use in mixed-metal cooling systems. This should be mixed in the correct ratio with clean, soft water. If you live in a hard water area use filtered rainwater that has been caught in a non-metallic container, or distilled water.

3  Before adding fresh antifreeze the cooling system should be completely drained and flushed and all hoses should be checked for condition and security.

4  The ratio of antifreeze to water should be maintained at the specified level all year round.

5  After filling with antifreeze a label should be attached to the expansion tank stating the type and concentration of antifreeze used and the date on which it was added. Any subsequent topping-up should be made with the same type and concentration of antifreeze.

6  Do not use engine antifreeze in the screen washer system as it will damage the vehicle's paintwork. Screen washer antifreeze is available from most motor accessory shops.

## 7  Cooling system hoses and connections – removal, refitting and inspection

**Note:** *Refer to the warnings given in Section 1 of this Chapter before starting work.*

1  The hoses should be inspected periodically and renewed if any sign is discovered of perishing, cracking or other damage. The most likely area for this is around the clips which secure each hose to its unions. Check also the clips themselves and all joint faces and gaskets in the system (photo).

2  Particular attention should be given if regular topping-up has become necessary. Since the cooling system is semi-sealed the only normal coolant loss should be in minute amounts (due to evaporation) through the expansion tank filler cap. If significant quantities have vanished the system must be leaking at some point, and the source of the leak must be investigated promptly.

3  To disconnect the hoses use a screwdriver (or pliers, as applicable) to slacken the clips, then move them along the hose clear of the union spigot. Carefully work the hose off its spigots (photos). While the hoses can be removed with relative ease when new or hot, **do not** attempt to disconnect any part of the system when it is still hot (Sec 1).

4  Note that the radiator hose unions are fragile, so **do not use excessive force** when attempting to remove the hoses. If a hose proves stubborn, try to release it by rotating it on its unions before attempting to work it off. If all else fails cut the hose with a sharp knife then slit it at each union so that it can be peeled off in two pieces. While expensive, this is preferable to buying a new radiator.

5  Serious leakage will be self-evident, but slight leakage may be more difficult to cure. It is likely that the leak will be apparent only while the engine is running and the system is under pressure, and even then the rate of escape may be such that the hot coolant evaporates as soon as it reaches the atmosphere, although traces of antifreeze should reveal the source of the leak in most cases. If not, it will be necessary to pressurise the system when cold, thereby enabling the source of the leak to be pinpointed. The vehicle should be taken to a Lada dealer or similar who has the necessary pressure-testing equipment.

6  In some cases the leak may be due to a broken head gasket. If this is suspected it will be necessary to remove the cylinder head (Chapter 1) to investigate.

7.1 Tightening coolant feed pipe-to-cylinder block bolts

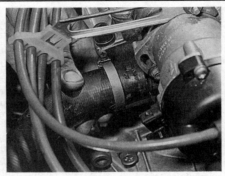

7.3A Disconnecting radiator top hose from coolant return hose union

7.3B Disconnecting radiator bottom hose from thermostat assembly

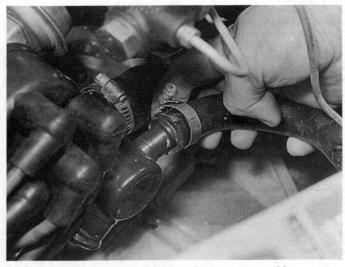

7.8 Connecting expansion tank hose to thermostat assembly

7    Other possible sources of leakage are the water pump and its gasket, the thermostat assembly, or the cylinder block fittings and core plugs. These should be examined and renewed if necessary as described in the relevant Sections of this Chapter and of Chapter 1.

8    When refitting a hose, first slide its clips on to the hose, then work the hose on to its unions (photo). If the hose is stiff, use soap as a lubricant or soften it by soaking it in boiling water, but take care to prevent scalding.

9    Work each hose end fully on to its spigot, check that the hose is settled correctly and is properly routed, then slide each clip along the hose until it is behind the spigot flared end before tightening it securely (photos).

10   Check carefully for leaks as soon as possible after disturbing any part of the cooling system.

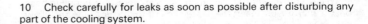

**8   Radiator and expansion tank – removal, inspection and refitting**

### Radiator – removal and refitting

1    Drain the cooling system (Sec 3).
2    Disconnect the battery negative lead.
3    Disconnect the electric cooling fan thermostatic switch wires and unclip the main wiring loom from the cooling fan shroud.
4    Remove the electric cooling fan assembly (Sec 10).
5    Pull the radiator backwards at the top edge so that the expansion tank hose, the top hose and the bottom hose can be disconnected (photos).
6    Withdraw the radiator. It is seated on two pegs on its bottom edge which locate in rubber bushes (photos).
7    Refitting is the reverse of the removal procedure. Ensure that the radiator is seated correctly and without strain on its mountings and carefully position the hose clips so that they do not foul the cooling fan shroud.
8    Refill the cooling system (Sec 5).

### Radiator – inspection

9    If the radiator was removed because of overheating caused by clogging, then try reverse flushing (Sec 4) or, in severe cases, use a radiator cleanser strictly in accordance with the manufacturer's instructions, ensuring that the cleanser is suitable for use in an aluminium radiator.
10   Use a soft brush and an air line or garden hose to clear the radiator matrix of leaves, insects etc.
11   In an emergency, minor leaks from the radiator can be cured by using a radiator sealant such as Holts Radweld. A permanent repair is a job best left to a specialist radiator repairer.
12   Check the mountings for condition and renew them if necessary.

7.9A Connecting heater feed hose to coolant return hose union

7.9B Connecting heater return hose to coolant feed pipe union

7.9C Tightening coolant return hose union/thermostat assembly coupling hose clip

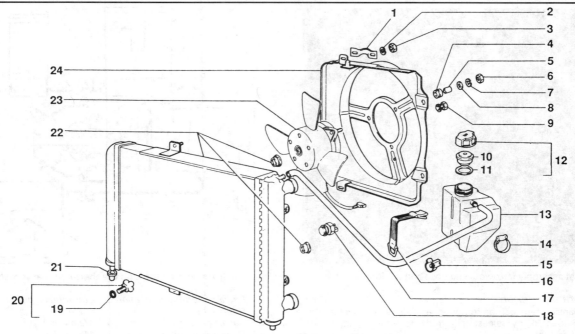

**Fig. 2.2 Radiator and electric cooling fan (Secs 8 and 10)**

| | | | | | |
|---|---|---|---|---|---|
| 1 | Top mounting clamp | 7 | Spring washer | 13 | Expansion tank |
| 2 | Spring washer | 8 | Washer | 14 | Clip |
| 3 | 5 mm nut | 9 | Bolt | 15 | Hose guide |
| 4 | Rubber bush | 10 | Valve | 16 | Rubber strap |
| 5 | Spacer | 11 | Sealing ring | 17 | Expansion tank/radiator hose |
| 6 | 5 mm nut | 12 | Expansion tank filler cap | 18 | Electric cooling fan |

| | |
|---|---|
| 19 | Sealing ring |
| 20 | Radiator drain plug |
| 21 | Mounting rubber bush |
| 22 | Radiator assembly |
| 23 | Electric cooling fan and motor assembly |
| 24 | Cooling fan shroud |

18  Electric cooling fan
    thermostatic switch

8.5A Disconnecting expansion tank hose from radiator

8.5B Disconnecting radiator top hose ...

8.5C ... and bottom hose

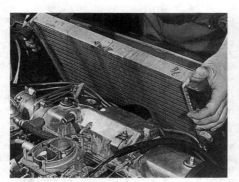

8.6A Removing the radiator

8.6B Check radiator bottom mounting bushes for wear

9.3 Thermostat assembly (arrowed) and hose connections

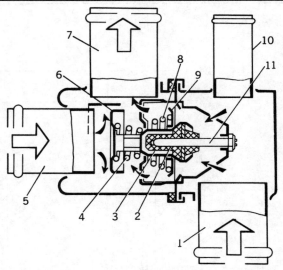

**Fig. 2.3 Cross-section through the thermostat assembly (Sec 9)**

| | | | |
|---|---|---|---|
| 1 | Radiator bottom hose union | 7 | Coolant feed pipe coupling |
| 2 | Rubber insert | | union |
| 3 | Solid, heat-sensitive filler | 8 | Main valve spring |
| 4 | Bypass valve spring | 9 | Main valve |
| 5 | Coolant return hose | 10 | Expansion tank hose |
| | coupling union | | union |
| 6 | Bypass valve | 11 | Main valve piston |

*Expansion tank – general*

13   The expansion tank can be removed, as soon as the system has been drained (Sec 3), by releasing it from its retaining strap and disconnecting its hoses.
14   Empty any coolant from the tank and flush it with fresh water to clean it. If the tank is leaking it must be renewed, but it is worth first attempting a repair using a proprietary sealant or suitable adhesive.
15   Refitting is the reverse of the removal procedure. Ensure that the hoses, especially that between the tank and the radiator, are correctly routed with no kinks or sharp bends.
16   Refill the cooling system (Sec 5).

*Expansion tank filler cap*

17   The cap should be cleaned and checked whenever it is removed. Check that its sealing surfaces and threads are clean and undamaged and that they mate correctly with those of the expansion tank.
18   The cap's performance can be checked only using a cap pressure-tester (cooling system tester) with a suitable adaptor. On applying pressure, the cap's pressure relief valve should hold until the specified pressure is reached, at which point the valve should open.
19   If there is any doubt about the cap's performance, it must be renewed, but note that the valve and sealing ring are available separately.
20   If the cap is to be renewed, ensure that the replacement is of exactly the correct type and rating.

**9   Thermostat – removal, testing and refitting**

1   If the thermostat is thought to be faulty, the simplest test is to check that, when the engine is started from fully cold, the radiator bottom hose remains cold to the touch until the coolant temperature reaches 87 to 92°C whereupon it rapidly warms up as the thermostat opens and allows water to flow around the radiator. If the thermostat is to be renewed, or tested further, it must be removed as follows:
2   Drain the cooling system (Sec 3).
3   Disconnect the radiator bottom hose, the expansion tank hose and the coolant feed pipe coupling hose from the thermostat assembly, then slacken its clip and remove the assembly from its coupling hose (photo).
4   If the thermostat remains in the open position at room temperature it is faulty and must be renewed as a matter of course. Since the valve itself is difficult to see clearly, block the assembly's expansion tank hose union with a finger and blow through its radiator bottom hose union. If the valve is open, air will be felt emerging from the remaining two unions.
5   To test it fully, boil a pan of water. Connect a long hose to the assembly's radiator bottom hose union, temporarily plug its expansion tank union and immerse the assembly in the water, without letting it touch the pan, so that you can blow through the hose (without splashing boiling water on to your face) to check exactly when the valve opens. On lowering the assembly into the water the valve should open. Remove

the assembly from the water and allow it to cool down, when the valve should close.
6   For a more accurate test, suspend a thermometer beside the assembly and heat the water from cold while checking the exact temperature at which the valve opens, then stop heating the water and note the temperature at which the valve closes on cooling down. The opening temperature should be within the tolerance specified, while the closing temperature should be approximately 5°C below that.
7   If the valve does not open and close as described, if it sticks in either position, or if it does not open and close at the specified temperatures the complete assembly must be renewed.
8   Refitting is the reverse of the removal procedure. Refill the cooling system (Sec 5).

**10   Electric cooling fan – testing, removal and refitting**

*Testing*

1   The cooling fan motor is supplied with current directly from the battery via fuse 8 and the cooling fan relay (K9). The relay is energised by a switching voltage from the battery via the ignition switch and fuse 4, this circuit being completed by the radiator-mounted thermostatic switch.
2   If the fan motor runs quietly and at a reduced speed, or if its operation is affected by (or itself affects) the brightness of the head-lamps and/or front sidelamps, then it is possible that the common earth points are faulty. See paragraph 4 below.
3   If the fan does not appear to work at all, run the engine until normal operating temperature is reached, then allow it to idle. If the fan does not cut in within a few minutes, switch off the ignition and disconnect the two wires from the thermostatic switch. Bridge these two wires with a length of spare wire and switch on the ignition. If the fan now operates the thermostatic switch is probably faulty and must be tested further (Sec 11).
4   If the fan still fails to operate, check that full battery voltage is available at the white/black wire terminal. If not, check the feed for a blown fuse or faulty relay (check also the fan motor feed circuit). If the feed is good, check that there is continuity between the black wire terminal and a good earth point on the body. If not, then the earth connection is faulty and must be remade (Chapter 11, Section 1). The thermostatic switch circuit earth connection is under one of the right-hand headlamp assembly retaining nuts, that for the cooling fan motor

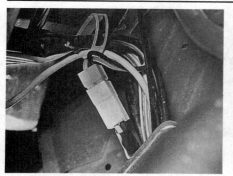

10.8 Electric cooling fan motor wiring connector plug

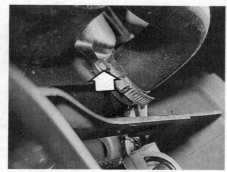

10.10 Electric cooling fan shroud mounting bolt (one arrowed)

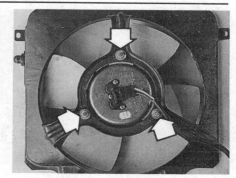

10.11 Unscrew nuts (arrowed) to separate fan/motor from shroud

circuit is at the same point on the left-hand headlamp assembly. Each earth point also serves the lamps on that side. If one earth is found to be faulty, both should be remade.

5   If the switch and wiring are in good condition, the fault must be in the motor itself. This can be checked by disconnecting it from the wiring loom and connecting a 12 volt supply directly to it. If the motor does not work it must be renewed.

### Removal and refitting

6   Disconnect the battery negative lead.
7   Unclip the main wiring loom from the cooling fan shroud.
8   Disconnect the fan motor wires (photo).
9   Unscrew from underneath the bonnet lock platform the two nuts securing the shroud top mounting, then withdraw their spring washers, followed by the clamp. Note that this mounting is shared with the radiator itself (see Fig. 2.2 for details) and is awkward to reach, so careful work is required if damage is to be avoided.
10   Unscrew the remaining mounting nut and two bolts (photo), then withdraw the cooling fan assembly. Take care not to damage the radiator matrix.
11   The fan and motor assembly can be unbolted from the shroud, if required (photo). Remove the retaining nut to separate the fan from the motor.
12   Refitting is the reverse of the removal procedure.

---

### 11   Cooling system electrical switches – testing, removal and refitting

### Electric cooling fan thermostatic switch

1   Refer to Section 10, paragraph 3, for details of a quick test which

should eliminate most faulty switches. If the switch is to be renewed, or to be tested thoroughly, it must be removed as follows.
2   When the engine and radiator are **cold**, either drain the cooling system (Sec 3) down to the level of the switch or unscrew the expansion tank filler cap to release any remaining pressure and have ready a suitable plug that can be used temporarily to stop the escape of coolant while the switch is removed. If the latter method is used, take care not to damage the radiator and do not use anything which will leave foreign matter inside the radiator.
3   Disconnect the battery negative lead.
4   Disconnect the switch wires (photo) and unscrew the switch from the radiator.
5   On refitting, apply a suitable sealant to the switch threads and tighten it securely. Reconnect the switch and battery, then refill the cooling system (Sec 5) or check the coolant level (Sec 2) as necessary.
6   To test the switch thoroughly, use two spare wires to connect to it either a multimeter (set to the resistance function) or a battery and bulb test circuit. Suspend the switch in a pan of water which is being heated. Measure the temperature of the water with a thermometer. Do not let either the switch or the thermometer touch the pan itself.
7   The switch contacts should close to the 'On' position (ie. continuity should exist) when the water reaches the temperature specified. Stop heating the water and allow it to cool down, and the switch contacts should open at the temperature specified.
8   If the switch's performance is significantly different from that specified, or if it does not work at all, it must be renewed.

### Coolant temperature gauge sender unit

9   The coolant temperature gauge mounted in the instrument panel is controlled by the sender unit screwed into the left-hand end of the cylinder head, underneath the distributor (photo).
10   The sender unit contains a thermistor, which is an element whose

11.4 Disconnecting electric cooling fan thermostatic switch wires

11.9 Location of coolant temperature gauge sender unit (arrowed)

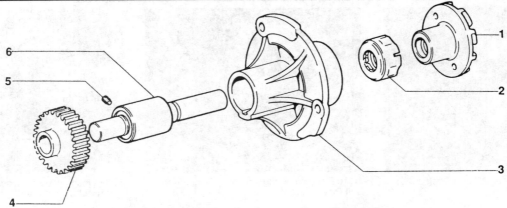

**Fig. 2.4 Water pump components (Sec 12)**

| | | | | | | | |
|---|---|---|---|---|---|---|---|
| 1 | *Impeller* | 3 | *Pump body* | 5 | *Grub screw* | 6 | *Spindle and bearing assembly* |
| 2 | *Seal* | 4 | *Toothed pulley* | | | | |

electrical resistance decreases at a predetermined rate as its temperature rises. If the unit is faulty it must be renewed.

11   If the gauge needle remains at the beginning of the scale (fully cold), disconnect the sender unit wire and earth it to the cylinder head. If the needle then deflects when the ignition is switched on the sender unit is proven faulty and must be renewed. If the needle still does not move, remove the instrument panel (Chapter 11) and use a spare length of wire to earth terminal 2 of the panel's white connector plug (wires still connected and ignition switched on). If the needle then moves, the wire between the sender unit and gauge is faulty. If the needle still does not move, then the gauge is faulty and the instrument panel must be renewed.

12   If the gauge needle remains at the 'hot' end of the scale, disconnect the sender unit wire. If the needle then returns to the beginning of the scale when the ignition is switched on the sender unit is proven faulty and must be renewed. If the needle still does not move, remove the instrument panel (Chapter 11) and disconnect its white connector plug. Use spare lengths of wire to earth the panel's terminal 5 and to connect the terminal 12 to the battery positive terminal and switch on the ignition. If the needle then moves, the wire between the sender unit and gauge is faulty. If the needle still does not move, then the gauge is faulty and the instrument panel must be renewed.

13   To remove and refit the sender unit, proceed as follows.

14   When the engine and radiator are **cold**, either drain the cooling system (Sec 3) down to the level of the sender unit or unscrew the expansion tank filler cap to release any remaining pressure and have ready a suitable plug that can be used temporarily to stop the escape of coolant while the unit is removed. If the latter method is used, take care not to damage the threads and do not use anything which will leave foreign matter inside the cooling system.

15   Disconnect the battery negative lead.

16   Disconnect the unit's wire and unscrew the unit from the cylinder head.

17   On refitting, apply a suitable sealant to the unit threads and tighten it securely. Reconnect the unit and battery, then refill the cooling system (Sec 5) or check the coolant level (Sec 2) as necessary.

## 12   Water pump – removal, overhaul and refitting

**Note:** *Refer to the warnings given in Section 1 of this Chapter before starting work.*

1   Water pump failure is usually indicated by coolant leaking from the gland behind the pump's bearing, or by rough and noisy operation, usually accompanied by excessive pump spindle play. If the pump shows any of these symptoms it must be renewed or overhauled as follows, but note that overhaul will require the renewal, at least, of the pump toothed pulley, the gasket and the seal. Check that these components are available **before** work starts.

2   Drain the cooling system (Sec 3).

3   Remove the air cleaner assembly and disconnect or move out of the way the accelerator and choke cables (Chapter 3).

4   Remove the timing belt cover, the belt itself and its tensioner assembly (Chapter 1, Section 7).

5   Remove the camshaft toothed pulley and the timing belt left-hand cover (Chapter 1, Section 7).

6   Withdraw the water pump (photo) and discard its gasket which should never be re-used. Carefully clean the cylinder block mating surface and the pump socket.

7   To dismantle the pump, unscrew the bearing locating grub screw, then draw off the toothed pulley from the pump spindle (photos). Discard the pulley, as the manufacturer recommends that the pulley be renewed whenever it is disturbed in this way.

8   Drive the spindle, impeller and bearing out of the pump body as a single unit, then draw the impeller off the spindle and withdraw the seal. Discard the seal, which should never be re-used.

9   Carefully clean all components and check them for signs of wear or damage. Check the body for cracks or distortion, then check that the bearing rotates smoothly and easily, with no signs of free play or of rough running. Renew any component that is worn or damaged, noting that the spindle and bearing can be renewed only as a single unit. Renew as a matter of course the toothed pulley, gasket and seal.

10   On reassembly, press the new seal into the body. Press the spindle into the body so that the bearing's locating hole aligns with the hole in the body. Refit the grub screw and tighten it securely to locate the bearing, then use a centre punch to stake the screw in place.

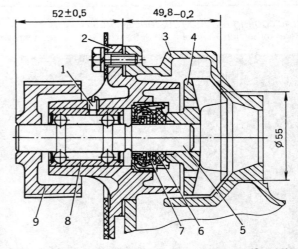

**Fig. 2.5 Cross-section through the water pump (Sec 12)**

| | | | |
|---|---|---|---|
| 1 | *Grub screw* | 6 | *Seal thrust ring* |
| 2 | *Pump body* | 7 | *Seal rubber* |
| 3 | *Cylinder block* | 8 | *Bearing* |
| 4 | *Impeller* | 9 | *Toothed pulley* |
| 5 | *Spindle* | | |

12.6 Removing water pump assembly

12.7A Unscrewing bearing location grub screw

12.7B Toothed pulley must be renewed whenever it is removed from pump spindle

11    Press the impeller on to the spindle, then the new toothed pulley, ensuring that both are installed according to the dimensions shown in Fig. 2.5. The pulley, when installed, should be fixed on the spindle so that it does not slip when a torque of 24.5 Nm (18 lbf ft) is applied.

12    On refitting, install the pump using a new gasket. The remainder of the refitting procedure is the reverse of removal; refer to the relevant sections of this Chapter as well as Chapters 1 and 3.
13    Refill the cooling system (Sec 5).

## 13    Fault diagnosis – cooling system

| Symptom | Reason(s) |
| --- | --- |
| Overheating | Low coolant level (may be the result of overheating or other reasons, such as neglect or leakage)<br>Faulty temperature gauge (gauge or sender unit) showing incorrect reading<br>Radiator blockage (internal or external) or grille restricted<br>Coolant flow restriction due to kinked or collapsed hose or clogged engine waterway<br>Faulty water pump<br>Faulty thermostat<br>Faulty electric cooling fan thermostatic switch<br>Faulty electric cooling fan motor<br>Faulty expansion tank filler cap<br>Engine oil level low or oil of incorrect grade<br>New engine not yet run-in<br>Cylinder head gasket blown<br>Cylinder head or block distorted or cracked<br>Fuel system fault (weak mixture) – see Chapter 3<br>Ignition system fault (ignition timing incorrect or faulty distributor) – see Chapter 4<br>Exhaust system partially blocked<br>Brakes binding – see Chapter 8 |
| Overcooling | Faulty temperature gauge (gauge or sender unit) showing incorrect reading<br>Faulty thermostat |
| Coolant loss – external* | Loose hose clips<br>Perished or cracked hoses<br>Radiator core leaking<br>Heater matrix leaking<br>Faulty expansion tank filler cap<br>Expansion tank leaking<br>Water pump leaking<br>Thermostat assembly leaking<br>Core plug leaking – see Chapter 1<br>Other joint face leak<br>Boiling due to overheating |
| Coolant loss – internal* | Cylinder head gasket blown<br>Cylinder head, block or inlet manifold distorted or cracked |
| Excessive corrosion | Infrequent draining and flushing of system<br>Use of incorrect coolant mixture ingredients, especially antifreeze<br>Combustion gases contaminating coolant |

*If source of coolant loss is not evident, have system pressure-tested*

**Note**: *This Section is not intended to be an exhaustive guide to fault diagnosis but summarises the more common faults which may be encountered during a vehicle's life. Consult a dealer for more specific advice.*

# Chapter 3 Fuel, exhaust and emission control systems

## Contents

## Specifications

### Fuel type
Minimum octane rating ................................................................ 93 RON (unleaded) ie unleaded Premium
Tank capacity ............................................................................ 43 litres (9.5 Imp gallons)

### Air cleaner
Element..................................................................................... Champion W106

### Fuel filter
Element..................................................................................... Champion L101

### Fuel pump
Type.......................................................................................... Mechanical, operated from eccentric on camshaft, hand priming lever
Delivery pressure ....................................................................... 0.2 to 0.3 bar
Output (@ 2000 ± 40 camshaft rpm) ............................................. 1.0 litre per minute (minimum)

### Carburettor (general)
Type.......................................................................................... Solex, built under licence in USSR
Identification number:
    1100.................................................................................. 21081-1107010
    1300.................................................................................. 2108-1107010
    1500.................................................................................. 21083-1107010
Choke type ................................................................................ Manual

### Carburettor calibration
Idle speed ................................................................................. 850 rpm
CO level at idle speed:
    1100.................................................................................. 1.0 to 1.5%
    1300.................................................................................. 1.0 to 1.5%
    1500.................................................................................. 1.5 to 1.8%
Choke vacuum pull-down clearance ('B', Fig. 3.9):
    1100.................................................................................. 2.0 mm
    1300, 1500.......................................................................... 2.5 mm
Fast idle speed .......................................................................... 1400 to 1600 rpm
Primary throttle valve fast idle clearance ('C', Fig. 3.9):
    1100.................................................................................. 1.0 mm
    1300, 1500.......................................................................... 1.1 mm

## Carburettor calibration (continued)

| | Primary | Secondary |
|---|---|---|
| Float chamber fuel level | 27.5 mm | |
| Float height | 1.0 ± 0.2 mm | |
| Float needle valve | 1.80 | |
| Float maximum weight | 6.23 g | |
| Accelerator pump injection capacity – per 10 cycles | 11.5 cc | |
| Mixing chamber diameter | 32 mm | 32 mm |
| Venturi diameter | 21 mm | 23 mm |
| Main jet: | | |
| 1100, 1500 | 95 | 97.5 |
| 1300 | 97.5 | 97.5 |
| Main air jet: | | |
| 1100 | 165 | 135 |
| 1300 | 165 | 125 |
| 1500 | 155 | 125 |
| Emulsion tube | 225299 or 23 | 22316 or ZC |
| Idle jet: | | |
| 1100, 1500 | 40 or 45 | – |
| 1300 | 42 or 45 | – |
| Idle air jet | 170 | |
| Power duty economiser jet | 40 | N/Av |
| Power duty economiser diaphragm pushrod minimum length | 6.0 mm | N/Av |
| Progression system jet | – | 50 |
| Progression system air jet | – | 120 |
| Full load enrichment (Econostat) jet: | | |
| 1100, 1500 | – | 70 |
| 1300 | – | 60 |
| Full load enrichment (Econostat) atomiser diameter | – | 0.03 mm |
| Accelerator pump spray tube | 35 | 40 |

## Torque wrench settings

| | Nm | lbf ft |
|---|---|---|
| Float needle valve | 14.5 | 11 |
| Fuel cut-off solenoid valve | 3.5 | 2.5 |
| Carburettor mounting nuts* | 13 to 16 | 9.5 to 12 |
| Inlet and exhaust manifold retaining nuts | 21 to 26 | 15 to 19 |
| Exhaust downpipe-to-manifold nuts | 21 to 26 | 15 to 19 |
| Exhaust system clamp nuts | 16 to 22.5 | 12 to 16.5 |

*Tighten **only** when engine and carburettor are cold

---

### 1 General description

The fuel system consists of a rear-mounted fuel tank, a mechanical fuel pump that is driven off the camshaft and the carburettor.

The fuel tank is of steel on early models, plastic components being introduced late in 1990. To minimise the escape into the atmosphere of unburned hydrocarbons, an evaporative emissions control system is fitted. The fuel tank filler cap is sealed and a separator unit is mounted above the filler cap to collect the petrol vapours, condense them, and return them to the tank. The tank breathes through the separator unit, with a non-return valve being fitted to ensure that fumes and neat petrol cannot escape into the atmosphere.

The fuel pump is of the mechanically-operated diaphragm type, with a hand priming lever. Apart from the filter screens fitted to the carburettor and pump, there is also a renewable filter fitted in the fuel feed pipe near the pump. Surplus fuel at the carburettor is returned to the tank, and a one-way valve is fitted in the return pipe to ensure that fuel cannot pass through it from the tank back up to the carburettor.

The carburettor is a twin-venturi (choke), downdraught Solex-type built under licence in the Soviet Union. It is fitted with a manual choke and an electronically-operated system to cut off the fuel feed on the overrun.

The carburettor primary throttle valve area and the cast aluminium alloy inlet manifold are coolant-heated to improve the atomisation of the fuel-air mixture.

The air cleaner uses a renewable, pleated-paper filter element and incorporates an automatically-controlled intake air temperature regulator. This uses an element which alters the position of a flap valve through a spring-loaded operating rod, according to the temperature of the intake air.

The exhaust system comprises the cast iron exhaust manifold, the downpipe (single on 1100 models, twin on 1300 and 1500 models), the mid-section with the aluminium-clad primary silencer and the tailpipe with a stainless steel main silencer.

To reduce the emission into the atmosphere from the crankcase of unburned hydrocarbons, the engine is sealed and the blow-by gases and oil vapour are drawn form the crankcase, through an oil separator in the cylinder head cover, into the inlet track to be burned by the engine during normal combustion.

**Warning:** *Many of the procedures in this Chapter require the removal of fuel lines and connections which may result in some fuel spillage. Before carrying out any operation on the fuel system refer to the precautions given in* Safety First! *at the beginning of this manual and follow them implicitly. Petrol is a highly dangerous and volatile liquid and the precautions necessary when handling it cannot be overstressed.*

---

### 2 Routine maintenance

**Note:** *Refer to the warnings given in Section 1 of this Chapter before starting work.*

1 Carry out the following procedures at the intervals given in *'Routine maintenance'* at the beginning of this manual.

#### Renew the air cleaner element
2 Refer to Section 3.

#### Renew the fuel filter
3 Refer to Section 6.

#### Clean the carburettor and fuel pump filters
4 Refer to Sections 18 and 7.

#### Check the tightness of the manifold and carburettor mounting nuts and carburettor top mounting screws
5 Referring where necessary to the relevant Sections of this Chapter, use a torque wrench to ensure that the inlet and exhaust manifold nuts

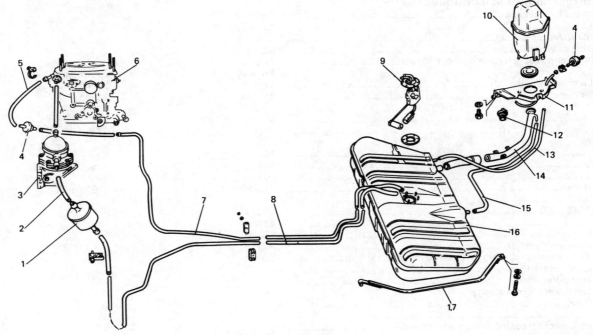

**Fig. 3.1 Fuel system (Sec 1)**

1 Fuel filter
2 Fuel hose
3 Fuel pump
4 One-way valve
5 Fuel hose (return)

6 Carburettor
7 Fuel pipe (return)
8 Fuel pipe (feed)
9 Fuel gauge sender unit

10 Evaporative emissions control
   system separator
11 Separator shield
12 Filler cap
13 Tank-to-separator breather hose

14 Filler tube
15 Filler tube breather hose
16 Fuel tank
17 Tank retaining strap

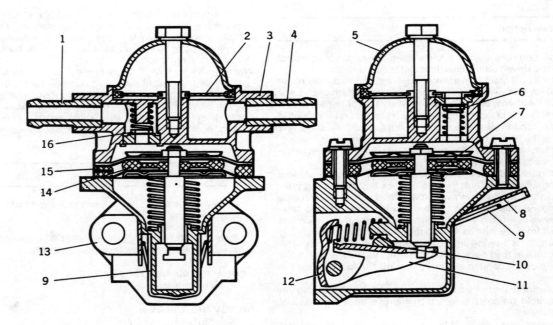

**Fig. 3.2 Cross-section through the fuel pump (Sec 1)**

1 Fuel feed (delivery) union
2 Filter gauze
3 Pump upper body
4 Fuel feed (suction) union

5 Cover
6 Suction valve
7 Pullrod
8 Hand priming lever

9 Spring
10 Cam
11 Balance arm
12 Operating lever

13 Pump lower body
14 Inner distance gasket
15 Outer distance gasket
16 Delivery valve

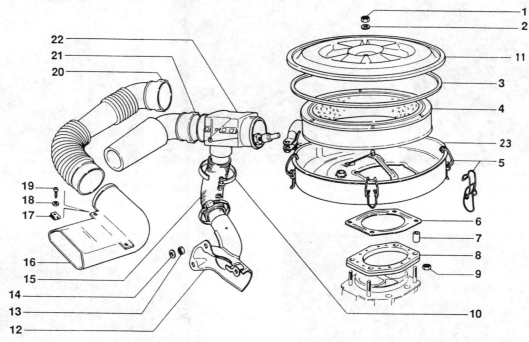

**Fig. 3.3 Air cleaner components (Secs 3, 4 and 5)**          AH 23221

| | | | | | |
|---|---|---|---|---|---|
| 1 | 6 mm nut | 7 | Spacer | 13 | 8 mm nut |
| 2 | Washer | 8 | Rubber gasket | 14 | Washer |
| 3 | Gasket | 9 | 5 mm nut | 15 | Warm air inlet hose |
| 4 | Element | 10 | Clip | 16 | Cold air inlet nozzle * |
| 5 | Spring clip | 11 | Air cleaner cover | 17 | Captive nut * |
| 6 | Metal plate | 12 | Warm air collector box | 18 | Washer * |

| | |
|---|---|
| 19 | Screw * |
| 20 | Connecting hose * |
| 21 | Cold air inlet nozzle |
| 22 | Intake air temperature regulator |
| 23 | Air cleaner body |
| * | Alternative fitting – later models only |

are correctly tightened. Remove the air cleaner (Sec 4), then check that the carburettor mounting nuts and top securing screws are securely tightened. Note that the engine and carburettor must be cold before these are checked.

### Lubricate the accelerator and choke cables and carburettor linkage
6   Removing the air cleaner (Sec 4) if better access is required, check the condition, adjustment and operation of both control cables (Sec 11 or 13) then apply a few drops of light machine oil (Duckhams Home Oil) to the exposed lengths of cable inner wire and to the carburettor linkage pivots and bearing surfaces.

### Check and adjust the idle speed and mixture
7   Refer to Section 16.

### Check and adjust the carburettor fuel level
8   Refer to Section 16.

### Check the exhaust system
9   With the vehicle over an inspection pit or supported on axle stands, check the exhaust system and mountings for security and condition. Any signs of a leak can be confirmed by running the engine at idle speed and temporarily placing a wad of rag over the tailpipe end. The leak will then be more obvious due to the exhaust gases blowing from the hole.

### Clean the crankcase emission control system
10   Refer to Section 22.

---

### 3  Air cleaner element – renewal

1   Noting the arrows stamped in the air cleaner cover and its body, release the spring clips, unscrew the central retaining nut and lift the cover from the air cleaner (photos).
2   Lift out the element and discard it (photo).
3   Wipe clean the inside of the air cleaner body and cover.

3.1A Note arrows stamped in air cleaner cover and body (arrowed)

3.1B Unscrew retaining nut

3.2 Withdrawing air cleaner element

4.2 Disconnecting crankcase breather hose from cylinder head cover

4.4A Unscrew retaining nuts ...

4.4B ... then remove metal plate, rubber gasket and spacers

4.5 Removing the air cleaner assembly

6.1 Location of fuel filter (arrowed)

4    Place the new element in the air cleaner and refit the cover, ensuring that the arrows align and that the cover gasket seals properly on the body lip.

5    Tighten the nut securely without distorting the cover and refasten the spring clips.

### 4   Air cleaner – removal and refitting

1    Remove the air cleaner element (Sec 3). Pack a clean rag into the carburettor mouth to prevent objects dropping in.

2    Slacken the clips securing the warm air inlet hose to the air cleaner body and the crankcase breather hose to the cylinder head cover (photo).

3    Where the cold air inlet is extended to the radiator grille, either unfasten the inlet nozzle from the bonnet lock platform, allowing the complete assembly to be withdrawn, or disconnect the connecting hose so the nozzle remains in place.

4    Unscrew the four nuts securing the air cleaner body to the carburettor and withdraw the metal plate, the rubber gasket and the spacers (photos).

5    Withdraw the air cleaner assembly, disconnecting the warm air inlet and crankcase breather hoses (photo)

6    Refitting is the reversal of the removal procedure.

### 5   Air cleaner air temperature control system – testing

1    To check the operation of the system, slacken the clamp bolt and withdraw the regulator from the air cleaner body.

2    With the engine cold and stopped, check that the regulator flap is fully closed across the cold air inlet.

3    Temporarily refit the regulator, start the engine and fully warm it up to normal operating temperature, then stop it. Check that the regulator flap is now fully closed across the warm air inlet.

4    If the flap does not move as described a certain amount of adjustment is possible by screwing the regulator element in or out. Use a spot of enamel paint applied to its threads to lock the element's threaded rod, once the correct setting is achieved.

5    If the flap does not move at all, or if alignment does not restore correct operation, the regulator assembly must be renewed.

### 6   Fuel filter – renewal

1    The in-line fuel filter is fitted in the fuel feed pipe, near the pump (photo).

2    With some rag ready to catch any spilt petrol, note which way round the filter is fitted before slackening its clamp screws and disconnecting its hoses. Withdraw and discard the filter.

3    Fit the new filter using the reverse of the removal procedure.

8.5A Disconnecting fuel feed (suction) hose from fuel pump

8.5B Disconnecting fuel feed (delivery) hose from fuel pump

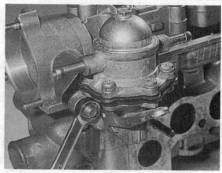

8.5C Unscrew retaining nuts to remove fuel pump

8.6A Withdraw pump and peel off gasket ...

8.6B ... remove pushrod and insulating spacer ...

8.6C ... noting number and thickness of gaskets behind spacer

### 7  Fuel pump – cleaning

1    With some rag ready to catch the petrol that will spill out, unscrew the pump cover retaining bolt, withdraw the cover and lift out the filter gauze (see Fig. 3.2 for details).
2    Clean the filter gauze using compressed air or a soft-bristled brush and clean petrol, then check it for splits or other damage. Clean the pump filter chamber and cover and check for signs of wear or damage.
3    If any of the pump's components is worn or damaged, the complete pump assembly must be renewed, as individual parts are not available.
4    On reassembly, ensure that the filter is seated correctly and that the cover seals properly on its gasket. Do not overtighten the cover bolt.

### 8  Fuel pump – testing, removal and refitting

1    The pump can be checked for correct operation by disconnecting the fuel feed hose from the carburettor and directing it into a container. Having checked that there is sufficient fuel in the tank, operate the hand priming lever and check that a regular, well-defined spurt of petrol emerges from the hose end with every stroke of the lever.
2    If there is any doubt about the pump drive mechanism, the same test can be carried out while turning the engine over on the starter motor, but the ignition system must first be disabled by disconnecting the distributor wiring connector plug and great care is required to avoid the risk of a spark igniting the petrol or its vapour. If the equipment is available, the pump's delivery pressure can be checked and compared with the specified value.
3    If there is no output from the pump, disconnect the fuel feed (suction) hose from the pump and operate the hand priming lever (or turn the engine over on the starter, as above) with a finger placed over the pump union. If there is no suction the pump is faulty and must be renewed. If suction is felt, check the fuel filter is not clogged, then check for blockages in the feed from the fuel tank.
4    If the pump is faulty or if its output is incorrect it must be renewed,

as individual parts are not available with which it can be reconditioned. Check first, however, that the fault is not due to a clogged pump filter gauze or to a fault in the pump drive mechanism.
5    To remove the pump, disconnect and plug the fuel feed hoses at the pump unions, unscrew the mounting nuts and withdraw the pump (photos).
6    Peel off the pump gasket, withdraw the pushrod and the insulating spacer, then peel off the gasket(s), noting carefully the number and thickness of gaskets fitted between the spacer and the cylinder head extension (photos).
7    Clean carefully the mating surfaces and renew any component that is worn or damaged. Check carefully the pushrod tips and cam lobe.

8.9 Measuring pump pushrod minimum protrusion

9.3 Cover plate in vehicle's floor protects sender unit

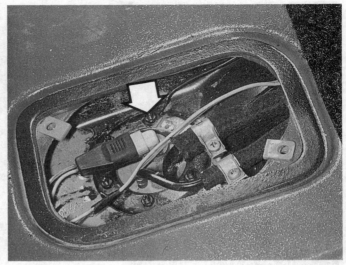

9.4 Do not forget earth wire (arrowed)when disconnecting unit wiring

8    To ensure correct pump operation, the pushrod minimum pro-trusion must be set by adding or removing gaskets between the spacer and cylinder head extension. Gaskets are available in three thicknesses:

    Gasket A 0.27 to 0.33 mm
    Gasket B 0.70 to 0.80 mm
    Gasket C 1.10 to 1.30 mm

**Note** that the spacer-to-pump joint should always be sealed by the thinnest gasket (A).
9    If starting from scratch, refit the spacer with a gasket B between it and the cylinder head extension and a gasket A on its pump face. Using a ruler and vernier calipers (photo) or similar, measure the pushrod's minimum protrusion beyond the gasket face, rotating the crankshaft slowly through one or two full turns to obtain an accurate reading.
10    The pushrod minimum protrusion should be 0.8 to 1.3 mm beyond the gasket face. If the figure measured is less than 0.8 mm, replace the gasket B with a gasket A and recheck the protrusion. If the setting is still not correct, carefully check the pushrod and cam lobe for wear.
11    If the protrusion is more than 1.3 mm, replace the gasket B with a gasket C (or more, as necessary until the correct setting is obtained).
12    When the pushrod protrusion is correct, use a thin smear of grease to stick the gaskets in place, noting that the spacer-to-pump joint should be sealed only by one of the thinnest gaskets (A). Refit the pump using the reverse of the removal procedure.

3    Remove the retaining screws and lift the cover plate from the vehicle's floor (photo).
4    Disconnect the wiring from the unit, not forgetting the earth wire under one of the unit's mounting nuts (photo).
5    Disconnect the fuel hoses from the unit, slackening their clamps and noting that the feed hose is of larger bore than the return.
6    Unscrew the retaining nuts, collect the washers and withdrawn the unit, taking care not to bend the float arm. Cover the tank opening while the unit is removed.
7    Refitting is the reverse of the removal procedure, but ensure that the unit's gasket is renewed if it is damaged or distorted.
8    To test the fuel gauge side of the unit, connect a multimeter (set to its resistance function) between the pink wire terminal and the unit's body and measure the resistance with the float in various positions. When the float is lowered to the 'empty' position a reading of between 315 and 345 ohms should be obtained, decreasing steadily to a reading of no more than 7 ohms when the float is raised to the 'full' position.
9    To test the fuel reserve warning lamp side of the unit, connect the multimeter between the blue/red wire terminal and the unit's body and check that the circuit is completed only when the float arm reaches the lower part of its travel. The lamp should light when there is approxi-mately 4.0 to 6.5 litres (1 Imp gallon) or less remaining in the tank.
10    If the unit is faulty it must be renewed.

## 9   Fuel gauge sender unit – removal, testing and refitting

1    Disconnect the battery negative terminal.
2    Tilt the rear seat base cushion forwards (Hatchback) or lift the floor mat (Van).

## 10   Fuel tank – removal, repair and refitting

1    If possible, run the vehicle until the tank is nearly empty of petrol before removing it. There is no drain plug, so either any remaining petrol

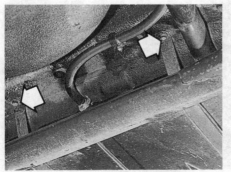

10.7A Unscrew bolts (arrowed) from fuel tank rear mountings ...

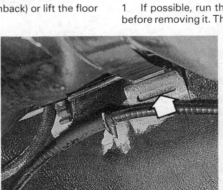

10.7B ... and unhook straps from front mountings (arrowed)

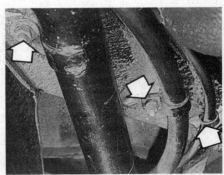

10.8 Fuel filler tube and breather hose fastenings (arrowed)

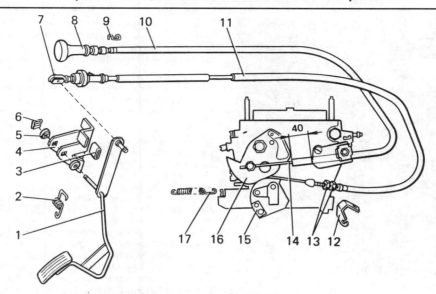

**Fig. 3.4 Accelerator and choke controls (Secs 11, 12 and 13)**

| | | | | |
|---|---|---|---|---|
| 1 | Accelerator pedal | 6 | Clip | 11 Accelerator cable | 15 Accelerator cable pulley |
| 2 | Return spring | 7 | Cable end fitting | 12 Cylinder head cover adjuster | 16 Choke valve control arm |
| 3 | Pedal stop rubber | 8 | Choke control knob |     bracket | 17 Return spring |
| 4 | Pedal bracket | 9 | Clip | 13 Adjusting nuts | |
| 5 | Bush | 10 | Choke cable | 14 Choke cable inner wire | |

must be syphoned out before the tank is removed or the tank must be removed with petrol still inside, which obviously increases the risk of fire and the difficulty of handling the tank.

2  Disconnect the battery negative terminal.

3  Tilt the rear seat base cushion forwards (Hatchback) or lift the floor mat (Van). Remove the cover plate from the vehicle's floor, then disconnect the wiring and fuel hoses from the fuel gauge sender unit (Sec 9). Do not forget the earth wire under one of the unit's mounting nuts.

4  Raise the rear of the vehicle and support it securely on axle stands (see 'Jacking, towing and wheel changing').

5  Slacken their clips using screwdrivers or pliers, as applicable, and disconnect the filler tube and breather hose and the separator hose.

6  Support the weight of the tank with a jack and interposed block of wood.

7  Unscrew the mounting bolts at the rear of the tank, unhook the retaining straps from their front mountings (photos) and lower the tank to the ground.

8  If required, the filler tube and breather hoses can be released by unbolting their mountings or clips from the underbody (photo).

9  If the tank contains sediment, swill it out with fuel or have it steam cleaned. Any repairs should be left to a specialist. **Do not** under any circumstances attempt to solder or weld a fuel tank.

10  Refitting is the reversal of the removal procedure, but ensure that the hoses are correctly refitted.

## 11  Accelerator cable – removal, refitting and adjustment

1  Remove the air cleaner (Sec 4).

2  Slacken the cable adjusting nuts on each side of the cylinder head cover adjuster bracket and release the cable from the bracket (photo).

3  Disconnect the return spring and cable from the pulley (photo).

4  Working inside the vehicle, disconnect the cable from the accelerator pedal, then withdraw the cable into the vehicle's interior.

5  Refitting is the reversal of the removal procedure (photo).

6  Adjust the cable so that when the accelerator pedal is fully depressed the primary throttle valve is fully open and the pulley has no further travel. When the pedal is released the primary throttle valve should return to the fully closed position and some free play should be evident.

7  The accelerator cable is adjusted by slackening the nuts at the cylinder head cover adjuster bracket and rotating them as necessary to reposition the cable (photo).

11.2 Disconnecting accelerator cable from cylinder head cover adjuster bracket

11.3 Disconnecting accelerator cable and return spring from cable pulley

11.5 Accelerator cable and return spring correctly installed on pulley

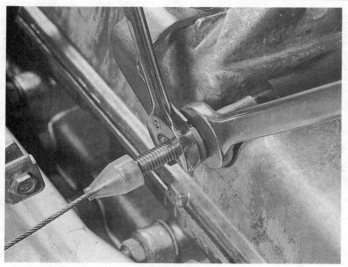

11.7 Adjusting accelerator cable

---

## 12   Accelerator pedal – removal and refitting

1   Disconnect the accelerator cable from the pedal (Sec 11).
2   Extract the clip, unhook the return spring and withdraw the pedal from its pivot, noting the bushes.
3   Refitting is the reversal of the removal procedure, but apply a little grease to the pedal pivot and cable end fittings.

---

## 13   Choke cable – removal, refitting and adjustment

1   Remove the air cleaner (Sec 4).
2   Slacken the cable inner and outer clamp bolts, then disconnect the cable from the carburettor (photo).
3   Working inside the vehicle, pull out the choke control knob until it can be unhooked from the choke inner wire (photo).
4   Remove the retaining screw and withdraw the cable from under the facia, then disconnect the choke warning lamp switch wire (photo). Withdraw the cable into the vehicle's interior.
5   Refitting is the reverse of the removal procedure. As a preliminary setting, gently tighten the cable outer clamp bolt when 40 mm of cable outer protrudes beyond the clamp (Fig. 3.4), then check that the choke valve control arm (item 16, Fig. 3.4) is returned fully clockwise before connecting the cable inner wire to its clamp bolt. Gently tighten the clamp bolt and check the cable adjustment as described below.
6   Start by checking that the choke operating mechanism is correctly set (Sec 16, paragraphs 24 to 26).
7   Adjust the cable so that when the choke knob is pulled fully out the choke valve is fully closed and the choke valve control arm has no

further travel. When the knob is pushed fully in the choke valve should return to the fully open position and some free play should be evident.
8   The choke cable is adjusted by slackening the clamp bolts at the carburettor and repositioning the cable inner or outer as necessary.

---

## 14   Unleaded petrol – general

**Note:** *The information given in this Chapter and in Chapter 4 is correct at the time of writing and applies only to petrols currently available in the UK. If updated information is thought to be required check with a good Lada dealer. If travelling abroad consult one of the motoring organisations (or a similar authority) for advice on the petrols available and their suitability for your vehicle.*

1   The fuel recommended by Lada for Samara models, and the equivalent petrol currently on sale in the UK is given in the Specifications of this Chapter.
2   RON and MON are different testing standards. RON stands for Research Octane Number (also written as RM), while MON stands for Motor Octane Number (also written as MM).
3   It will be helpful, before describing individual requirements, to clarify the various terms used for petrol types.
4   **Leaded petrol:** In addition to the natural lead content of crude oil, an amount of lead is added during refining to increase the octane rating. In the early 1970s this amount was 0.640 gm/litre (maximum) but by 1985 (BS 4040:1985) it had been reduced progressively to 0.150 gm/litre (maximum), thus bringing it into the **'low-lead'** classification. Since the disappearance in 1988/9 from UK forecourts of 2- and 3-star petrol, the only petrol remaining on sale in this category is **4-star**: Minimum octane rating 97 RON/86 MON. Can be used in Samara models (but see paragraph 9 below).
5   **Unleaded petrol:** Contains only the natural lead content of crude oil, which must be no more than 0.013 gm/litre (BS 7070:1985). Petrols in this category are:
**Super/Super Plus:** Recently introduced and not yet covered by BS 7070 but claimed by the oil companies to have an octane rating at least the equivalent of 4-star (ie 97/98 RON). Can be used in Samara models (but see paragraph 9 below).
**Premium:** Minimum octane rating 95 RON/85 MON – The first to be introduced and is currently the only unleaded petrol universally available. It is recommended for Samara models.
**Regular:** Minimum octane rating 90 RON/80MON – Not yet available in the UK. When it is introduced the ignition timing on all Samara models will have to be retarded before it can be used, so check with a Lada dealer for details.
6   **Lead-free petrol:** Contains no lead at all, as that naturally present is refined out and none is added. Not currently available in the UK and should not be confused with unleaded.
7   The use of unleaded petrol is generally believed to cause accelerated wear of conventional valve seats (particularly the exhaust) due to the loss of the lead's lubricating effect. All Samara models, in common with most USSR-built vehicles, have the hardened valve seats which enable them to use unleaded fuels continuously.
8   Also, Samara models are designed to run on 93 RON octane petrol. No 'adjustment' is required, therefore, to allow them to use the Premium grade 95 RON unleaded petrol currently available in the UK.

13.2 Choke inner and outer cable clamp bolts (arrowed)

13.3 Unhooking choke control knob from inner cable

13.4 Disconnecting choke warning lamp switch wire

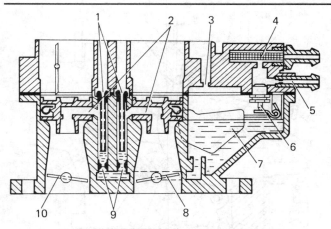

Fig. 3.5 Carburettor main fuel system (Sec 15)

| | | | |
|---|---|---|---|
| 1 | Main air jets and emulsion tubes | 6 | Float needle valve assembly |
| 2 | Atomisers | 7 | Float assembly |
| 3 | Float chamber vent | 8 | Secondary throttle valve |
| 4 | Fuel filter gauze | 9 | Main jets |
| 5 | Fuel return union | 10 | Primary throttle valve |

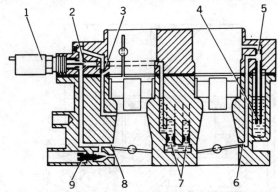

Fig. 3.6 Carburettor idle and progression fuel systems (Sec 15)

| | | | |
|---|---|---|---|
| 1 | Fuel cut-off system solenoid valve | 6 | Secondary venturi progression system orifice |
| 2 | Idle jet | 7 | Main jets |
| 3 | Idle air jet | 8 | Idle system bypass port |
| 4 | Secondary venturi progression system jet | 9 | Idle mixture adjusting screw |
| 5 | Secondary venturi progression system air jet | | |

9  Four-star (leaded) and Super/Super Plus (unleaded) petrols can be used in Samara models without modification, if nothing else is available. However, they will not produce any noticeable improvement in performance or economy and the higher price will merely result in a waste of the driver's money.

**Note:** *The only vehicles which* **must** *use unleaded petrol at all times are those with catalytic converters. None of the vehicles covered in this manual are so equipped.*

## 15  Carburettor – description and operation

The carburettor's sub-systems function as follows.

The main fuel system (Fig. 3.5) draws fuel from the float chamber to the main jets, where it is mixed with air from the main air jets and emulsion tubes and passes through the atomisers into the carburettor venturis (chokes). The throttle valves are linked to open progressively. Initial opening is made by the primary throttle valve until it is about two-thirds open, after which the secondary throttle valve opens as well (unless the choke valve is still closed, see below).

The idle system (Fig. 3.6) draws fuel from the emulsion well, above the main jets, through a passage to the idle jet and the fuel cut-off solenoid valve. The fuel is mixed with air drawn from the primary venturi, through the idle air jet, and passed into the venturi downstream of the primary throttle valve, through a passage controlled by the idle mixture screw.

As engine speed increases, in the transition period before the throttle valve opens, the idle system starts to admit mixture to the venturi through a bypass port (item 8, Fig. 3.6). The secondary venturi has a progression system which functions in a similar way to the idle system (see above). As inlet manifold depression increases it becomes sufficient to draw fuel up so that it mixes with air through the (primary and secondary) main air jets and emulsion tubes and passes through the atomisers into the carburettor venturis.

To combine good economy and reasonable power output, both venturis are provided with forms of full load enrichment (power valve), in which additional fuel is delivered through a sub-system to each venturi only when the throttle valve is fully open. This enables the normal main system to be jetted weaker than would otherwise be the case, for economy, while the sub-system caters for power requirements.

The primary venturi's system is the power duty economiser, in which a diaphragm-controlled ball valve (item B, Fig. 3.7) remains closed until the depression downstream of the throttle valve decreases to the

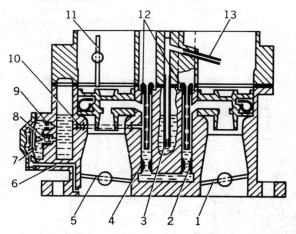

Fig. 3.7 Carburettor power duty economiser and Econostat systems (Sec 15)

| | | | |
|---|---|---|---|
| 1 | Secondary throttle valve | 8 | Ball valve |
| 2 | Secondary main jet | 9 | Power duty economiser jet |
| 3 | Econostat jet | 10 | Fuel passage |
| 4 | Primary main jet | 11 | Choke valve |
| 5 | Primary throttle valve | 12 | Main air jets and emulsion tubes |
| 6 | Power duty economiser vacuum passage | 13 | Econostat orifice |
| 7 | Diaphragm | | |

point at which the valve is opened by the spring and admits additional fuel through the economiser jet to the main system's main air jet/emulsion tube.

The secondary venturi's system is the Econostat, which is a simple jet positioned so that it does not draw fuel (from the float chamber) until the airflow across its orifice reaches a speed high enough to do so.

An accelerator pump is provided to inject extra fuel into both venturis when the primary throttle valve is opened (Fig. 3.8). One non-return ball valve ensures that fuel only passes from the float chamber to the pump, while a second valve ensures that fuel is not drawn from the spray tubes by air passing over them during normal operation.

The choke mechanism (Fig. 3.9) is manually operated to provide a rich mixture and fast idle speed on starting. To minimise the possibility of flooding, a vacuum pull-down assembly is provided that is connected to the venturi downstream of the throttle valve. When the inlet manifold depression increases sufficiently the pull-down diaphragm retracts its

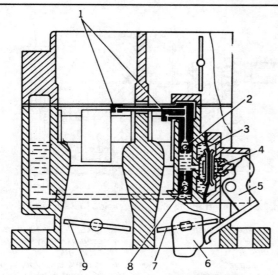

**Fig. 3.8 Carburettor accelerator pump (Sec 15)**

| | |
|---|---|
| 1 Spray tubes | 6 Pump cam |
| 2 Non-return ball valve | 7 Primary throttle valve |
| 3 Pump diaphragm | 8 Non-return ball valve |
| 4 Pushrod | 9 Secondary throttle valve |
| 5 Operating lever | |

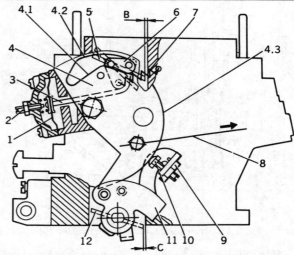

**Fig. 3.9 Choke vacuum pull-down and fast idle mechanism (Sec 15)**

| | |
|---|---|
| 1 Vacuum pull-down diaphragm | 5 Choke valve |
| 2 Adjusting screw | 6 Choke valve arm |
| 3 Vacuum pull-down rod | 7 Return spring |
| 4 Choke valve control arm | 8 Choke cable inner wire |
| 4.1 Choke valve opening control contour | 9 Adjusting screw stop |
| 4.2 Choke valve opening contour | 10 Primary throttle valve adjusting screw |
| 4.3 Throttle valve fast idle contour | 11 Throttle valve operating lever |
| | 12 Primary throttle valve |

To improve economy and to reduce emissions of unburned hydrocarbons, an electronically-controlled system is provided to cut off the fuel feed through the idle system when the throttle valve operating lever is fully closed. The system consists of a switch on the throttle valve operating lever/idle speed screw, a solenoid valve screwed into the carburettor body and a control module which is mounted on the engine compartment bulkhead, above the brake vacuum servo unit. If the throttle is closed at engine speeds of more than 2100 rpm, the solenoid valve is switched off and the idle system fuel passage is closed by its plunger. If the engine speed falls to 1900 rpm, the solenoid is switched on and the fuel supply is gradually restored until normal idle speed begins. The system is activated only when the throttle is fully released (ie the switch contacts are closed).

**Fig. 3.10 Carburettor external components (Sec 15)**

| | |
|---|---|
| 1 Accelerator cable pulley | 10 Fuel feed union |
| 2 Secondary throttle interlock lever pin | 11 Fuel return union |
| 3 Primary throttle valve adjusting screw | 12 Choke cable outer casing clamp |
| 4 Choke cable inner wire clamp bolt | 13 Secondary throttle valve adjusting screw |
| 5 Choke valve control arm | 14 Secondary throttle valve arm |
| 6 Choke valve arm | 15 Secondary throttle valve operating arm |
| 7 Return spring | 16 Primary throttle valve return spring |
| 8 Vacuum pull-down rod | 17 Throttle valve operating lever |
| 9 Fuel cut-off system solenoid valve | |

## 16  Carburettor – adjustments and checks

### Idle mixture

1  **Note** that an exhaust gas analyser (CO meter) will be required to check the mixture and to set it with the necessary standard of accuracy. If such equipment is not available a basic setting procedure is given.

2  The idle mixture is set at the factory and should require no further adjustment. If, due to a change in engine characteristics (carbon build-up, bore wear etc) or after a major carburettor overhaul, the mixture becomes incorrect it can be reset as follows.

3  First ensure that the valve clearances and compression pressures are correct (Chapter 1), that the ignition timing is accurate and the spark plugs are in good condition and correctly gapped (Chapter 4), and that the air cleaner element is clean (Sec 3). Start the engine and warm it up to normal operating temperature, then check that the choke valve is fully open.

4  Using a sharp implement, prise out the tamperproof plug sealing the idle mixture adjusting screw aperture (photo). Ensure that all electrical components are switched off, start the engine and allow it to idle.

5  If an exhaust gas analyser is available, follow its manufacturer's instructions to check the CO level. If adjustment is required, turn the idle mixture adjusting screw in very small increments until the level is correct.

operating rod so that the choke valve is opened slightly. Also, the valve itself is kept fully closed by a light spring so that it can be opened slightly at any time by the flow of air alone. The mechanism has an interlock (Fig. 3.10) so that the secondary throttle valve cannot be opened until the choke is fully open.

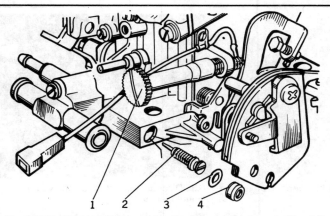

**Fig. 3.11 Carburettor idle speed and mixture adjustments (Sec 16)**

1   Idle speed adjusting screw
2   Idle mixture adjusting
    screw
3   Sealing ring
4   Tamperproof plug

6    If an exhaust gas analyser is not available, the following basic setting procedure will serve until the vehicle can be checked by a competent mechanic using proper test equipment.

7    With the vehicle prepared as described in paragraphs 3 and 4 above, slowly turn the idle mixture adjusting screw in small amounts first one way, then the other, until the position is found at which the engine runs fastest and smoothest. If the idle speed rises significantly, use the idle speed adjusting screw to restore it to the specified value.

8    If adjustments take more than three minutes, clear any excess fuel from the inlet manifold by racing the engine two or three times to between 2000 and 3000 rpm, then allow it to idle again.

9    Check the idle speed and reset if necessary. Do not forget to have the mixture checked as soon as possible.

10   When the mixture is correct, press in a new tamperproof plug.

### Idle speed

11   While the idle speed can be reset without removing the air cleaner assembly, if the accelerator cable is incorrectly adjusted (which can affect the idle speed considerably) the air cleaner must be removed so that the adjustment can be corrected (Sec 11).

12   First ensure that the valve clearances and compression pressures are correct (Chapter 1), that the ignition timing is accurate and the spark plugs are in good condition and correctly gapped (Chapter 4), and that the air cleaner element is clean (Sec 3). Start the engine and warm it up to normal operating temperature, then check that the choke valve is fully open.

13   If an accurate setting is required, connect a tachometer to the engine following its manufacturer's instructions. Ensure that all electrical components are switched off, then start the engine and allow it to idle.

14   Using the tachometer, check that the idle speed is as specified. If not, alter it using the idle speed adjusting screw. Race the engine (see paragraph 16) and check that the idle speed remains unchanged.

15   If a tachometer is not available, use the idle speed adjusting screw to set the idle speed to the point at which the engine ticks over smoothly and steadily. The speed should be as low as possible, but ensure that the engine does not falter and die if the accelerator pedal is depressed sharply and released.

16   If adjustments take more than three minutes, clear any excess fuel from the inlet manifold by racing the engine two or three times to between 2000 and 3000 rpm, then allow it to idle again.

### Fuel level

17   Warm the engine up to normal operating temperature and park the vehicle on smooth, level ground. Remove the air cleaner (Sec 4), disconnect the choke cable (Sec 13), disconnect and plug the fuel feed and return hoses at the carburettor unions, disconnect the fuel cut-off system's solenoid valve wire, then remove the carburettor cover (Sec 18).

18   Check that the cover gasket is in good condition. If it is broken or distorted in any way, sufficient to affect the distance between the carburettor body and cover, it must be renewed (Sec 18) and the engine

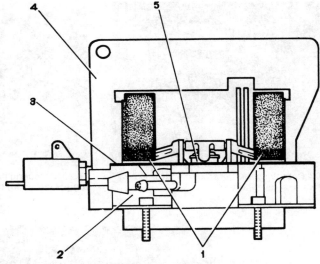

**Fig. 3.12 Checking float height (Sec 16)**

1   Floats
2   Carburettor cover
3   Gasket
4   Gauge
5   Float needle valve
    assembly

run to establish a true fuel level before the float height is altered.

19   Measure the distance from the carburettor body-to-cover mating surface to the top of the fuel in the float chamber. If the fuel level is not as specified, the float height must be adjusted as follows.

20   Invert the carburettor cover and hold it horizontally, so that the floats are uppermost, then measure the distance from the top of each float to the gasket (pressed firmly on to the cover). A gauge can be used to ensure accuracy (Fig. 3.12). Make measurements at several points on each float, to ensure an accurate reading. The float height should be within the range specified (photo).

21   If adjustment is required, gently bend the tongue of the float assembly which bears against the tip of the float needle. Ensure that the tongue is smooth and undamaged and that it is square to the needle.

22   When the setting is correct, reassemble the carburettor following the reverse of the removal procedure.

### Vacuum pull-down and fast idle settings

23   Remove the air cleaner (Sec 4). If the accelerator and choke cables are incorrectly adjusted, slacken their adjusters fully (Sec 11 or 13, as appropriate), check and adjust the linkage if required, then adjust the cables correctly.

24   Check that when the choke valve control arm (item 4, Fig. 3.9) is rotated fully anti-clockwise the choke valve itself is closed fully by its return spring (item 7, Fig. 3.9).

25   With the choke valve fully closed, press the vacuum pull-down rod (item 3, Fig. 3.9) fully into the diaphragm assembly and check that the choke vacuum pull-down clearance ('B', Fig. 3.9) opens to the specified amount. Use a drill bit (or similar) of suitable size to check the clearance. If adjustment is necessary, slacken its locknut and turn the adjusting screw (item 2, Fig. 3.9) until the setting is correct. Tighten the locknut and recheck the clearance.

26   Check that the cables are correctly adjusted and refit the air cleaner (Sec 4).

27   If a tachometer is available, the fast idle speed can be checked on restarting the engine and compared with the specified value.

28   If the fast idle setting requires adjustment, remove the carburettor (Sec 17) and close the choke valve fully (paragraph 24 above), then use a drill bit (or similar) of suitable size to check that the primary throttle valve fast idle clearance ('C', Fig. 3.9) opens to the specified amount. To adjust, turn the primary throttle valve adjusting screw (item 10, Fig. 3.9) until the clearance is correct. Refit the carburettor and recheck the setting.

### Accelerator pump

29   With the engine stopped, remove the air cleaner cover. Check that the nut securing the pump cam (item 6, Fig. 3.8) is correctly tightened.

30   Open the throttle valve operating lever fully and check that the pump injects fuel smoothly and strongly.

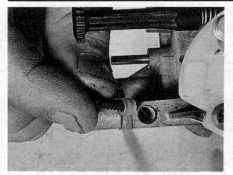

16.4 Removing tamperproof plug from idle mixture screw aperture

16.20 Measuring float height – bend float tongue (arrowed) to adjust

16.33 Disconnecting fuel cut-off system solenoid valve

16.34 Disconnecting fuel cut-off system throttle switch

16.35 Locating of fuel cut-off system control module

31    If a fault is found, dismantle the pump and check it for wear or damage (Sec 180) as no adjustment is possible.

### Fuel cut-off system

32    If the system is thought to be faulty, check that its wires are securely connected and in good condition before proceeding. Remove the air cleaner (Sec 4).

33    To test the system, connect a test lamp or a voltmeter between the solenoid valve terminal (valve grey/red wire still connected) and an earth point on the engine (photo).

34    Disconnect the green wire from the throttle switch wire (photo) and use a spare length of wire to earth the green wire (and therefore the control module) to one of the carburettor air cleaner studs. Connect a tachometer to the engine following its manufacturer's instructions.

35    Start the engine and note the system's operation at the different engine speeds. The system should cycle (the test lamp should flash on and off, or the voltmeter readings should go from at least 10 volts to no more than 0.5 volts) between 2100 and 1900 rpm as the control module (photo) switches the valve on and off.

36    Disconnect the earth lead and reconnect the throttle switch wire. Increase engine speed to 3000 rpm (the valve should stay switched on) then release the throttle (the valve should be switched off as the speed drops then switched on again at 1900 rpm.)

37    If the solenoid valve is dirty it can be unscrewed and cleaned (Sec 18), but if any (electrical) part of the system is faulty it must be renewed.

### Improving low-speed running

38    Some Samara models, especially those with 1500 engines, may suffer from poor low-speed running which cannot be cured by attention to the normal settings. If such a case is encountered, two modifications may be made to the carburettor which should provide a cure, but it must be stressed that these should be carried out only after seeking advice of a Lada dealer and may invalidate the vehicle's warranty (where applicable).

39    **Always** check first that the valve clearances and compression pressures are correct (Chapter 1), that the ignition timing is accurate and the spark plugs are in good condition and correctly gapped (Chapter 4),

that the air cleaner filter element is clean (Sec 3) and that the idle speed and mixture are **exactly** correct (using an exhaust gas analyser and tachometer). Check also the fuel level and accelerator pump (see above), the choke cable operation and adjustment (Sec 13) and ensure that the idle jet is clean and a proper fit on the fuel cut-off solenoid valve (Sec 18).

40    Most problems will be cured by correcting one or more of these settings. The modifications are to be carried out only on vehicles that still have a problem when they are otherwise perfect and are **not** a substitute for poor servicing work.

41    Remove the air cleaner (Sec 4), disconnect the choke cable (Sec 13), disconnect and plug the fuel feed and return hoses at the carburettor unions, disconnect the fuel cut-off system's solenoid valve wire, then remove the carburettor cover (Sec 18).

42    Unscrew the fuel cut-off solenoid valve, remove the idle jet and use a pin-drill holder to open the jet's orifice to 0.45 mm, or obtain a 45 idle jet from a Lada dealer. Clean off any swarf and refit the jet and valve.

43    Remove the accelerator pump valve and spray tube assembly (Sec 18) and cut (vertically) the longer spray tube at the point where it passes through the groove in the carburettor body casting (see photos 18.13a and 18.13b for details). Seal the cut end with solder and refit the assembly.

44    Reassemble the carburettor, check and re-adjust the idle mixture using an exhaust gas analyser, then road test the vehicle. It may prove worthwhile to reduce slightly the fast idle speed (see paragraph 26 above).

### 17   Carburettor – removal and refitting

**Note:** *The engine and carburettor* **must** *be cold before work can start.*

1    Remove the air cleaner (Sec 4).

2    Disconnect the accelerator cable (Sec 11) and the choke cable (Sec 13).

3    Either remove its retaining screw (photo) and withdraw the heater from the carburettor body or remove the expansion tank filler cap to

17.3 Carburettor heater retaining screw (arrowed)

17.5 Disconnecting fuel return hose from carburettor – note one-way valve (arrowed)

17.7 Fuel feed hose (A), crankcase breather hose (B), carburettor heater hose (C), distributor vacuum hose (D)

17.8A Check inlet manifold mating surface is clean and flat, then fit a new gasket ...

17.8B ... the insulating spacer ...

17.8C ... and the carburettor gasket

17.9A Refitting the carburettor

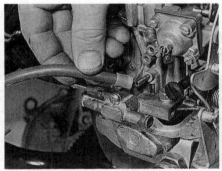

17.9B Connecting the distributor vacuum hose to its carburettor union

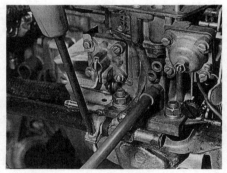

17.9C Tighten securely all hose clamps

release any residual cooling system pressure, prepare to catch the small amount of coolant that will be spilt (Chapter 2) and disconnect the carburettor heater's two hoses.

4    Disconnect the fuel cut-off system's solenoid valve and throttle switch wires.

5    Disconnect and plug the fuel feed and return hoses (photo).

6    Disconnect the crankcase breather hose from the carburettor.

7    Disconnect the distributor vacuum hose (photo).

8    Unscrew the four mounting nuts and remove the carburettor. Plug the inlet port with a wad of clean cloth, then check that the manifold, insulating spacer and carburettor mating surfaces are clean and flat and renew the gaskets if necessary (photos).

9    Refitting is the reverse of the removal procedure (photos). If the cooling system was disturbed, refill it or check the coolant level as required, then wash off any spilt coolant (Chapter 2). Check, and adjust if necessary, the cable adjustments and idle speed and mixture.

## 18   Carburettor – overhaul

1    Note that it is rare for a carburettor to require a complete overhaul, and in fact it may prove more economical to completely renew such a worn instrument. Check the price and availability of a replacement carburettor and of its component parts before starting work. Note that most sealing washers, screws and gaskets are available in kits, as are some of the major sub-assemblies themselves. In most cases it will be sufficient to remove the carburettor cover and to clean the jets.

2    If symptoms of undue richness or weakness have been encountered, check the fuel level (Sec 16) before the carburettor is removed.

3    Remove the carburettor (Sec 17) and clean away all external dirt.

4    Remove the retaining screws and lift off the carburettor cover, taking care not to tear the gasket or to damage the floats and fuel feed tubes. Note the sealing ring fitted to one of the feed tubes (photos).

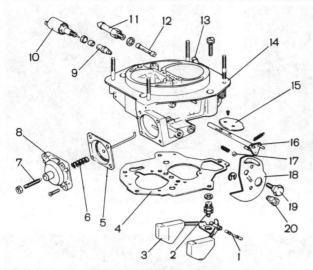

**Fig. 3.13 Carburettor cover components (Sec 18)**

| | |
|---|---|
| 1  Float assembly pivot pin | 11  Fuel feed union |
| 2  Float needle valve | 12  Fuel filter gauze |
|     assembly | 13  Fuel return union |
| 3  Float assembly | 14  Carburettor cover |
| 4  Cover gasket | 15  Choke valve |
| 5  Vacuum pull-down | 16  Choke valve spindle and |
|     diaphragm and rod |     arm |
| 6  Spring | 17  Detent ball |
| 7  Adjusting screw | 18  Choke valve control arm |
| 8  Vacuum pull-down | 19  Arm pivot bolt |
|     diaphragm cover | 20  Choke cable inner wire |
| 9  Idle jet |     clamp |
| 10  Fuel cut-off system | |
|     solenoid valve | |

5    Drift out the pivot pin and withdraw the float assembly. Peel off the gasket, noting its locating pegs, and unscrew the float needle valve assembly, noting its sealing washer (photos).

6    Check the floats for wear or damage. If they weigh any more than the specified value they have been leaking and must be renewed. Check that the valve assembly is free to move and shows no signs of wear.

7    Unscrew the fuel feed union, noting its sealing washer, and from the opposite side of the cover unscrew the filter plug and withdraw the sealing washer and the filter gauze (photos).

8    Clean the filter gauze using compressed air or a soft-bristled brush and clean petrol, then check it for splits or other damage. Clean the carburettor filter chamber and passages.

9    Unscrew the fuel cut-off solenoid valve and remove it, noting the idle jet (photos). The jet should be a light press-fit in the valve body. Its split end may be opened **gently** (only if necessary) to ensure this.

10   The choke valve control arm can be unbolted if required (note the detent ball and spring behind the arm) but if the choke valve spindle or its bearing surfaces are worn, the complete carburettor must be renewed.

11   Remove the four screws and withdraw the vacuum pull-down diaphragm cover, noting the spring behind it, then withdraw the diaphragm and pull-down rod (photos). Renew the diaphragm if it is split or torn.

12   Working on the carburettor body, remove the four screws and dismantle the accelerator pump assembly, noting the spring (photos). Renew the diaphragm if it is split or torn.

13   Very carefully prise the accelerator pump valve and spray tube assembly out of its housing and withdraw it, taking care not to bend the spray tubes (photos). Check that the ball valve is free to move.

14   Marking them with a felt-tip pen or similar to ensure that they are refitted in their original locations, remove the atomisers from the venturis (photo).

15   Remove the three screws and dismantle the power duty economiser assembly, noting the spring (photos). Renew the diaphragm if it is split or torn, or if the pushrod is worn to less than the specified amount (measured from end to end). Note that the economiser jet can be unscrewed for cleaning, but not the ball valve, which can only be cleaned using compressed air.

16   Being careful to keep them in separate, clearly-marked containers

18.4A Remove screws and remove carburettor cover ...

18.4B ... noting sealing ring (arrowed) on cover mating surface

18.5A Driving out float pivot pin

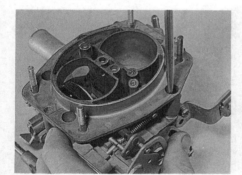

18.5B Renew cover gasket if damaged ...

18.5C ... noting gasket locating pegs (one arrowed)

18.5D Unscrew float needle valve assembly ...

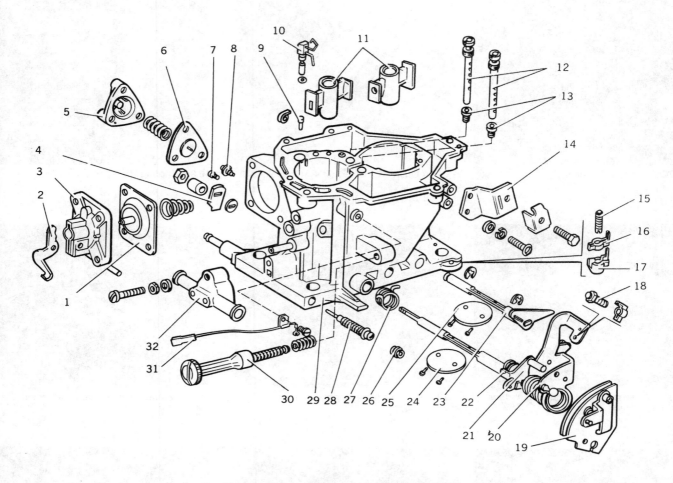

**Fig. 3.14 Carburettor body components (Sec 18)**

| 1 | Accelerator pump diaphragm | 10 | Accelerator pump valve and spray tube assembly | 18 | Primary throttle valve adjusting screw | 25 | Secondary throttle valve |
|---|---|---|---|---|---|---|---|
| 2 | Operating lever | 11 | Atomisers | 19 | Accelerator cable pulley | 26 | Tamperproof plug |
| 3 | Accelerator pump cover | 12 | Main air jets and emulsion tubes | 20 | Primary throttle valve spindle and operating lever | 27 | Secondary throttle valve operating arm return spring |
| 4 | Pump cam | 13 | Main jets | 21 | Secondary throttle interlock arm | 28 | Idle mixture adjusting screw |
| 5 | Power duty economiser cover | 14 | Choke cable outer casing clamp | 22 | Interlock arm spring | 29 | Carburettor body |
| 6 | Economiser diaphragm | 15 | Secondary throttle valve adjusting screw | 23 | Secondary throttle valve spindle and arm | 30 | Idle speed adjusting screw |
| 7 | Economiser jet | 16 | Adjusting screw lock | 24 | Primary throttle valve | 31 | Fuel cut-off system throttle switch |
| 8 | Economiser ball valve | 17 | Lock cap | | | 32 | Carburettor heater |
| 9 | Accelerator pump non-return ball valve | | | | | | |

18.5E ... noting sealing washer

18.7A Unscrew fuel feed union ...

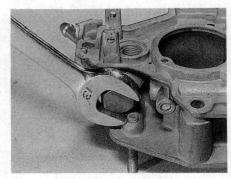

18.7B ... followed by fuel filter plug ...

18.7C ... to clean filter gauze

18.9A Unscrew fuel cut-off system solenoid valve ...

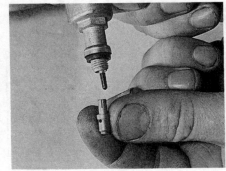

18.9B ... noting idle jet on valve end

18.11A When removing vacuum pull-down diaphragm cover ...

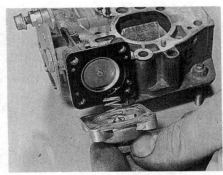

18.11B ... note how spring engages on diagphragm

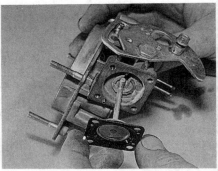

18.11C Withdrawing vacuum pull-down diaphragm and rod

18.12A Removing accelerator pump cover screws ...

18.12B ... remove pump cover and diaphragm, noting spring

18.12C Note how diaphragm engages in pump cover

18.13A Be careful not to bend spray tubes when ...

18.13B ... removing accelerator pump valve and spray tube assembly

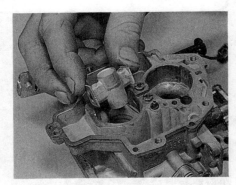

18.14 Removing atomiser from secondary venturi

18.15A Removing power duty economiser cover screws ...

18.15B ... remove economiser cover, noting spring ...

18.15C ... note how diaphragm pushrod engages with ball valve

18.15D Economiser jet only can be unscrewed for cleaning

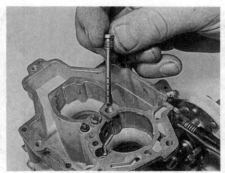

18.16A Removing a main air jet and emulsion tube

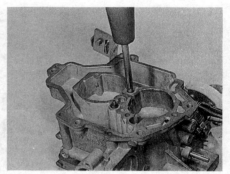

18.16B Insert screwdriver into main air jet passage ...

18.16C ... to unscrew main jet

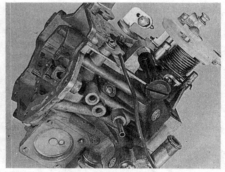

18.17 Do not disturb throttle linkage except for lubrication

so that they are correctly refitted, unscrew the main air jets and emulsion tubes, followed by the main jets (photos).

17   The throttle valve linkage can be dismantled if required but if either spindle or its bearing surfaces are worn, the complete carburettor must be renewed (photo).

18   Do not disturb the idle mixture adjusting screw unless absolutely necessary. If cleaning is required, first use a sharp implement to remove the tamperproof plug. Screw in the screw until it bottoms lightly, counting the **exact** number of turns necessary to do this, then unscrew the screw. On refitting, reverse the procedure to restore the screw to its original setting. Remember to have the idle mixture checked as soon as the carburettor is refitted.

19   Thoroughly clean all components, check them for wear or damage and renew them where necessary. Renew as a matter of course all gaskets, sealing washers and rings. Use compressed air only to dry the components and to blow clear all passages and jets. Never use wire to probe clear such components or their calibration will be ruined.

20   Refitting is the reverse of the removal procedure, noting the following points.

21   Do not overtighten any components, and note the torque wrench settings specified for some.

22   When reassembling the accelerator pump, refit the spring, diaphragm and cover, lightly tighten the cover screws, then press the operating lever fully in to seat the components before fully tightening the screws.

23   While reassembling the carburettor, check the fuel level and the vacuum pull-down and fast idle settings (Sec 16).

24   Refit the carburettor to the vehicle (Sec 17).

## 19   Inlet manifold – removal and refitting

**Note:** *While the inlet and exhaust manifolds can be removed independently of each other, **both** must be removed if the (two-piece) manifold gasket is to be renewed (see also Sec 20).*

1   It is preferable to completely drain the cooling system. Alternative-

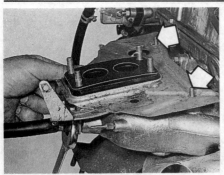

19.3 Slacken carburettor heater feed hose union and unscrew mounting nuts (arrowed) to release heat shield

19.6A Unscrew nuts to release engine lifting eye ...

19.6B ... warm air collector box ...

19.6C ... and inlet manifold-to-coolant feed pipe bracket (arrowed)

19.7 Inlet manifold can be removed separately from exhaust ...

ly, remove the expansion tank filler cap to release any residual cooling system pressure, then prepare to catch the coolant which will be spilt from the carburettor heater and inlet manifold (Chapter 2).

2    Remove the carburettor, disconnecting its heater hoses (Sec 17).

3    Unscrewing its two retaining nuts and slackening the carburettor heater feed hose union, withdraw the heat shield (photo).

4    Remove the carburettor insulating spacer and gaskets.

5    Disconnect from the manifold the econometer hose and the brake vacuum servo unit vacuum hose.

6    Unscrew the retaining nuts and remove the engine lifting eye, the warm air collector box and the inlet manifold-to-coolant feed pipe bracket (photos).

7    Unscrew the remaining nuts and withdraw the inlet manifold (photo).

8    If the gasket is to be renewed (as is good practice) remove the exhaust manifold (Sec 20) to permit this (photos).

9    On refitting, install a new (two-piece) gasket and check that the mating surfaces are clean and flat.

10    Refitting is the reverse of the removal procedure, noting the following points.

11    Tighten the manifold retaining nuts evenly, to the specified torque wrench setting (photo).

12    Refill the cooling system or check the coolant level as required, then wash off any spilt coolant (Chapter 2).

### 20    Exhaust manifold – removal and refitting

**Note:** *While it is possible to remove the exhaust manifold independently of the inlet manifold, access (especially to some of the retaining nuts) is very awkward and it is far easier to remove both manifolds together. Also, **both** manifolds **must** be removed if the (two-piece) manifold gasket is to be renewed (see also Sec 19).*

1    Remove the exhaust downpipe (Sec 21).

2    Unscrew the retaining nuts and remove the engine lifting eye, the

19.8A ... but exhaust manifold must be removed as well ...

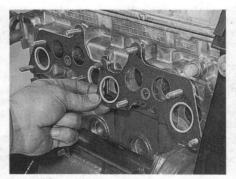

19.8B ... to permit renewal of (two-piece) manifold gasket

19.11 Tighten manifold nuts to torque wrench setting specified

21.3 Flatten lockwasher tabs to unscrew downpipe-to-manifold nuts (three arrowed)

warm air collector box and the inlet manifold-to-coolant feed pipe bracket (Sec 19).
3   Unscrew the remaining nuts and withdraw the exhaust manifold.
4   If the gasket is to be renewed (as is good practice) remove the inlet manifold (Sec 19) to permit this.

5   On refitting, install a new (two-piece) gasket and check that the mating surfaces are clean and flat.
6   Refitting is the reverse of the removal procedure. Tighten evenly and to their specified torque wrench settings the manifold retaining nuts, the downpipe-to-manifold nuts and the exhaust system clamp nuts.

## 21   Exhaust system – removal and refitting

1   The exhaust system is in three sections with a flexible joint beneath the passenger compartment. The sections are connected by clamps with tapered sealing rings.
2   Position the vehicle over an inspection pit or raise it and support it on axle stands (see *'Jacking, towing and wheel changing'*).
3   Flatten back the raised tabs of their lockwashers and unscrew the downpipe-to-manifold nuts (photo). **Note** that if these are not of the brass/copper self-locking type, they must be renewed whenever they are disturbed.
4   Either unscrew the downpipe clamp nuts and withdraw the clamp, or unbolt the bracket from the cylinder block/crankcase (photo).
5   Slacken the downpipe-to-mid-section clamp nuts or dismantle the clamp completely and withdraw the tapered ring (photos). Withdraw the downpipe.
6   Slacken the mid-section-to-tailpipe clamp nuts or dismantle the clamp completely and withdraw the tapered ring (photo).
7   Unhook the five rubber mountings (photo) and remove the two parts of the system.
8   Holts Flexiwrap and Holts Gun Gum exhaust repair systems can be used for effective repairs to exhaust pipes and silencer boxes, including

21.4 Exhaust downpipe to cylinder block/crankcase bracket and clamp mountings (arrowed)

21.5A Exhaust downpipe-to-mid-section clamp bolts (arrowed)

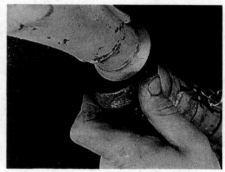

21.5B Exhaust system joints are sealed by tapered rings

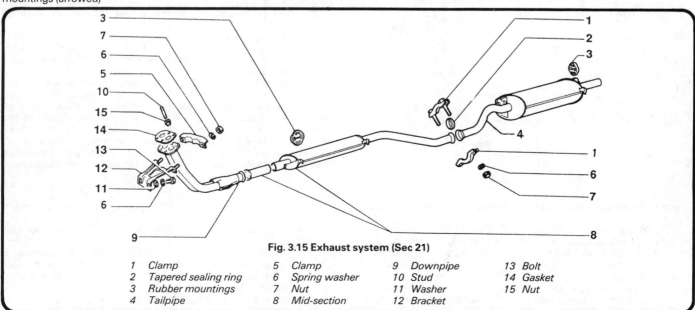

Fig. 3.15 Exhaust system (Sec 21)

| | | | |
|---|---|---|---|
| 1  Clamp | 5  Clamp | 9  Downpipe | 13  Bolt |
| 2  Tapered sealing ring | 6  Spring washer | 10  Stud | 14  Gasket |
| 3  Rubber mountings | 7  Nut | 11  Washer | 15  Nut |
| 4  Tailpipe | 8  Mid-section | 12  Bracket | |

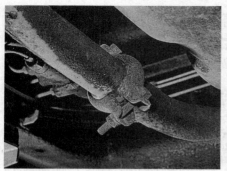

21.6 Exhaust mid-section-to-tailpipe clamp

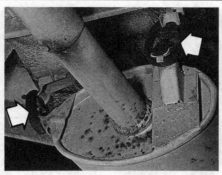

21.7 Exhaust system is supported by five rubber mountings (two arrowed)

21.8 Renew downpipe-to-manifold gasket whenever it is disturbed

ends and bends. Holts Flexiwrap is an MOT approved permanent exhaust repair.

9    On refitting, renew as a matter of course the downpipe-to-manifold gasket (photo) and, if they are of the appropriate type, the manifold nuts. Check, and renew if necessary, standard-type manifold nuts and lock-washers, the clamps and sealing rings and the rubber mountings.

10    Refitting is the reverse of the removal procedure, noting the following points.

11    Apply a smear of anti-seize compound (such as Holts Copaslip) to the threads of all nuts (except self-locking nuts) and bolts as well as to the sealing rings.

12    Assemble the system loosely on its mountings and check that it cannot touch any part of the body or suspension, even when deflected within the full extent of the flexible mountings.

13    Tighten evenly and to their specified torque wrench settings the new downpipe-to-manifold nuts and the exhaust system clamp nuts. Secure each of the manifold nuts by bending an unused portion of the lockwasher up against one of their flats, then securely tighten the downpipe-to-cylinder block/crankcase bracket mountings.

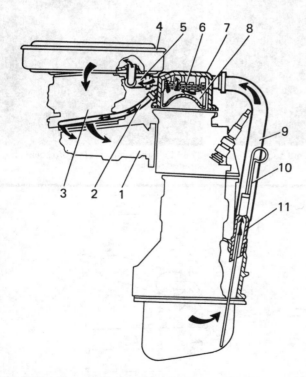

**Fig. 3.16 Crankcase emission control system components (Sec 22)**

| | |
|---|---|
| 1   Inlet manifold | 7   Cylinder head cover |
| 2   Breather hose (cylinder head cover-to-carburettor) | 8   Oil separator body |
| 3   Carburettor | 9   Breather hose (cylinder block/crankcase-to-cylinder head cover) |
| 4   Air cleaner | |
| 5   Breather hose (cylinder head cover-to-air cleaner) | 10  Engine oil level dipstick |
| 6   Oil separator screens | 11  Breather hose union |

## 22   Emission control systems – general

1    Apart from their ability to use unleaded petrol and features such as the fuel cut-off system which help to minimise emissions, Samara models have two other emission control systems.

### Evaporative emissions control

2    Refer to Section 1 and Fig. 3.1 for a description of the system and the location of its components.

3    The system requires no maintenance other than a check, whenever the fuel tank or separator are removed, that the two hoses are not kinked, blocked or split.

4    If any part of the system is damaged or faulty it must be renewed.

5    The filler cap can be tested only by the substitution of a new component.

6    The non-return valve can be tested by checking that air can only pass into the separator, not out of it. If the valve is clogged or leaking, release it from its clamp and disconnect the hose, then remove the plastic cap (photo).

7    To remove the separator, first remove the rear bumper (Chapter 10), then remove (working inside the luggage compartment) the single nut securing the separator and shield to the wheel arch. Unbolt the shield, disconnect the hoses from the separator and lower the shield until the separator can be withdrawn. It may be necessary to unbolt their mountings or clips so that the filler tube and breather hoses can be released far enough for the shield to be moved. Renew the separator if it is damaged or faulty. Refitting is the reversal of the removal procedure.

### Crankcase emission control

8    Refer to Section 1 and Fig. 3.16 for a description of the system and the location of its components.

9    To clean the system, remove the three hoses and the cylinder head cover (Chapter 1).

10    Check that the hoses are clear and free from splits, damage or wear, and renew them if necessary. Check also that the unions are clear.

11    Unbolt the separator body from the cylinder head cover and use a suitable solvent to flush clean the separator screens, then reassemble the separator and refit the cylinder head cover (photos). Ensure that the hoses are correctly routed and properly secured.

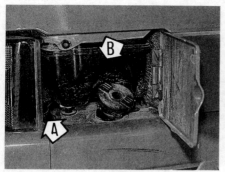

22.6 Evaporative emissions control system non-return valve 'A', and separator 'B'

22.11A Remove cylinder head cover and unbolt oil separator body ...

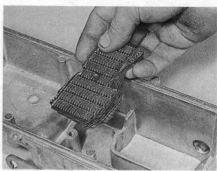

22.11B ... so that separator screens can be cleaned

## 23  Fault diagnosis – fuel system

**Note:** *High fuel consumption and poor performance are not necessarily due to fuel system faults. Make sure that the ignition system is properly adjusted, that the brakes are not binding and that the engine is in good mechanical condition before tampering with the fuel system.*

| Symptom | Reason(s) |
|---|---|
| Fuel consumption excessive | Air cleaner choked, giving rich mixture<br>Leak from fuel tank, pump or pipes/hoses<br>Float chamber flooding due to incorrect fuel level or worn needle valve<br>Carburettor incorrectly adjusted<br>Idle speed too high<br>Choke mechanism faulty or sticking<br>Excessively worn carburettor |
| Lack of power, stalling or difficult starting | Faulty fuel pump<br>Leak on suction side of pump or in fuel line<br>Inlet manifold or carburettor flange gaskets leaking<br>Carburettor incorrectly adjusted<br>Faulty fuel cut-off system<br>Choke mechanism faulty or sticking |
| Poor or erratic idling | Weak mixture<br>Leak in inlet manifold<br>Leak in distributor vacuum hose<br>Leak in crankcase breather hose<br>Leak in vacuum servo unit vacuum hose<br>Carburettor incorrectly adjusted<br>Faulty fuel cut-off system<br>Choke mechanism faulty or sticking |

**Note:** *This Section is not intended to be an exhaustive guide to fault diagnosis but summarises the more common faults which may be encountered during a vehicle's life. Consult a dealer for more specific advice.*

# Chapter 4 Ignition system

## Contents

## Specifications

### General

| | |
|---|---|
| System type ...................................................... | Electronic, Hall-effect, incorporating contactless distributor and separate amplifier module |
| Firing order........................................................ | 1 – 3 – 4 – 2 (No 1 cylinder at timing belt end) |
| Direction of crankshaft rotation ............................ | Clockwise (seen from right-hand side of vehicle) |

### Distributor

| | |
|---|---|
| Type.................................................................. | Hall-effect |
| Identification: | |
| 1100................................................................ | 40.3706-10 |
| 1300, 1500 ....................................................... | 40.3706 or 40.3706-01 |
| Direction of rotor arm rotation .............................. | Anti-clockwise (seen from left-hand side of vehicle) |
| Rotor arm resistance ........................................... | 1 K ohm (built-in) |
| Centrifugal advance commences: | |
| 1100................................................................ | 800 to 1200 rpm |
| 1300, 1500 ....................................................... | 800 to 1300 rpm |
| Maximum centrifugal advance: | |
| 1100................................................................ | 27° to 31° @ 5000 rpm |
| 1300, 1500 ....................................................... | 22° to 26° @ 5600 rpm |
| Vacuum advance commences: | |
| 1100................................................................ | 90 to 110 mbar |
| 1300, 1500 ....................................................... | 120 to 150 mbar |
| Maximum vacuum advance: | |
| 1100................................................................ | 8° to 12° @ 160 mbar |
| 1300, 1500 ....................................................... | 12° to 16° @ 240 mbar |

**Note:** *Degree and speed values to be measured at crankshaft*

### Ignition HT coil

| | |
|---|---|
| Type: | |
| Early models .................................................... | 27.3705 (USSR-built) |
| Later models .................................................... | Lucas DLB 198 or equivalent |
| Primary resistance: | |
| Russian unit..................................................... | 0.45 ± 0.05 ohm |
| Intermotor unit ................................................. | 0.8 to 1.1 ohm |
| Secondary resistance: | |
| Lucas .............................................................. | 5.0 ± 1.0 K ohms |
| Soviet.............................................................. | 4.0 ± 0.5 K ohms |
| Minimum insulation resistance.............................. | 50 M ohms |

### Ignition timing

*At idle speed, vacuum hose connected:*

| | |
|---|---|
| 1100................................................................ | 6° ± 1° BTDC |
| 1300................................................................ | 1° ± 1° BTDC |
| 1500................................................................ | 4° ± 1° BTDC |

## Spark plugs
Type.................................................................................... Champion N9YCC or N9YC
Electrode gap...................................................................... 0.8 mm (0.032 in)

## HT leads
Resistance (original equipment, blue leads) ........................... 2 K ohm per lead max
Type (replacement)................................................................ Champion CLS4 (boxed set)

## Torque wrench settings

| | Nm | lbf ft |
|---|---|---|
| Spark plugs ................................................... | 31.5 to 39 | 23 to 29 |

---

### 1  General description

The ignition system is of the electronic type, incorporating a contact-less distributor (driven off the camshaft left-hand end) and an amplifier module as well as the spark plugs, HT leads, ignition HT coil and associated wiring. The system is divided into two circuits; primary (low tension/LT) and secondary (high tension/HT). The primary circuit consists of the battery, ignition switch, ignition HT coil secondary windings, ignition amplifier module, distributor signal generating system and wiring. The secondary circuit consists of the ignition HT coil secondary windings, the distributor cap and rotor arm, the spark plugs and the HT leads connecting these.

The distributor incorporates features which advance the ignition timing both mechanically and by vacuum operation. Its signal generating system consists of a Hall-effect sensor which sends a signal to the ignition amplifier module whenever the cut-out in a shaped rotor passes across its magnetic gate. The rotor is mounted on the centre part of a mechanical governor whose two weights move outwards under centrifugal force as engine speed rises, the amount of advance being controlled by light springs. The sensor is mounted on a baseplate that is able to rotate under the control of the vacuum capsule mounted on the side of the distributor. The capsule consists of a diaphragm, one side of which is connected via a small-bore hose to the carburettor and the other side to the baseplate. Inlet manifold depression, which varies with engine speed and throttle position, causes the diaphragm to move thus rotating the baseplate and advancing or retarding the spark.

Refer to Chapter 11 for details of the ignition switch.

**Warning:** *The voltages produced by the electronic ignition system are considerably higher than those produced by conventional systems. Extreme care must be taken when working on the system with the ignition switched on. Persons with surgically-implanted cardiac pacemaker devices should keep well clear of the ignition circuits, components and test equipment.*

---

### 2  Routine maintenance

**Note:** *Refer to the warnings given in Section 1 of this Chapter before starting work.*

1    Carry out the following procedures at the intervals given in *Routine maintenance* at the beginning of this manual.

### Check the spark plugs
2    If the appropriate type of spark plug is fitted, remove and check the plugs and reset the electrode gap if necessary (Sec 9).

### Renew the spark plugs
3    At the specified intervals the spark plugs must be renewed, irrespective of their apparent condition, to preserve the engine's performance and economy and to help minimise pollution.
4    Remove the old plugs (Sec 9), noting their condition and taking corrective action where necessary, then discard them.
5    Ensuring that the new plugs are of the correct grade, as specified in this manual or by Lada, set the electrode gap and install them as described in Section 9.

### Check the ignition timing
6    Refer to Section 5.

---

### 3  Distributor – removal and refitting

1    Disconnect the battery negative terminal.
2    Releasing its wire clip, unplug the wiring connector from the distributor (photo).
3    Disconnect and plug the vacuum hose (photo).
4    Remove the rubber plug from the bellhousing aperture (Sec 5). Using a spanner applied to the alternator drive pulley bolt, rotate the crankshaft clockwise until the flywheel mark aligns with the scale's notch and longer (centre) line. Numbers 1 and 4 cylinders are now at TDC (Top Dead Centre), one of them on the compression stroke.
5    Mark the relationship of the distributor cap to the body, then remove the screws and withdraw the cap (photo). Mark the relationship of the rotor arm to the distributor body. Its brass segment should be aligned with the distributor cap's number 1 or 4 cylinder HT lead segment.
6    Mark the relationship of the distributor body to the cylinder head extension, using as references the scale on the distributor's mounting flange and the extension's raised rib.
7    Unscrew the three retaining nuts and secure the HT lead guide out of the way, then withdraw the distributor. Do not disturb the crankshaft setting while the distributor is removed, or rotate the distributor shaft (unless the unit is to be overhauled).
8    Check the distributor body sealing ring and renew it if it is worn or damaged.

3.2 Disconnecting distributor wiring

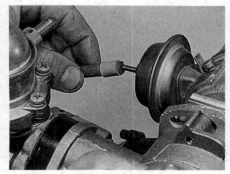
3.3 Disconnecting vacuum hose

3.5 Note position of cap before removing

3.10 Distributor drive dogs will fit only one way in camshaft slots

9    On refitting, first check that numbers 1 and 4 cylinders are at TDC (paragraph 4), then check that the rotor arm is in the position noted on removal (paragraph 5).
10    Aligning the marks made on removal, refit the distributor. If necessary, rotate the rotor arm very slightly to help the distributor drive dogs locate in the camshaft slots, which are offset and will fit only one way (photo). Refit the HT lead guide and retaining nuts.
11    Refit the distributor cap, ensuring it is correctly located, then reconnect the HT leads.
12    Reconnect the vacuum hose and distributor wiring.

13    Check the ignition timing and adjust if necessary (Sec 5).
14    Note that if a new distributor is to be fitted (or no marks were made on removal), the following procedure will produce a basic setting which will enable the engine to start and run while the ignition timing is set accurately.
15    Remove the cylinder head cover (Chapter 1). Using a spanner applied to the alternator drive pulley bolt, rotate the crankshaft clockwise until number 1 cylinder inlet valve has opened and closed again, then slowly rotate it further until the flywheel mark aligns with the bellhousing scale's notch and longer (centre) line. With number 1 cylinder now at TDC on the compression stroke, rotate the crankshaft slightly anti-clockwise until the flywheel mark aligns with the appropriate scale mark (see Specifications), so that the engine is in the firing position.
16    Rotate the distributor rotor arm until its brass segment is aligned with the distributor cap's number 1 cylinder HT lead segment.
17    Refit the distributor (see paragraph 10 above), positioning its body so that the centre mark of its mounting flange's scale is aligned with the cylinder head extension's raised rib.
18    Check the ignition timing and adjust if necessary (Sec 5).

### 4   Distributor – overhaul

1    Remove the distributor (Sec 3).
2    Remove the rotor and the shield (photos).
3    Prise out the retaining circlip and disconnect the vacuum capsule arm from the baseplate, then remove the screws and withdraw the capsule (photos).

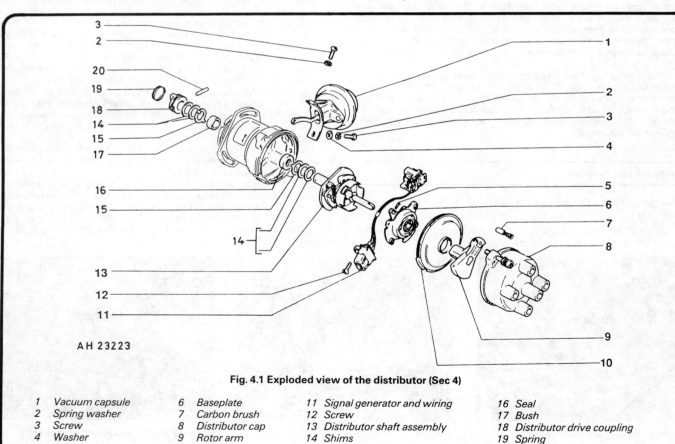

AH 23223

**Fig. 4.1 Exploded view of the distributor (Sec 4)**

| | | | | | | |
|---|---|---|---|---|---|---|
| 1 | Vacuum capsule | 6 | Baseplate | 11 | Signal generator and wiring | 16 | Seal |
| 2 | Spring washer | 7 | Carbon brush | 12 | Screw | 17 | Bush |
| 3 | Screw | 8 | Distributor cap | 13 | Distributor shaft assembly | 18 | Distributor drive coupling |
| 4 | Washer | 9 | Rotor arm | 14 | Shims | 19 | Spring |
| 5 | Circlip | 10 | Shield | 15 | Washer | 20 | Pin |

4.2A Removing motor arm ...

4.2B ... and shield

4.3A Prise out circlip to disconnect vacuum capsule arm from baseplate

4.3B Remove retaining screws to release vacuum capsule

4.4A Remove retaining screw to release wiring connector ...

4.4B ... unscrew baseplate mounting screws ...

4.4C ... and withdraw assembly

4.5 Measuring distributor shaft endfloat

4    Remove the screws and withdraw the baseplate, signal generator and wiring as a single unit (photos).
5    Measure the distributor shaft endfloat (photo), which should not exceed 0.35 mm.
6    Remove the spring from the distributor drive coupling, then drive out the pin and remove the coupling, noting the shims and washer behind it (photos).
7    Withdraw the shaft, noting the shims and washer underneath the mechanical advance assembly (photo).
8    While the advance mechanism can be dismantled by removing the circlip (photo), this is only for lubrication purposes. If renewal is necessary, the assembly is available only as a single unit.
9    Clean and examine all components, renewing any that are worn or damaged. The distributor shaft bush and seal can be renewed separately if required. Add or remove shims as required to bring the shaft endfloat within the set limit.
10   Wipe clean the distributor cap and check it for cracks or for signs of

fine black lines from any of the HT lead terminal segments, which might indicate 'tracking'. Renew the cap if either condition is found and check that the cap's carbon brush is unworn, free to move against spring pressure and making good contact with the rotor arm. Renew it if necessary.
11   If a suitable insulation tester is available, check that the resistance between any two terminal segments is a minimum of 50 M ohm. Similarly, check that there is no continuity between the rotor arm body and its brass segment, noting that the arm has a specified built-in resistance.
12   Refitting is the reverse of the removal procedure, noting the following points.
13   Apply high melting-point grease to the advance mechanism pivots and springs, to the shaft bearing surfaces and to the baseplate bearing surface.
14   Refit the distributor (Sec 3).

4.6A Remove spring ...

4.6B ... drive out pin ...

4.6C ... and remove coupling, noting shims and washer behind

4.7 Remove distributor shaft, noting shims and washer

4.8 Advance mechanism can be dismantled for lubrication

## 5  Ignition timing – checking and adjusting

**Note:** *Refer to the warnings given in Section 1 of this Chapter before starting work. To prevent any risk of shocks, make up a distributor earth from a spare length of wire with a female Lucar connector crimped on each end and connect this between the battery negative terminal and the distributor body* **whenever** *the distributor mounting nuts are slackened while the engine is running. Male earth terminals are provided for this purpose, one on the battery earth strap and the other on one of the distributor vacuum capsule mounting screws.*

1    Ignition timing marks are provided on the alternator drive pulley and timing belt cover (Fig. 4.2) or on the flywheel and bellhousing scale, the bellhousing aperture being sealed by a rubber plug (photos). Use **only** the flywheel/bellhousing marks for ignition timing as the other set are for reference only, during engine servicing.
2    The flywheel mark is a single line. The scale has several marks, the (longer) centre line, which may be emphasised by a notch, indicating TDC (Top Dead Centre). The short lines each correspond to one crank-shaft degree before or after TDC (BTDC/ATDC), while the medium-length lines show five degrees (BTDC/ATDC). Using white paint or similar, emphasise the flywheel mark and the correct scale mark (see Specifications) appropriate to the engine concerned.
3    Start the engine and warm it up to normal operating temperature.
4    Stop the engine and connect the distributor earth (see note above) and a timing light, according to the manufacturer's instructions.
5    Start the engine, allow it to idle and aim the timing light at the timing marks, when the emphasised marks should stand out clearly.
6    Check that the flywheel mark aligns with the correct scale mark, or within the specified tolerance.
7    If adjustment is required, slacken the distributor mounting nuts until the distributor body is just able to rotate, then turn the body clockwise (viewed from the vehicle's left-hand side) to advance the ignition timing, anti-clockwise to retard it. Tighten the nuts when the setting is correct and recheck the ignition timing to ensure that it has not altered.
8    Note that the distributor body mounting flange has a scale em-bossed on it, with the raised rib on the cylinder head extension serving

as the fixed reference point (photo). This is to facilitate ignition timing adjustment, each mark on the scale corresponding to five crankshaft degrees.
9    Increase engine speed and check that the flywheel mark advances out of sight, which shows that the centrifugal advance mechanism is functioning. A detailed check, however, must be left to a Lada dealer who has the necessary equipment.
10   Unplug and reconnect the vacuum hose. The ignition timing

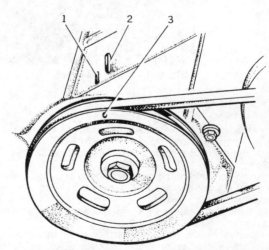

**Fig. 4.2 Timing marks on timing belt cover (Sec 5)**

*1   5° BTDC mark*      *3   Alternator drive pulley*
*2   TDC mark*              *mark*
                                   **Note:** *Shown for reference only –* **do not** *use to check ignition timing*

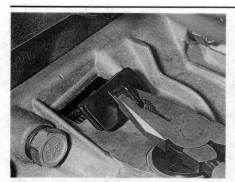

5.1A Remove rubber plug from bellhousing to expose timing marks

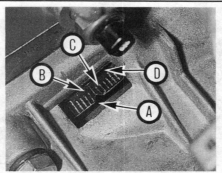

5.1B Flywheel/bellhousing timing marks, showing flywheel mark (A), TDC mark (B), 1° BTDC mark (C) and 5° BTDC mark (D)

5.8 Slacken mounting nut to turn distributor – note scale and earth terminal (arrowed)

should retard, then advance as the hose is reconnected. If the ignition timing does not alter, check that the hose is clear of blockages or kinks and that it is not leaking. Suck on the carburettor end of the hose. If there is no effect on the ignition timing, then the vacuum capsule is faulty and must be renewed. Again, any more detailed tests must be left to a Lada dealer.

11   When the ignition timing is correct, stop the engine and disconnect the timing light and earth.

*Running on Premium grade unleaded petrol*

12   In common with most USSR-built vehicles, all Samara models are designed to run on 93 RON octane petrol and have the hardened valve seats which enable them to use unleaded fuels. No adjustment is required, therefore, to allow them to use the Premium grade (95 RON) unleaded petrol currently available in the UK.

## 6   Ignition HT coil – description and testing

1   The coil is mounted on the left-hand side of the engine compartment (photo).
2   Testing of the coil consists of using a multimeter set to its resistance function or a low-wattage test lamp to check the primary and secondary windings for continuity. If the meter is used the resistance of each circuit can be checked and compared with the specified values. Note that since the readings obtained will vary slightly with temperature, the coil should be tested (where possible) after the engine has been running for at least 15 minutes so that the coil is at its normal operating temperature.

3   If a suitable insulation tester is available, check that the resistance between the HT lead terminal and the coil body is a minimum of 50 M ohm.
4   If the coil is faulty it must be renewed.

## 7   Ignition amplifier module – removal and refitting

**Note:** *Refer to the warnings given in Section 1 of this Chapter before starting work. To prevent any risk of shocks, or of damage to the module,* **always** *switch off the ignition before disconnecting the module's wires and* **never** *disconnect the battery when the engine is running.*

1   The amplifier module is mounted on the left-hand end of the engine compartment bulkhead, between the vacuum servo unit and the left-hand front suspension strut mounting (photo).
2   The module itself cannot be tested without special equipment, so if the process of elimination indicates that the module might be faulty the vehicle must be taken to a Lada dealer for the complete ignition system to be checked.
3   If the module is faulty it must be renewed.
4   To remove the module, unscrew the two retaining nuts and collect the washers (noting the earth wires under one of the nuts), withdraw the module and disconnect its wires.
5   Refitting is the reverse of the removal procedure. Ensure that the mounting points are cleaned back to bare metal and treated and that the earth wires are correctly secured. Do not overtighten the nuts.

6.1 Disconnecting distributor HT lead from ignition HT coil

7.1 Location of ignition amplifier module

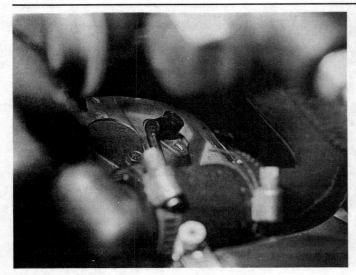

8.0A TDC sensor mounted on bellhousing rear face

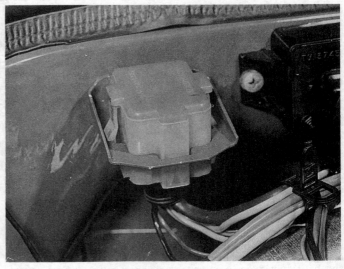

8.0B Diagnostic system socket on bulkhead

## 8    TDC sensor – general

The TDC sensor mounted in the bellhousing is not part of the ignition system itself, but is instead a part of the built-in diagnostic system which allows electronic test equipment (available only to Lada dealers) to be plugged into the socket on the engine compartment bulkhead to check all electrical equipment, including the alternator and voltage regulator, the battery and the ignition system (photos).

## 9    Spark plugs and HT leads – general

**Note:** *Refer to the warnings given in Section 1 of this Chapter before starting work.*

1    The correct functioning of the spark plugs is vital for the correct running and efficiency of the engine. It is essential that the plugs fitted are appropriate for the engine, and the suitable type is specified at the beginning of this Chapter. If Champion 'Double Copper' spark plugs (CC suffix) are used and the engine is in good condition, the spark plugs should not need attention between scheduled replacement intervals. All other types of spark plug should be checked at the more frequent interval given in *Routine maintenance* at the beginning of this manual. Spark plug cleaning is rarely necessary and should not be attempted unless specialised equipment is available, as damage can easily be caused to the firing ends.
2    To remove the plugs, first open the bonnet and mark the HT leads one to four to correspond to the cylinder the lead serves (number 1 cylinder is at the timing belt end of the engine). Pull the HT leads from the plugs by gripping the end fitting, not the lead, otherwise the lead connection may be fractured.
3    It is advisable to remove the dirt from the spark plug recesses using a clean brush, vacuum cleaner or compressed air before removing the plugs, to prevent the dirt dropping into the cylinders (photo).
4    Unscrew the plugs using a spark plug spanner, suitable box spanner or a deep socket and extension bar. As each plug is removed, examine it as follows.
5    Examination of the spark plugs will give a good indication of the condition of the engine. If the insulator nose of the spark plug is clean and white, with no deposits, this is indicative of a weak mixture or too hot a plug (a hot plug transfers heat away from the electrode slowly, a cold plug transfers heat away quickly).
6    If the tip and insulator nose are covered with hard black looking deposits, then this is indicative that the mixture is too rich. Should the plug be black and oily, then it is likely that the engine is fairly worn, as well as the mixture being too rich.
7    If the insulator nose is covered with light tan to greyish brown deposits, then the mixture is correct and it is likely that the engine is in good condition.

8    The spark plug gap is of considerable importance as, if it is too large or too small, the size of the spark and its efficiency will be seriously impaired. For the best results the spark plug gap should be set in accordance with the Specifications at the beginning of this Chapter.
9    To set it, measure the gap with a feeler gauge, and then bend open or close, the outer plug electrode until the correct gap is achieved. The centre electrode should never be bent, as this may crack the insulation and cause plug failure, if nothing worse.
10    Special spark plug electrode gap adjusting tools are available from most motor accessory shops.
11    Also, check the HT leads for any signs of chafing or damage and ensure that they are routed correctly, clear of any hot or moving components, and secured in the guide provided. Wipe clean the leads (including the HT coil lead) over their entire length. If any sign of corrosion can be seen, especially inside the end fittings, it must be carefully cleaned away.
12    If any lead is obviously damaged or faulty it must be renewed. Occasionally a misfire can be caused by tracking from the leads, especially in damp weather. This can be checked by looking closely at the leads when the engine is run at night, the dark making more obvious the tiny sparks created by tracking. **Warning:** *If tracking is suspected, do not touch any part of the system while the ignition is switched on (Sec 1).*
13    To test an HT lead, remove it and use an ohmmeter or similar to check its resistance from one end fitting to the other. Check for breaks or intermittent faults by wiggling the lead as it is tested. All the leads should show the same resistance value, and if any differs significantly

9.3 Blow clean recesses before unscrewing spark plugs

from the others, or if the values measured are different from those specified, the lead(s) must be renewed. Note that to ensure the continued reliability and efficiency of the ignition system, it is good practice to renew the leads as a set, even if only one is actually faulty.

14   Before fitting the spark plugs check that the threaded connector sleeves (where used) are tight and that the plug exterior surfaces and threads are clean. Apply a thin smear of graphite grease or anti-seize compound (eg Holts Copaslip) to the plug threads.

15   Screw in the spark plugs by hand where possible, then tighten them to the specified torque wrench setting. If a torque wrench is not available, screw in each plug by hand only until it seats lightly on its gasket, then tighten it by a maximum of a quarter of a turn with the plug spanner. **Do not** overtighten the spark plugs and take extra care to enter each plug's threads correctly, as the cylinder head is of aluminium alloy.

16   Reconnect the HT leads in their correct order.

---

## 10   Fault diagnosis – ignition system

1   Electronic ignition systems are normally very reliable. Faults are most likely to be due to loose or dirty connections or to 'tracking' of HT voltage due to dirt, dampness or damaged insulation.

2   The old practice of checking for a spark by holding the live end of an HT lead a short distance away from the engine is not recommended by the manufacturer. Not only is there a high risk of a powerful electric shock, but the HT coil or amplifier module may be damaged. Similarly, do not try to 'diagnose' misfires by pulling off one HT lead at a time.

### Engine will not start

3   If the engine either will not turn over at all, or only turns very slowly, check the battery and starter motor. Connect a voltmeter across the battery terminals (meter positive probe to battery positive terminal), disconnect the ignition coil HT lead from the distributor cap and earth it, then note the voltage reading obtained while turning over the engine on the starter for no more than ten seconds. If the reading obtained is less than 9.6 volts, check the battery, starter motor and charging system (Chapter 11).

4   If the engine turns over at normal speed but will not start, check the HT circuit by connecting a timing light and turning the engine over on the starter motor. If the light flashes, voltage is reaching the spark plugs,

so these should be checked first. If the light does not flash, check the HT leads themselves (Sec 9), followed by the distributor cap, carbon brush and rotor arm (Sec 4).

5   If the fault is still not located, check the ignition HT coil (Sec 6). If the coil is in good condition, disconnect the coil's HT lead from the distributor cap and connect it to a spark plug that is firmly earthed on the engine. Disconnect the distributor wiring, switch on the ignition and briefly bridge (using a split pin) the green and white/black wires in the plug disconnected from the distributor, when a spark should occur at the plug electrodes. If so, the amplifier module, HT coil and wiring are proven to be working and the fault must lie in the distributor itself. Check first that 6 to 12 volts is available at the distributor red wire, indicating that the supply from the module is working.

6   If no spark appears, the fault is in either the distributor or the amplifier module. Both of these can be tested only by a Lada dealer using special test equipment. The only alternative open to the ordinary owner is to try the effect of substituting a known good unit.

7   If the engine fails to start due to either damp HT leads or distributor cap, a moisture dispersant, such as Holts Wet Start, can be very effective. To prevent the problem re-occurring, Holts Damp Start can be used to provide a sealing coat, so excluding any further moisture from the ignition system. In extreme difficulties, Holts Cold Start will help to start a car when only a very poor spark occurs.

### Engine misfires

8   An irregular misfire suggests either a loose connection or intermittent fault on the primary circuit, or an HT fault on the coil side of the rotor arm.

9   With the ignition switched off, check carefully through the system, ensuring that all connections are clean and securely fastened. Check also that the HT coil, the distributor cap and the HT leads are clean and dry. Check the leads themselves and the spark plugs (by substitution, if necessary) (Sec 9).

10   Check the distributor cap, carbon brush and rotor arm (Sec 4).

11   Regular misfiring is almost certainly due to a fault in the distributor cap, HT leads or spark plugs. Use a timing light (paragraph 4 above) to check whether HT voltage is present at all leads.

12   If HT voltage is not present on any particular lead, the fault will be in that lead or in the distributor cap. If HT is present on all leads, the fault will be in the spark plugs. Check them, and renew them if there is any doubt about their condition (Sec 9).

13   If no HT is present, check the HT coil, as its secondary windings may be breaking down under load.

# Chapter 5 Clutch

## Contents

## Specifications

**Type** ...................................................................................... Single dry plate, with diaphragm spring, cable-operated

**Pedal travel**
Standard .................................................................................. 125 to 130 mm
Maximum ................................................................................. 160 mm

**Friction plate**
Nominal thickness.................................................................... 8.3 mm
Friction material wear limit – minimum distance from rivet heads to
friction material surface ...........................................................  0.2 mm
Friction material maximum run-out........................................... 0.5 mm

**Torque wrench settings**

| | Nm | lbf ft |
|---|---|---|
| Cable adjuster nuts | 14.5 to 20 | 11 to 14.5 |
| Cover assembly bolts | 19 to 31 | 14 to 23 |

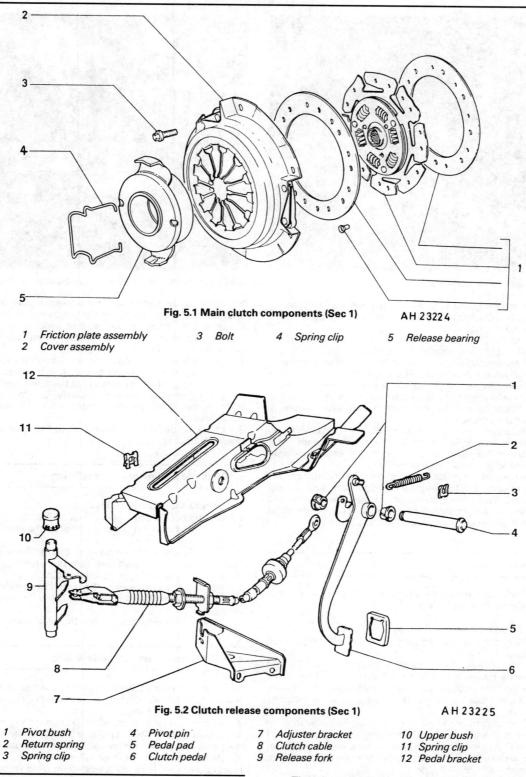

**Fig. 5.1 Main clutch components (Sec 1)**

AH 23224

| | | | | | |
|---|---|---|---|---|---|
| 1 | Friction plate assembly | 3 | Bolt | 4 | Spring clip | 5 | Release bearing |
| 2 | Cover assembly | | | | |

**Fig. 5.2 Clutch release components (Sec 1)**

AH 23225

| | | | | | | | |
|---|---|---|---|---|---|---|---|
| 1 | Pivot bush | 4 | Pivot pin | 7 | Adjuster bracket | 10 | Upper bush |
| 2 | Return spring | 5 | Pedal pad | 8 | Clutch cable | 11 | Spring clip |
| 3 | Spring clip | 6 | Clutch pedal | 9 | Release fork | 12 | Pedal bracket |

## 1   General description

All models are fitted with a dry single plate diaphragm spring clutch to provide the driver with a means of smoothly taking up the drive on starting off and of interrupting the drive when changing gear.

The clutch consists of a friction plate, a cover assembly, a release bearing and the release mechanism. All of these components are contained in the large cast aluminium alloy bellhousing sandwiched between the engine and the transmission and all use UK design technol-

ogy. The release mechanism is mechanical, being operated by a cable.

The friction plate is fitted between the engine flywheel and the clutch pressure plate and is allowed to slide on the transmission input shaft splines. It consists of two circular facings of friction material riveted in position to provide the clutch bearing surface and a spring-cushioned hub to damp out transmission shocks.

The cover assembly is bolted to the engine flywheel and is located by three dowel pins. It comprises the clutch cover, the diaphragm spring and the pressure plate. When the engine is running drive is transmitted from the crankshaft via the flywheel and clutch cover to the friction

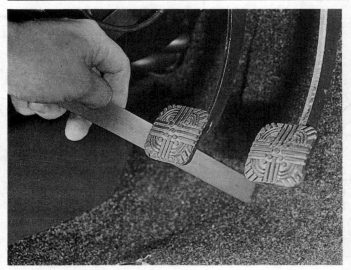

2.5 Measuring clutch pedal travel

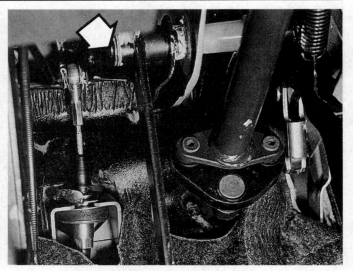

3.3 Clutch pedal is retained by a spring clip (arrowed)

plate (these last three components being clamped securely together by the pressure plate and diaphragm spring) and from the friction plate to the transmission input shaft.

To interrupt the drive the spring pressure must be relaxed. This is achieved by a sealed, ball-race release bearing which is fitted concentrically around the transmission input shaft. When the driver depresses the clutch pedal the release bearing is pressed against the fingers at the centre of the diaphragm spring. Since the spring is held by rivets between two annular fulcrum rings the pressure at its centre causes it to deform so that it flattens and thus releases the clamping force it exerts, at its periphery, on the pressure plate.

Depressing the clutch pedal pulls the control cable inner wire and rotates the release fork by acting on the lever at the fork's upper end, above the bellhousing. The fork itself is located on the left of the release bearing and is secured to it by a wire spring clip.

As the friction plate facings wear, the pressure plate moves towards the flywheel. This causes the diaphragm spring fingers to push against the release bearing, thus raising the height of the clutch pedal and increasing its travel. To ensure correct operation, the clutch cable must be adjusted periodically to restore the specified pedal travel.

## 2  Routine maintenance

Carry out the following procedures at the intervals given in *'Routine maintenance'* at the beginning of this manual.

### Lubricate the clutch cable
1    Check that the clutch pedal moves slowly and easily through its full travel, with no signs of stiffness.
2    If excessive effort is required to operate the clutch, check first that the cable is correctly routed and undamaged, then remove the pedal (Sec 3) to ensure that it is properly greased before suspecting a fault in the cable itself. If the cable is worn or damaged it must be renewed (Sec 4).
3    If the cable is fit for further use, slide up the rubber sleeve from the bulkhead bracket and lubricate the cable using a light machine oil (Duckhams Home Oil). Operate the clutch pedal to spread the oil down the cable's inner wire, refit the sleeve, then apply a few drops of oil or some grease to both cable end fittings.

### Check and adjust the clutch pedal travel
4    Check that the clutch pedal moves smoothly and easily through its full travel and that the clutch itself functions correctly with no trace of slip or drag.
5    Fully depress the clutch pedal to the floor then release it steadily, using a ruler placed alongside (photo) to measure the travel (at the centre of the pedal pad) from the fully-depressed to the fully-released positions. Repeat this check twice and note the average of the three measurements.

6    Note that the pedal travel will increase in service from the standard specified value, but no adjustment is required until the maximum value is reached. If, therefore, the average pedal travel measured exceeds 160 mm (6.3 in), then the cable must be adjusted to restore the travel to within the limits of the standard value.
7    To adjust the cable, open the bonnet and slacken the adjuster nuts on each side of the bracket bolted to the transmission. Rotate both adjuster nuts to alter the cable's effective length until the pedal travel is correct. Tighten the two nuts securely, but do not overtighten them (note the torque wrench setting specified) and ensure that the setting is not altered.
8    Check the pedal travel again (para 5) to ensure that it is correct, and re-adjust if necessary.

## 3  Clutch pedal – removal and refitting

1    Unhook the return spring from the pedal.
2    Disconnect the cable from the pedal (Sec 4).
3    Remove the spring clip and withdraw the pedal from the pivot pin (photo).
4    Carefully clean all components and renew any that are worn or damaged. Check with particular care the return spring and the bearing surfaces of the pivot bushes and pivot pin.
5    Refitting is the reverse of the removal procedure, but apply a thin smear of the specified multi-purpose grease to the pedal pivot bearing surfaces.
6    Check, and adjust if necessary, the pedal travel (Sec 2).

## 4  Clutch cable – removal and refitting

1    Working in the engine compartment, slacken the adjuster nuts until there is sufficient slack for the cable end fitting to be unhooked from the release fork lever (photos).
2    Release the cable from the bracket bolted to the transmission.
3    Working inside the car, remove the spring clip securing the cable to the pedal and disconnect the cable from the pedal (photo).
4    Remove the spring clip or nut securing the cable to the bulkhead bracket and peel back the carpet (removing retaining screws where necessary) until the rubber grommet is exposed at the point where the cable passes through the bulkhead. Disengage the cable from the bulkhead bracket and push the grommet into the engine compartment.
5    Return to the engine compartment and withdraw the cable forwards through the bulkhead aperture.
6    Examine the cable, looking for worn end fittings or a damaged outer casing and for signs of fraying of the inner wire. To test the cable's operation, check that the inner wire moves smoothly and easily through the outer casing, but remember that a cable that appears serviceable when tested off the car may well be much heavier in operation when

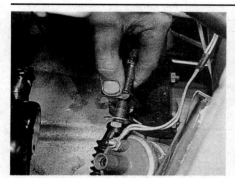

4.1A Slacken adjuster nuts to release cable from bracket ...

4.1B ... so that cable end can be unhooked from release fork lever

4.3 Clutch cable is secured by spring clips (arrowed) to pedal and bulkhead

5.6 Friction plate is fitted as shown

5.7 Cover assembly is located on three dowels (one arrowed)

5.9 Using a clutch aligning tool to centralise the friction plate

compressed into its working position. Renew the cable if it shows any signs of excessive wear or of damage.

7    Refitting is the reverse of the removal procedure, but apply a thin smear of the specified multi-purpose grease to the cable end fittings. Ensure that the cable is routed correctly, with no sharp bends or kinks, and that it is secured clear of the exhaust downpipe and components such as brake pipes, coolant hoses and wiring.

8    Check, and adjust if necessary, the pedal travel (Sec 2).

## 5  Clutch assembly – removal and refitting

**Warning:** *Dust created by clutch wear and deposited on the clutch components may contain asbestos which is a health hazard. DO NOT blow it out with compressed air or inhale any of it. DO NOT use petrol or petroleum-based solvents to clean off the dust. Brake system cleaner or methylated spirit should be used to flush the dust into a suitable receptacle. After the clutch components are wiped clean with rags, dispose of the contaminated rags and cleaner in a sealed, marked container.*

1    Unless the complete engine/transmission unit is to be removed from the car and separated for major overhaul (see Chapter 1), the clutch can be reached only after the transmission has been removed (Chapter 6).

2    Before disturbing the clutch use chalk or a felt-tip pen to mark the relationship of the cover assembly to the flywheel.

3    Working in a diagonal sequence, slacken the cover assembly bolts by half a turn at a time until spring pressure is released and the bolts can be unscrewed by hand.

4    Prise the cover assembly off its locating dowels and collect the friction plate, noting which way round the friction plate is fitted.

5    On reassembly, ensure that the bearing surfaces of the flywheel and pressure plate are completely clean, smooth and free from oil or grease. Use solvent to remove any protective grease from new components.

6    Fit the friction plate so that the longer part of its central, splined, boss is towards the flywheel and so that its spring hub assembly faces away from the flywheel (photo).

7    Refit the cover assembly, aligning the marks made on dismantling (if the original cover is re-used) and locating the cover on its three locating dowels (photo). Fit the mounting bolts, but tighten them only finger-tight so that the friction plate can still be moved.

8    The friction plate must now be centralised so that when the transmission is refitted its input shaft will pass through the splines at the centre of the friction plate.

9    Centralisation can be achieved by passing a screwdriver or other long bar through the friction plate and into the hole in the crankshaft. The friction plate can then be moved around until it is centred on the crankshaft hole. Alternatively, a clutch aligning tool (photo) can be used to eliminate the guesswork. These can be obtained from most accessory shops or can be made up from a length of metal rod or wooden

5.10 Tighten cover assembly bolts evenly and in a diagonal sequence

dowel which fits closely inside the crankshaft hole and has insulating tape wound around it to match the diameter of the friction plate splined hole.

10　When the friction plate is centralised, tighten the cover assembly bolts evenly and in a diagonal sequence to the specified torque setting (photo).

11　Apply a thin smear of molybdenum disulphate grease to the splines of the friction plate and the transmission input shaft, also to the release bearing contact surface and diaphragm spring fingers.

12　Refit the transmission (Chapter 6).

---

**6　Clutch assembly – inspection**

**Warning:** *Dust created by clutch wear and deposited on the clutch components may contain asbestos which is a health hazard. DO NOT blow it out with compressed air or inhale any of it. DO NOT use petrol or petroleum-based solvents to clean off the dust. Brake system cleaner or methylated spirit should be used to flush the dust into a suitable receptacle. After the clutch components are wiped clean with rags, dispose of the contaminated rags and cleaner in a sealed, marked container.*

**Note:** *Due to the amount of work necessary to remove and refit clutch components, it is usually considered good practice to renew as a matched set the clutch friction plate, cover assembly and release bearing, even if only one of these is actually worn enough to require renewal.*

1　Remove the clutch assembly (Sec 5).

2　When cleaning clutch components, first read the warning above. Although some friction materials may no longer contain asbestos it is safest to assume that they do and to take precautions accordingly.

3　Check the friction plate facings for signs of wear, damage or oil contamination. If the distance from the friction material surface to any of the rivets is less than that specified, if the friction material is cracked, burnt, scored or damaged, or if it is contaminated with oil or grease (shown by shiny black patches), the friction plate must be renewed.

4　If the friction material is still serviceable, check that the centre boss splines are unworn, that the torsion springs are in good condition and

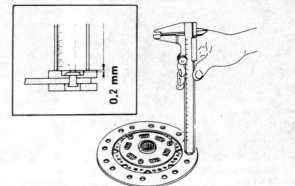

**Fig. 5.3 Using a vernier gauge to measure distance from friction material surface to rivet heads (Sec 6)**

securely fastened and that all the rivets are tightly fastened. If any wear or damage is found, the friction plate must be renewed.

5　If the friction material is fouled with oil, this must be due to an oil leak either from the crankshaft left-hand oil seal or sump/cylinder block joint or from the transmission input shaft. Renew the seal or repair the joint, as appropriate, as described in Chapter 1 or 6.

6　Check the cover assembly for obvious signs of wear or damage, and shake it to check for loose rivets or worn or damaged fulcrum rings. If the diaphragm spring is worn or damaged, or if its pressure is in any way suspect, the cover assembly should be renewed.

7　Examine closely the machined bearing surfaces of the pressure plate and of the flywheel. These should be clean, completely flat and free from scratches or scoring. If either is discoloured from excessive heat or shows signs of cracks it should be renewed, although minor damage of this nature can sometimes be polished away using emery paper.

8　Check the release bearing as described in Section 8 of this Chapter.

7.3 Disengage spring clip ends to permit removal of release bearing

7.4A Lever out release fork upper bush ...

7.4B ... and peel back rubber boot ...

7.4C ... to remove release fork

7.8 Position spring clip ends as shown to secure release bearing

## 7  Clutch release mechanism – removal and refitting

**Warning:** *Dust created by clutch wear and deposited on the clutch components may contain asbestos which is a health hazard. DO NOT blow it out with compressed air or inhale any of it. DO NOT use petrol or petroleum-based solvents to clean off the dust. Brake system cleaner or methylated spirit should be used to flush the dust into a suitable receptacle. After the clutch components are wiped clean with rags, dispose of the contaminated rags and cleaner in a sealed, marked container.*

### Removal and refitting

1   Unless the complete engine/transmission unit is to be removed from the car and separated for major overhaul (see Chapter 1), the clutch release mechanism can be reached only after the transmission has been removed (Chapter 6).
2   Refitting is as described in Chapter 6.

### Dismantling and reassembly

3   Prising the spring clip ends clear of the release bearing tongues, pull the release bearing off its guide sleeve (photo). Withdraw the spring clip, noting how it is fitted.
4   Lever the release fork upper (black) bush from the bellhousing and withdraw the release fork (photos).
5   On refitting, apply a thin smear of molybdenum disulphide grease to the release fork bearing surfaces and install it, then grease the upper bush and press it into place. Check that the fork pivots smoothly and easily.
6   Press the spring clip into place on the release fork.
7   Apply a thin smear of molybdenum disulphide grease to the release

bearing guide sleeve, to the release fork ends and spring clip and to the release bearing itself, both at its centre bore and at its contact surface with the diaphragm spring fingers. Use only the thinnest possible smear of grease. Any surplus grease may melt and find its way on to the friction plate facings.
8   Fit the release bearing over the guide sleeve and press it into place, then lift both spring clip ends on to their respective bearing tongues (photo).

## 8  Clutch release mechanism – inspection

**Warning:** *Dust created by clutch wear and deposited on the clutch components may contain asbestos which is a health hazard. DO NOT blow it out with compressed air or inhale any of it. DO NOT use petrol or petroleum-based solvents to clean off the dust. Brake system cleaner or methylated spirit should be used to flush the dust into a suitable receptacle. After the clutch components are wiped clean with rags, dispose of the contaminated rags and cleaner in a sealed, marked container.*

1   Check the release mechanism, renewing any component which is worn or damaged. Check carefully all bearing surfaces and points of contact.
2   When checking the release bearing itself, note that it is often considered worthwhile to renew it as a matter of course (see Section 6). Check that the contact surface rotates smoothly and easily, with no sign of noise or roughness and that the surface itself is smooth and unworn, with no signs of cracks, pitting or scoring. If there is any doubt about its condition the bearing must be renewed.

## 9  Fault diagnosis – clutch

| Symptom | Reason(s) |
| --- | --- |
| Judder when taking up drive | Loose engine/transmission mountings<br>Badly worn or oil-contaminated friction material<br>Worn or corroded splines on transmission input shaft or friction plate centre boss<br>Worn or damaged cable<br>Faulty cover assembly |
| Clutch drag (failure to disengage – gears cannot be meshed) | Incorrect adjustment<br>Damaged cable<br>Friction plate sticking on transmission input shaft splines<br>Faulty cover assembly |
| Clutch slip (increase in engine speed does not result in corresponding increase in vehicle roadspeed – particularly on gradients) | Incorrect adjustment<br>Badly worn or oil-contaminated friction material<br>Release mechanism sticking or partially seized<br>Faulty or worn cover assembly |
| Noise evident on depressing clutch pedal | Dry, worn or damaged release bearing<br>Faulty release mechanism<br>Worn or corroded splines on transmission input shaft or friction plate centre boss<br>Faulty cover assembly |
| Noise evident on releasing clutch pedal | Broken friction plate torsion springs<br>Faulty cover assembly<br>Distorted or damaged friction plate<br>Dry or worn pedal pivot bushes<br>Transmission worn or damaged |

**Note:** *This Section is not intended to be an exhaustive guide to fault diagnosis but summarises the more common faults which may be encountered during a vehicle's life. Consult a dealer for more specific advice.*

# Chapter 6 Transmission

## Contents

## Specifications

### Type

Manual, five forwards speeds and reverse. Synchromesh on all forward speeds.

### Identification

Code number painted on transmission casing:

| | |
|---|---|
| No number | 4.333:1 (65/15 T) final drive |
| 01 | 3.938:1 (63/16 T) final drive |
| 02 | 4.063:1 (65/16 T) final drive |
| 03 | 3.706:1 (63/17 T) final drive |

### Ratios

Final drive:

| | |
|---|---|
| 1100 | 4.333:1 or 4.063:1 |
| 1300 | 3.938:1 or 4.063:1 |
| 1500 | 3.706:1 or 3.938:1 |
| 1st | 3.636:1 |
| 2nd | 1.950:1 |
| 3rd | 1.357:1 |
| 4th | 0.941:1 |
| 5th | 0.784:1 |
| Reverse | 3.530:1 |

### Transmission overhaul data

| | |
|---|---|
| Synchro-unit baulk ring-to-gear minimum clearance | 0.60 mm |
| Differential bearing preload | 0.25 ± 0.10 mm |
| Differential sun gear maximum endfloat | 0.30 mm |

### Lubrication

| | |
|---|---|
| Oil type/specification | Multigrade engine oil, viscosity SAE 10W/40 to 15W/50, to API SF or better (Duckhams QXR, Hypergrade, or 10W/40 Motor Oil) |
| Capacity | 3.0 litres (5.3 Imp pints) |

### Torque wrench settings

| | Nm | lbf ft |
|---|---|---|
| Oil filler/level and drain plugs | 28.5 to 46.5 | 21 to 34 |
| Gear lever mounting plate-to-body retaining bolts | 15.5 to 25.5 | 11.5 to 19 |
| Gearchange control rod clamp bolt nut | 15.5 to 25.5 | 11.5 to 19 |
| Universal joint-to-gear selector rod taper screw (cadmium-plated, 24 mm long) | 16.5 to 20 | 12 to 15 |
| Lever-to-gear selector rod taper screw (phosphated, 19.5 mm long) | 28.5 to 35 | 21 to 26 |
| Gear selector mechanism-to-bellhousing retaining bolts | 5 to 8 | 4 to 6 |
| Gear selector mechanism axle nut | 15.5 to 25.5 | 11.5 to 19 |
| Selector fork shaft detent assembly cover retaining bolts | 15.5 to 25.5 | 11.5 to 19 |
| Reverse gear detent threaded plug | 28.5 to 45.5 | 21 to 33.5 |
| Selector fork-to-fork shaft bolts | 11.5 to 18.5 | 8.5 to 13.5 |
| Reversing lamp switch | 28.5 to 45.5 | 21 to 33.5 |
| Speedometer drive retaining nut | 4.5 to 7.5 | 3.5 to 5.5 |
| Clutch release bearing guide sleeve bolts | 4 to 6 | 3 to 4.5 |
| Transmission casing-to-bellhousing nuts and bolt | 15.5 to 25.5 | 11.5 to 19 |
| Differential crownwheel bolts | 63.5 to 82.5 | 47 to 61 |
| Left-hand bearing thrustplate screws | N/Av | N/Av |
| Input and output shaft nuts | 121 to 149 | 89 to 110 |
| End cover-to-transmission casing retaining nuts | 15.5 to 25.5 | 11.5 to 19 |
| Transmission-to-cylinder block/crankcase fasteners: | | |
|     12 mm (thread size) nut | 54 to 87.5 | 40 to 64.5 |
|     12 mm (thread size) bolts | 54 to 87 | 40 to 64 |
| Engine/transmission left-hand mounting: | | |
|     Through-bolt retaining nut | 41.5 to 52.5 | 30.5 to 38.5 |
|     Mounting bracket-to-transmission casing nuts | 29 to 34 | 21 to 25 |
| Engine/transmission rear mounting: | | |
|     Bracket-to-transmission retaining nuts | 66.5 to 84 | 49 to 62 |
|     Mounting-to-body nuts or bolts | 27.5 to 34 | 20 to 25 |

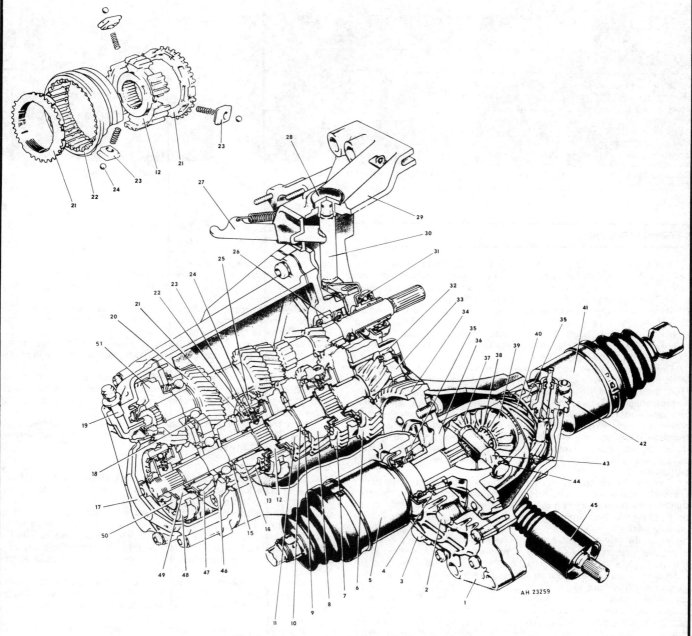

**Fig. 6.1 Cutaway view of the transmission (Sec 1)**

| | | | |
|---|---|---|---|
| 1 Transmission casing | 12 3rd/4th gear synchro-hub | 27 Clutch release fork lever | 40 Speedometer drivegear |
| 2 Filler/level plug | 13 Output shaft 4th gear pinion | 28 Clutch release fork upper bush | 41 Right-hand driveshaft |
| 3 Drain plug | 14 Needle-roller bearing | 29 Bellhousing | 42 Speedometer drive housing |
| 4 Differential bearing preload shim | 15 Thrustwasher | 30 Clutch release fork | 43 Planetary gear shaft |
| 5 Left-hand driveshaft | 16 Output shaft ball-bearing | 31 Clutch release bearing | 44 Circlip |
| 6 Output shaft 1st gear pinion | 17 Transmission left-hand end cover | 32 Output shaft roller bearing | 45 Rubber cover |
| 7 1st/2nd gear synchro-sleeve (with reverse gear) | 18 Input shaft ball-bearing | 33 Output shaft | 46 Left-hand bearing thrustplate |
| 8 Output shaft 2nd gear pinion | 19 Breather | 34 Differential crownwheel | 47 Output shaft 5th gear pinion |
| 9 Lockring | 20 Input shaft | 35 Differential side bearing | 48 5th gear synchro-sleeve |
| 10 Half-ring | 21 Baulk ring | 36 Differential case | 49 5th gear synchro-hub |
| 11 Output shaft 3rd gear pinion | 22 3rd/4th gear synchro-sleeve | 37 Differential planetary gear | 50 Metal plate |
| | 23 Shifting plate | 38 Driveshaft inboard locking ring | 51 Input shaft 5th gear pinion |
| | 24 Steel ball | 39 Differential sun gear | |
| | 25 3rd/4th gear selector fork | | |
| | 26 Input shaft roller bearing | | |

2.5 Location of filler/level plug (arrowed) –
seen from below

2.6 Topping-up the transmission oil

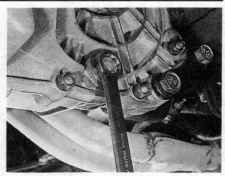

2.11 Unscrewing drain plug

## 1   General description

The transmission is contained in a cast aluminium alloy casing bolted to the engine's left-hand end and consists of the gearbox and final drive differential. Such a design is sometimes also called a transaxle. The gearbox enables the driver to select the gear ratio which will most closely match the engine's performance with the load imposed on the vehicle. Five forward gear ratios are provided, as well as the reverse gear and neutral position. The differential allows the roadwheels to rotate at different speeds (as they must do when the vehicle is cornering) while still maintaining drive to both.

Drive is transmitted from the crankshaft via the clutch to the input shaft, which has a splined extension to accept the clutch friction plate. From the input shaft drive is transmitted to the output shaft. Both shafts rotate in roller bearings at their right-hand ends and ball-bearings at their left-hand ends. From the output shaft the drive is transmitted to the differential crownwheel, which rotates with the differential case and planetary gears, thus driving the sun gears and driveshafts. The rotation of the planetary gears on their shaft allows the inner roadwheel to rotate at a slower speed than the outer roadwheel when the vehicle is cornering.

The input and output shafts are arranged side by side, parallel to the crankshaft and driveshafts, so that their gear pinion teeth are in constant mesh. In the neutral position the output shaft gear pinions rotate freely on needle-roller bearings so that drive cannot be transmitted to the crownwheel.

When the driver selects a gear, the selector mechanism causes the appropriate selector fork to move its respective synchro-sleeve along the shaft to lock the gear pinion to the synchro-hub. Since the synchro-hubs are splined to the output shaft, this locks the pinion to the shaft so that drive can be transmitted. To ensure that gearchanging can be made quickly and quietly a synchro-mesh system is fitted to all forward gears, consisting of baulk rings and spring-loaded shifting plates as well as the gear pinions and synchro-hubs. The synchromesh cones are formed on the mating faces of the baulk rings and gear pinions. Gear selection is by a floor-mounted lever acting through a remote control linkage on the selector mechanism.

## 2   Routine maintenance

**Note:** *The procedure given below for checking the transmission oil level and the quantity of oil specified for the transmission are the latest recommended by Lada Cars and supersede all previous versions.*

1   Carry out the following procedures at the intervals given in *'Routine maintenance'* at the beginning of this manual.

### Check for oil leaks

2   Carefully inspect the transmission and bellhousing joint faces and oil seals for signs of damage, deterioration or oil leakage. Check also the reversing lamp switch and other transmission casing fittings.

### Check the transmission oil level

3   Park the vehicle on level ground, switch off the ignition and apply the handbrake firmly. Do not start the engine or allow the vehicle to move while checking the oil level.

4   If the vehicle has been driven recently, allow it to cool for a few minutes, as the transmission oil can foam when hot, leading to a false level reading.

5   Wipe clean around the hexagon-headed filler/level plug, which is located at the rear of the transmission, next to the left-hand driveshaft inner constant velocity joint (photo). Unscrew the plug and clean it.

6   The oil level should reach the lower edge of the filler/level hole. If topping-up is required, add only good quality oil of the specified type (photo).

7   If the transmission has been overfilled so that oil flows out as soon as the filler/level plug is removed, check that the vehicle is completely level (front-to-rear and side-to-side) and allow the surplus to drain off into a suitable container.

8   When the level is correct, apply a smear of sealant to its threads and refit the filler/level plug, tightening it to the specified torque wrench setting. Wash off any spilt oil.

### Change the transmission oil

9   This operation is much quicker and more efficient if the vehicle is first taken on a journey of sufficient length to warm the engine/transmission up to normal operating temperature.

10   Park the vehicle on level ground, switch off the ignition and apply the handbrake firmly. For improved access, jack up the front of the vehicle and support securely on axle stands (see *'Jacking, towing and wheel changing'*). Note that the vehicle must be lowered to the ground and must be level, to ensure accuracy when checking the oil level after refilling.

11   Remove the filler/level plug (see above), then position a suitable container under the drain plug at the rear of the transmission, below the left-hand driveshaft inner constant velocity joint. Unscrew the plug and clean it (photo).

12   Allow the oil to drain completely into the container. If the oil is hot, take precautions against scalding.

13   When the oil has finished draining, clean the drain plug threads and those of the transmission casing, apply a smear of sealant to its threads and refit the drain plug, tightening it to the specified torque wrench setting. Where applicable, lower the vehicle to the ground.

14   Refilling the transmission is an extremely awkward operation, so allow plenty of time for the oil level to settle properly before checking it. In the workshop it was found that if the left-hand side of the vehicle is jacked up so that the left-hand front roadwheel is raised by 0.45 m (1.5 ft) it helps the oil to flow fully into the transmission casing. If this approach is used, take great care that the vehicle is securely supported at all times.

15   Refill the transmission with the exact amount of the specified type of oil. Allow time for the oil to settle. If it was raised for refilling, slowly lower the vehicle to the ground.

16   Check the oil level (see above). If the correct amount was poured into the transmission and a large amount flows out on checking the level, refit the filler/level plug and take the vehicle on a short journey so that the new oil is distributed fully around the transmission components, then check the level again.

17   Dispose safely of the old oil; **do not** pour it down a drain.

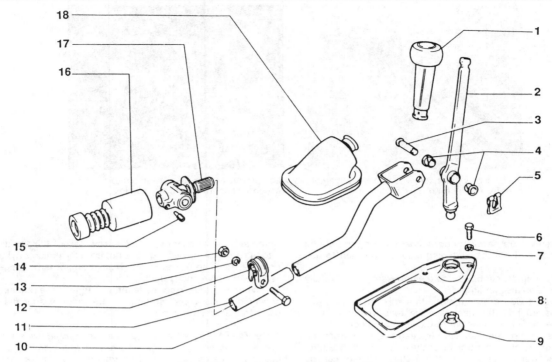

**Fig. 6.2 Gearchange lever and linkage (Sec 3)**

| | | | |
|---|---|---|---|
| 1 | Gear lever knob | 6 | Bolt |
| 2 | Gear lever | 7 | Washer |
| 3 | Pivot pin | 8 | Mounting plate |
| 4 | Pivot bush | 9 | Ball support |
| 5 | Clip | 10 | Bolt |
| 11 | Gearchange control rod | 16 | Rubber cover |
| 12 | Clamp | 17 | Universal joint |
| 13 | Spring washer | 18 | Rubber cover |
| 14 | Nut | | |
| 15 | Taper screw | | |

## 3  Gearchange lever and linkage – removal, examination and refitting

1   Park the vehicle on level ground, switch off the ignition and apply the handbrake firmly. Jack up the front of the vehicle and support it securely on axle stands (see *'Jacking, towing and wheel changing'*).
2   Working underneath the vehicle, use a hammer and a sharply-pointed punch to mark the relationship of the gearchange control rod to the universal joint, then slacken the clamp bolt and nut and disconnect the rod from the joint (photos).
3   **Do not** remove the universal joint unless absolutely necessary, as the (cadmium-plated) taper screw which secures it to the transmission gear selector rod is coated with a special sealing adhesive. If the joint must be removed, first disconnect the gearchange control rod (see above), then peel back the rubber cover and extract the taper screw (photo). The joint will fit only one way on the selector rod so there is no need to mark it before removal.

4   Working inside the passenger compartment, remove the centre console (Chapter 10). Prise out the retaining clip (photo), drive out the pivot pin and withdraw the gearchange control rod through the rubber cover.
5   To remove the gear lever, remove the centre console and disconnect the gearchange control rod (see above), then unbolt the mounting plate from the body and peel off the rubber cover to remove the assembly. Remove the ball support to separate the lever from the mounting plate.
6   Thoroughly clean all components and check them for wear or damage, renewing all worn or faulty items. Note that the gear lever/control rod pivot bushes can be renewed separately if necessary.
7   Refitting is the reverse of the removal procedure, noting the following points.
8   Apply a smear of grease to all pivots and bearing surfaces, and pack the gear lever ball support with grease.
9   Tighten all fasteners to their specified torque wrench settings.
10   When refitting the universal joint, degrease the rod threads and

3.2A Mark relationship of gearchange control rod to universal joint ...

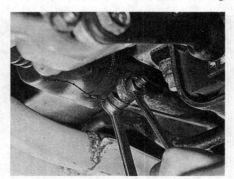

3.2B ... before slackening clamp bolt and nut ...

3.2C ... and disconnecting control rod from joint

3.3 Unscrew taper screw to release universal joint from selector rod

3.4 Remove clip (arrowed) and pin to disconnect control rod from gear lever

those of the taper screw, apply a few drops of thread-locking compound to the screw threads and refit it, tightening it to its specified torque wrench setting.

11    When reconnecting the control rod to the universal joint, carefully align the marks made on dismantling.

12    If no marks were made, ensure that the transmission is in neutral, then have an assistant hold the gear lever so that while its lower, cranked, length is exactly perpendicular to the vehicle's floor, the gear lever's knob is one-third of the distance between the seats from the driver's seat edge. Connect the control rod to the universal joint, tighten the clamp bolt and nut securely, then check that all gears can be selected and that the gear lever is correctly positioned before refitting the centre console.

Remove material only from that narrow part of the spindle which fits into the bellhousing bearing bore, not from the pinion's nylon gear teeth or supporting shoulders. Polish off any burrs or raised edges and reassemble the drive, then refit it.

7    When the drive is correctly refitted, tighten the retaining nut to the specified torque wrench setting, refit the metal washer and connect the cable to the transmission.

**Note:** *The speedometer drivegear can be checked visually by removing the pinion assembly and shining a torch into the aperture. If any of the gear teeth are damaged the transmission must be removed from the vehicle and dismantled so that the gear can be renewed. The gear is pressed on to the differential case.*

---

### 4    Speedometer drive – removal and refitting

1    Open the bonnet and disconnect the speedometer drive cable from the transmission (Chapter 11). Collect the metal washer (photo).

2    Unscrew the single retaining nut and withdraw the speedometer drive assembly (photos). Remove and discard the sealing O-ring, then withdraw the pinion itself.

3    Renew as a matter of course the O-ring and oil seal whenever they are disturbed.

4    Renew the pinion if its teeth are worn or damaged and check the housing for cracks or damage. If the housing is damaged, the complete drive assembly must be renewed.

5    On reassembly, fit the new oil seal and O-ring to the housing, then refit the pinion, applying a smear of grease to all components before installation. Insert the assembly into the transmission, rotating the pinion until it is felt to engage the teeth of the drivegear, then press the housing into place. **Do not** use excessive force or the drive components may be damaged.

6    If the drive is particularly difficult to fit, carefully grind or file a flat 2 mm wide along the extreme lower end of the pinion's spindle.

### 5    Transmission oil seals – removal and refitting

*Differential side (driveshaft) oil seals*

1    Jack up the front of the vehicle and support it securely on axle stands, then remove the roadwheel (see *'Jacking, towing and wheel changing'*).

2    Drain the transmission oil (Sec 2).

3    At the bottom of the hub carrier, unscrew the two bolts to separate the hub carrier from the suspension lower arm balljoint, then open the bonnet and slacken, by one or two turns only, each of the three suspension strut top mounting nuts (Chapter 9).

4    Remove the driveshaft from the transmission and support the differential sun gear (Chapter 7, Section 3 paragraphs 9 and 10), then secure the driveshaft to one side (complete with the suspension strut, the hub carrier and the brake caliper). Take care not to stretch or kink the brake hose.

5    Prise out the seal, taking care not to scratch the seal housing (photo). If difficulty is experienced, use an internally-expanding claw-type puller to extract the seal.

4.1 Note metal washer fitted to speedometer drive

4.2A Unscrew nut and remove washer ...

4.2B ... to release speedometer drive assembly

5.5 Prising out a differential side (driveshaft) oil seal

9   Reassemble the front suspension as described in the relevant Sections of Chapter 9, then lower the vehicle to the ground.
10   Refill the transmission with oil and check the level (Sec 2).

### Input shaft (clutch) oil seal

11   Remove the transmission from the vehicle (Sec 7).
12   Unbolt the clutch release bearing guide sleeve and measure the depth of the oil seal from the surrounding housing (photos).
13   Working as described in Section 9, dismantle the transmission until the input and output shafts are removed, then drive out the oil seal using a pin punch applied from the bellhousing's left-hand face (photo).
14   Dip the new seal in clean oil, fit it to the bellhousing aperture and drive it squarely into place (using as a drift a piece of tubing which bears only on the seal's hard outer edge) until the seal is 3.5 ± 0.2 mm below the surrounding housing (photos).
15   Refit the clutch release bearing guide sleeve, tightening its bolts to the specified torque wrench setting.
16   Before refitting the input shaft, check its seal rubbing surface for signs of burrs, scratches or other damage which caused the seal to fail in the first place. It may be possible to polish away faults of this sort using fine abrasive paper.
17   Ensuring that the input shaft is clean and greased to protect the seal lips on refitting, reassemble the transmission (Sec 11) and refit it to the vehicle (Sec 7).

### Selector rod oil seal

18   Remove the gearchange linkage universal joint (Sec 3).
19   Extract the seal housing and drive out the seal. Clean and check both housing and selector rod for signs of wear or damage which might have caused the seal to fail in the first place, and renew any damaged or worn components.
20   Dip the new seal in clean oil and drive it into the housing (using as a drift a piece of tubing which bears only on the seal's hard outer edge) then apply a smear of sealant to the housing and drive it into the transmission casing until it seats on its locating shoulder.
21   Reassemble the gearchange linkage (Sec 3), check the transmission oil level and top up if necessary (Sec 2), then wash off any spilt oil.

6   Dip the new seal in clean oil, fit it to the transmission aperture and drive it squarely into place, until it seats on its locating shoulder, using as a drift a piece of tubing which bears only on the seal's hard outer edge (photo).
7   Before refitting the driveshaft, check its seal rubbing surface for signs of burrs, scratches or other damage which caused the seal to fail in the first place. It may be possible to polish away faults of this sort using fine abrasive paper.
8   Ensuring that the driveshaft is clean, greased and that a new inboard locking ring is fitted, refit the driveshaft as described in Chapter 7, Section 3, paragraphs 12 to 15.

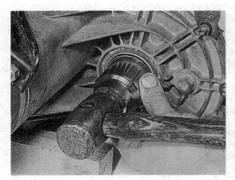

5.6 Installing an oil seal

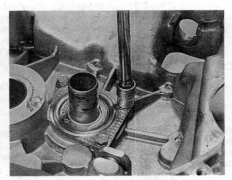

5.12A Unbolt clutch release bearing guide sleeve ...

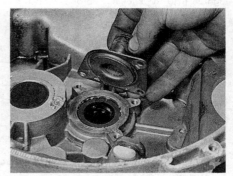

5.12B ... and note depth of oil seal from housing ...

5.13 ... before driving out oil seal from behind

5.14A Install new seal as shown ...

5.14B ... until it is at specified depth

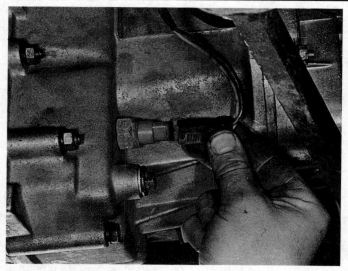

6.1 Location of reversing lamp switch

## 6  Reversing lamp switch – removal, refitting and testing

1    The reversing lamp circuit is controlled by a plunger-type switch that is screwed into the transmission casing (photo). The circuit feed is protected by fuse number 5.

2    To test the switch, disconnect its wires and use a multimeter (set to the resistance function) or a battery and bulb test circuit to check that there is continuity between the switch terminals only when reverse gear is selected. If this is not the case and there are no obvious breaks or other damage to the wires, the switch is faulty and must be renewed.

3    To remove the switch, disconnect its wires and unscrew it. Plug the hole temporarily to minimise the loss of oil.

4    On refitting, apply a smear of sealant to the switch threads and tighten it to the specified torque wrench setting, then reconnect its wires and test the circuit. If oil loss was significant, check the level and top up if necessary (Sec 2).

## 7  Transmission – removal and refitting

**Note:** *To carry out this task an adjustable engine hoist or similar will be required to support the engine and a second, similar, piece of equipment must be available to take the weight of the transmission while it is moved sideways and raised or lowered. A strong trolley jack would be useful in the latter case provided that a wooden spacer is available to spread the load and prevent the risk of damage to the transmission casing.*

1    Park the vehicle on firm, level ground and apply the handbrake firmly.

2    Open the bonnet and disconnect the battery negative terminal (Chapter 11).

3    Disconnect the starter motor wiring (Chapter 11).

4    Removing its single retaining screw, withdraw the TDC sensor from the bellhousing.

5    Disconnect the clutch cable (Chapter 5).

6    Disconnect the speedometer drive cable (Chapter 11).

7    Jack up the front of the vehicle and support it securely on axle stands, then remove the roadwheels (see *'Jacking, towing and wheel changing'*).

8    Drain the transmission oil (Sec 2).

9    Disconnect the engine/transmission earth lead from the transmission.

10    Disconnect the gearchange linkage control rod from the transmission (Sec 3, paragraph 2).

11    Disconnect the reversing lamp switch wires (Sec 6).

12    Unbolt the engine compartment left-hand undershield (Chapter 10).

13    Unbolt the bellhousing dust cover.

14    Remove the starter motor (Chapter 11).

15    At the bottom of each hub carrier, unscrew the two bolts to separate the hub carrier from its suspension lower arm balljoint, then slacken (by one or two turns only) the three top mounting nuts of each suspension strut (Chapter 9).

16    Remove both driveshafts from the transmission and support the differential sun gears (Chapter 7, Section 3 paragraphs 9 and 10), then secure the driveshafts (complete with suspension strut, hub carrier and brake caliper) clear of the transmission. Take care not to stretch or kink the brake hoses.

17    Support the engine's left-hand end, either using an engine hoist or an adjustable crosspiece (Fig. 6.3). Note that the support must be adjustable as it may be necessary to raise or lower the engine. Attach the lifting eye to the exhaust manifold left-hand mounting stud.

18    Support the weight of the transmission using a trolley jack and wooden spacer, an engine hoist, or similar.

19    Unbolt the engine/transmission rear and left-hand mountings from the vehicle's body. If the extra clearance is required, unfasten both mountings from the transmission (Chapter 1).

20    Unscrew the bolts and the nut securing the transmission to the cylinder block/crankcase. Check that all components have been removed or disconnected that might prevent the removal of the transmission.

21    Prise the transmission off the locating dowels and move it squarely away from the engine, ensuring that the clutch components are not damaged.

22    If the transmission is to be overhauled or renewed, unbolt the mountings (if not already removed), check them and renew them if necessary (Chapter 1).

23    Whenever the transmission is removed, overhaul the clutch components. If the transmission is to be overhauled or renewed, dismantle the clutch release mechanism (Chapter 5).

24    On refitting, check that the mating surfaces of the engine and transmission are completely clean and dry, that all clutch components are in good condition and correctly installed and that the engine/transmission adaptor plate is correctly installed on the locating dowels, which should be clean and lubricated with a smear of anti-seize compound (eg Holts Copaslip).

25    Apply a thin smear of molybdenum disulphide grease to the splines of the clutch friction plate and the transmission input shaft, also to the release bearing contact surface and diaphragm spring fingers.

26    Offer up the transmission to the engine and engage the input shaft with the clutch friction plate, ensuring that the transmission is absolutely square to the engine.

27    Push the transmission into full engagement with the engine, ensuring that it seats correctly on the dowels and that the adaptor plate is not displaced.

28    If the transmission proves reluctant to mate with the engine, try swivelling it slightly, or have an assistant rotate the crankshaft via the pulley bolt, until the input shaft splines engage with those of the friction plate.

29    Once the transmission is fully engaged, refit the bolts and nut securing it to the engine, then refit the engine/transmission mountings. Tighten all nuts and bolts to their specified torque wrench settings.

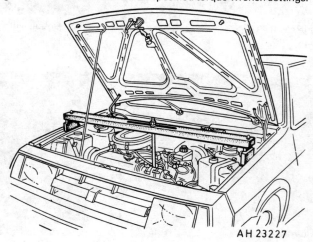

AH 23227

**Fig. 6.3 Supporting the engine left-hand end for transmission removal (Sec 7)**

30    The remainder of the refitting procedure is the reverse of removal, noting the following points.

31    Tighten all nuts and bolts to their specified torque wrench settings. Ensure that the engine/transmission earth lead makes good, metal-to-metal contact at each end before tightening it.

32    Ensuring that the driveshafts are clean, greased and that new inboard locking rings are fitted, refit the driveshafts as described in Chapter 7, Section 3 paragraphs 12 to 15.

33    Reassemble the front suspension as described in the relevant Sections of Chapter 9.

34    Adjust the clutch pedal travel (Chapter 5).

35    Refill the transmission with oil and check the level (Sec 2).

carry out most of the work and obtain all the parts required from the dealer, while his staff complete the operations that are beyond your scope.

If the transmission is to be overhauled, start by thoroughly cleaning its exterior using a suitable solvent.

Ensure that a clean, uncluttered working area is available, with a good supply of small containers for storing the various components. Always note or label any parts as they are removed, keep them strictly in their order and direction of removal (noting which way round they were fitted, where any could be installed in more than one way) and keep all related components together.

On reassembly, all components must be spotlessly clean and must be lubricated with the specified type of oil as they are refitted.

## 8  Transmission overhaul – general notes and precautions

Dismantling the transmission into its major assemblies is reasonably straightforward and can be carried out without using the manufacturer's special tools, although a comprehensive standard toolkit will be required. This will permit an initial assessment of any wear or damage that can be used to decide whether or not to proceed with an overhaul.

A common reason for transmission overhaul is to renew the synchromesh units. Wear or faults in these assemblies is indicated by the noise when changing gear, or by the synchromesh being easily beaten. Jumping out of gear or similar gear selection faults may mean the renewal of the selector mechanism, forks, or synchro-sleeves. General noise during operation on the road, however, may be due to worn bearings, shafts or gears the cumulative cost of renewing all worn components (see also note in Sec 12) may well make it more economical to renew the transmission complete.

To establish whether transmission overhaul is economically viable or not, first establish the cost of a complete replacement transmission, comparing the price of a new unit with that of an exchange reconditioned unit (if available) or even a good secondhand unit (with a guarantee) from a breaker. Compare this with the likely cost of the replacement parts that will be required if the existing transmission is overhauled.

If the time element is important, do not forget to establish the availability of the parts concerned, or their expected delivery times if, as is possible, they are not held in stock by your local dealer. Add to this your expected time to complete the work, including the time required to obtain any special tools or facilities that may be needed.

The final factor to be considered is that of your ability to carry out the work necessary in view of the equipment and facilities available to you and your experience in overhauling transmissions. Read carefully through the procedure in the following Sections so that you know exactly what to expect and can decide whether or not you can undertake the work. If you are in doubt about any procedure, seek the advice of a good Lada dealer. There are some tasks, such as the setting of the differential bearing preload (which requires a selection of shims that only a well-stocked dealer will have), that are best left to such a dealer. It may be possible to arrive at a compromise arrangement whereby you

## 9  Transmission – dismantling

### Dismantling into major assemblies

1    Remove the transmission from the vehicle (Sec 7).

2    Remove the clutch release mechanism (Chapter 5) and unbolt the engine/transmission mountings (Chapter 1).

3    Using a proprietary engine cleaner or similar solvent, thoroughly wash the exterior of the transmission, scrubbing away dirt with a stiff brush.

4    Stand the transmission upright on the bellhousing's engine mating surface.

5    Remove the speedometer drive (Sec 4) and the reversing lamp switch (Sec 6).

6    Unscrew the retaining nuts and remove the left-hand end cover (photo). Note the clutch cable adjuster bracket and discard the gasket.

7    Unscrew the 5ft gear selector fork-to-fork shaft bolt and press downwards (ie, towards the transmission casing) the selector fork to select 5th gear, then engage any other gear by moving the selector rod universal joint. This will lock the output and input shafts together and enable their nuts to be unscrewed.

8    Using a suitable punch or similar tool, relieve the staking on the output and input shaft nuts, then unscrew the nuts (photo). Note that it is good practice to renew these nuts as a matter of course whenever they are disturbed.

9    Remove the 5th gear synchro-unit and selector fork (photo), using a puller if required; note the synchro-unit's metal plate.

10    Withdraw the baulk ring, the 5th output shaft gear pinion, the thin spacer and the needle-roller bearing, followed by the input shaft 5th gear pinion (photos).

11    Using an impact driver, remove the retaining screws and withdraw the left-hand bearing thrustplate (photos).

12    Prise out the left-hand bearing locating rings (photo).

13    Unbolt the cover plate and remove the detent springs and balls (photos).

14    Unscrew the reverse gear detent plug and remove the detent spring and ball (photo).

15    Unscrew the transmission casing-to-bellhousing nuts and bolt and lift off the transmission casing (photos). Recover and clean the magnet from its location in the bellhousing. Peel off and discard the gasket.

9.6 Removing transmission left-hand end cover

9.8 Relieve staking to unscrew output and input shaft nuts

9.9 Removing 5th gear synchro-unit and selector fork

9.10A Removing baulk ring ...

9.10B ... and 5th output shaft gear pinion ...

9.10C ... followed by thin spacer, ...

9.10D ... needle-roller bearing ...

9.10E ... and input shaft 5th gear pinion

9.11A Use impact driver to remove thrustplate screws ...

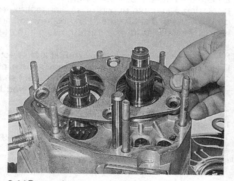

9.11B ... and remove thrustplate

9.12 Removing left-hand bearing locating rings

16   Unscrew the selector fork-to-fork shaft bolts, then rotate and lift out each shaft in turn until it can be removed, with its respective selector fork.

17   Withdraw its shaft and remove the reverse idler gear (photo).

18   Lift out as a pair the output and input shafts, then withdraw the differential (photos).

### Transmission casing

19   Remove the differential side oil seal as described in Section 5.

20   If the differential side bearing is to be renewed, heat the casing and extract the outer race using a puller, noting the shim(s) behind the outer race.

### Bellhousing

21   Remove the input shaft (clutch) and differential side oil seals as described in Section 5.

22   It is possible to remove the selector rod oil seal without disturbing the rod itself (see Section 5), but the operation would be easier if the rod were removed first, as described below.

23   If the differential side bearing is to be renewed, heat the casing and extract the outer race using a puller. A similar method can be used to extract the input and output shaft roller bearings, but note that once their oil seal (input) or blanking plug (output) have been removed (Sec 5), both these bearings can also be driven out from behind.

24   To remove the selector mechanism, unscrew the retaining bolts and withdraw it, noting how it engages with the selector rod lever. Note carefully the arrangement of springs before removing the axle nut and circlip to dismantle the mechanism (photos).

25   **Do not** remove the lever from the selector rod unless absolutely necessary as the phosphated taper screw which secures it is coated with a special sealing adhesive. If the lever must be removed, extract the taper screw. The lever will fit only one way on the selector rod so there is no need to mark it before removal.

26   Withdraw the selector rod (photo) and remove the oil seal (Sec 5).

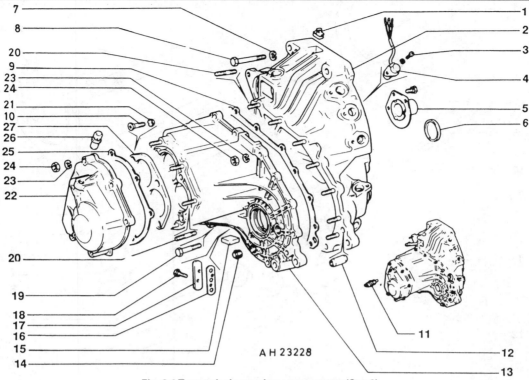

**Fig. 6.4 Transmission casing components (Sec 9)**

| | | | |
|---|---|---|---|
| 1 | Rubber plug | 8 | Bolt |
| 2 | Bellhousing | 9 | Gasket |
| 3 | Screw | 10 | Countersunk screw |
| 4 | TDC sensor | 11 | Reversing lamp switch |
| 5 | Clutch release bearing guide sleeve | 12 | Locating dowel |
| | | 13 | Transmission casing |
| 6 | Output shaft blanking plug | 14 | Filler/level or drain plug |
| 7 | Spring washer | | |

| | |
|---|---|
| 15 | Magnet |
| 16 | Gasket |
| 17 | Detent assembly cover |
| 18 | Bolt |
| 19 | Bolt |
| 20 | Stud |
| 21 | Lockwasher |

| | |
|---|---|
| 22 | Transmission left-hand end cover |
| 23 | Spring washer |
| 24 | Nut |
| 25 | Gasket |
| 26 | Breather |
| 27 | Left-hand bearing thrustplate |

### Input shaft

27   The input shaft is a one-piece unit, and the only dismantling possible is to draw the ball-bearing off the shaft's left-hand end (photo).

### Output shaft

28   Note that some of the shaft's components, especially the synchro-hubs, may be a tight fit and will require the use of a good-quality knife-edged bearing puller to remove them. The manufacturer recommends that the synchro-hubs are not removed unless absolutely necessary as this will slacken their fit on the shaft splines.

29   Clamp the shaft by its right-hand end in a soft-jawed vice and draw off the ball-bearing with the 5th gear pinion needle-roller bearing inner sleeve and thrustwasher (photos).

30   Remove the next thrustwasher, followed by the 4th gear pinion with its needle-roller bearing and thin spacer (photos).

31   Withdraw the baulk ring. Draw the 3rd/4th gear synchro-unit off its splines using a puller applied to the 3rd gear pinion, then remove the 4th gear pinion needle-roller bearing inner sleeve and the synchro-unit (photos).

32   Withdraw the baulk ring and the 3rd gear pinion, followed by its needle-roller bearing (photos).

33   The 2nd gear pinion is located by a lockring, two half-rings and steel ball(s). Remove these, withdraw the pinion and remove its needle-roller bearing (photos).

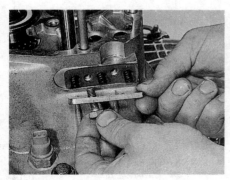

9.13A Unbolt detent assembly cover plate ...

9.13B ... to remove detent spring and balls

9.14 Unscrew threaded plug to remove reverse detent components

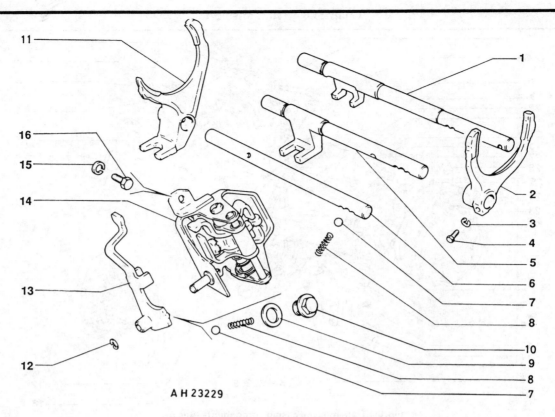

A H 23229

**Fig. 6.5 Selector mechanism and forks (Sec 9)**

| | | | | | | | |
|---|---|---|---|---|---|---|---|
| 1 | 5th gear selector fork shaft | 5 | 3rd/4th gear selector fork shaft | 9 | Sealing washer | 13 | Reverse gear selector fork |
| 2 | 5th gear selector fork | 6 | 1st/2nd gear selector fork shaft | 10 | Threaded plug | 14 | Selector mechanism |
| 3 | Spring washer | 7 | Steel ball | 11 | 1st/2nd gear selector fork | 15 | Spring washer |
| 4 | Bolt | 8 | Detent spring | 12 | Circlip | 16 | Bolt |

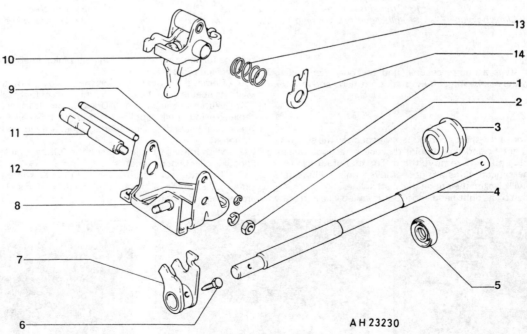

A H 23230

**Fig. 6.6 Selector mechanism and rod (Sec 9)**

| | | | | | | | |
|---|---|---|---|---|---|---|---|
| 1 | Spring washer | 5 | Oil seal | 9 | Circlip | 13 | Spring |
| 2 | Nut | 6 | Taper screw | 10 | Lever assembly | 14 | Thrustwasher |
| 3 | Oil seal housing | 7 | Selector rod lever | 11 | Selector arm axle | | |
| 4 | Selector rod | 8 | Selector mechanism | 12 | Interlock lever guide axle | | |

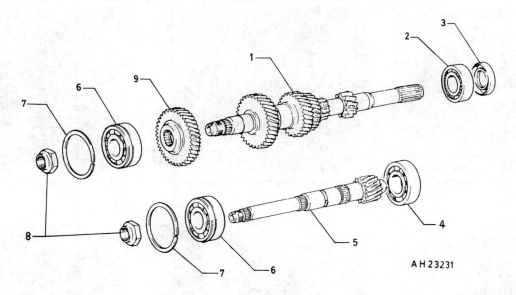

AH 23231

**Fig. 6.7 Input and output shafts (Sec 9)**

| | | | | | | | |
|---|---|---|---|---|---|---|---|
| 1 | Input shaft | 4 | Ball-bearing | 6 | Roller bearing | 8 | Nut |
| 2 | Ball-bearing | 5 | Output shaft | 7 | Locating ring | 9 | Input shaft 5th gear pinion |
| 3 | Oil seal | | | | | | |

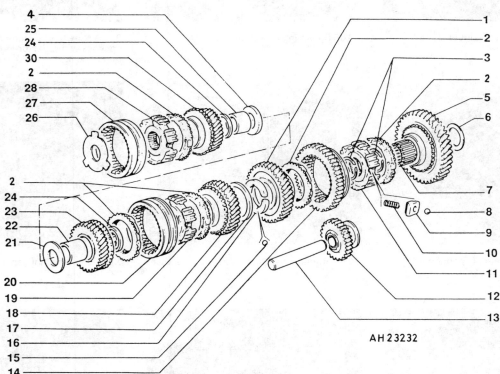

AH 23232

**Fig. 6.8 Output shaft components and reverse idler gear (Sec 9)**

| | | | | | | | |
|---|---|---|---|---|---|---|---|
| 1 | 2nd gear pinion (with needle-roller bearing) | 9 | Shifting plate | 16 | Half ring | 23 | 4th gear pinion |
| 2 | Baulk ring | 10 | Spring | 17 | Lockring | 24 | Thin spacer |
| 3 | Circlip | 11 | 1st/2nd gear synchro-hub | 18 | 3rd gear pinion (with needle-roller bearing) | 25 | Needle-roller bearing and inner sleeve |
| 4 | Thrustwasher | 12 | Reverse idler gear | 19 | 3rd/4th gear synchro-hub | 26 | Metal plate |
| 5 | 1st gear pinion | 13 | Reverse idler gear shaft | 20 | 3rd/4th gear synchro-sleeve | 27 | 5th gear synchro-sleeve |
| 6 | Thrustwasher | 14 | 1st/2nd gear synchro-sleeve (with reverse gear) | 21 | Thrustwasher | 28 | 5th gear synchro-hub |
| 7 | Needle-roller bearing | 15 | Steel ball | 22 | Needle-roller bearing and inner sleeve | 29 | 5th gear pinion |
| 8 | Steel ball | | | | | | |

9.15A Note location of retaining bolt ...

9.15B ... when removing transmission casing

9.17 Pull out reverse idler gear shaft to remove idler gear

9.18A Remove output and input shafts together

9.18B Removing the differential

9.24A Note how selector mechanism engages with selector rod lever before removing it

9.24B Note arrangement of springs and levers before dismantling selector mechanism

9.26 Withdrawing selector rod and universal joint

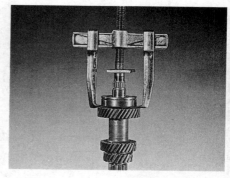

9.27 Removing input shaft left-hand ball-bearing

9.29A Draw off output shaft left-hand ball-bearing ...

9.29B ... to release needle-roller bearing inner sleeve ...

9.29C ... and thrustwasher

9.30A Remove next thrustwasher ...

9.30B ... followed by 4th gear pinion, ...

9.30C ... its needle-roller bearing ...

9.30D ... and the thin spacer

9.31A Remove baulk ring

9.31B Apply puller to 3rd gear pinion to draw 3rd/4th gear synchro-unit off shaft splines

9.31C Remove needle-roller bearing inner sleeve ...

9.31D ... and remove synchro-unit

9.32A Remove baulk ring ...

9.32B ... followed by 3rd gear pinion ...

9.32C ... and needle-roller bearing

9.33A Remove lockring ...

9.33B ... and note arrangement of half-rings and steel balls ...

9.33C ... before removing 2nd gear pinion ...

9.33D ... and needle-roller bearing

9.34A Remove baulk ring

9.34B Extract circlip locating 1st/2nd synchro-unit ...

9.35A ... and remove synchro-unit ...

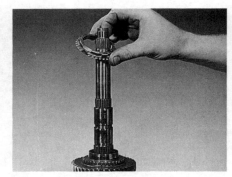

9.35B ... followed by baulk ring ...

9.35C ... and 1st gear pinion

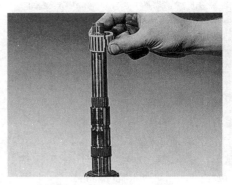

9.36A Needle-roller bearing has a split cage to permit removal over circlip ...

9.36B ... do not forget final thrustwasher

9.38A Remove circlip to release planetary gear shaft

9.38B Removing a differential sun gear

34   Withdraw the baulk ring and extract the circlip locating the 1st/2nd gear synchro-unit (photos).
35   Draw the 1st/2nd gear synchro-unit off its splines using, if necessary, a puller applied to the 1st gear pinion, then remove the baulk ring and the 1st gear pinion (photos).
36   The split-caged 1st gear pinion needle-roller bearing and the thrustwasher can be removed without disturbing the remaining circlip (photos).

*Differential*
37   Unbolt the crownwheel from the differential case.
38   Remove one of the retaining circlips and drive out the planetary gear shaft, then withdraw the gears (photos). Label each gear so that it can be returned to its original location.
39   Use a puller to draw off the bearing inner races, then withdraw the speedometer drivegear, noting its locating tangs.

## 10   Transmission – inspection

1   With the transmission completely dismantled, clean all components and check them for wear or damage.
2   Check the gears for chipped teeth and the bearings and inner sleeves for wear.
3   Check the shaft bearing journals for scoring or grooving.
4   Check the bearings for wear by spinning them with the fingers. If they shake or rattle, or show visible signs of wear or damage, they must be renewed.
5   Wear in the synchro-units will normally be revealed by noisy gearchanging, but even if this is not the case it is worthwhile to check the units whenever the transmission is dismantled. Note that some consider it good practice to renew the baulk rings as a matter of course, especially if the vehicle has covered a high mileage.
6   To check baulk ring wear, place each ring on its gear pinion's cone and twist it to ensure good contact between the surfaces, then use feeler gauges to measure the clearance between the ring's flat face and

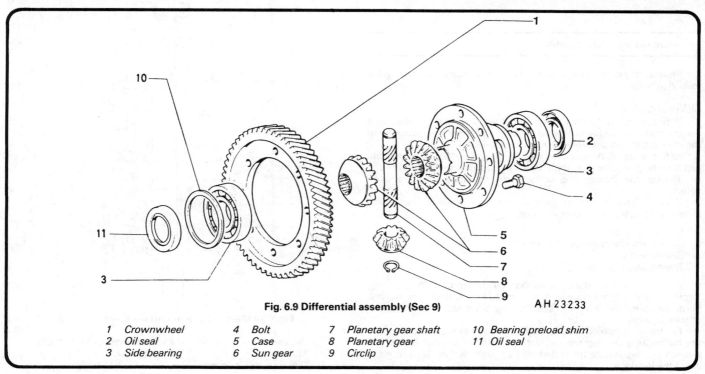

**Fig. 6.9 Differential assembly (Sec 9)**

AH 23233

| 1 Crownwheel | 4 Bolt | 7 Planetary gear shaft | 10 Bearing preload shim |
| 2 Oil seal | 5 Case | 8 Planetary gear | 11 Oil seal |
| 3 Side bearing | 6 Sun gear | 9 Circlip | |

10.6 Measuring baulk ring-to-gear pinion clearance

10.7A Mark hub/sleeve relationship before dismantling synchro-unit

10.7B Press hub out of sleeve until balls, plates and springs can be removed

that of the pinion (photo). If the clearance measured is reduced to the specified minimum or less, the baulk ring must be renewed.

7   To dismantle a synchro-unit, first mark the relationship of the hub to the sleeve so that they can be refitted in the same relative positions, then place the unit in a clear plastic bag to trap the components as the hub is pressed out of the sleeve (photos). Note that the steel balls should align with the deepest sockets in the sleeve. Collect the shifting plates, the steel balls and the springs. Check all items for wear or damage and renew them if necessary.

8   To reassemble a synchro-unit, use grease to stick the springs and balls in place in the hub, refit the shifting plates and use a tightly-wrapped elastic band to secure the assembly while it is refitted to the sleeve, ensuring that the marks made on removal are aligned. Use an electrical screwdriver or similar to press each shifting plate and ball in turn into the hub so that it engages correctly in the sleeve. If assembly is carried out in a clear plastic bag the balls will not be lost if they fly clear.

9   Renew as a matter of course all O-rings, seals, gaskets and circlips disturbed on dismantling; these should never be re-used. The same applies to the output and input shaft nuts (refer to Section 9, paragraph 8.)

8   Use a dial gauge (Fig. 6.10) to measure the differential endfloat.

9   The thickness of the shims required is the sum of the endfloat recorded, plus 1.25 mm (the constant value required for the measure procedure) **plus** a further 0.25 mm (the specified preload). If possible, make up the required thickness using one thick shim rather than several thinner ones. Shims are available from Lada dealers over a range of thicknesses from 1.65 mm to 2.65 mm.

10   To ensure correct tooth meshing, the shim(s) must be fitted only between the differential left-hand side bearing outer race and the transmission casing. Remove the outer race and withdraw the test shim, then insert the selected shims and refit the outer race.

11   To check the preload setting, measure the differential turning torque. With the differential only refitted to the transmission casing, refit the bellhousing and tighten the nuts and bolt to the specified torque wrench setting. Rotate the differential through two or three turns to settle the bearings.

12   Using Lada service tool 02.7812.9501 applied to the differential planetary gear shaft through the driveshaft aperture, rotate the differential several times clockwise and note the effort required to do so. A

## 11   Transmission – reassembly

1   Reassembly is the reverse of the dismantling procedure, noting the following points.

### Differential

2   Refit the speedometer drivegear and press on the new bearings using a mandrel that bears only on the bearing's inner race. Ensure that the inner races seat securely on the case shoulders.

3   Refit the planetary gears, followed by the sun gears, then lubricate and refit the planetary gear shaft. Fit a new circlip to secure the shaft.

4   Tighten the crownwheel bolts to the specified torque wrench setting.

5   If any of the following components have been renewed, the differential bearing preload must be reset:

   *Differential case*
   *Differential side bearings*
   *Bellhousing*
   *Transmission casing*

6   Press the right-hand side bearing outer race into the bellhousing. Replacing the original shim with one of 1.25 mm thickness for test purposes, press the left-hand side bearing outer race into the transmission casing.

7   Fit the reassembled differential into the transmission casing, refit the bellhousing and tighten the nut and bolt to the specified torque wrench setting. Rotate the differential through two or three turns to settle the bearings.

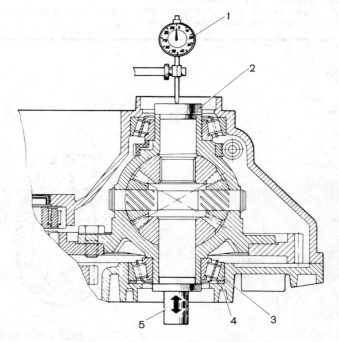

**Fig. 6.10 Measuring differential endfloat (Sec 11)**

| | |
|---|---|
| 1   *Dial gauge* | 4   *Test shim (1.25 mm thick)* |
| 2   *Mandrel* | 5   *Mandrel* |
| 3   *Differential side bearing* | |

11.14 When reassembling output shaft, check that thrustwasher, bearing and first circlip are fitted as shown

11.15 Fit a new circlip as shown to secure 1st/2nd gear synchro-unit

11.16A Note different lengths of projections on baulk ring inner faces (arrows) ...

11.16B ... ensure shorter projections are aligned with synchro-hub grooves and shifting plates (arrows)

11.19 Using a long tube to drive 3rd/4th gear synchro-unit on to shaft

turning torque figure of between 1.5 and 3.5 Nm should be obtained if new bearings have been fitted. If the original bearings are being re-used the figure should be at least 0.3 Nm.

## Output shaft

13 Note that while in most cases the synchro-units can be tapped on to the shafts using a long tube, if any were a tight fit on the shaft splines they must be heated to 100°C so that they can be installed without causing the shaft/hub fit to slacken. The units must be fitted in their assembled state. To prevent the baulk rings from being trapped as the components cool down, make up a forked spacer to fit between the baulk ring and gear pinion end faces (when they are cold) so that the baulk ring-to-gear pinion clearance is maintained at its cold state when the components are heated. Ensure that the spacers are removed only when the components are fully cooled down.

14 Mount the shaft in a soft-jawed vice and refit the thrustwasher, followed by the split-caged 1st gear pinion needle-roller bearing, ensuring that the first circlip is correctly seated (photo).
15 Refit the 1st gear pinion and the baulk ring, followed by the 1st/2nd gear synchro-unit and its second baulk ring. Fit a new circlip to secure the synchro-hub (photo).
16 When refitting baulk rings to their synchro-units, align the **shorter** projections on the ring inner face with the hub grooves and shifting plates (photos). If care is not taken to ensure this, it will not be possible to select gears when the transmission is reassembled.
17 Refit the 2nd gear pinion and its needle-roller bearing, locate the steel ball(s) in their groove and refit the two half-rings, followed by the lockring. Ensure that the lockring fits around the half-rings.
18 Refit the 3rd gear pinion and its needle-roller bearing, followed by the baulk ring.
19 Aligning the baulk ring as described above, refit the 3rd/4th gear synchro-unit (photo), followed by its second baulk ring.
20 Refit the 4th gear pinion needle-roller bearing inner sleeve, fol-

11.21A Ensure that left-hand ball-bearing is fitted as shown ...

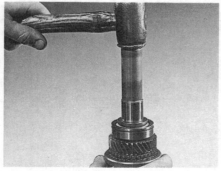
11.21B ... before refitting thrustwasher and needle-roller bearing inner sleeve

11.25 If selector rod lever is disturbed, refit carefully (see text)

11.26 Tighten selector mechanism bolts to specified torque wrench setting

11.31 Engage reverse idler gear on selector fork before refitting shaft

11.32 Refitting 5th gear selector fork

11.33A Locate 3rd/4th gear selector fork on synchro-sleeve ...

11.33B ... then rotate shaft to engage with selector mechanism ...

11.33C ... before refitting fork-to-fork shaft bolt

lowed by the thin spacer, the bearing itself, the pinion and the thrust-washer.

21    Refit the thrustwasher, the ball-bearing (ensuring that its groove is to the left) and the 5th gear pinion needle-roller bearing inner sleeve and thrustwasher (photos).

### Input shaft

22    When refitting its ball-bearing to the shaft's left-hand end, ensure that the bearing's groove is to the left.

### Bellhousing

23    If the bearings (or their outer races, as applicable) are to be installed, heat the casting and drive in the bearings, ensuring that they are kept square to their housing, until they seat firmly on the locating shoulder. Use a mandrel which bears only on the bearing's outer race.

24    Refit the oil seals as described in Section 5.

25    Lubricate the selector rod bearing surfaces and insert the rod into the bellhousing, rotate it until it is correctly aligned, then degrease the rod threads and those of the taper screw. Refit the selector rod lever, apply a few drops of thread-locking compound to the taper screw threads and refit it, tightening it to its specified torque wrench setting (photo).

26    Ensure that the selector mechanism engages correctly with the selector rod lever when refitting. Tighten the bolts to the specified torque wrench setting (photo).

### Transmission casing

27    Refit the differential side bearing outer race as described in para-

graph 23 above, noting the shim(s) behind the outer race.

28    Refit the differential side oil seal as described in Section 5.

### General reassembly

29    Refit the differential to the bellhousing. To hold the sun gears, insert into the bellhousing aperture a clean metal rod or wooden dowel of the same diameter as the driveshaft (approximately 27 mm) until the gear is securely supported.

30    Meshing together their gear teeth, refit the input and output shafts as a single unit.

31    Refit the reverse idler gear, engaging it on the reverse selector fork (photo), then refit the reverse idler gear shaft.

32    Insert the 5th gear selector fork into its bellhousing bore, then rotate the shaft until it engages with the selector mechanism (photo).

33    With its fork loosely in place, refit the 3rd/4th gear selector fork shaft so that the fork engages on its synchro-sleeve, then insert the shaft into its bellhousing bore and rotate it until it engages with the selector mechanism. Refit the fork-to-shaft bolt (photos).

34    Place the 1st/2nd gear selector fork on its synchro-sleeve, rotate it to engage with the selector mechanism, then refit its shaft (photo).

35    Tighten the fork-to-fork shaft bolts to the specified torque wrench setting (photo).

36    Insert the cleaned magnet into its location and fit a new gasket (photos).

37    Refit the transmission casing and tighten the nuts and bolt to the specified torque wrench settings (photo).

38    Using grease to stick them in place, refit the detent balls and springs and tighten the detent cover bolts and threaded plug to their specified torque wrench settings (photos).

39    Refit the left-hand bearing locating rings followed by the bearing thrustplate, then use an impact driver to tighten the retaining screws securely (photo).

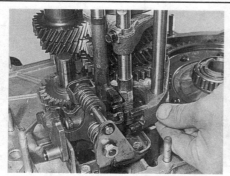

11.34 Locate 1st/2nd gear selector fork on synchro-sleeve and selector mechanism, then refit shaft

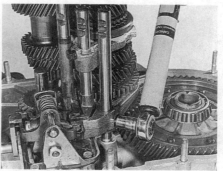

11.35 Tighten fork-to-fork shaft bolts to specified torque wrench setting

11.36A Clean magnet before refitting ...

11.36B ... and install a new gasket – note locating dowel (arrowed)

11.37 Note location of lifting eye when tightening transmission casing fasteners

11.38A Refit reverse detent steel ball ...

11.38B ... and spring

11.38C Fit new sealing washer before refitting reverse detent threaded plug

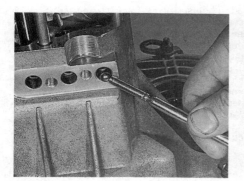

11.38D Use grease to stick detent steel balls in position ...

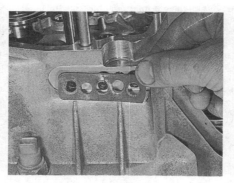

11.38E ... refit detent springs and new cover gasket ...

11.38F ... followed by detent assembly cover

11.39 Thrustplate is secured by countersunk screws – note lockwashers

11.41 Metal plate's tongues must cover synchro-unit shifting plates and springs

11.42 Input and output shaft nuts should always be renewed

11.43A Tighten nuts to specified torque wrench setting ...

11.43B ... then secure by staking nut collar into shaft groove

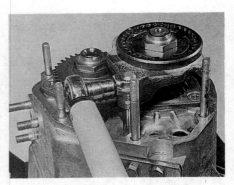

11.44 Tighten fork-to-fork shaft bolt to specified torque wrench setting

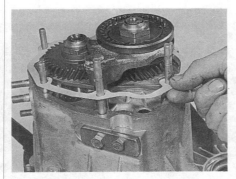

11.45A Fit a new gasket to seal end cover joint

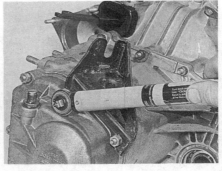

11.45B Note location of adjuster bracket when tightening end cover nuts

40   Refit the input shaft 5th gear pinion, followed by the needle-roller bearing. The thin spacer fits above (ie to the left of) the bearing cage and is followed by the 5th output shaft gear pinion and its baulk ring.

41   Refit as an assembly the 5th gear synchro-unit and selector fork. Do not forget to align the baulk ring with the synchro-unit correctly (see paragraph 16 above). Fit the synchro-unit's metal plate, covering the shifting plates and springs with the plate's locating tongues (photo).

42   Refit the input and output shaft nuts (photo). Note that owners are advised **always** to renew these nuts whenever they are disturbed.

43   Locking together the two shafts as described in Section 9, paragraph 7, tighten the shaft nuts to their specified torque wrench setting. Using a hammer and punch, secure each nut by staking its collar into the shaft groove. The staking must be 3.5 to 4 mm long and should not

damage the shaft threads (photos).

44   Raise to its correct position the 5th gear synchro-unit and selector fork, select neutral, then refit and tighten the fork-to-fork shaft bolt to the specified torque wrench setting (photo).

45   Using a new gasket, refit the left-hand end cover. Ensuring that the clutch cable adjuster bracket is correctly located, refit and tighten to the specified torque wrench setting the retaining nuts (photos).

46   Refit the speedometer drive (Sec 4), the reversing lamp switch (Sec 6), the clutch release mechanism (Chapter 5) and the engine/transmission mountings (Chapter 1).

47   Rotating the input shaft to aid selection, check that all gears can be selected with relative ease, then refit the transmission (Sec 7).

## 12  Fault diagnosis – transmission

**Note:** *It is sometimes difficult to decide whether it is worthwhile removing and dismantling the transmission for a fault which may be nothing more than a minor irritant. Transmissions which howl, or where the synchromesh can be beaten by a quick gearchange, may continue to perform for a long time in this state. A worn transmission usually needs a complete rebuild to eliminate noise as the various gears, if re-aligned on new bearings, will continue to howl when different bearing surfaces are presented to each other. The decision to overhaul, therefore, must be considered with regard to time and money available, relative to the degree of noise or malfunction that the driver has to suffer (see also Sec 8).*

| Symptom | Reason(s) |
| --- | --- |
| Transmission noisy in neutral | Oil level low or oil of incorrect grade<br>Worn input shaft or bearing(s)<br>Clutch fault – see Chapter 5 |
| Transmission noisy only when moving (in all gears) | Oil level low or oil of incorrect grade<br>Worn input shaft or bearing(s)<br>Worn output shaft or bearing(s)<br>Worn differential side bearing(s)<br>Incorrect differential side bearing preload<br>Worn or chipped output shaft/differential crownwheel gear teeth |
| Transmission noisy only when moving (one gear only) | Worn, damaged or chipped gear teeth<br>Worn gear pinion bearing |
| Transmission jumps out of gear | Worn or damaged selector mechanism<br>Weak, worn or damaged selector mechanism detent components (especially springs)<br>Selector fork shaft detent grooves worn<br>Worn or damaged selector forks<br>Worn or damaged synchro-units |
| Gearchanging noisy | Worn or damaged synchro-units (especially baulk rings and cones)<br>Oil of incorrect grade<br>Clutch fault – see Chapter 5 |
| Difficulty in engaging gears | Clutch fault – see Chapter 5<br>Worn or damaged gearchange linkage<br>Worn or damaged selector mechanism<br>Worn or damaged synchro-units |

**Note:** *This Section is not intended to be an exhaustive guide to fault diagnosis but summarises the more common faults which may be encountered during a vehicle's life. Consult a dealer for more specific advice.*

# Chapter 7 Driveshafts

## Contents

## Specifications

**Type** ............................................................................ Unequal-length solid (left-hand) or tubular (right-hand) steel shafts, splined to inner and outer constant-velocity joints

**Lubrication (overhaul only – see text)**
Lubricant type ............................................................... Lada special grease or multi-purpose molybdenum disulphide grease (Duckhams LBM 10)

Lubricant quantity:
  Inner joint................................................................ 80 cc
  Outer joint............................................................... 40 cc

**Torque wrench settings**

|  | Nm | lbf ft |
|---|---|---|
| Driveshaft nut | 225.5 to 247 | 166 to 182 |
| Front suspension lower arm balljoint mounting bolts | 49 to 61.5 | 36 to 45.5 |
| Front suspension strut top mounting nuts | 19.5 to 24 | 14.5 to 18 |
| Roadwheel bolts | 58.5 to 72 | 43 to 53 |

## 1 General description

The drive is transmitted from the differential sun gears to the front roadwheels by two unequal-length steel driveshaft assemblies. While the left-hand driveshaft is solid, the (longer) right-hand driveshaft is tubular and of larger diameter to reduce harmonic vibrations and resonance. UK design technology was employed during their development.

Both driveshafts are splined at their outer ends to accept the wheel hubs and are threaded so that each hub can be fastened by a large nut. The inner end of each driveshaft is splined to accept the differential sun gear and has a groove to accept the locking ring which secures the driveshaft to the sun gear.

Two constant velocity joints are fitted to each driveshaft to ensure the smooth and efficient transmission of drive at all the angles possible as the roadwheels move up and down with the suspension and as they turn from side to side under steering. Both joints are of the Birfield-Rzeppa ball-and-cage type, but the inner joints are plunge-accepting, to allow for the differences in driveshaft effective length at the extremes of suspension travel.

**Note:** *The only replacement parts listed are the bare shafts themselves, the outer constant velocity joint assemblies, the rubber bellows and their clips and the various locking rings, thrust rings and retainers. If any of the joints is worn or damaged it cannot be reconditioned but* **must** *be renewed. In the case of the inner joints, this means that the complete driveshaft assembly must be renewed.*

## 2 Routine maintenance

1  At regular intervals (see *Routine maintenance*) carry out a thorough inspection of the driveshafts and joints as follows.
2  Jack up the front of the vehicle and support it securely on axle stands.
3  Slowly rotate each roadwheel in turn and inspect the condition of the outer joint rubber bellows. Check for signs of cracking, splits or deterioration of the rubber which may allow the grease to escape and lead to the entry of water and dirt into the joint. Also check the security and condition of the bellows clips. Repeat these checks on the inner joints. If any damage or deterioration is found, the bellows must be renewed (Sec 5).
4  Continue rotating the roadwheel and check for any distortion or damage to the driveshaft. Check for any free play in the joints by holding the driveshaft firmly and attempting to rotate the roadwheel. Repeat this check whilst holding the inner joint body. Any noticeable movement indicates wear in the joints or driveshaft splines or a loose driveshaft nut.
5  Lower the vehicle to the ground and remove the roadwheel trim, then prise off the hub dust cap. If the staking is still effective, the driveshaft nut should be correctly tightened. If in doubt, use a torque wrench to check that the nut is securely fastened and then re-stake it (Sec 3), then refit the dust cap and trim. Repeat this check on the remaining driveshaft nut.
6  Road test the vehicle and listen for a metallic clicking from the front as the vehicle is driven slowly in a circle on full lock. If a clicking noise is heard this indicates wear in the outer constant velocity joint, which must be renewed (Sec 4).

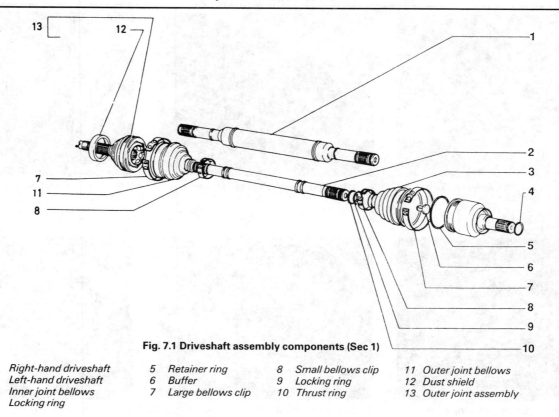

**Fig. 7.1 Driveshaft assembly components (Sec 1)**

| | | | |
|---|---|---|---|
| 1  Right-hand driveshaft | 5  Retainer ring | 8  Small bellows clip | 11  Outer joint bellows |
| 2  Left-hand driveshaft | 6  Buffer | 9  Locking ring | 12  Dust shield |
| 3  Inner joint bellows | 7  Large bellows clip | 10  Thrust ring | 13  Outer joint assembly |
| 4  Locking ring | | | |

7    If vibration, consistent with road speed, is felt through the vehicle when accelerating, there is a possibility of wear in the inner constant velocity joints. Remove the driveshafts, then dismantle them and check the joints as described in the relevant Sections of this Chapter.

## 3   Driveshafts – removal and refitting

**Note:** *If both driveshafts have been removed, the vehicle should* **not** *be moved or the front hub bearings may be damaged. If it is absolutely necessary to move the vehicle either refit both driveshafts temporarily and tighten the driveshaft nuts correctly or preload the bearings using a bolt, nut and washers to clamp the bearing inboard inner race against the hub itself.*
*As well as any other parts which may be required, ensure that new inboard locking ring(s) and driveshaft nuts are available* **before** *the driveshafts are removed.*

1    With the vehicle standing on its wheels, apply the handbrake firmly and select first or reverse gear.
2    Remove the roadwheel trim (where fitted) and prise off the hub dust cap. Relieve the staking of the driveshaft nut using a hammer and punch or (if necessary) an electric drill, then use a suitable socket, a strong T-bar and a long extension tube to slacken the nut, but do not completely unscrew it yet.
3    Slacken the roadwheel bolts, then jack up the front of the vehicle and support it securely on axle stands. Remove the roadwheel, then unscrew the driveshaft nut and remove the metal washer. Note that it is good practice to renew these nuts as a matter of course whenever they are disturbed.
4    Open the bonnet and slacken, by one or two turns only, each of the three suspension strut top mounting nuts.
5    At the bottom of the hub carrier, unscrew the two bolts to separate the hub carrier from the suspension lower arm balljoint.
6    Sharply tug the hub carrier outwards off the driveshaft splines. It may be necessary to use a soft-faced mallet (having first refitted the driveshaft nut to protect the shaft's threaded end) to tap the driveshaft out of the hub. Note the dust shield fitted at the driveshaft's outer end and take care not to stretch or kink the flexible brake hose.

7    Tie or wedge the strut assembly, complete with the hub carrier and brake caliper, clear of the driveshaft end.
8    Drain the transmission oil (Chapter 6).
9    Taking care not to damage the dust shield fitted to the inboard end of each driveshaft, use a suitable lever or a hammer and punch, as appropriate, to prise or drift out the driveshaft (photo) until the locking ring compresses into its groove and is released from the differential sun gear.
10    Withdraw the driveshaft assembly, then remove and discard the locking ring from its inboard end (photo). To prevent the risk of the sun gear falling down inside the transmission, insert into the transmission aperture a clean metal rod or wooden dowel of the same diameter as the driveshaft (approximately 27 mm) until the gear is securely supported.
11    Refitting is the reverse of the removal procedure, noting the following points.

3.9 Levering the driveshaft from the transmission

3.10 Always renew inboard end locking ring whenever it is disturbed

3.14 Refitting driveshaft to transmission

3.16A Do not forget metal washer behind driveshaft nut

3.16B Driveshaft nut should be renewed whenever it is disturbed

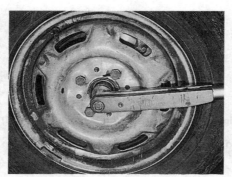

3.18A Tighten driveshaft nut to specified torque setting ...

3.18B ... and stake into two grooves to secure it

12  Thoroughly clean the driveshaft itself and the apertures in the transmission and hub carriers to prevent the entry of dirt during reassembly. Apply a thin film of grease to the oil seal lips and to the driveshaft splines and shoulders. Check that the bellows clips are securely fastened.

13  Note that the locking ring fitted to the inboard end of each driveshaft **must** be renewed whenever it is disturbed. Ensure that the new ring is located securely in its groove. Remove the sun gear support.

14  Taking care not to damage the oil seal lips, insert the driveshaft into the transmission and engage its splines with those of the sun gear (photo). Press the driveshaft firmly into place until the locking ring engages correctly behind (inboard of) the sun gear. If it is necessary to use tools to tap the driveshaft into place, be very careful not to damage the rubber bellows.

15  Check that the locking ring is properly engaged by firmly grasping the inner joint body and trying to pull the driveshaft out of the sun gear.

16  Refit the driveshaft to the hub carrier and install the metal washer and the driveshaft nut (photos). Note that owners are advised **always** to renew a driveshaft nut whenever it is disturbed. Each nut is secured by being staked at two points and the manufacturer specifies that it must be refitted so that the original staking points are **not** re-used, even if this means fitting a new nut, or one that has been used on another vehicle.

17  Refit the hub carrier to the suspension lower arm balljoint and tighten the balljoint mounting bolts to the specified torque setting. Similarly tighten the suspension strut top mounting nuts.

18  Refit the roadwheel, lower the vehicle to the ground and tighten the driveshaft nut and roadwheel bolts to their specified torque settings. Using a hammer and punch, secure the driveshaft nut by staking its collar into the two driveshaft grooves (photos).

19  Refit the hub dust cap and roadwheel trim (where fitted).

20  Refill the transmission with oil (Chapter 6).

**4  Driveshafts – overhaul**

**Note:** *Before attempting to overhaul either of the driveshafts, note the*

comments made in Section 1 concerning the availability of replacement parts.

*Removal and refitting – general*

1  Remove the driveshaft to be overhauled (Sec 3). Note, however, that it is possible to dismantle an outer joint without removing the driveshaft from the transmission. If an outer joint only is to be serviced, refer to Section 3, paragraphs 1 to 7.

2  Refitting is the reverse of the removal procedure.

*Outer joints*

3  Remove the bellows clips, then slide the bellows off the joint and towards the middle of the driveshaft.

4  Using a sharply-pointed punch or scribing tool, mark the relationship of the joint body to the driveshaft itself, then use a hammer and a drift (applied to the joint inner race only) to tap the joint off the shaft splines until the locking ring compresses into its groove and is released from the inner race.

5  Withdraw the joint from the driveshaft and slide off the bellows. If the bellows is to be re-used, wrap insulating tape around the shaft to protect it from any sharp edges. Check the bellows for splits, cracking or other signs of damage and renew it if necessary. Similarly check both clips and renew them if cracked or damaged.

6  Remove and discard the locking ring.

7  To check the joint for wear, dismantle it as follows.

8  First use a sharply-pointed punch or scribing tool to mark the relationship of both the joint's inner race and its cage to its body, then clamp the joint's splined section in a vice with padded jaws.

9  Tilt the race and cage so that one of the balls is pushed as far as possible out of the body groove (see Fig. 7.4), then use a wooden rod or similar to eject the ball without marking it. Repeat this procedure to remove all the balls in turn. It is permissible to tap the race or cage gently in an attempt to dislodge any of the balls, but **never** use excessive force or the balls may be locked in place.

10  With all balls removed, align the cage's elongated holes with the projections on the joint body (see Fig. 7.5) and withdraw the cage and race from the body. Align one of the projections on the race with one of

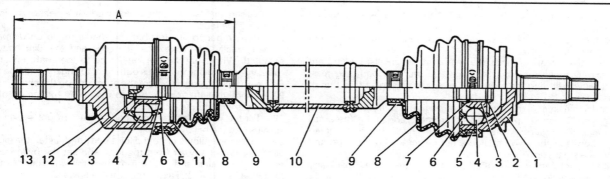

**Fig. 7.2 Cutaway drawing of (right-hand) driveshaft assembly (Sec 4)**

| 1 | Outer joint body | 5 | Large bellows clip | 9 | Small bellows clip | 12 | Inner joint body |
|---|---|---|---|---|---|---|---|
| 2 | Locking ring | 6 | Joint cage | 10 | Driveshaft | 13 | Driveshaft inboard end |
| 3 | Joint inner race | 7 | Thrust ring | 11 | Retainer ring | | locking ring |
| 4 | Steel ball | 8 | Bellows | | | | |

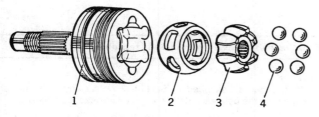

**Fig. 7.3 Outer joint components (Sec 4)**

| 1 | Outer joint body | 3 | Joint inner race |
|---|---|---|---|
| 2 | Joint cage | 4 | Steel balls |

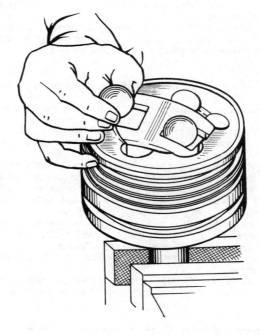

**Fig. 7.4 Removing outer joint steel ball from joint cage (Sec 4)**

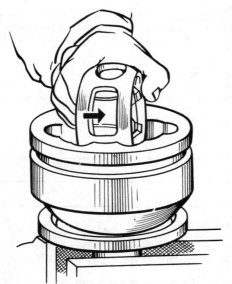

**Fig. 7.5 Removing outer joint cage and race from joint body (Sec 4)**

the cage's elongated holes (see Fig. 7.6) and remove the race from the cage.

11   Thoroughly clean all components using a suitable solvent to remove all traces of grease, then dry them and check for signs of wear, damage or corrosion. If any such signs are found, the joint assembly must be renewed. In particular check the balls themselves and their tracks in the race, cage and body. The manufacturer states that the joint must be renewed if wear at these points exceeds 0.1mm. In practice, if any wear is visible to the naked eye then the joint is excessively worn and should be renewed. Remember, however, that the balls and their tracks will acquire a fine polish during normal operation, which should not be confused with wear.

12   Check the splined section for signs of wear or damage, and also the

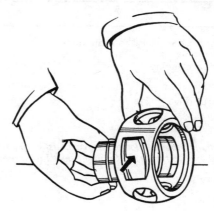

**Fig. 7.6 Removing outer joint race from cage (Sec 4)**

threaded end. Renew the joint if any faults are found at these points.

13   On reassembly, apply a good coat of grease to all components. If Lada's special lubricant is not available, a good-quality molybdenum

disulphide grease (such as Duckhams LBM 10) will serve as an adequate substitute.

14 Refitting is the reverse of the removal procedure, noting the following points.

15 Remember to ensure that the marks made on dismantling are aligned exactly when the race, the cage and the joint body are reassembled. When refitting the balls, tilt the race to an angle twice that of the cage.

16 Wind a thin layer of insulating tape around the shaft to protect the bellows from the shaft splines and other sharp edges. Fit the small bellows clip, then slide on the bellows and check that it is seated correctly between the two shoulders before removing the tape and fastening the small clip.

17 Fill the joint with the specified amount of grease, and pack any surplus into the bellows.

18 Ensuring that the thrust ring is securely located in its groove, fit a new locking ring to the groove nearest the driveshaft's end, apply a smear of grease and press the outer joint into place so that the driveshaft end, the locking ring and the joint inner race are all aligned. Using a soft-faced mallet and protecting the joint's threaded end by refitting temporarily the driveshaft nut, tap the outer joint on to the driveshaft until the locking ring compresses into its groove and passes through the inner race.

19 Check that the locking ring is correctly engaged by trying to pull the joint off the shaft, then position the bellows on the joint and expel all air from the bellows before fastening the large bellows clip.

### Inner joints

20 Remove the bellows from the joint as described in paragraph 3 above.

21 Using a sharply-pointed punch or scribing tool, mark the relationship of the joint body to the driveshaft itself. Prise the retainer ring from the joint body, then pull the joint body off the driveshaft end, leaving the balls, cage and inner race in place on the shaft. Remove and discard the locking ring.

22 Mark the relationship of both the joint's inner race and its cage to the shaft, then remove the balls as described in paragraph 9 above. Withdraw the cage and race from the shaft and check all components for wear as described in paragraphs 11 and 12 above. Remove and check the bellows as described in paragraph 5 above.

23 On reassembly, apply a good coat of grease to all components. If Lada's special lubricant is not available, a good quality molybdenum disulphide grease will serve as an adequate substitute.

24 Refitting is the reverse of the removal procedure, noting the following points.

25 Wind a thin layer of insulating tape around the shaft to protect the bellows from the shaft splines and other sharp edges. Fit the small

bellows clip, then slide on the bellows until it is clear of the joint, before removing the tape.

26 Remember to ensure that the marks made on dismantling are aligned exactly when the race, the cage and the joint body are reassembled. When refitting the inner race to the shaft, ensure that the circular recess in one end faces outboard, to engage with the thrust ring. Fit a new locking ring to secure the assembly on the shaft.

27 Check that the joint is free to move the full length of the body grooves, then refit the retainer.

28 Fill the joint with the specified amount of grease, and pack any surplus into the bellows.

29 Slide the bellows on to the joint body and fasten the large bellows clip, then expel any air from the joint and set the bellows so that its outboard (smaller) end is 210 mm from the driveshaft's inboard end (distance 'A', Fig. 7.2). Fasten the small bellows clip.

### Driveshafts – inspection

30 Once both constant velocity joints have been removed (as described above), the driveshaft itself can be checked for worn splines or locking ring grooves or for signs of cracking, bending or twisting.

31 If any such signs are found the driveshaft must be renewed.

---

### 5 Driveshaft bellows – removal and refitting

### General

1 If the checks described in Section 2 reveal any splits or other damage then the bellows must be renewed as described below.

### Outer joint bellows

2 Separate the suspension components from the driveshaft as described in Section 3, paragraphs 1 to 7.

3 Dismantle the joint and remove the bellows as described in Section 4, paragraphs 3 to 5.

4 Fit the new bellows, add grease to replace any that has been lost and reassemble the joint as described in Section 4, paragraphs 16 to 19.

5 Reassemble the front suspension as described in Section 3, paragraphs 16 to 19.

### Inner joint bellows

6 Remove the driveshaft (Sec 3).

7 Dismantle the joint and renew the bellows, then reassemble the joint (Sec 4).

8 Refit the driveshaft (Sec 3).

---

### 6 Fault diagnosis – driveshafts

| Symptom | Reason(s) |
| --- | --- |
| Vibration and/or noise, especially on tight turns | Worn outer constant velocity joint(s) |
| Vibration when accelerating | Worn inner constant velocity joint(s)<br>Bent or distorted driveshaft(s) |
| Noise on taking up drive | Worn driveshaft or constant velocity joint splines<br>Worn constant velocity joints<br>Loose driveshaft nut |

**Note:** *This Section is not intended to be an exhaustive guide to fault diagnosis but summarises the more common faults which may be encountered during a vehicle's life. Consult a dealer for more specific advice.*

# Chapter 8 Braking system

**Contents**

**Specifications**

**System type**............................................................... Hydraulically-operated diagonally split dual circuit with pressure regulator to rear brakes, vacuum servo-assisted, discs front, (automatically adjusted) drums rear. Handbrake cable-operated on rear drums.

**Front brakes**

Type................................................................... Disc, with single-piston sliding caliper
Disc diameter ........................................................ 239 mm
Disc minimum thickness ............................................. 10.8 mm
Disc maximum run-out ............................................... 0.15 mm
Front brake friction material minimum thickness ..................... 1.5 mm (0.060 in)

**Rear brakes**

Type................................................................... Self-adjusting single leading shoe drum
Drum internal diameter:
    Nominal ......................................................... 200.0 mm
    Maximum permissible after machining ......................... 201.0 mm
    Maximum permissible......................................... 201.5 mm
Brake shoe friction material minimum thickness ..................... 1.5 mm (0.060 in)

## Vacuum servo unit
Pushrod protrusion (beyond master cylinder mating surface) .................. 1.25 – 0.2 mm

## Brake pedal
Free play (engine switched off)......................................................... 3 to 5 mm (0.12 to 0.20 in)

## Handbrake
Fully applied at.............................................................................. 4 to 5 sector teeth (clicks)

## Brake fluid
Type/specification.......................................................................... Hydraulic fluid to SAE J1703 or DOT 4 (Duckhams Universal Brake and Clutch Fluid)

## Torque wrench settings

| | Nm | lbf ft |
|---|---|---|
| Brake pedal crossover rod mounting bracket-to-bulkhead retaining nuts ......... | 10 to 15.5 | 7 to 11.5 |
| Vacuum servo unit mounting bracket-to-bulkhead retaining nuts........... | 10 to 15.5 | 7 to 11.5 |
| Vacuum servo unit-to-mounting bracket nuts .......................... | 26.5 to 32.5 | 19.5 to 23.5 |
| Master cylinder-to-vacuum servo unit nuts ......................... | 26.5 to 32.5 | 19.5 to 23.5 |
| Brake pipe union nuts ........................... | 15 to 18 | 11 to 13 |
| Brake flexible hose unions........................... | 29.5 to 33.5 | 21.5 to 24.5 |
| Pressure regulator threaded plug........................... | 39 to 49 | 29 to 36 |
| Front brake caliper: | | |
|   Caliper body Allen bolts ........................... | 115 to 150 | 85 to 110.5 |
|   Guide pin bolts........................... | 31 to 38 | 23 to 28 |
|   Mounting bracket-to-hub carrier bolts ........................... | 31 to 38 | 23 to 28 |
| Rear stub axle/brake backplate-to-trailing arm bolts........................... | 34.5 to 42.5 | 25 to 31 |

## 1   General description

The braking system is hydraulically-operated and incorporates a vacuum servo unit and master cylinder mounted on the left-hand side of the engine compartment bulkhead, with a disc brake caliper at each front wheel and a drum brake wheel cylinder at each rear wheel. Both front and rear brakes are adjusted automatically to compensate for pad/shoe friction material wear. The system uses UK design technology.

The brake pedal operates the vacuum servo unit through a crossover linkage.

The master cylinder is of the tandem type and, with the connecting metal hydraulic pipes and flexible hoses, provides a diagonally-split dual

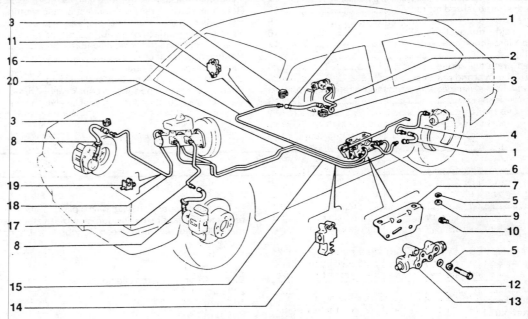

**Fig. 8.1 Layout of braking system components (Sec 1)**

| | | | | | | | |
|---|---|---|---|---|---|---|---|
| 1 | Flexible hose | 6 | Metal hydraulic pipe | 11 | Clamp | 16 | Metal hydraulic pipe |
| 2 | Metal hydraulic pipe | 7 | Pressure regulator | 12 | Washer | 17 | Metal hydraulic pipe |
| 3 | Spring clip | | mounting bracket | 13 | Pressure regulator | 18 | Metal hydraulic pipe |
| 4 | Metal hydraulic pipe | 8 | Flexible hose | 14 | Clamp | 19 | Clamp |
| 5 | Spring washer | 9 | Nut | 15 | Metal hydraulic pipe | 20 | Metal hydraulic pipe |
| | | 10 | Bolt | | | | |

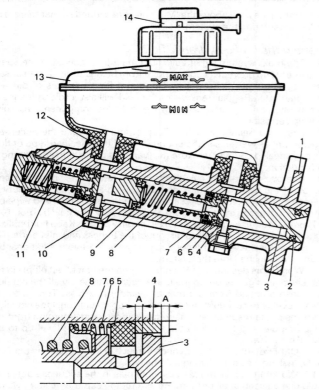

**Fig. 8.2 Cross-section through the master cylinder (Sec 1)**

| | | | |
|---|---|---|---|
| 1 | Master cylinder body | 9 | Washer |
| 2 | Seal | 10 | Stop screw |
| 3 | Primary circuit piston | 11 | Secondary circuit piston |
| 4 | Spacer | 12 | Seal |
| 5 | Seal | 13 | Reservoir body |
| 6 | Spring | 14 | Filler cap/fluid level switch |
| 7 | Spring seat | A | Operating clearance |
| 8 | Piston return spring | | |

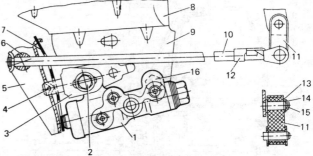

**Fig. 8.3 Pressure regulator operating linkage (Sec 1)**

| | | | |
|---|---|---|---|
| 1 | Pressure regulator | 9 | Mounting bracket |
| 2 | Mounting bolt | 10 | Operating arm |
| 3 | Operating lever bracket | 11 | Operating arm link |
| 4 | Dowel pin | 12 | Clip |
| 5 | Operating lever | 13 | Washer |
| 6 | Operating lever pivot | 14 | Circlip |
| 7 | Leaf spring | 15 | Pivot pin |
| 8 | Underbody | 16 | Mounting bolt |

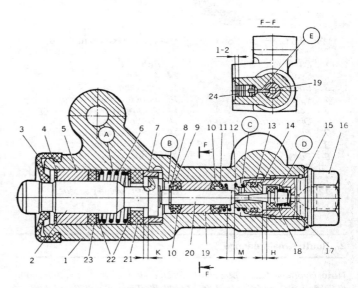

**Fig. 8.4 Cross-section through the pressure regulator (Sec 1)**

| | | | |
|---|---|---|---|
| 1 | Pressure regulator body | 17 | Valve spring |
| 2 | Piston | 18 | Valve |
| 3 | Rubber protective cap | 19 | Pushrod bush |
| 4 | Circlip | 20 | Pushrod |
| 5 | Piston sleeve | 21 | Piston head seal |
| 6 | Spring | 22 | Washer |
| 7 | Body bush | 23 | Piston rod seal |
| 8 | Circlip | 24 | Plug |
| 9 | Washer | A,D | Chambers linked to master |
| 10 | Seal | | cylinder |
| 11 | Spring seat | B | Chamber linked to R/H |
| 12 | Spring | | wheel cylinder |
| 13 | Seal | C | Chamber linked to L/H |
| 14 | Valve seat | | wheel cylinder |
| 15 | Sealing washer | E | Passage |
| 16 | Threaded plug | H,K,M | Operating clearances |

circuit system. The primary circuit operates the left-hand front and right-hand rear brakes while the secondary operates the right-hand front and left-hand rear. Thus in the event of hydraulic failure of one of the circuits full brake pressure will still be available at two of the wheels.

To prevent the rear wheels locking under heavy braking, a load-sensitive pressure regulator is fitted which uses the height of the rear suspension to control the amount of hydraulic pressure at the rear brakes. The heavier the load, the greater the pressure that can be applied to the rear brakes.

The handbrake operates the rear brakes through a lever assembly bolted to the floor and a single cable to each brake backplate.

A handbrake warning lamp is included in the instrument panel, activated by a plunger switch mounted at the base of the lever, and also a brake fluid level warning lamp (operated by a float-type switch in the master cylinder reservoir filler cap) which lights whenever the fluid level falls to a dangerously low level.

The vacuum servo unit uses inlet manifold depression (generated only while the engine is running) to boost the effort applied by the driver at the brake pedal and transmits this increased effort to the master cylinder pistons.

The front brake calipers are of the single-piston sliding type in which the main caliper body slides on a mounting bracket that is rigidly attached to the hub carrier. Full braking efficiency relies on the ability of the body to slide easily on its mounting bracket, as well as on the condition of the pads and the caliper bore, piston and seals.

The rear brakes consist of the drum, (fastened to the hub and roadwheel) and the backplate which is mounted on the rear torsion beam axle to carry the shoes and wheel cylinder. The wheel cylinder incorporates a mechanism which adjusts the clearance between the shoes and drums automatically.

**Note:** When servicing any part of the system, work carefully and method-

ically and observe scrupulous cleanliness when overhauling any part of the hydraulic system. Always renew components (in axle sets, where applicable) if in doubt about their condition and use only genuine Lada replacement parts, or at least those of known good quality. Note the warnings given in 'Safety First' and at relevant points in this Chapter concerning the dangers of asbestos dust and hydraulic fluid.

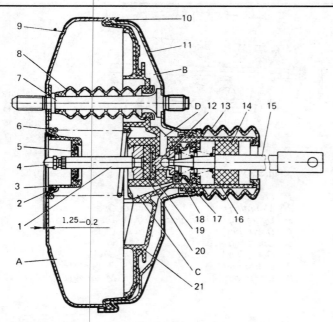

**Fig. 8.5 Cross-section through the vacuum servo unit (Sec 1) —**

| | | | |
|---|---|---|---|
| 1 | Pushrod | 13 | Rubber boot |
| 2 | Sealing ring | 14 | Air filter |
| 3 | Body cup | 15 | Input rod |
| 4 | Pushrod tip | 16 | Input rod return spring |
| 5 | Seal | 17 | Control valve return spring |
| 6 | Diaphragm return spring | 18 | Control valve |
| 7 | Pin | 19 | Control valve body bush |
| 8 | Seal | 20 | Pushrod buffer |
| 9 | Body | 21 | Control valve body |
| 10 | Diaphragm | A | At inlet manifold pressure |
| 11 | Body cover | B | At atmospheric pressure |
| 12 | Piston | C,D | Control valve passages |

## 2  Routine maintenance

**Note:** *Hydraulic fluid is poisonous; wash off immediately and thoroughly in case of skin contact and seek immediate medical advice if any fluid is swallowed or gets into the eyes. It is also an effective paint stripper and will attack plastics. If any is spilt, it should be washed off immediately using copious quantities of fresh water. Finally, it is hygroscopic (it absorbs moisture from the air) – old fluid may be contaminated and unfit for further use. When topping-up or renewing the fluid, always use a good quality fluid of the specified type and ensure that it comes from a freshly-opened sealed container.*

1   Carry out the following procedures at the intervals given in *'Routine maintenance'* at the beginning of this manual.

### Check the brake hydraulic fluid level

2   Check that the fluid level in the master cylinder translucent reservoir is between the 'Max' and 'Min' lines marked on the side of the reservoir. If the level is below the 'Min' line, top up to between the lines using the good quality fluid of the specified type from a freshly-opened sealed container (photo).

3   If frequent topping-up is necessary, check carefully for signs of fluid leaks from the various components of the system. Any leaks found must be cured immediately by the renewal of the seal or component concerned.

4   Note that the fluid level should drop steadily in service as the brake friction material wears. Thus, since a steady lowering of the level is to be expected, only sudden changes require immediate investigation.

5   Note also that it is not necessary to top up to the 'Max' level line unless all brake pads and shoes have been renewed. It is quite sufficient

to maintain the level above the 'Min' line as described so that there is no risk of air entering the system.

### Renew the brake hydraulic fluid

6   The brake system's hydraulic fluid must be renewed at the specified interval to prevent its boiling point from being reduced to an unsafe level by contamination from moisture and from particles of dirt and foreign matter. Regular renewal of the fluid will also prolong the life of the master cylinder and caliper/wheel cylinder components by minimising corrosion.

7   First read Section 8 of this Chapter and assemble the necessary equipment as well as a sufficient quantity of the specified type of fluid (in new, sealed containers). Note the warnings given at the beginning of this Section.

8   Remove the master cylinder reservoir cap and examine the condition of the fluid. If it is dark and dirty, with a significant quantity of sludge at the bottom of the reservoir, syphon out the fluid and wipe out the reservoir using a lint-free cloth. **Do not** syphon the fluid by mouth, as it is poisonous; use a syringe or an old poultry baster. Keep fluid spillage to a minimum and try to keep dirt out of the bypass and inlet ports. Top up to the 'Max' level with new fluid, which will prevent additional dirt from being flushed into the system.

9   Working as described in Section 8, open the first bleed nipple in the sequence and gently pump the brake pedal until nearly all the old fluid has been emptied from the master cylinder reservoir. Top up to the 'Max' level with new fluid and continue pumping until only the new fluid remains in the reservoir and new fluid can be seen emerging from the bleed nipple. Tighten the nipple and top the reservoir level up to the 'Max' level line.

10   Old hydraulic fluid is invariably much darker in colour than the new, making it easy to distinguish the two.

11   Work through all the remaining nipples in the sequence until new fluid can be seen at all of them. Be careful to keep the master cylinder reservoir topped up to above the 'Min' level at all times or air may enter the system and greatly increase the length of the task.

12   When the operation is complete, check that all nipples are securely tightened and that their dust caps are refitted. Wash off all traces of spilt fluid and recheck the master cylinder reservoir fluid level.

13   Check the operation of the brakes before taking the vehicle on the road. If the pedal feels spongy air may be present in the system and must be removed immediately.

### Check the adjustment of the brake pedal and stop-lamp switch

14   Check that the brake pedal pivot is properly greased and that the pedal moves smoothly and easily through its full travel. If the pedal action is stiff or spongy, do not forget to check the crossover linkage pivots (Sec 3).

15   When the engine is switched off, the pedal should have the specified amount of free play, measured at the pedal pad.

16   If adjustment is required, slacken the two nuts securing the stop-lamp switch and reposition the switch until the play is correct. Tighten the two nuts. Switch on the ignition and check the operation of the stop-lamps.

17   If the pedal free play is correct but there is evidence of brake drag, then it is possible that the vacuum servo unit pushrod is incorrectly adjusted. See Section 5.

### Check the operation of the vacuum servo unit

18   Refer to Sections 4 and 6.

### Check the metal hydraulic pipes and flexible hoses

19   Refer to Section 9.

### Check the brake pads and the caliper operation

20   Refer to Section 12. At regular intervals the discs themselves should be checked (Sec 15).

### Check the brake shoes and the wheel cylinder condition

21   Refer to Section 20. At regular intervals the drums themselves should be checked (Sec 19).

### Check the pressure regulator operation and condition

22   With the vehicle on a lift or over an inspection pit (unladen, except for a half-full fuel tank), bounce the rear of the vehicle to settle the rear

2.2 Use only good quality hydraulic fluid when topping-up master cylinder reservoir

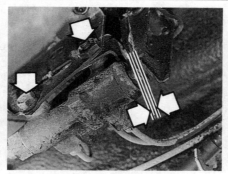

2.27 Slacken regulator mounting bolts (arrowed) to adjust regulator linkage

2.32 Handbrake adjusting nut 'A' and locknut 'B'

suspension, then clean any dirt from the pressure regulator and its linkage. Check that there is no obvious damage, fluid leakage or corrosion.

23   The plug (item 24, Fig. 8.4) should be at a depth of 1 to 2 mm in the body and there should be no free play evident in the linkage pivots or bearings.

24   Have an assistant apply pressure to the brake pedal. The piston (item 2, Fig. 8.4) should protrude by 1.6 to 2.4 mm from the body and compress the leaf spring until it bears against the operating lever, which should then rotate about its pivot.

25   With pedal pressure relaxed, the gap, at the piston, between the lever and the leaf spring (items 5 and 7, Fig. 8.3) should be 2.0 to 2.1 mm.

26   If piston travel is not as described then the regulator is probably faulty and should be overhauled or renewed (Sec 18).

27   If adjustment is required, slacken the regulator mounting bolts and move the regulator assembly until the setting is correct, then retighten the bolts (photo).

28   Road test the vehicle to check that the pedal pressure and front-to-rear brake bias are correct.

### Check the handbrake operation and adjustment

29   Note that, since the rear brakes are of the self-adjusting type, the only adjustments to the handbrake mechanism that are required are to the cables themselves.

30   The handbrake should be capable of holding the parked vehicle stationary even on steep slopes, when applied with moderate force. The mechanism should be firm and positive in feel with no trace of stiffness or sponginess from the cables and should release immediately the handbrake lever is released. If the mechanism is faulty in any of these respects it must be checked immediately.

31   To check the setting, apply the handbrake firmly several times to establish correct shoe-to-drum clearance, then fully release the lever. Applying normal, moderate pressure, pull the handbrake lever to the fully- applied position and count the number of clicks required to do so. If the number of clicks is more or less than that specified, adjustment is required.

32   To adjust the handbrake, first fully release the lever then pull it up by one or two clicks. Chock the front wheels, jack up the rear of the vehicle and support it on axle stands. The handbrake adjuster is beneath the rear of the vehicle, just above the exhaust system primary silencer (photo).

33   Slacken the adjuster locknut and rotate the adjusting nut until the brake shoes can just be heard to be rubbing on the drums, then tighten the locknut securely. If the adjustment was too tight, slacken the adjusting nut fully until the brake shoes are clear of the drums, then tighten the nut until the setting is correct.

34   Check that the roadwheels rotate easily and with no sound of brake shoe-to-drum contact when the handbrake lever is fully released.

35   Lower the vehicle to the ground and recheck the setting (para 31), which should now be correct.

### Renew the brake flexible hoses

36   Refer to Section 9.

### 3   Brake pedal and crossover linkage – removal and refitting

1   Since the Samara was designed as a left-hand drive (LHD) vehicle and was 'converted' to right-hand drive for the UK, the brake pedal operates the vacuum servo unit through a crossover linkage which is mounted on the passenger compartment side of the bulkhead, behind the heater. Refer to the relevant sub-Section below for information.

### Brake pedal

2   Unhook the return spring from the pedal.

3   Remove its spring clip and withdraw the clevis pin from the link to separate the pedal from the link (photo).

4   Remove its spring clip and tap out the pivot pin, then withdraw the brake pedal. The clutch pedal should remain in place.

5   Carefully clean all components and renew any that are worn or damaged, checking with particular care the return spring and the bearing surfaces of the pivot bushes and pivot pin.

6   Refitting is the reverse of the removal procedure, but apply a thin smear of multi-purpose grease to all pivots and bearing surfaces.

7   Check the pedal action and adjust its free play if necessary (Sec 2).

### Crossover linkage

8   Either disconnect the brake pedal from the link or remove the pedal completely (see above).

3.3 Brake pedal-to-link clevis pin (arrowed)

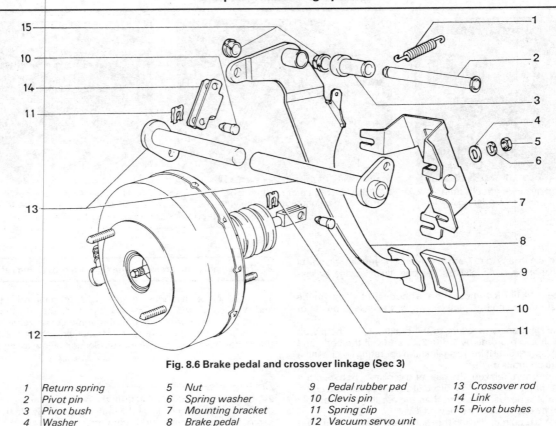

**Fig. 8.6 Brake pedal and crossover linkage (Sec 3)**

| | | | | | | | |
|---|---|---|---|---|---|---|---|
| 1 | Return spring | 5 | Nut | 9 | Pedal rubber pad | 13 | Crossover rod |
| 2 | Pivot pin | 6 | Spring washer | 10 | Clevis pin | 14 | Link |
| 3 | Pivot bush | 7 | Mounting bracket | 11 | Spring clip | 15 | Pivot bushes |
| 4 | Washer | 8 | Brake pedal | 12 | Vacuum servo unit | | |

9    Remove the centre console (Chapter 10). Peel back the carpet, removing the retaining screws where necessary, until the linkage left-hand end is visible next to the heater.

10    Remove its spring clip and withdraw the clevis pin joining the crossover rod to the vacuum servo unit input rod.

11    Unscrew the four retaining nuts and withdraw the mounting bracket, followed by the crossover rod itself (photo).

12    Refitting is the reverse of the removal procedure, but apply a thin smear of the specified multi-purpose grease to all pivots and bearing surfaces.

13    Check the pedal action and if necessary adjust its free play (Sec 2).

3.11 Unscrew nuts (arrowed) to remove crossover rod mounting bracket

## 4   Vacuum servo unit – checking

**Note:** *Do not attempt to dismantle the unit or to clean or renew the air filter. The unit is sealed and no components are available to make reconditioning viable.*

1    In normal use any failure of the vacuum servo unit will be evident to the driver due to the increased pedal effort required to achieve normal braking. To test the unit, park the vehicle on level ground and release the handbrake, then proceed as follows.

2    Switch off the engine and destroy the vacuum in the unit by depressing the brake pedal five to six times. Check that there is no significant change in pedal travel after the first two or three strokes.

3    Apply normal pressure to the brake pedal and maintain it while the engine is started. If the unit is operating correctly the pedal should move down slightly as vacuum is restored in the unit.

4    To check whether the unit is completely airtight, start the engine and run it for one or two minutes, then switch off the ignition. Depress the brake pedal slowly several times using the same, normal, pressure at each stroke. If the unit is airtight the pedal should go down to the normal depressed height on the first one or two strokes, but after that the depressed height should gradually rise as the vacuum is destroyed and the level of assistance decreases.

5    Finally start the engine again, apply normal pressure to the brake pedal and maintain it while the engine is switched off. There should be no change in pedal height for at least thirty seconds.

6    If the vacuum servo unit proves faulty as a result of the above tests it must be renewed, although it is worth checking first that the non-return check valve is not faulty (Sec 6) or that the vacuum hose from the inlet manifold is not kinked, blocked or leaking.

## 5   Vacuum servo unit – removal and refitting

1    Working inside the vehicle, disconnect the crossover rod from the vacuum servo unit input rod (Sec 3).

5.4 Vacuum servo unit mounting bracket-to-bulkhead nuts (two arrowed)

2 Working in the engine compartment, unplug the non-return check valve from the unit.
3 Unscrew the two nuts securing the master cylinder to the vacuum servo unit and very carefully move the master cylinder forwards clear of the servo unit studs and pushrod, taking great care not to kink or damage the metal hydraulic pipes. If there is any risk of kinking or damaging any of the pipes, disconnect them until the master cylinder can be moved forwards or removed, as required.
4 Unscrew the four nuts securing the servo unit's mounting bracket to the bulkhead (photo) and withdraw the assembly.
5 If the vacuum servo unit is faulty it must be renewed (see the note at the beginning of Sec 4). It can be unbolted from the mounting bracket if required. If necessary, renew the seal fitted to the bulkhead aperture.
6 Refitting is the reverse of the removal procedure. Tighten all nuts and bolts securely, to the specified torque wrench settings, where

given. If any pipes were disconnected, bleed any air from the system (Sec 8) and wash off any spilt hydraulic fluid.
7 Check that the pushrod is correctly adjusted. If its tip does not protrude by the specified amount beyond a straight-edge placed across the master cylinder mating surface, it must be adjusted by holding the rod with one spanner while its tip is screwed in or out until the setting is correct. The pushrod can be pulled slightly to the front so that ordinary spanners can be used to make the adjustment. Refit the master cylinder.
8 Check the pedal action and adjust its free play if necessary (Sec 2).

### 6 Vacuum servo unit non-return check valve – testing

1 When testing the valve, remember that its function is to allow air to flow in one direction only, **out of** the servo unit. If it allows air to flow in both directions, or in neither, it is faulty and must be renewed.
2 To test the valve, blow through it from the servo unit end, when air should pass freely through the valve. Now suck hard on the same end and there should be no leakage at all back through the valve.

### 7 Vacuum servo unit non-return check valve – removal and refitting

1 The valve is at the end of the vacuum hose from the inlet manifold and is plugged into the front of the vacuum servo unit (photo).
2 To remove the valve, unplug it from the servo unit, slacken the clip and pull it out of the vacuum hose.
3 Refitting is the reverse of the removal procedure. As soon as the engine is restarted, check that there are no signs of air leaks.

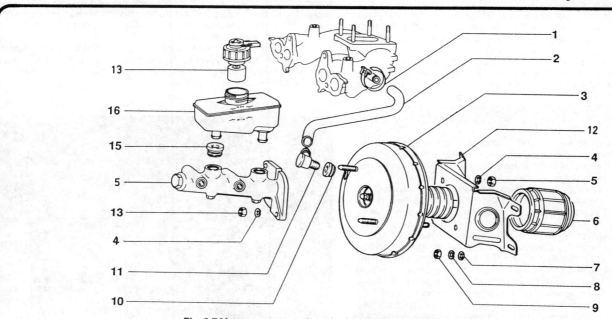

**Fig. 8.7 Vacuum servo unit and related components (Secs 4,5,6 and 7)**

| | | | |
|---|---|---|---|
| 1 Cable tie | 5 10 mm nut | 9 8 mm nut | 13 Filler cap/fluid level switch |
| 2 Vacuum hose | 6 Seal | 10 Seal | 14 Master cylinder |
| 3 Vacuum servo unit | 7 8 mm washer | 11 Non-return check valve | 15 Seal |
| 4 10 mm spring washer | 8 8 mm spring washer | 12 Mounting bracket | 16 Reservoir body |

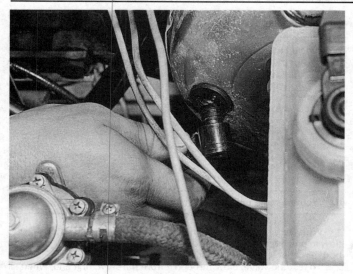

7.1 Unplugging non-return check valve from vacuum servo unit

## 8   Hydraulic system – bleeding

**Note:** *Hydraulic fluid is poisonous; wash off immediately and thoroughly in case of skin contact and seek immediate medical advice if any fluid is swallowed or gets into the eyes. It is also an effective paint stripper and will attack plastics. If any is spilt, it should be washed off immediately using copious quantities of fresh water. Finally, it is hygroscopic (it absorbs moisture from the air) – old fluid may be contaminated and unfit for further use. When topping-up or renewing the fluid, always use a good quality fluid of the specified type and ensure that it comes from a freshly-opened sealed container.*

### General

1    The correct operation of any hydraulic system is only possible after removing all air from the components and circuit by bleeding the system.
2    During the bleeding procedure, add only clean, new hydraulic fluid of the specified type. **Never** re-use fluid that has already been bled from the system. Ensure that sufficient new fluid is available before starting work.
3    If there is any possibility of incorrect fluid being already in the system, the brake components and circuit must be flushed completely with uncontaminated, correct fluid and new seals should be fitted to the various components.
4    If hydraulic fluid has been lost from the system, or if air has entered, because of a leak, ensure that the fault is cured before proceeding further.
5    Park the vehicle on level ground, switch off the engine and select first or reverse gear, then chock the wheels and release the handbrake.
6    Check that all pipes and hoses are secure, unions tight and bleed nipples closed. Clean any dirt from around the bleed nipples.
7    Top the master cylinder reservoir up to the 'Max' level line. Refit the cap loosely and remember to maintain the fluid level at least above the 'Min' level line throughout the procedure or there is a risk of further air entering the system.
8    There are a number of one-man, do-it-yourself brake bleeding kits currently available from motor accessory shops. It is recommended that one of these kits is used whenever possible as they greatly simplify the bleeding operation and also reduce the risk of expelled air and fluid being drawn back into the system. If such a kit is not available the basic two-man method must be used which is described in detail below.
9    If a kit is to be used, prepare the vehicle as described in paragraphs 5 and 6 of this Section and then follow the kit manufacturer's instructions as the procedure may vary slightly according to the type being used, but generally they are as outlined below in the relevant sub-section.
10    Whichever method is used, the same sequence must be followed (paras 11 and 12) to ensure the removal of all air from the system.

### Bleeding sequence

11    If the system has been only partially disconnected and suitable precautions were taken to minimise fluid loss, it should be necessary only to bleed that part of the system (ie, primary or secondary circuit).
12    If the complete system is to be bled, then it should be done working in the following sequence:

    (a)    *Left-hand rear brake*
    (b)    *Right-hand front brake*
    (c)    *Right-hand rear brake*
    (d)    *Left-hand front brake*

### Bleeding – basic two-man method

13    Collect a clean glass jar, a suitable length of plastic or rubber tubing which is a tight fit over the bleed nipples and a ring spanner to fit the nipples. The help of an assistant will also be required.
14    Remove the dust cap from the first nipple in the sequence. Fit the spanner and tube to the nipple, place the other end of the tube in the jar and pour in sufficient fluid to cover the end of the tube.
15    Ensure that the master cylinder reservoir fluid level is maintained at least above the 'Min' level line throughout the procedure.
16    Have the assistant fully depress the brake pedal several times to build up pressure, then maintain it on the final stroke.
17    While pedal pressure is maintained, unscrew the bleed nipple (approximately one turn) and allow the compressed fluid and air to flow into the jar (photo). The assistant should maintain pedal pressure, following it down to the floor if necessary and should not release it until instructed to do so. When the flow stops, tighten the bleed nipple again, release the pedal slowly and recheck the reservoir fluid level.
18    Repeat the steps given in paragraphs 16 and 17 until the fluid emerging from the bleed nipple is free from air bubbles. If the master cylinder has been drained and refilled and air is being bled from the first nipple in the sequence, allow approximately five seconds between cycles for the master cylinder passages to refill. See also Sec 10.
19    When no more air bubbles appear, securely tighten the bleed nipple, remove the tube and spanner and refit the dust cap. **Do not** overtighten the bleed nipples.
20    Repeat the procedure on all the remaining nipples in the sequence until all air is removed from the system and the brake pedal feels firm again.

### Bleeding – using a one-way valve kit

21    As their name implies, these kits consist of a length of tubing with a one-way valve fitted which prevents expelled air and fluid from being drawn back into the system. Some kits include a translucent container which can be positioned so that the air bubbles can be more easily seen flowing from the end of the tube.
22    Such a kit is connected to the bleed nipple, which is then opened. The user returns to the driver's seat and depresses the brake pedal with a smooth, steady stroke and slowly releases it. This is repeated until the expelled fluid is clear of air bubbles.

8.17 Bleeding air from hydraulic system at front brake caliper bleed nipple

23 These kits simplify work so much that it is easy to forget the master cylinder reservoir fluid level, so ensure that this is maintained at least above the 'Min' level line at all times.

### Bleeding – using a pressure bleeding kit

24 These kits are usually operated by the reservoir of pressurised air contained in the spare tyre.

25 By connecting a pressurised, fluid-filled container to the master cylinder reservoir, bleeding can be carried out simply by opening each nipple in turn and allowing the fluid to flow out until no more air bubbles can be seen in the expelled fluid.

26 This method has the advantage that the large reservoir of fluid provides an additional safeguard against air being drawn into the system during bleeding.

27 Pressure bleeding is particularly effective when bleeding 'difficult' systems or when bleeding the complete system at the time of routine fluid renewal.

### All methods

28 When bleeding is complete and a firm pedal feel is restored, wash off any spilt fluid, tighten the bleed nipples securely and refit their dust caps. **Do not** overtighten the bleed nipples.

29 Check the hydraulic fluid level and top up if necessary (Sec 2).

30 Discard any hydraulic fluid that has been bled from the system, as it will not be fit for re-use.

31 Check the feel of the brake pedal. If it feels at all spongy, air must still be present in the system and further bleeding is required. Failure to bleed satisfactorily after a reasonable repetition of the bleeding procedure may be due to worn master cylinder seals.

### 9 Hydraulic pipes and hoses – inspection, removal and refitting

1 The brake hydraulic system consists of a number of metal hydraulic pipes which run from the master cylinder around the engine compartment to the front brakes and along the underbody to the pressure regulator and rear brakes. Flexible hoses are fitted at front and rear to cater for steering and suspension movement (see Fig. 8.1).

2 When checking the system, first look for signs of leakage at the pipe or hose unions, then examine the flexible hoses for signs of cracking, chafing or deterioration of the rubber. Bend them sharply between the fingers (but do not actually bend them double or the casing may be damaged) and check that this does not reveal previously hidden cracks, cuts or splits. Check that all pipes and hoses are securely fastened in their clips.

3 Carefully work along the length of the metal hydraulic pipes looking for dents, kinks, damage of any sort or corrosion. Corrosion should be polished off, but if the depth of pitting is significant the pipe must be renewed.

4 If any pipe or hose is to be renewed, minimise fluid loss by removing the master cylinder reservoir cap and then tightening it down on to a piece of polythene to obtain an airtight seal. If a flexible hose is to be disconnected, unscrew the hydraulic pipe union nut before removing the spring clip which secures the hose to its mounting bracket.

5 To unscrew the union nuts it is preferable to obtain a brake pipe spanner of the correct size. These are available from most large motor accessory shops. Failing this, a close-fitting open-ended spanner will be required, though if the nuts are tight or corroded their flats may be rounded-off if the spanner slips. In such a case a self-locking wrench is often the only way to unscrew a stubborn union, but it follows that the pipe and the damaged nuts must be renewed on reassembly. Always clean a union and surrounding area before disconnecting it. If disconnecting a component with more than one union make a careful note of the connections before disturbing any of them.

6 If a hydraulic pipe is to be renewed, it can be obtained, cut to length and with the union nuts and end flares in place, from Lada dealers. All that is then necessary is to bend it to shape, following the line of the original, before fitting it to the vehicle. Alternatively, most motor accessory shops can make up hydraulic pipes from kits, but this requires very careful measurement of the original to ensure that the replacement is of the correct length. The safest answer is usually to take the original to the shop as a pattern.

7 On refitting, do not overtighten the union nuts. The specified torque wrench settings are not high and it is not necessary to exercise brute

force to obtain a sound joint. When refitting flexible hoses, always renew any sealing washers used, again noting the torque settings specified.

8 Ensure that the pipes and hoses are correctly routed with no kinks and that they are secured in the clips or brackets provided. After fitting, remove the polythene from the reservoir and bleed the hydraulic system (Sec 8). Wash off any spilt fluid and check carefully for fluid leaks.

### 10 Master cylinder – removal and refitting

**Note:** *Hydraulic fluid is poisonous; wash off immediately and thoroughly in case of skin contact and seek immediate medical advice if any fluid is swallowed or gets into the eyes. It is also an effective paint stripper and will attack plastics, so if any is spilt, it should be washed off immediately using copious quantities of fresh water. Finally, it is hygroscopic (it absorbs moisture from the air) – old fluid may be contaminated and unfit for further use. When topping-up or renewing the fluid, always use a good quality fluid of the specified type and ensure that it comes from a freshly-opened sealed container.*

1 Remove the master cylinder reservoir cap and syphon the hydraulic fluid from the reservoir. **Do not** syphon the fluid by mouth, as it is poisonous; use a syringe or an old poultry baster. Alternatively, open any convenient bleed nipple in the system and gently pump the brake pedal to expel the fluid through a plastic tube connected to the nipple (Sec 8).

2 Unscrew the union nuts and disconnect the metal hydraulic pipes (photo). Try to keep fluid spillage to a minimum and wash off any spilt fluid as soon as possible.

3 Unscrew the two nuts securing the master cylinder to the vacuum servo unit and withdraw it.

4 Refitting is the reverse of the removal procedure, noting the following points.

5 Refill the reservoir with new fluid and bleed the system (Sec 8).

6 If a new master cylinder has been fitted (or the original was fully drained) start the bleeding procedure by disconnecting each metal hydraulic pipe union in turn (working from front to rear) and gently pumping the brake pedal until only clear hydraulic fluid emerges. Catch the ejected fluid in a container or a rag placed under the master cylinder.

7 In very difficult cases, disconnect all of the metal hydraulic pipes, plug their unions with the fingers (protected by clean rags), then uncover each one in turn as the brake pedal is depressed and plug it again as the pedal is released, so that fluid is forcibly drawn down from the reservoir. Refit and tighten all pipe unions securely as soon as the master cylinder is clear of air and is pumping correctly, then proceed with the normal bleeding procedure.

10.2 Metal hydraulic pipe unions at master cylinder

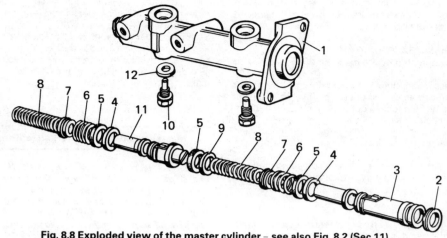

**Fig. 8.8 Exploded view of the master cylinder – see also Fig. 8.2 (Sec 11)**

| | | | | | | |
|---|---|---|---|---|---|---|
| 1 | Master cylinder body | 4 | Spacer | 7 | Spring seat | 10 Stop screw |
| 2 | Seal | 5 | Seal | 8 | Piston return spring | 11 Secondary circuit piston |
| 3 | Primary circuit piston | 6 | Spring | 9 | Washer | 12 Sealing washer |

## 11  Master cylinder – overhaul

**Note:** *Before attempting to overhaul the unit, check the price and availability of individual components and the price of a new or reconditioned unit, as overhaul may not be viable on economic grounds alone. Also, read through the procedure and check that the special tools and facilities required are available.*

1    Remove the master cylinder from the vehicle (Sec 10). Clean it thoroughly.
2    Prise the reservoir from the master cylinder body, then remove the two seals.
3    Unscrew the two stop screws and discard their sealing washers.
4    Noting the order of removal and the direction of fitting of each component, withdraw the piston assemblies with their springs and seals. If necessary, clamp the master cylinder body in a vice (fitted with soft jaw covers) and unscrew the threaded plug at the front of the body so that the pistons can be pushed out (using only a wooden rod).
5    Thoroughly clean all components using as a cleaning medium only methylated spirit, isopropyl alcohol or clean hydraulic fluid. Never use mineral-based solvents such as petrol or paraffin, which will attack the hydraulic system's rubber components. Dry the components immediately using compressed air or a clean, lint-free cloth.
6    As a matter of course, renew all seals and sealing washers disturbed on dismantling. They should never be re-used.

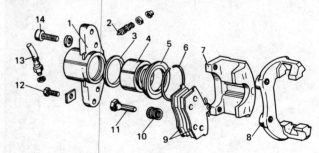

**Fig. 8.9 Exploded view of a brake caliper (Secs 12, 13 and 14)**

| | | | |
|---|---|---|---|
| 1 | Caliper body – cylinder half | 8 | Mounting bracket |
| 2 | Bleed nipple | 9 | Brake pads |
| 3 | Piston seal | 10 | Rubber dust cover |
| 4 | Piston | 11 | Guide pin |
| 5 | Dust seal | 12 | Guide pin bolt |
| 6 | Retainer ring | 13 | Flexible hose |
| 7 | Caliper body – caliper half | 14 | Caliper body Allen bolt |

7    Check all other components and renew any that are worn or damaged, particularly the cylinder bores and pistons. If these are scratched, worn or corroded, the complete assembly should be renewed. If there is any doubt about the condition of the assembly or of any of its components, renew it. Check that the body's inlet and bypass ports are clear.
8    On reassembly, soak the pistons and the new seals in clean hydraulic fluid. Smear clean fluid into the cylinder bore.
9    Fit the new seals to their pistons using only the fingers to manipulate them into the grooves.
10    Insert the pistons into the bore using a twisting motion to avoid trapping the seal lips. Ensure that all components are refitted in the correct order and the right way round.
11    Using new sealing washers, refit and securely tighten the stop screws and threaded plug (if removed).
12    Press new seals into the body ports, then refit the reservoir.
13    Refit the master cylinder to the vehicle (Sec 10).

## 12  Front brake pads – inspection and renewal

**Warning:** *Disc brake pads must be renewed on both front wheels at the same time – never renew the pads on only one wheel as uneven braking may result. Also, the dust created by wear of the pads may contain asbestos, which is a health hazard. Never blow it out with compressed air and don't inhale any of it. An approved filtering mask should be worn when working on the brakes. DO NOT use petroleum based solvents to clean brake parts. Use brake cleaner or methylated spirit only.*

1    Jack up the front of the vehicle and support it securely on axle stands, then remove the roadwheel (see 'Jacking, towing and wheel changing').
2    For a quick check, the thickness of friction material remaining on each brake pad can be measured through the slot in the caliper body (photo). If any pad's friction material is worn to the specified thickness or less, all four pads must be renewed.
3    For a comprehensive check, the brake pads should be removed and cleaned. This should be carried out, at every specified service interval, as follows.
4    Pull the caliper body outwards to compress the piston into the cylinder, then check that the caliper body slides smoothly and easily in the mounting bracket. If not, the guide pins must be cleaned, checked for wear and lubricated before reassembly.
5    Flatten back the raised tab of its lockwasher and unscrew the caliper bottom guide pin bolt, if necessary using a slim open-ended spanner to counterhold the head of the guide itself. Pivot the caliper body upwards to expose the brake pads (photos). **Do not** depress the brake pedal until

12.2 Thickness of brake pad friction material can be checked through slot in caliper body

12.5A Counterhold guide pin while unscrewing guide pin bolt

12.5B Pivot up caliper body to expose brake pads – note anti-rattle springs

12.6 Withdrawing one of the brake pads ...

12.7 ... and measuring the remaining thickness of friction material

12.10 Guide pins must be clean, unworn and properly greased

the caliper is reassembled. Renew the lockwasher if all of its tabs have been used.

6 Noting the exact location of the anti-rattle spring on each, withdraw the brake pads (photo). Mark them so that they will be refitted in their original locations, but do not be tempted to interchange pads to compensate for uneven wear.

7 First measure the thickness of friction material remaining on each brake pad (photo). If either is worn at any point to the specified minimum thickness or less, all four pads must be renewed (see the warning above and note that replacement pads are available from Lada dealers only as an axle set). Also, the pads should be renewed if any are fouled with oil or grease, as there no truly satisfactory way of de-greasing friction material.

8 If any of the brake pads are worn unevenly or fouled with oil or grease, trace and rectify the cause before reassembly.

9 If the brake pads are still serviceable, carefully clean them using a clean, fine wire brush or similar, paying particular attention to the sides and back of the metal backing. Clean out the grooves in the friction material (where applicable) and pick out any large embedded particles of dirt or debris. Carefully clean the anti-rattle springs and the pad locations in the caliper body and mounting bracket.

10 If there is any doubt about the ability of the caliper to slide in the mounting bracket, dismantle, clean and lubricate the guide pins as described in Section 14 (photo). Check the brake disc (Sec 15).

11 On reassembly, fit the anti-rattle springs to the brake pads and apply a thin smear of high-temperature brake grease (silicone- or BPC/ Poly Butyl Cuprysil-based) or anti-seize compound (eg Holts Copaslip) to the sides and back of each pad's metal backing and to those surfaces of the caliper body and mounting bracket which bear on the pads. **Do not** allow the lubricant to foul the friction material.

12 Refit the brake pads, ensuring that the friction material is against the disc.

13 If new brake pads have been fitted, the caliper piston must be pushed back into the cylinder to make room for them. Either use a G-clamp or similar tool, or use suitable pieces of wood as levers. Provided that the master cylinder reservoir has not been overfilled with hydraulic fluid there should be no spillage, but keep a careful watch on

12.14 Bending up lockwasher tab to secure guide pin bolt

the fluid level while retracting the piston. If the fluid level rises above the 'Max' level line at any time the surplus should be syphoned off or ejected via a plastic tube connected to the bleed nipple (see Section 10, paragraph 1).

14 Pivot down the caliper body over the brake pads, refit the bottom guide pin bolt and tighten it to the specified torque wrench setting, then bend an unused portion of the lockwasher up against one of its flats (photo).

15 Check that the caliper body slides smoothly in the mounting bracket, then repeatedly depress the brake pedal until the pads are pressed into firm contact with the brake disc and normal (non-assisted) pedal pressure is restored. Refit the roadwheel.

16    Repeat the full procedure on the opposite brake caliper, then lower the vehicle to the ground and tighten the roadwheel bolts to the specified torque wrench setting.
17    Check the brake hydraulic fluid level (Sec 2).

### 13  Front brake caliper – removal and refitting

**Warning:** *Dust created by the braking system may contain asbestos, which is a health hazard. Never blow it out with compressed air and don't inhale any of it. An approved filtering mask should be worn when working on the brakes. DO NOT use petroleum based solvents to clean brake parts. Use brake cleaner or methylated spirit only. Read also the note at the beginning of Section 10 concerning the dangers of hydraulic fluid.*

1    Jack up the front of the vehicle and support it securely on axle stands, then remove the roadwheel (see *'Jacking, towing and wheel changing'*).
2    Minimise fluid loss either by removing the master cylinder reservoir cap and then tightening it down on to a piece of polythene to obtain an airtight seal, or by using a brake hose clamp, a G-clamp or similar tool to clamp the flexible hose.
3    Clean the area around the union, unclip the flexible hose from the suspension strut bracket, then slacken the flexible hose union.
4    Unscrew the two caliper mounting bracket-to-hub carrier bolts.
5    Withdraw the brake caliper assembly, unscrew it from the flexible hose union and collect the sealing washer. Slip a clean wooden spacer (of the same thickness as the brake disc) between the brake pads to retain them.
6    Refitting is the reverse of the removal procedure, noting the following points.
7    Tighten all nuts and bolts to the specified torque wrench settings. As a matter of course, renew the flexible hose union sealing washer.
8    Ensure that the flexible hose is correctly routed and secured in the clip provided without being twisted.
9    Bleed any air from the system (Sec 8), then check the brake hydraulic fluid level (Sec 2).

### 14  Front brake caliper – overhaul

**Warning:** *Dust created by the braking system may contain asbestos, which is a health hazard. Never blow it out with compressed air and don't inhale any of it. An approved filtering mask should be worn when working on the brakes. DO NOT use petroleum based solvents to clean brake parts. Use brake cleaner or methylated spirit only. Read also the note at the beginning of Section 10 concerning the dangers of hydraulic fluid.*

1    Jack up the front of the vehicle and support it securely on axle stands, then remove the roadwheel (see *'Jacking, towing and wheel changing'*).
2    Minimise fluid loss either by removing the master cylinder reservoir

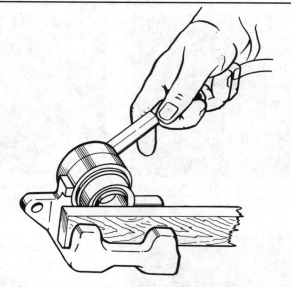

**Fig. 8.10 Using compressed air to eject caliper piston (Sec 14)**

cap and then tightening it down on to a piece of polythene to obtain an airtight seal, or by using a brake hose clamp, a G-clamp or similar tool to clamp the flexible hose.
3    Clean the area around the union, unclip the flexible hose from the suspension strut bracket, then slacken the flexible hose union.
4    Flatten back the lockwasher raised tabs and unscrew the caliper guide pin bolts, if necessary using a slim open-ended spanner to counterhold the head of each guide pin. Withdraw the caliper body, unscrew it from the flexible hose union and collect the sealing washer (photo).
5    Remove and check the brake pads (Sec 12).
6    Extract the guide pins, if necessary by screwing their bolts into them and pulling on the head of each bolt using a self-locking wrench or similar. Peel off the rubber dust cover from each guide pin.
7    Unbolt the caliper mounting bracket from the hub carrier (photo).
8    Prise off the retainer ring which secures the piston dust seal to the caliper body. Place a small block of wood in the jaws of the caliper body and remove the piston, including dust seal, by applying a jet of low-pressure compressed air (such as that from a tyre pump) to the fluid entry port (see Fig. 8.10).
9    Peel the dust seal off the piston and use a blunt instrument such as a knitting needle to extract the piston seal from the caliper cylinder bore.
10    **Do not** disturb the caliper body Allen bolts. While the caliper body can be separated into two parts, these cannot be obtained separately. If either part of the body is worn or damaged in any way the complete caliper assembly must be renewed.
11    Thoroughly clean all components using as a cleaning medium only methylated spirit, isopropyl alcohol or clean hydraulic fluid. Never use mineral-based solvents such as petrol or paraffin, which will attack the hydraulic system's rubber components. Dry the components immedi-

**14.4 Using a brake hose clamp to prevent fluid loss while caliper body is unscrewed from flexible hose**

**14.7 Unbolting caliper mounting bracket from hub carrier**

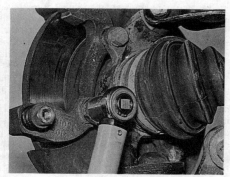

**14.17 Tighten all nuts and bolts to specified torque wrench settings**

ately using compressed air or a clean, lint-free cloth. Use compressed air to blow clear the fluid passages.

12    As a matter of course, renew all rubber seals, dust covers and caps, and the sealing washers disturbed on dismantling, which should never be re-used.

13    Check all other components and renew any that are worn or damaged. Check particularly the cylinder bore and piston, which should be renewed (even if this means the renewal of the complete assembly) if they are scratched, worn or corroded in any way. Similarly check the condition of the guide pins and their bores in the mounting bracket. Both guide pins should be undamaged and (when cleaned) a reasonably tight sliding fit in the mounting bracket bores. If there is any doubt about the condition of any of the components, renew it.

14    On reassembly, ensure that all components are absolutely clean and dry.

15    Soak the piston and the new piston seal in clean hydraulic fluid. Smear clean fluid into the cylinder bore.

16    Fit the new piston seal using only the fingers to manipulate it into the cylinder bore groove. Fit the new dust seal to the piston and refit it to the cylinder bore, using a twisting motion and ensuring that the piston enters squarely into the bore. Press the piston fully into the bore, then refit the retainer ring to secure the dust seal to the caliper body.

17    Refit the caliper mounting bracket to the hub carrier, tightening the two bolts to the specified torque wrench setting (photo).

18    Fit a new rubber dust cover to each guide pin and apply a thin smear of high-temperature brake grease (silicone- or PBC/Poly Butyl Cuprysil-based) or anti-seize compound (eg Holts Copaslip) to the guide pins before refitting them to their bores.

19    Refit the brake pads (Sec 12).

20    Using a new sealing washer, screw the caliper body on to the flexible hose union and tighten it securely. Fit the caliper body over the mounting bracket/brake pads, refit the guide pin bolts and tighten them to the torque wrench setting specified, then bend an unused portion of its lockwasher up against one of each bolt's flats.

21    Check that the caliper body slides smoothly in the mounting bracket.

22    Bleed any air from the system (Sec 8), then depress the brake pedal repeatedly until the pads are pressed into firm contact with the brake disc and normal (non-assisted) pedal pressure is restored. Refit the roadwheel. Wash off any spilt fluid and check for any fluid leaks while an assistant applies full pressure to the brake pedal.

23    Repeat the full procedure on the opposite brake caliper, then lower the vehicle to the ground and tighten the roadwheel bolts to the specified torque wrench setting.

24    Check the brake hydraulic fluid level (Sec 2). Check for any fluid leaks which might subsequently appear.

## 15  Front brake disc – inspection, removal and refitting

**Warning:** *Dust created by the braking system may contain asbestos, which is a health hazard. Never blow it out with compressed air and don't inhale any of it. An approved filtering mask should be worn when working on the brakes. DO NOT use petroleum based solvents to clean brake parts. Use brake cleaner or methylated spirit only.*

1    Jack up the front of the vehicle and support it securely on axle stands, then remove the roadwheel (see *'Jacking, towing and wheel changing'*).

2    Slowly rotate the brake disc so that the full area of both sides can be checked. Light scoring is normal in the area swept by the brake pads, but if heavy scoring is found the disc must be renewed. The only alternative to this is to have the disc surface-ground until it is flat again, but this must not reduce the disc to less than the minimum thickness specified.

3    It is normal to find a lip of rust and brake dust around the disc's perimeter, and this can be scraped off if required. If, however, a lip has formed due to excessive wear of the brake pad swept area then the disc's thickness must be measured using a micrometer. Take measurements at four places around the disc at the inside and outside of the pad swept area. If the disc has worn at any point to the specified minimum thickness or less, it must be renewed.

4    If the disc is thought to be warped it can be checked for run-out (in the centre of the pad swept area) either using a dial gauge mounted on any convenient fixed point, while the disc is slowly rotated (see Fig. 8.11), or by using feeler gauges to measure (at several points all around

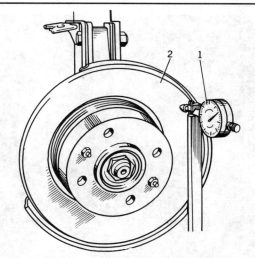

**Fig. 8.11 Measuring brake disc run-out (Sec 15)**

*1    Dial gauge     2    Brake disc*

the disc) the clearance between the disc and a fixed point such as the caliper mounting bracket. If the measurements obtained are at the specified maximum or beyond, the disc is excessively warped and must be renewed, though it is worth checking first that the hub bearing is in good condition (Chapter 9, Sections 2 and 4). Also try the effect of removing the disc and turning it through 180° to reposition it on the hub. If run-out is still excessive the disc must be renewed.

5    Check the disc for cracks, especially around the bolt holes, and any other wear or damage. Renew it if any of these are found.

6    Note that to ensure even and consistent braking, both discs should be renewed at the same time, even if only one is faulty.

### Removal and refitting

7    Jack up the front of the vehicle and support it securely on axle stands, then remove the roadwheel (see *'Jacking, towing and wheel changing'*).

8    With reference to Section 13, unscrew the two bolts securing the brake caliper mounting bracket to the hub carrier and unclip the brake flexible hose from the suspension strut bracket, then withdraw the caliper assembly and secure it out of harm's way without stretching or kinking the brake hose. Place a clean spacer (of the same thickness as the brake disc) between the pads to prevent them being dislodged.

9    Use chalk or paint to mark the relationship of the disc to the hub, then unscrew the disc retaining screws/roadwheel guide pins (photo) and withdraw the disc.

15.9 Unscrewing disc retaining screw/roadwheel guide pin

15.10 Ensure that disc/hub mating surfaces are clean and flat

10   Refitting is the reverse of the removal procedure, noting the following points. Ensure that the mating surfaces of the disc and hub are clean and flat (photo), and (if applicable) align the marks made on removal. If a new disc has been fitted, use a suitable solvent to wipe any preservative coating from the disc before refitting the caliper.

### 16   Front brake disc shield – removal and refitting

1   Remove the brake disc (Sec 15).
2   Unbolt the brake disc shield from the hub carrier and withdraw it.
3   Refitting is the reverse of the removal procedure.

### 17   Pressure regulator – removal and refitting

**Note:** *Hydraulic fluid is poisonous; wash off immediately and thoroughly in case of skin contact and seek immediate medical advice if any fluid is swallowed or gets into the eyes. It is also an effective paint stripper and will attack plastics. If any is spilt, it should be washed off immediately using copious quantities of fresh water. Finally, it is hygroscopic (it absorbs moisture from the air) – old fluid may be contaminated and unfit for further use. When topping-up or renewing the fluid, always use a good quality fluid of the specified type and ensure that it comes from a freshly-opened sealed container.*

1   Minimise fluid loss by removing the master cylinder reservoir cap and then tightening it down on to a piece of polythene to obtain an airtight seal.
2   Jack up the rear of the vehicle and support it securely on axle stands (see *'Jacking, towing and wheel changing'*).
3   Clean the area around the pressure regulator, especially the metal hydraulic pipe unions, and make a careful note of the pipe connections before disturbing any of them.
4   Prise off the circlip and withdraw the washer to release the operating arm link from the rear suspension torsion beam axle (photo).
5   Unscrew in turn each of the metal hydraulic pipe union nuts and disconnect the pipes from the regulator without distorting them. Be prepared to catch the spilt fluid.
6   Unscrew the two nuts securing the pressure regulator mounting bracket to the underbody (photo), then withdraw the assembly.
7   Refitting is the reverse of the removal procedure, noting the following points.
8   Ensure that the linkage pivots and bearing surfaces are clean and properly lubricated before refitting.
9   Loosely refit the assembly to the underbody, connect the linkage to the rear suspension torsion beam axle and adjust it (Sec 2) before tightening the mounting nuts and bolts securely.
10   Ensure that each metal hydraulic pipe is connected to its correct union on the regulator (photo) and tighten the union nuts to the specified torque wrench settings.
11   Lower the vehicle to the ground and bleed any air from the system (Sec 8). Note, however, that it may take several attempts (and a larger than usual amount of hydraulic fluid) to clear all the air from a new regulator. This is one of the cases where a pressure bleeding kit would be most useful.

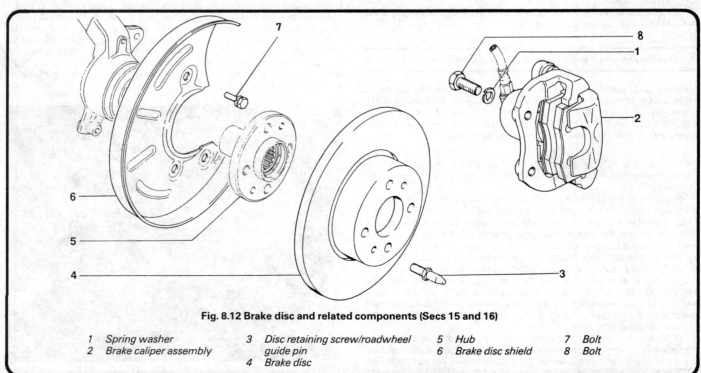

**Fig. 8.12 Brake disc and related components (Secs 15 and 16)**

| 1 | Spring washer | 3 | Disc retaining screw/roadwheel | 5 | Hub | 7 | Bolt |
| 2 | Brake caliper assembly | | guide pin | 6 | Brake disc shield | 8 | Bolt |
| | | 4 | Brake disc | | | | |

17.4 Pressure regulator operating arm link to torsion beam axle (arrowed)

17.6 Pressure regulator mounting bracket-to-underbody nuts (arrowed)

17.10 Ensure pressure regulator pipes are correctly connected

12 Wash off any spilt fluid and check for any fluid leaks while an assistant applies full pressure to the brake pedal.

13 Check the brake hydraulic fluid level (Sec 2). Check for any fluid leaks which might subsequently appear.

## 18 Pressure regulator – overhaul

**Note:** *Before attempting to overhaul the unit, check the price and availability of individual components and the price of a new or reconditioned unit, as overhaul may not be viable on economic grounds alone. Also, read through the procedure and check that the special tools and facilities required are available.*

1 If one or both rear roadwheels lock repeatedly under heavy braking, first check that this is not due to adverse road conditions or to incorrectly inflated or badly-worn tyres, then check the regulator adjustment (Sec 2) and the condition of all four brake assemblies before suspecting a regulator fault. If the fault persists, overhaul the regulator as follows.

2 Remove the pressure regulator from the vehicle (Sec 17). Clean it thoroughly.

3 Unbolt the mounting bracket from the regulator body. Dismantle, clean and grease the linkage pivots and bearing surfaces.

4 Mount the regulator in a soft-jawed vice and unscrew the threaded plug from its rear end. Remove and discard the sealing washer, then tip out the coil spring and spring seat.

5 From the regulator's front end, remove the rubber protective cap. Press the piston sleeve into the regulator body to compress the piston spring, extract the retaining circlip and slowly allow spring pressure to push the piston sleeve out of the body.

6 Withdraw the piston, noting the piston seals, the spring, and the washer at each end.

7 Remove the pushrod and pushrod bush with their seals and washers.

8 The body bush is not available separately and so should not be disturbed.

9 Thoroughly clean all components using as a cleaning medium only methylated spirit, isopropyl alcohol or clean hydraulic fluid. Never use mineral-based solvents such as petrol or paraffin which will attack the hydraulic system's rubber components. Dry the components immediately using compressed air or a clean, lint-free cloth.

10 As a matter of course, renew all seals and sealing washers disturbed on dismantling. They should never be re-used.

11 Check all other components and renew any that are worn or damaged, particularly the body bore and matching bearing surfaces.

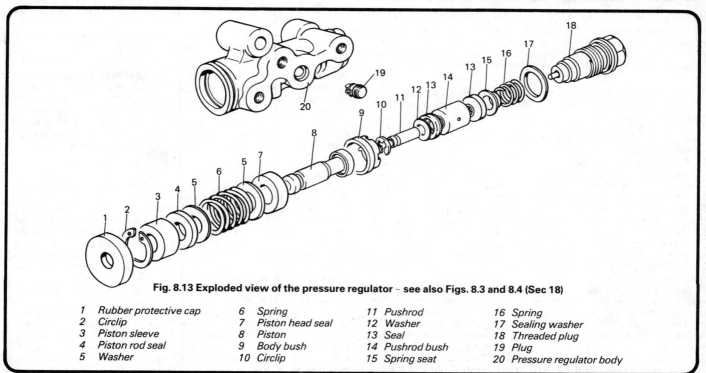

**Fig. 8.13 Exploded view of the pressure regulator – see also Figs. 8.3 and 8.4 (Sec 18)**

| | | | | | | | |
|---|---|---|---|---|---|---|---|
| 1 | Rubber protective cap | 6 | Spring | 11 | Pushrod | 16 | Spring |
| 2 | Circlip | 7 | Piston head seal | 12 | Washer | 17 | Sealing washer |
| 3 | Piston sleeve | 8 | Piston | 13 | Seal | 18 | Threaded plug |
| 4 | Piston rod seal | 9 | Body bush | 14 | Pushrod bush | 19 | Plug |
| 5 | Washer | 10 | Circlip | 15 | Spring seat | 20 | Pressure regulator body |

19.4 Unscrewing drum retaining screw/roadwheel guide pin

19.5 Using retaining screws/roadwheel guide pins to remove brake drum

19.12 Clean and prepare drum/hub mating surfaces (arrowed) before refitting drum

The complete assembly must be renewed if these are scratched, worn or corroded. If there is any doubt about the condition of the assembly or of any of its components, renew it. Check that the body's ports are clear. The plug (item 24, Fig. 8.4) should be at a depth of 1 to 2 mm in the body.

12   On reassembly, soak the components and the new seals in clean hydraulic fluid. Smear clean fluid into the body bore.

13   Fit the new head seal to the piston, followed by the first washer, the spring, the second washer, the piston rod seal and the piston sleeve. Refit the assembly to the body and press it fully into place until the spring is compressed and the circlip can be refitted. Apply a smear of brake assembly grease to the sleeve and piston before fitting the new rubber protective cap.

14   Fit the washer to the pushrod, followed by a new seal, the pushrod bush, a second new seal and the spring seat. Refit the assembly to the body, followed by the spring. Using a new sealing washer, refit and tighten the threaded plug to the specified torque wrench setting.

15   Refit the mounting bracket, tightening its bolts only lightly until the regulator is refitted to the vehicle and adjusted.

16   Refit the pressure regulator to the vehicle (Sec 17).

## 19   Rear brake drum – removal, inspection and refitting

**Warning:** *Dust created by the braking system may contain asbestos, which is a health hazard. Never blow it out with compressed air and don't inhale any of it. An approved filtering mask should be worn when working on the brakes. DO NOT use petroleum based solvents to clean brake parts. Use brake cleaner or methylated spirit only.*

1   Note that the rear brake drums are aluminium alloy castings with a cast iron sleeve which require some care in handling if they are not to be cracked or distorted.

2   Jack up the rear of the vehicle and support it securely on axle stands, then remove the roadwheel (see 'Jacking, towing and wheel changing').

3   Use chalk or paint to mark the relationship of the drum to the hub.

4   With the handbrake firmly applied to prevent drum rotation, unscrew the two drum retaining screws/roadwheel guide pins (photo). Release the handbrake fully and withdraw the drum.

5   If the drum will not pull away, first check that the handbrake is fully released. If the drum still cannot be moved, it is probably stuck to the hub flange with corrosion. Screw the two retaining screws/roadwheel guide pins into the holes threaded into the drum (not into the hub) and tighten them evenly and carefully to jack the drum off the hub (photo).

6   Working carefully (see warning above), remove all traces of brake dust from the drum.

7   Scrub clean the outside of the drum and check it for obvious signs of wear or damage such as cracks around the roadwheel bolt holes or damage to the various threads. Renew the drum if necessary.

8   Examine carefully the inside of the drum. Light scoring of the friction surface is normal, but if heavy scoring is found the drum must be renewed. It is usual to find on the drum's inboard edge a lip which consists of a mixture of rust and brake dust. This should be scraped away to leave a smooth surface which can be polished with fine (120 to

150 grade) emery paper. If, however, the lip is due to the friction surface being recessed by excessive wear, then the drum must be renewed.

9   If the drum is thought to be excessively worn, or oval, its internal diameter must be measured at several points using an internal micrometer. Take measurements in pairs, the second at right angles to the first, and compare the two to check for signs of ovality. Provided that it does not enlarge the drum to beyond the specified maximum internal diameter, it may be possible to have the drum refinished by skimming or grinding. If this is not possible, the drum must be renewed.

10   If either drum requires renewal, both should be renewed at the same time to ensure even and consistent braking.

11   On fitting a new brake drum, use a suitable solvent to remove any preservative coating that may have been applied to its interior.

12   On reassembly, use a clean wire brush to remove all traces of dirt, brake dust and corrosion from the mating surfaces of the drum and the hub flange, then apply a thin smear of anti-seize compound (eg Holts Copaslip) to those surfaces (photo).

13   Refitting is the reverse of the removal procedure. Tighten the drum retaining screws/roadwheel guide pins evenly and securely and tighten the roadwheel bolts to the specified torque wrench setting.

14   Depress the brake pedal several times until the wheel cylinder(s) and brake shoes have taken up their correct working positions and normal (non-assisted) pedal pressure is restored. Check the handbrake adjustment (Sec 2) and ensure that the roadwheels rotate easily, with no (or very slight) sound of brake shoe-to-drum contact.

## 20   Rear brake shoes – inspection and renewal

**Warning:** *Drum brake shoes must be renewed on both rear wheels at the same time - never renew the shoes on only one wheel as uneven braking may result. Also, the dust created by wear of the shoes may contain asbestos, which is a health hazard. Never blow it out with compressed air and don't inhale any of it. An approved filtering mask should be worn when working on the brakes. DO NOT use petroleum based solvents to clean brake parts. Use brake cleaner or methylated spirit only.*

1   Remove and check the brake drum (Sec 19).

2   Working carefully (see warning above) remove all traces of brake dust from the brake drum, backplate and shoes.

3   Measure at several points the thickness of friction material remaining on each brake shoe. If either shoe is worn at any point to the specified minimum thickness or less, all four shoes must be renewed (see the warning above and note that replacement shoes are available from Lada dealers only as an axle set). Also, the shoes should be renewed if any are fouled with oil or grease, as there is no truly satisfactory way of degreasing friction material.

4   If any of the brake shoes are worn unevenly or fouled with oil or grease, trace and rectify the cause before reassembly.

5   To remove the brake shoes, first prise forwards the handbrake operating lever until the handbrake cable can be disconnected, then unhook the brake shoe retaining springs. Release the shoes one at a time from the bottom anchor point, remove the bottom return spring and withdraw the shoes from the backplate (photos). Do not depress the brake pedal until the brakes are reassembled.

20.5A Disconnect handbrake cable ...

20.5B ... unhook shoe retaining springs ...

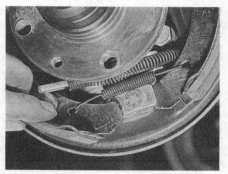

20.5C ... release shoes from bottom anchor point ...

20.5D ... and withdraw shoes from backplate

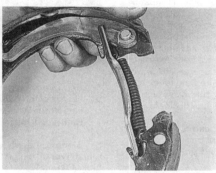

20.6A Remove handbrake operating strut ...

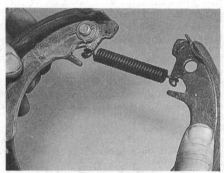

20.6B ... and unhook top return spring to separate shoes

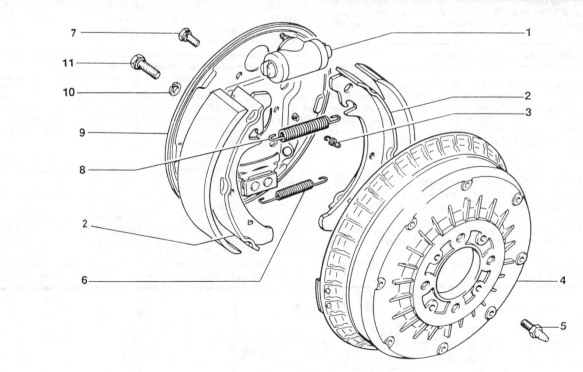

**Fig. 8.14 Exploded view of a rear brake assembly (Secs 19, 20, 21 and 23)**

| | | | |
|---|---|---|---|
| 1 Wheel cylinder | 4 Brake drum | 6 Shoe bottom return spring | 9 Brake backplate |
| 2 Brake shoes | 5 Drum retaining screw/roadwheel | 7 Bolt | 10 Spring washer |
| 3 Shoe retaining spring | guide pin | 8 Shoe top return spring | 11 Bolt |

6  Carefully note the exact fitted positions of the brakes shoes, return springs and handbrake operating linkage to ensure correct reassembly, then remove the handbrake operating strut and unhook the return spring to separate the shoes (photos). Remove the split pin and withdraw the handbrake operating lever, pivot pin and spacer.

7  Clean the backplate and apply a thin smear of high-temperature brake grease (silicone- or PBC/ Poly Butyl Cuprysil-based) or anti-seize compound (eg Holts Copaslip) to all those surfaces of the backplate which bear on the shoes, particularly the bottom anchor point and the wheel cylinder pistons. If the shoes are not renewed, check that the pivots of the handbrake operating linkage are properly lubricated. **Do not** allow the lubricant to foul the friction material.

8  Peel back the rubber protective caps and check the wheel cylinder for fluid leaks or other damage (Sec 22).

9  To reassemble the brake shoes, transfer the handbrake operating lever (if new shoes are being fitted) to the rear (trailing) shoe, grease the pivot pin and refit it, followed by the spacer and a new split pin. Assemble the leading shoe and top return spring, then refit the handbrake operating strut and bottom return spring.

10  If new shoes are to be fitted, the wheel cylinder pistons must be compressed into the cylinder to a depth of 4.5 to 4.8 mm so that the distance between the grooves (photo) is no more than 67 mm (see Fig. 8.16). Use a G-clamp or similar to compress the pistons, but be careful not to damage them or to force them at an angle into the cylinder.

11  Provided that the master cylinder reservoir has not been overfilled with hydraulic fluid there should be no spillage, but keep a careful watch on the fluid level while compressing the pistons. If the fluid level rises above the 'Max' level line at any time the surplus should be syphoned off or ejected via a plastic tube connected to the bleed nipple (see Section 10, paragraph 1).

12  Fit the shoe assembly to the backplate, being careful not to get grease on to the friction material. Ensure that the shoe ends engage properly with the wheel cylinder piston grooves and on the bottom anchor point.

13  Hook the retaining springs on to the brake shoes, then connect the handbrake cable to the operating lever. Tap the shoes to centralise them on the backplate.

14  Refit the drum and depress the brake pedal several times until the wheel cylinder(s) and brake shoes have taken up their correct working positions and normal (non-assisted) pedal pressure is restored (Sec 19).

### 21  Rear wheel cylinder – removal and refitting

**Warning:** *Dust created by the braking system may contain asbestos, which is a health hazard. Never blow it out with compressed air and don't inhale any of it. An approved filtering mask should be worn when working on the brakes. DO NOT use petroleum based solvents to clean brake parts. Use brake cleaner or methylated spirit only. Read also the note at the beginning of Section 17 concerning the dangers of hydraulic fluid.*

1  Minimise fluid loss either by removing the master cylinder reservoir cap and then tightening it down on to a piece of polythene to obtain an airtight seal, or by using a brake hose clamp, a G-clamp or similar tool to clamp the flexible hose.

2  Jack up the rear of the vehicle and support it securely on axle stands, then remove the roadwheel (see 'Jacking, towing and wheel changing').

3  Clean the area around the wheel cylinder mountings, especially the metal hydraulic pipe union.

20.10 Measuring distance between piston grooves to permit fitting of new brake shoes

4  Remove the brake drum and shoes (Secs 19 and 20).

5  Unscrew the union nut and disconnect the metal hydraulic pipe.

6  Unbolt the wheel cylinder and withdraw it.

7  Refitting is the reverse of the removal procedure, noting the following points.

8  Tighten the wheel cylinder mounting bolts securely, connect the metal hydraulic pipe to the cylinder and refit the brake shoes and drum (Secs 20 and 19).

9  When the brakes are reassembled, bleed any air from the system (Sec 8) and check for leaks while an assistant applies full pressure to the brake pedal.

10  Check the brake hydraulic fluid level (Sec 2). Check for any fluid leaks which might subsequently appear.

### 22  Rear wheel cylinder – overhaul

**Note:** *Before attempting to overhaul the unit, check the price and availability of individual components and the price of a new or reconditioned unit, as overhaul may not be viable on economic grounds alone. Also, read through the procedure and check that the special tools and facilities required are available.*

1  Remove the wheel cylinder from the vehicle (Sec 21). Clean it thoroughly.

2  Mount the wheel cylinder in a soft-jawed vice and remove the rubber protective caps. Extract the piston assemblies.

3  Holding the head of the stop screw to prevent it from rotating, use a screwdriver applied to the piston groove to unscrew the piston from the stop screw. Remove the piston seal, seat, spring and collets, then separate the thrust ring from the stop screw.

4  Thoroughly clean all components using as a cleaning medium only methylated spirit, isopropyl alcohol or clean hydraulic fluid. Never use

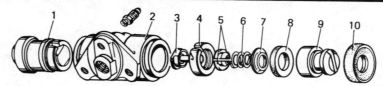

**Fig. 8.15 Exploded view of a wheel cylinder (Sec 22)**

| | | | |
|---|---|---|---|
| 1  *Piston assembly (complete)* | 4  *Thrust ring* | 7  *Seal seat* | 9  *Piston* |
| 2  *Wheel cylinder body* | 5  *Collets* | 8  *Seal* | 10  *Rubber protective cap* |
| 3  *Stop screw* | 6  *Spring* | | |

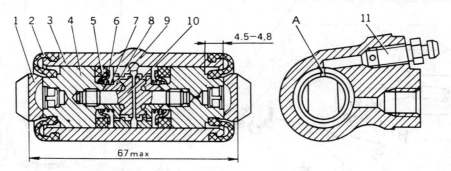

**Fig. 8.16 Cross-section through a wheel cylinder (Sec 22)**

| | | | | | | |
|---|---|---|---|---|---|---|
| 1 | Shoe stop | 4 | Piston | 7 | Spring | 10 Stop screw |
| 2 | Rubber protective cap | 5 | Seal | 8 | Collets | 11 Bleed nipple |
| 3 | Wheel cylinder body | 6 | Seal seat | 9 | Thrust ring | A Thrust ring slot |
| | | | | | | Dimensions in mm |

mineral-based solvents such as petrol or paraffin, which will attack the hydraulic system's rubber components. Dry the components immediately using compressed air or a clean, lint-free cloth.

5   As a matter of course, renew the rubber protective caps, dust caps and seals disturbed on dismantling. They should never be re-used.

6   Check all other components and renew any that are worn or damaged, particularly the cylinder bore and pistons. The complete assembly must be renewed if these are scratched, worn or corroded. If there is any doubt about the condition of the assembly or of any of its components, renew it. Check that the fluid entry port is clear.

7   The self-adjusting mechanism depends on the condition of the thrust rings, which can be assessed only by measuring the force required to insert the complete piston assembly into the cylinder (see paragraph 10). If the force required is less than 35 kgf the thrust ring is too weak and must be renewed. The test requires the use of Lada service tool 67.7823.9532, but if this is not available a spring balance and suitable hook may serve as an adequate substitute. If there is any doubt about the operation of the mechanism, renew its components as a matter of course.

8   On reassembly, soak the components and the new seals in clean hydraulic fluid. Smear clean fluid into the cylinder bore.

9   Fit the new seal and the seat to the piston, followed by the spring and the collets. Refit the stop screw to the thrust ring and tighten the stop screw to a torque setting of 4 to 7 Nm (3 to 5 lbf ft) in the piston.

10   Insert the completed piston assembly into the cylinder so that the thrust ring slot faces upwards (no more than 30° either side of the vertical), to align with the bleed nipple port (see Fig. 8.16). Ensuring that the seal is not distorted, press the piston into the cylinder to a depth of 4.5 to 4.8 mm.

11   Repeat the above procedure to fit the second piston assembly. The distance between the piston grooves should be no more than 67 mm (see Fig. 8.16).

12   Check that each piston has 1.25 to 1.65 mm free play in the cylinder.

13   Apply a smear of brake assembly grease to each piston before fitting the new rubber protective caps.

14   Refit the wheel cylinder to the vehicle (Sec 21).

## 23   Rear brake backplate – removal and refitting

**Warning:** *Dust created by the braking system may contain asbestos, which is a health hazard. Never blow it out with compressed air and don't inhale any of it. An approved filtering mask should be worn when working on the brakes. DO NOT use petroleum based solvents to clean brake parts. Use brake cleaner or methylated spirit only. Read also the note at the beginning of Section 17 concerning the dangers of hydraulic fluid.*

1   Remove the rear wheel cylinder (Sec 21).

2   Disconnect the handbrake cable from the backplate, unbolting the

handbrake cable clips from the rear suspension torsion beam axle if necessary.

3   Unscrew the four bolts securing the stub axle and brake backplate to the torsion beam trailing arm, then withdraw the stub axle/hub assembly (Chapter 9, Section 11).

4   Withdraw the brake backplate.

5   Refitting is the reverse of the removal procedure. Refer to the relevant Sections of Chapter 9 as well as this Chapter for detailed instructions.

## 24   Handbrake lever – removal and refitting

1   Remove the centre console (Chapter 10).

2   Chock the front wheels, jack up the rear of the vehicle and support it on axle stands. Release the handbrake lever fully.

3   Slacken the handbrake adjustment (Sec 2) and disconnect the cables from the yoke. Peel back the rubber grommet from the body.

4   Unbolt the lever assembly from the floor (photo), then lift the lever into the passenger compartment until the adjuster rod can be disconnected by prising off the circlip and removing the pivot pin.

5   Refitting is the reverse of the removal procedure, but apply a smear of grease to all pivots, the yoke and cable end fittings and the adjuster threads. Adjust the handbrake (Sec 2).

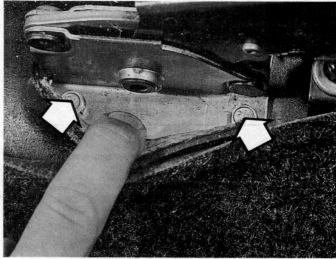

24.4 Peel back carpet to expose handbrake lever assembly mounting nuts (arrowed)

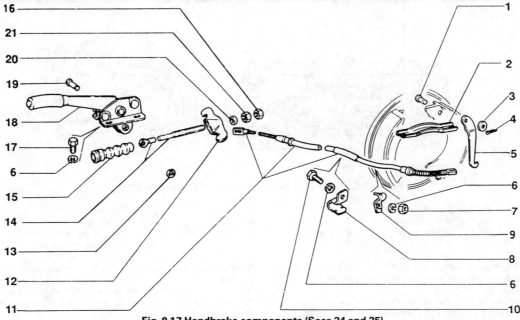

**Fig. 8.17 Handbrake components (Secs 24 and 25)**

| | | | | | | | |
|---|---|---|---|---|---|---|---|
| 1 | Pivot pin | 7 | Nut | 12 | Adjuster yoke | 17 | Bolt |
| 2 | Operating strut | 8 | Cable clip | 13 | Circlip | 18 | Handbrake lever |
| 3 | Spacer | 9 | Cable clip | 14 | Adjuster rod | | assembly |
| 4 | Split pin | 10 | Bolt | 15 | Rubber grommet | 19 | Pivot pin |
| 5 | Operating lever | 11 | Handbrake cable | 16 | Adjuster locknut | 20 | Washer |
| 6 | Spring washer | | | | | 21 | Adjusting nut |

## 25   Handbrake cables – removal and refitting

1   Remove the brake shoes and disconnect the cable from the brake backplate (Sec 20).
2   Unbolt the handbrake cable clips from the rear suspension torsion beam axle and from the underbody.
3   Slacken the handbrake adjustment (Sec 2) and disconnect the cables from the yoke. Withdraw the cable.
4   Check the cable for wear or damage and renew it if necessary.
5   Clean the adjuster threads thoroughly and apply a smear of grease to the yoke. Check and lubricate the operating linkage (Sec 20).
6   On refitting, connect the cable to the yoke and route the cable back along the underbody, clear of components such as the exhaust system and rear suspension. Refit the cable to the brake backplate, then secure the cable to the underbody and torsion beam axle using the clips provided.
7   Connect the cable end to the operating linkage and refit the brake shoes (Sec 20), then refit the brake drum (Sec 19).
8   Check the handbrake adjustment (Sec 2).

## 26   Brake system warning lamps – general

### Stop-lamp
1   The stop-lamp circuit is controlled by a plunger-type switch mounted on the brake pedal bracket (photo). Note that since the switch is permanently live, **always** disconnect the battery negative terminal before disconnecting the switch wires.
2   Check and adjust the switch setting as described in Section 2 of this Chapter.
3   If the switch is thought to be faulty it can be tested by disconnecting its wires (see note above) and connecting either a multimeter (set to the resistance function) or a battery and bulb test circuit across the switch terminals. The switch should allow current to flow only when it is extended. If the switch is faulty it must be renewed.

4   To remove the switch, disconnect its wires (see note above) and unscrew the securing nuts.
5   Refitting is the reverse of the removal procedure, but also adjust the switch setting (Sec 2).

### Handbrake warning lamp
6   The handbrake warning lamp is activated by a plunger switch mounted at the base of the lever (photo) and flashes whenever the handbrake is applied.
7   The switch is not adjustable and is secured by a single screw. To remove it, unscrew the screw and withdraw the switch until the rubber boot can be peeled back and the switch wire can be disconnected.
8   To test the switch, remove it and use the equipment described in

26.1 Stop-lamp switch is mounted on brake pedal bracket

26.6 Handbrake warning lamp switch is mounted at base of lever

paragraph 3 to check that current can flow between the switch's terminal and its body only when the plunger is extended. If the switch is faulty it must be renewed.

9    Refitting is the reverse of the removal procedure.

10    Note that the lamp's flashing is controlled by the unit plugged into the rear of the instrument panel (Chapter 11).

### Brake fluid level warning lamp

11    The brake fluid level warning lamp is operated by a float-type switch in the master cylinder reservoir filler cap, and lights whenever the fluid level falls to a dangerously low level.

12    The switch is a discrete assembly, only available with the master cylinder reservoir filler cap. If the switch is faulty the complete assembly must be renewed.

13    To test the switch, remove it and use the equipment described in paragraph 3 to check that current can flow between the switch's terminals only when the float is at the bottom of its travel.

## 27   Fault diagnosis – braking system

| Symptom | Reason(s) |
|---|---|
| Brake pedal feels spongy | Air in hydraulic system<br>Stiff brake pedal crossover linkage<br>Faulty master cylinder<br>Weak flexible hose(s) |
| Excessive pedal travel | Incorrect pedal adjustment<br>Faulty, sticking or seized brake caliper (front brakes)<br>Faulty wheel cylinder self-adjusting mechanism (rear brakes)<br>Faulty master cylinder<br>Air in hydraulic system<br>Primary or secondary circuit failure<br>Worn hub bearings (Chapter 9)<br>Distorted or worn brake disc or drum |
| Pedal sinks to floor during sustained application | Hydraulic fluid leak – check first the caliper/wheel cylinder piston seals<br>Master cylinder seals leaking |
| Excessive pedal pressure required to stop vehicle | Vacuum hose leaking or disconnected<br>Faulty non-return check valve<br>Faulty vacuum servo unit<br>Partially seized caliper or wheel cylinder<br>Seized or worn caliper guide pins<br>Brake pad or shoe friction material glazed, worn or contaminated, or (if recently renewed) of wrong grade<br>New brake pad or shoe friction material not yet bedded in<br>Primary or secondary circuit failure |
| Vehicle pulls to one side when brakes applied | Brake pad or shoe friction material contaminated with oil or grease (on opposite side)<br>Partially seized caliper or wheel cylinder (on opposite side)<br>Distorted or worn brake disc or drum<br>Faulty wheel cylinder self-adjusting mechanism (rear brakes)<br>Brakes overhauled on one side only<br>Tyre fault – incorrect types fitted, incorrect pressures or excessively worn on one side<br>Steering or suspension defect (Chapter 9) |
| Rear wheels lock when brakes applied | Pedal pressure greater than required<br>Adverse road conditions<br>Tyres incorrectly inflated or badly worn<br>Front brakes inefficient, or rear brakes grabbing<br>Faulty pressure regulator |

| Symptom | Reason(s) |
| --- | --- |
| Brakes grab | Brake pad or shoe friction material wet – apply brakes gently until they are dry |
|  | Brake pad or shoe friction material worn out |
|  | Distorted, cracked or worn brake disc or drum |
|  | Brake components loose |
|  | Worn hub bearings (Chapter 9) |
| Judder felt through brake pedal or steering wheel when brakes applied | Distorted, cracked or worn brake disc or drum, particularly at front |
|  | Hubs distorted or hub bearings worn (Chapter 9) |
|  | Brake pad or shoe friction material glazed, worn or contaminated |
|  | Worn brake caliper guide pins |
|  | Brake components loose |
|  | Steering or suspension defect (Chapter 9) |
| Squealing noise when brakes applied | Roadwheel wobble or vibration (Chapter 9) |
|  | Brake pad or shoe friction material glazed |
|  | Excessive brake dust in brake assembly |
|  | Foreign matter caught between brake pads and disc |
|  | Brake pad or shoe friction material (if recently renewed) of wrong grade |
| Brakes bind or drag | Stiff brake pedal crossover linkage |
|  | Vacuum servo unit pushrod incorrectly adjusted (Sec 5) |
|  | Partially seized caliper or wheel cylinder |
|  | Handbrake incorrectly adjusted |
|  | Seized handbrake cable or operating mechanism |
|  | Master cylinder reservoir filler cap breather hole blocked |
|  | Faulty master cylinder |
|  | Metal hydraulic pipe(s) crushed or blocked; flexible hose(s) kinked or twisted |
|  | Air in hydraulic system |

**Note**: *This Section is not intended to be an exhaustive guide to fault diagnosis but summarises the more common faults which may be encountered during a vehicle's life. Consult a dealer for more specific advice.*

# Chapter 9 Suspension and steering

## Contents

## Specifications

### Front suspension

Type ................................................................................................. Independent, with MacPherson struts and coil springs, anti-roll bar

### Rear suspension

Type ................................................................................................. Semi-independent, with torsion beam axle

## Steering
Type................................................................................................ Rack and pinion
Turns lock to lock............................................................................ 3.5
Steering wheel maximum free play.................................................. 5°
Steering gear lubricant:
    Type............................................................................................ Molybdenum disulphide grease (Duckhams LBM 10)
    Quantity...................................................................................... 20 to 30 g

## Wheel alignment and steering angles
*All measurements are with vehicle at kerb weight (see 'General dimensions, weights and capacities')*
Toe-out in turns .............................................................................. Inside roadwheel 23°, Outside roadwheel 20°
Camber angle ................................................................................. 0° to 0° 30' negative
Castor angle ................................................................................... 1° to 1° 30' positive
Steering axis inclination/SAI (also known as kingpin inclination/KPI) ....... 13° 4'
Toe setting ...................................................................................... 3 ± 1 mm (0.12 ± 0.04 in) toe-in

## Roadwheels
Type................................................................................................ Forged steel, four-bolt fastening
Size................................................................................................. 5½J x 13 (4J x 13 on some models)
Maximum run-out at rim:
    Radial ......................................................................................... 0.7 mm
    Axial........................................................................................... 1.0 mm

## Tyres
Type................................................................................................ Tubed or tubeless steel-braced radial
Size................................................................................................. 165/70 SR 13 (165/70) R 13, 155/80 R 13 or I75/70 R 13 permissible)
Pressures (cold) – front and rear:
    155/80 R 13, 175/70 R 13.......................................................... 1.9 bar (28 psi)
    165/70 SR 13, 165/70 R 13 – normal load ................................ 2.0 bar (29 psi)
    165/70 SE 13, 165/70 R 13 – full load ...................................... 2.1 bar (30 psi)
**Note:***Pressures apply only to original equipment tyres and may vary if any other make or type is fitted. Check with the tyre manufacturer or supplier for correct pressures if necessary.*

## Torque wrench settings

| | Nm | lbf ft |
|---|---|---|
| *Front suspension* | | |
| Strut top mounting nuts | 19.5 to 24 | 14.5 to 18 |
| Strut piston rod nut | 66 to 81 | 48.5 to 60 |
| Strut-to-hub carrier clamp bolt nuts | 77.5 to 96 | 57 to 71 |
| Lower arm balljoint retaining nut | 77.5 to 96 | 57 to 71 |
| Lower arm balljoint mounting bolts | 49 to 61.5 | 36 to 45.5 |
| Lower arm pivot bolt nut | 77.5 to 96 | 57 to 71 |
| Tie-bar front and rear nuts | 160 to 176.5 | 118 to 130 |
| Tie-bar front bracket-to-body bolts | 42 to 52 | 31 to 38 |
| Anti-roll bar-to-body mounting nuts | 13 to 16 | 9.5 to 12 |
| Anti-roll bar link-to-lower arm bolt retaining nut | 42 to 52 | 31 to 38 |
| | | |
| *Rear suspension* | | |
| Suspension unit top mounting nut | 50 to 61.5 | 37 to 45.5 |
| Suspension unit bottom mounting bolt retaining nut | 74.5 to 96 | 55 to 71 |
| Torsion beam axle pivot bracket retaining nuts | 31.5 to 39 | 23 to 29 |
| Torsion beam axle pivot bolt nut | 66.5 to 82.5 | 49 to 61 |
| Stub axle/brake backplate-to-torsion beam trailing arm bolts | 34.5 to 42.5 | 25 to 31 |
| Stub axle nut | 198 to 242 | 146 to 178.5 |
| | | |
| *Steering* | | |
| Steering wheel nut | 31.5 to 51 | 23 to 37.5 |
| Steering column mounting nuts | 15 to 18.5 | 11 to 13.5 |
| Steering column mounting bolts | Tighten until heads shear off | |
| Steering column lower joint pinch-bolt | 18 | 13 |
| Steering gear mounting nuts | 15 to 18.5 | 11 to 13.5 |
| Steering gear pinion nut | 45 to 55 | 33 to 40.5 |
| Track rod-to-steering gear bolts | 69 to 85 | 51 to 62.5 |
| Track rod threaded sleeve locknuts | 121 to 149.5 | 89 to 110 |
| Track rod balljoint retaining nut: | | |
|   1st stage | 27 to 33.5 | 20 to 24.5 |
|   2nd stage (if required) | Tighten (through no more than 60°) until split pin can be inserted | |
| | | |
| *Roadwheels* | | |
| Mounting bolts | 58.5 to 72 | 43 to 53 |

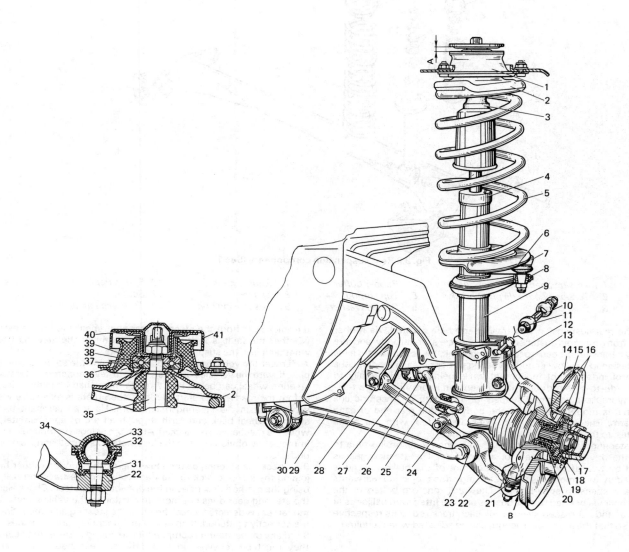

**Fig. 9.1 Front suspension components (Sec 1)**

| | | | |
|---|---|---|---|
| 1 | Strut top mounting | 12 | Strut bracket |
| 2 | Spring upper seat | 13 | Hub carrier |
| 3 | Rubber buffer and dust cover | 14 | Brake disc shield |
| 4 | Buffer seat | 15 | Brake disc |
| 5 | Spring | 16 | Retaining circlips |
| 6 | Spring lower seat | 17 | Dust cap |
| 7 | Track rod balljoint | 18 | Driveshaft |
| 8 | Strut steering arm | 19 | Brake disc retaining |
| 9 | Suspension strut | | screw/roadwheel guide pin |
| 10 | Eccentric washer | 20 | Hub bearing |
| 11 | Strut-to-hub carrier clamp bolt | 21 | Lower arm balljoint |

| | | | |
|---|---|---|---|
| 22 | Suspension lower arm | 31 | Lower arm balljoint rubber |
| 23 | Castor adjusting shim | | dust cover |
| 24 | Anti-roll bar connecting link | 32 | Balljoint bearing |
| 25 | Anti-roll bar | 33 | Balljoint tapered stud |
| 26 | Anti-roll bar mounting rubber | 34 | Balljoint body |
| | bushes | 35 | Strut piston rod |
| 27 | Anti-roll bar mounting clamp | 36 | Top mounting outer case |
| 28 | Suspension lower arm inboard | 37 | Top mounting inner case |
| | mounting | 38 | Top mounting ball-bearing |
| 29 | Tie-bar | 39 | Top mounting rubber |
| 30 | Tie-bar front mounting clamp | 40 | Strut top cap |

## 1    General description

The front suspension is fully independent, using MacPherson struts, and the rear suspension is semi-independent, using a torsion beam axle. Steering is by rack-and-pinion.

On the front suspension the roadwheel hub carriers are clamped to the bottom of each strut and are located transversely, via a balljoint, by the suspension lower arms. The lower arms pivot on rubber bushes and are located in the fore-and-aft direction by tie bars which have rubber bushes at each end. An anti-roll bar is fastened to the body via rubber bushes and joined to both suspension lower arms by connecting links.

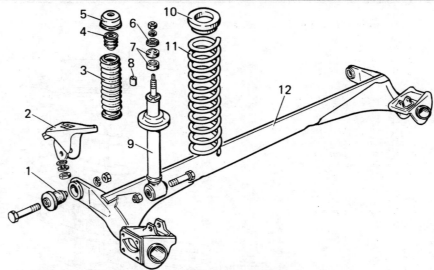

**Fig. 9.2 Rear suspension components (Sec 1)**

| | | | |
|---|---|---|---|
| 1 | Torsion beam axle pivot bush | 4 | Rubber buffer | 7 | Rubber pads | 10 | Spring upper seat |
| 2 | Torsion beam axle pivot bracket | 5 | Top shroud | 8 | Spacer | 11 | Spring |
| 3 | Dust cover | 6 | Dished washer | 9 | Suspension unit | 12 | Torsion beam axle |

On the rear suspension two trailing arms are pivoted, via rubber bushes, from brackets fastened to the vehicle's underbody and are linked by a transverse beam to form a single unit, the torsion beam axle. This is designed to allow enough twisting to permit each roadwheel a measure of independent movement while being braced laterally to prevent side-to-side movement. Suspension is provided by a telescopic, hydraulically-damped suspension unit with a concentric coil spring that is mounted between the body and the rear end of each trailing arm. The roadwheel stub axles are bolted, with the brake backplates, to the rear ends of the trailing arms.

The steering wheel is of the collapsible, energy-absorbing type to protect the driver in the event of an accident. The steering gear is clamped by two rubber bushes to the front of the bulkhead and is connected by two track rods to the steering arms projecting rearwards from the suspension strut bodies. The track rods are bolted to the steering gear via bonded rubber bushes and are fitted with balljoints at their outer ends; threaded sleeves link each track rod to its respective balljoint so that the assembly's length can be adjusted when required.

## 2  Routine maintenance

1    Carry out the following procedures at the intervals given in 'Routine maintenance' at the beginning of this manual.

### Check the steering gear and linkage

2    Apply the handbrake, jack up the front of the vehicle and support it securely on axle stands.
3    Visually inspect the steering gear rubber gaiter and the rubber dust covers over the track rod balljoints. Renew any component showing signs of grease leakage, wear or damage, referring to the relevant Sections of this Chapter for details.
4    Check that the steering column lower joint pinch-bolt is tight and ensure that the joint is correctly positioned on the steering gear pinion shaft. If necessary unscrew the bolt, reposition the joint so that the pinch-bolt bore is aligned exactly with the pinion shaft groove, then refit the bolt and tighten it to the specified torque setting.
5    Check that the steering gear mount nuts, the track rod-to-steering gear bolts and the track rod balljoint retaining nuts are tight. Check also that the track rod bolts are correctly secured by their locking plate and that the balljoint retaining nut split pins are correctly fitted.
6    Ensure that the steering wheel spokes are horizontal when the roadwheels are in the straight-ahead position and check that the steering wheel and column are securely fastened. Check that there is no stiffness apparent, or undue noises to be heard, when the steering is moved from lock to lock. If the steering is stiff or awkward, disconnect

the track rods from the steering gear and repeat the test to establish whether the fault is in the steering column or the steering gear, or whether it is in the suspension components.
7    Lower the vehicle to the ground and check the steering wheel free play. If, with the vehicle parked on smooth, level concrete or tarmac, the steering wheel can be rotated through more than 5° (either direction) before the roadwheels start to move, then there is excessive wear at some point in the steering mechanism. Have an assistant turn the steering wheel back and forth through an arc of approximately 20° while the mechanism is checked. Any worn or loose components will be immediately obvious due to the lost motion as the steering is operated under load.
8    Check the steering column lower joint, the bonded rubber bushes joining the steering rack to the track rods and the track rod balljoints, using the method described in the previous paragraph. Check also that the steering gear does not move in relation to the vehicle body. If any movement is detected, check first that the steering gear mounting nuts are correctly tightened, then renew the mounting rubber bushes.
9    If any of the steering components are found to be worn or damaged they must be renewed immediately, as described in the relevant Sections of this Chapter.

### Check the suspension, roadwheels and tyres

10    With the vehicle standing on its wheels on level ground, bounce it at each corner to test the performance of the front suspension struts and of the rear suspension units. If each is working properly the body will return once to its normal position and stop after being depressed. If the body oscillates more than once, with signs of uncontrolled movement, the strut or unit is probably suspect and should be renewed, especially if the vehicle's handling has deteriorated.
11    While bouncing the vehicle listen carefully for any groans, squeaks, rattles or creaks from the suspension components which will require further investigation when the vehicle is jacked up.
12    Open the bonnet and remove the cap from the top of each front suspension strut. Load the vehicle with four passengers, or their equivalent weight (320 kg) then turn the steering wheel until the clearance ('A', Fig 9.1) is equal at all points between the stop and the rubber part of the top mounting. Measure the clearance; if it exceeds 10 mm at any point the mounting's rubber is weakened and the mounting must be renewed. Check the opposite side mounting in the same way, then refit the top caps.
13    Apply the handbrake, jack up the front of the vehicle and support it securely on axle stands.
14    Visually inspect all front suspension components, looking for obvious signs of wear, damage or loose mountings. Check the rubber dust covers over the suspension lower arm balljoints. If a cover is damaged, split or showing signs of grease leakage it must be renewed.

### Fig. 9.3 Steering components – LHD shown, RHD mirror-image (Sec 1)

| | | |
|---|---|---|
| 1   Track rod balljoint | 14   Rubber bush | 27   Steering column jacket tube |
| 2   Balljoint dust cover | 15   Rubber ring | 28   Housing end cap |
| 3   Suspension strut steering | 16   Rack supporting bush | 29   Pinion roller bearing |
|      arm | 17   Rack | 30   Pinion |
| 4   Locknuts | 18   Steering gear housing | 31   Pinion ball-bearing |
| 5   Threaded sleeve | 19   Steering column lower joint | 32   Lockring |
| 6   Track rod |        pinch-bolt | 33   Protective washer |
| 7   Track rod-to-steering gear | 20   Steering column lower joint | 34   Sealing ring |
|      bolts | 21   Steering column top cover | 35   Pinion nut |
| 8   Track rod | 22   Steering wheel collapsible | 36   Lockwasher |
| 9   Steering gear mounting |        section | 37   Sealing ring |
|      clamp | 23   Steering wheel | 38   Lockring |
| 10   Rubber bush | 24   Ball-bearing | 39   Slipper |
| 11   Rubber gaiter | 25   Steering column | |
| 12   Connecting plate | 26   Steering column bottom | |
| 13   Lockplate |        cover | |

| | |
|---|---|
| 40   Coil spring | A   Pinion dust guard |
| 41   Slipper adjuster |       projection |
| 42   Balljoint tapered stud | B   Steering gear housing |
| 43   Balljoint dust cover |       raised mark |
| 44   Balljoint bearing | |

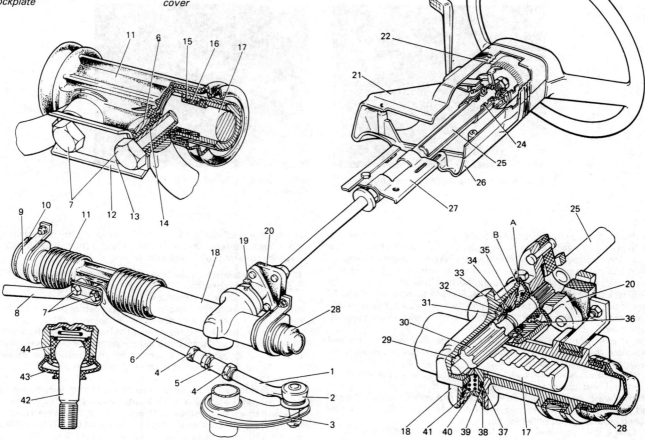

15   Check each suspension strut for signs of oil leaks or other damage, and renew them if necessary.

16   Grasp each roadwheel at the 12 o'clock and 6 o'clock positions and try to rock it. If any free play is evident, check the tightness of the roadwheel bolts first, then the driveshaft nut (Chapter 7). If these are correctly fastened, repeat the check with an assistant applying firm pressure to the brake pedal. If the movement is eliminated or significantly reduced it is likely that the hub bearing is worn, but if not, then there is wear in one or more of the suspension components, especially the suspension lower arm balljoint.

17   Spin each roadwheel by hand and listen carefully. If the wheel rotates smoothly and easily with no signs of noise and if it slows down and stops with no signs of jerkiness the hub bearing is in good order. If there is any doubt about its condition, it must be renewed (Sec 4).

**Note:** If either bearing is found to have free play present, **do not** overtighten the driveshaft nut beyond the specified torque in an attempt to 'adjust' the bearing.

18   Using a large screwdriver or a flat bar, check for wear in the suspension bushes and mounting points by carefully levering against them to check for free play. Note that some free play is to be expected even from new rubber bushes, but excessive wear should be obvious. If free play is found, first check the tightness of the mounting nuts or bolts, using a torque wrench, then renew any worn components as described in the relevant Sections of this Chapter.

19   Also check the strut top and bottom mountings, the lower arm and tie-bar bushes and mountings, the anti-roll bar mountings and connecting links and the suspension lower arm balljoint, using the method described in the previous paragraph. When checking the balljoint, if the clearance ('B', Fig 9.1) between the end of the suspension lower arm and the brake disc shield varies by more than 0.8 mm as a result of rocking the suspension, then the balljoint is excessively worn and must be renewed.

20   Lower the vehicle to the ground and select first or reverse gear. Chock the front wheels, jack up the rear of the vehicle and support it on

3.2 Unclip the brake flexible hose from the suspension strut bracket

3.3A Mark positions of eccentric washer on hub carrier (arrowed) ...

3.3B ... before removing hub carrier assembly

3.6A Grease clamp bolts before refitting ...

3.6B ... ensure washer cut-out locates correctly on upper clamp bolt

axle stands. Release the handbrake for the rear hub bearing checks.

21   Working as described in paragraphs 14, 15 and 18 above, check the condition and security of all rear suspension components. Check the torsion beam axle pivot bracket mountings and the pivot bushes, and also the suspension unit mountings and bottom bushes.

22   Check the rear hub bearings as described in paragraphs 16 and 17 above. If any free play is detected, check the tightness of the stub axle nut and of the stub axle/brake backplate mounting bolts before suspecting the bearing itself.

**Note:** *If either bearing is found to have free play present,* **do not** *overtighten the stub axle nut beyond the specified torque setting in an attempt to 'adjust' the bearing.*

23   When the suspension checks are complete, lower the vehicle to the ground and check the tyre tread wear. If there is any sign of abnormal wear, or if the vehicle's steering and handling have deteriorated in any way, the wheel alignment and steering angles should be checked as soon as possible (Sec 25).

24   Check the roadwheels themselves, referring to Section 26 for further details. Check for obvious signs of cracks, wear or damage, particularly around the bolt holes and the rims. Check that the roadwheel bolts are securely fastened to the specified torque setting. Check that the balance weights are secure, and if any are missing or if the roadwheels are thought to be out of balance, have the wheels balanced as soon as possible.

25   With reference to Section 26 for further details, check all five tyres for signs of tread wear or damage. Ensure that a sound cap is fitted to each valve. If a tyre repeatedly loses pressure, do not forget to check that the valve is not leaking before suspecting a puncture. If any of the tyres require renewal, puncture repair or other professional attention ensure that this is done as soon as possible, in the interests of safety.

---

**3  Front hub carrier – removal and refitting**

**Note:** *The bolts securing the hub carrier to the suspension strut are also used to adjust the camber angle and should* **not** *be disturbed unless*

*absolutely necessary. If they must be disturbed, mark their exact positions before removal and return them to this position on refitting, then have the camber angle checked as soon as possible.*

1   Separate the hub carrier from the driveshaft as described in Chapter 7, Section 3, paragraphs 1 to 7.

2   With reference to Chapter 8, unscrew the two bolts securing the brake caliper mounting bracket to the hub carrier and unclip the brake flexible hose from the suspension strut bracket (photo), then withdraw the caliper assembly and secure it out of harm's way without stretching or kinking the brake hose. Place a clean spacer (of the same thickness as the brake disc) between the pads to prevent them being dislodged. If the hub carrier is to be dismantled, the brake disc should now be removed.

3   Each hub carrier is clamped to its respective suspension strut by two bolts, the upper of which is located by an eccentric washer at each end to permit the adjustment of the camber angle. Using a hammer and pin punch, white paint or similar, mark the relationship of both eccentric washers to the strut bracket. Unscrew the retaining nuts, tap out the bolts and remove the hub carrier from the vehicle (photos).

4   Remove and refit the brake disc shield and hub bearing, if required (Sec 4).

5   On refitting, clean and grease the strut-to-hub carrier clamp bolts, then clean the mating surfaces of the hub carrier and strut.

6   Offer up the hub carrier to the strut, refit both bolts from front to rear, then refit and lightly tighten the lower bolt's retaining nut. Ensuring that its shaped cut-out engages correctly on the bolt's shank, refit the eccentric washer to the upper bolt, then refit and lightly tighten the retaining nut (photos).

7   Rotate the upper bolt until the marks that were made on removal are aligned. While this should restore the camber angle to its previous setting, it is essential that the angle is checked properly as soon as possible (Sec 25). Remember to tighten the two retaining nuts to the specified torque setting, as soon as adjustment is complete, or before the vehicle is driven to have the adjustment carried out.

8   Refit the brake disc and caliper (Chapter 8).

9   Reassemble the front suspension as described in Chapter 7, Section 3, paragraphs 16 to 19. Tighten all nuts and bolts to the specified torque

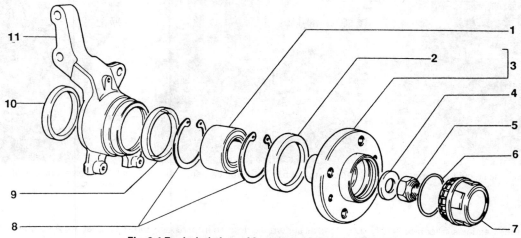

**Fig. 9.4 Exploded view of front hub and bearing (Sec 4)**

| | | | | | | | |
|---|---|---|---|---|---|---|---|
| 1 | Bearing | 4 | Washer | 7 | Dust cap | 10 | Driveshaft dust shield |
| 2 | Outboard grease seal | 5 | Driveshaft nut | 8 | Retaining circlips | 11 | Hub carrier |
| 3 | Hub | 6 | Sealing ring | 9 | Inboard grease seal | | |

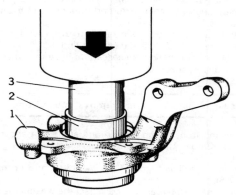

**Fig. 9.5 Pressing bearing into hub carrier (Sec 4)**

| | | | |
|---|---|---|---|
| 1 | Hub carrier | 3 | Mandrel |
| 2 | Bearing | | |

settings (when given) and do not forget to have the camber angle
checked as soon as possible.

## 4   Front hub and bearing – removal and refitting

**Note:** *The bearing is sealed, of the (non-adjustable) double-row ball
journal type and is intended to last the vehicle's entire service life without
maintenance or attention.* **Do not** *attempt to remove the bearing unless
absolutely necessary, as it probably will be damaged during the removal
operation.*

*The bearing's inner race is an interference fit on the hub, so a press will
be required to dismantle and rebuild the assembly. If a press is not
available, a large bench vice and suitable spacers will serve as an
adequate substitute.*

1   Remove the hub carrier from the vehicle (Sec 3).
2   The brake disc shield can be removed if required. It is secured to the
carrier by three bolts (photo).
3   Press the hub out of the hub carrier assembly (photo). If the
bearing's outboard inner race remains on the hub, use a proprietary
general-purpose bearing puller to remove it. Two special hollows are
provided in the hub for·this purpose.
4   Noting which way round each is fitted, carefully prise the driveshaft
dust shield and the inboard and outboard grease seals out of the hub
carrier.

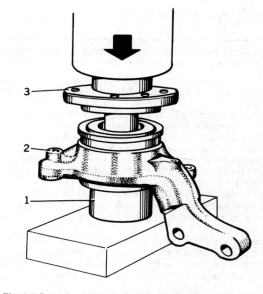

**Fig. 9.6 Pressing hub into bearing/hub carrier (Sec 4)**

| | | | |
|---|---|---|---|
| 1 | Bearing inner race support | 3 | Hub |
| 2 | Hub carrier | | |

5   Extract the two retaining circlips from the hub carrier and press out
the bearing.
6   Thoroughly clean the bearing, the hub carrier and the hub. Check all
components for signs of wear or damage and renew them if necessary.
Check with particular care the roadwheel bolt threads. The bearing
should be renewed as a matter of course whenever it is disturbed (see
the note at the beginning of this Section), but if it appears fit for further
service it can be examined as follows. Check that it rotates smoothly
and easily, with no signs of noise or roughness. If the races and balls can
be seen, check them for signs of scoring, pitting or flaking.
7   Renew the grease seals as a matter of course whenever they are
disturbed and check that the circlips are fit for re-use.
8   On reassembly, check (as far as possible) that the bearing is packed
with grease, refit the first circlip to the hub carrier outboard groove then
press in the bearing as shown in Fig. 9.5, until it seats against the circlip.
Ensure that pressure is applied only to the bearing's outer race or the
bearing may be damaged.
9   Refit the second circlip to the hub carrier inboard groove, then apply
a thin smear of grease to the lips of the new grease seals, and install the
seals (photo), ensuring that they are fitted the correct way round.

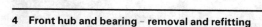

4.2 Removing brake disc shield from hub carrier

4.3 Pressing out hub from hub carrier

4.9 Ensure second circlip and grease seal are located as shown

10   Ensuring that the bearing's inner race is fully supported as shown in Fig. 9.6, press the hub into the hub carrier. Temporarily refit the hub carrier to the driveshaft, tighten the driveshaft nut to the specified torque setting and check that the bearing rotates smoothly and easily, with no trace of free play.
11   Refit the driveshaft dust shield and the brake disc shield, if renewed.
12   Refit the hub carrier (Sec 3).

## 5   Front suspension lower arm balljoint – removal and refitting

1   Jack up the front of the vehicle and support it securely on axle stands, then remove the roadwheel (see *'Jacking, towing and wheel changing'*).
2   At the bottom of the hub carrier, unscrew the two bolts to separate the hub carrier from the suspension lower arm balljoint.
3   Either pull the hub carrier (complete with the strut, the driveshaft and the brake caliper) away from the suspension lower arm to secure it, or disconnect the anti-roll bar from the lower arm (Sec 8) and slacken the lower arm (pivot bolt) and tie-bar (front and rear nuts) so that the arm and bar can be lowered clear of the hub carrier.
4   Slacken the balljoint retaining nut and unscrew it until it is flush with the end of the stud thread, then use a universal balljoint separator tool (if necessary) to remove the balljoint from the suspension lower arm (photo).
5   Renew the balljoint if its movement is sloppy (more than 0.7 mm free play) or if it is too stiff. Slight grease leakage is permissible from the circular slot in the top of the balljoint body but none should be evident from the rubber dust cover. The dust cover can be renewed separately if

it is split, perished, torn or damaged. Also check the stud taper and threads for damage.
6   On reassembly, degrease the tapers of the balljoint stud and of the lower arm, then pack the balljoint with the specified grease and refit its cover and plate before pressing the assembly into the lower arm. Refit and tighten the retaining nut.
7   Reassemble the front suspension and tighten the balljoint mounting bolts (photo), and any other disturbed nuts or bolts to the specified torque settings.
8   Refit the roadwheel, lower the vehicle to the ground and tighten the roadwheel bolts to the specified torque setting.
9   Remember that it may be necessary to have the wheel alignment and steering angles checked.

## 6   Front suspension lower arm – removal and refitting

1   Jack up the front of the vehicle and support it securely on axle stands, then remove the roadwheel (see *'Jacking, towing and wheel changing'*).
2   Separate the balljoint either from the lower arm or from the hub carrier (Sec 5).
3   Unscrew the tie-bar rear nut and collect the washer (Sec 7).
4   Unbolt the anti-roll bar connecting link from the lower arm.
5   Unscrew the lower arm pivot bolt nut and remove the bolt (photo). Withdraw the arm from its pivot and pull it off the tie-bar. Do not lose any washers or shims from the tie-bar.
6   Thoroughly clean the arm and the underbody areas around its mountings, removing all traces of dirt, and of underseal if necessary, then check it carefully for cracks, distortion or any other signs of wear or

5.4 Using balljoint separator tool to remove lower arm balljoint

5.7 Be careful not to damage rubber dust cover when tightening balljoint mounting bolts

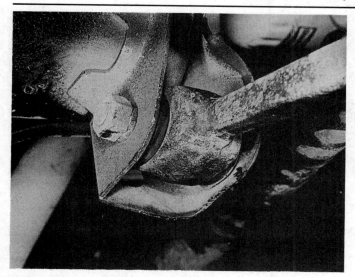

6.5 Suspension lower arm inboard mounting

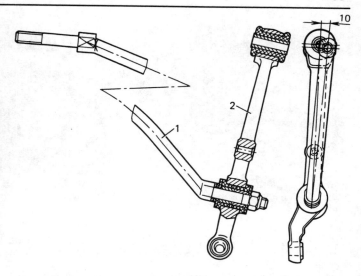

Fig. 9.7 Aligning lower arm and tie-bar before refitting (Sec 7)

1   Tie-bar   2   Lower arm

damage. Do not forget to check the pivot bolt and nut. Renew any worn or damaged component.

7   Check the pivot and tie-bar bushes and renew them if they are cracked, worn, split or perished. Both must be removed and refitted using a press, although it may be possible to achieve the required result using a strong bench vice and sockets or pieces of tubing. Soak the old bush in penetrating fluid before attempting removal and use liquid soap or petroleum jelly as a lubricant on pressing in the new bush. Ensure that new bushes are located symmetrically and note that the manufacturer recommends that newly fitted bushes should be left to settle for 24 hours before being installed on the vehicle.

8   Refitting is the reverse of the removal procedure, noting the following points.

9   If the lower arm and tie-bar have both been removed and are to be refitted together, refer to Section 7, paragraph 12 to ensure that they are aligned correctly relative to each other before being refitted.

10   All other fasteners should be tightened only lightly at first until the suspension is reassembled and the vehicle is lowered to the ground. When all the vehicle's weight is back on its wheels, rock it to settle the suspension and load it with four people (or the equivalent weight, 320 kg) plus 40 kg in the luggage compartment, then tighten all disturbed nuts and bolts to the specified torque wrench settings.

11   It will be necessary to have the wheel alignment and steering angles checked (Sec 25) on completion.

## 7   Front suspension tie-bar – removal and refitting

1   If the vehicle is to be raised for the tie-bar to be removed, ensure that it is supported securely on axle stands before starting work (see 'Jacking, towing and wheel changing').

2   Unscrew the tie-bar front and rear nuts and collect the washers.

3   Unbolt the tie-bar front mounting bracket from the body and pull the bracket off the bar, noting the washer behind it as well as any adjusting shims. Note carefully the number of shims and their fitted direction.

4   Withdraw the tie-bar from the lower arm, again noting the presence of a washer as well as any shims (photos).

5   Thoroughly clean the bar and the underbody areas around its mountings, removing all traces of dirt, and of underseal if necessary, then check it carefully for cracks, distortion or any other signs of wear or damage. Do not forget to check the bracket, the bolts and the nuts. Renew any worn or damaged component.

6   Check the rubber bushes and renew them if they are cracked, worn, split or perished (photo). Both must be removed and refitted using a press, although it may be possible to achieve the required result using a strong bench vice and sockets or pieces of tubing. Soak the old bush in penetrating fluid before attempting removal and use liquid soap or petroleum jelly as a lubricant on pressing in the new bush. The front bracket bushes must be installed so that the larger-diameter shoulder (which has a marked end face for easy identification) will face forwards when the bracket is refitted to the vehicle. Ensure that new bushes are located symmetrically and note that the manufacturer recommends that newly fitted bushes should be left to settle for 24 hours before being installed on the vehicle.

7   Refitting is the reverse of the removal procedure, noting the following points.

8   Each adjusting shim and large washer has a chamfer on one inner edge which must face away from the rubber bush, towards the tie-bar's centre section.

9   When refitting the bar to the lower arm, ensure that the adjusting

7.4A When removing tie-bar, note washers at rear ...

7.4B ... and front of mountings, also any shims

7.6 Tie-bar rear mounting rubber bush

7.10A When reassembling tie-bar front mounting, do not forget shim(s) and washer ...

7.10B ... refit front washer and tighten nut loosely ...

7.10C ... then refit to body and tighten bolts and nuts

shims and washer are correctly positioned (see above), then tighten the rear nut lightly, using an adjustable spanner to prevent the bar from rotating.

10    When refitting the bracket to the bar's front end, again ensure that the shims and washer are correctly positioned, then offer up the bracket to the body and carefully (so as not to damage the threads in the body captive nuts) refit the three bolts. Tighten the bolts to the specified torque wrench setting, refit the front nut and washer and tighten them lightly (photos).

11    Lower the vehicle to the ground if necessary. When all the vehicle's weight is back on its wheels, rock it to settle the suspension and load it with four people (or the equivalent weight, 320 kg) plus 40 kg in the luggage compartment, then rotate the tie-bar until it is aligned correctly. It should be square to its mountings, so that neither bush is twisted, and almost parallel to the ground. When it is correct, use an adjustable spanner to hold the tie-bar, and tighten the front and rear nuts to the specified torque setting.

12    If the lower arm and tie-bar have both been removed and are to be refitted together, they must be aligned correctly relative to each other before being refitted. Clamp the lower arm in a vice and refit the tie-bar rear end (see para 9 above), tightening the rear nut lightly. Rotate the tie-bar in the bush until its front end is offset from the lower arm's pivot centre by 10 mm (see Fig. 9.7). Use an adjustable spanner to prevent the bar from rotating and tighten the rear nut to its specified torque setting. Remove the assembly from the vice, refit the bracket to the tie-bar front end (ensuring that the shims and washer are correctly positioned), then refit the assembly to the vehicle and tighten all remaining fasteners to the specified torque settings when the suspension is fully loaded, as described above.

13    It will be necessary to have the wheel alignment and steering angles checked on completion (Sec 25).

## 8   Front suspension anti-roll bar – removal and refitting

1    Jack up the front of the vehicle and support it securely on axle stands (see '*Jacking, towing and wheel changing*').

2    Unbolt both anti-roll bar connecting links from the suspension lower arms and pull the links off each bar end (photo).

3    Unbolt both clamps from the body (photo) and manoeuvre the bar from above the exhaust system until it can be withdrawn from the vehicle.

4    Thoroughly clean all components and the underbody areas around the mountings, removing all traces of dirt, and of underseal if necessary, and check the components for signs of wear or damage – renew if necessary.

5    Check the rubber bushes and renew them if they are cracked, worn, split or perished. The connecting link bushes must be removed and refitted using a press, although it may be possible to achieve the required result using a strong bench vice and sockets or pieces of tubing. Soak the old bush in penetrating fluid before attempting removal and use liquid soap or petroleum jelly as a lubricant on pressing in the new bush. The clamp bushes, if disturbed, must be refitted 350 mm each side of the bar's centre point, with the split to the front.

6    On refitting, manoeuvre the bar into place and reassemble the connecting links, then align the clamp bushes with the body mounting studs before refitting the clamps.

7    With the clamp nuts and link bolts lightly fastened, check that the anti-roll bar is correctly installed and centred on the body without distorting the clamp bushes.

8    Lower the vehicle to the ground. When all the vehicle's weight is back on its wheels, rock it to settle the suspension and load it with four people (or the equivalent weight, 320 kg) plus 40 kg in the luggage compartment, then tighten the nuts and bolts as follows.

8.2 Anti-roll bar-to-lower arm connecting link

8.3 Anti-roll bar mounting clamp on underbody

9.4A Remove the strut top cap, unscrew the strut top mounting nuts ...

9.4B ... and withdraw the suspension strut

9.9 Tighten fasteners to torque wrench settings specified

9   Using the specified torque wrench settings, tighten first the clamp front nuts (next to the bush split), followed by the rear nuts, ensuring that the bush splits are fully closed but that the bushes are not distorted when the clamps are secured.
10   Finally, tighten the link bolts to the specified torque wrench setting.

## 9   Front suspension strut – removal and refitting

**Note:** *The bolts securing the hub carrier to the suspension strut are also used to adjust the camber angle and should **not** be disturbed unless absolutely necessary. If they must be disturbed, mark their exact positions before removal and return them to this position on refitting, then have the camber angle checked as soon as possible.*

1   Separate the hub carrier from the driveshaft as described in Chapter 7, Section 3, paragraphs 1 to 7.
2   With reference to Chapter 8, unscrew the two bolts securing the brake caliper mounting bracket to the hub carrier and unclip the brake flexible hose from the suspension strut bracket, then withdraw the caliper assembly and secure it out of harm's way without stretching or kinking the brake hose. Place a clean spacer (of the same thickness as the brake disc) between the pads to prevent them being dislodged.
3   Disconnect the track rod balljoint from the strut (Sec 24).
4   Remove the strut top cap, unscrew the three suspension strut top mounting nuts and withdraw the strut, complete with the hub carrier, from under the front wing (photos).
5   Do not separate the strut and hub carrier unless necessary (see the note above).
6   On refitting, thoroughly clean the underwing area and all mounting points.
7   Offer up the strut/hub carrier assembly and refit the top mounting nuts and washers.
8   Connect the track rod balljoint to the strut (Sec 24) and refit the brake caliper to the hub carrier (Chapter 8).
9   Reassemble the front suspension as described in Chapter 7, Section 3, paragraphs 16 to 19. Tighten all nuts and bolts to the specified torque settings, when given (photo).
10   Remember that it may be necessary to have the wheel alignment and steering angles checked on completion.

## 10   Front suspension strut – overhaul

**Warning:** *Before attempting to dismantle the suspension strut, a suitable tool must be obtained to hold the coil spring safely in compression. Adjustable coil spring compressors are readily available and are recommended for this operation. Any attempt to dismantle the strut without such a tool is likely to result in damage or personal injury. **Do not** attempt to undo the piston rod nut with the strut in place on the vehicle.*

1   Remove the suspension strut and spring from the vehicle (Sec 9) and thoroughly clean the assembly.

2   The hub carrier can be removed and refitted, if required, as described in Section 3.
3   Note that the suspension strut piston rod nut is difficult to remove and refit without special tools. After reading the procedure given below, owners may prefer to have the strut overhauled by a Lada dealer.
4   Using Lada service tool 67.7812.9535 to prevent the piston rod from rotating, **slacken**, but **do not** unscrew, the piston rod nut using Lada service tool 67.7812.9533 (Churchill Tools numbers A-677812-9533/1 and A-677812-9533/2 respectively). If these tools are not available, the holding tool can be fabricated from scrap metal to produce a T-handled instrument that fits closely over the piston rod upper end. The spanner can be fabricated by cutting up a 22 mm box spanner and welding a handle (at least 1 ft long) to it.
5   Fit spring compressors (available from most motor accessory shops) to each side of the spring and tighten them evenly to compress the spring until there is no pressure on the spring upper seat or the strut top mounting.
6   Unscrew the piston rod nut and remove the compression stroke stop, the top mounting, the spring upper seat, the rubber buffer, the dust cover and the spring (photos).
7   Visually inspect all components of the strut and renew any that are showing obvious signs of wear or damage. Check particularly the top mounting components, looking for cracks, distortion or deterioration of the rubber itself.
8   Check the top mounting's ball-bearing, which should rotate smoothly and easily with no signs of free play. If it shows signs of stiffness, corrosion or free play the bearing must be renewed. Note that

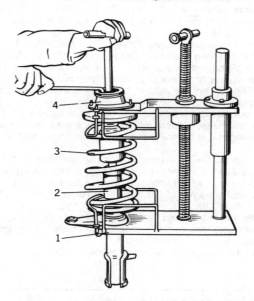

**Fig. 9.8 Unscrewing strut piston rod nut (Sec 10)**

| | |
|---|---|
| *1   Coil spring compressor* | *3   Spring* |
| *2   Strut* | *4   Strut top mounting* |

10.6A Unscrew piston rod nut and remove compression stroke stop ...

10.6B ... withdraw top mounting and spring upper seat ...

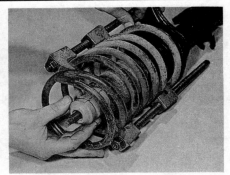

10.6C ... followed by rubber buffer, dust cover and spring

the mounting's inner sleeve is clenched over in four places to retain the bearing. Once this has been tapped back the bearing can be driven out using a hammer and punch or a press, provided that the inner sleeve is securely supported. The new bearing can be installed using either a press or a strong bench vice and a socket or piece of tubing which bears only on the bearing's outer race. When the bearing is securely seated, use a hammer and punch to clench over the inner sleeve at four points different from those previously used. Check that the bearing is securely fixed, with no free play evident.

9   If any of the top mounting studs require renewal, ensure that the mounting plate is securely supported so that it does not distort as the stud is tapped in or out; a suitable socket (photo) is ideal.

10   If the spring is obviously broken or damaged it must of course be renewed, but if it is thought to have sagged, seek the advice of a Lada dealer. Most UK-specification Samara models are fitted with shortened springs, so a suspect spring can be checked only (in the absence of sufficient accurate information) by direct comparison with a new spring of the correct type. Note that if either of the front springs requires renewal, it is good practice to renew both together as a matched pair. Ensure that the spring colour code (painted on the outside of the middle coils) is the same on both front struts and matches that on the rear suspension.

11   Check the strut's damping action by mounting it upright in a vice and moving the piston rod fully up and down. Firm, even resistance should be felt in both directions. If the damping is weak, if the strut shows signs of oil leaks at any point or if the piston rod is bent, scored or damaged the complete suspension strut must be renewed, as individual components are not available to permit repairs. Note that if either of the front struts requires renewal, it is good practice to renew both together as a matched pair.

12   Always store suspension struts in an upright position. If a strut is to be fitted after a long period of storage, mount it upright in a vice and move the piston rod fully up and down several times to prime the damper passages and restore full damping action.

13   Refitting is the reverse of the removal procedure, noting the following points.

14   Pull out the piston rod to its full extent and ensure that the spring is correctly compressed before refitting it. Locate the upper seat on the spring correctly and ensure that the top mounting is refitted the right way up.

15   To tighten the piston rod nut to the specified torque wrench setting use a spring balance or similar to apply a measured force to the spanner handle at a corresponding distance from the nut's centre (for example, applying a pull of 48.5 to 60 lb at a distance of 1 ft is the same as 24 to 30 lb at 2 ft).

16   When the nut is correctly tightened, slacken the spring compressors evenly until they can be disengaged from the spring, then check that the top mounting is free to rotate.

17   Refit the strut assembly to the vehicle (Sec 9).

---

**11   Rear stub axle – removal and refitting**

**Note:** If the rear hub is to be dismantled, the stub axle nut will be easier to slacken when all the vehicle's weight is on the ground (Sec 12).

10.9 Renewing strut top mounting stud

1   Jack up the rear of the vehicle and support it securely on axle stands, then remove the roadwheel (see 'Jacking, towing and wheel changing').

2   Remove the brake drum (Chapter 8). The handbrake cables and brake hydraulic pipes need not be disturbed unless required.

3   Unscrew the four bolts securing the stub axle and brake backplate to the torsion beam trailing arm, then withdraw the stub axle/hub assembly.

4   Remove and refit the hub bearing, if required (Sec 12).

5   Refitting is the reverse of the removal procedure. Tighten the various nuts and bolts to the specified torque wrench settings. Refer to the relevant Sections of Chapter 8 to ensure that the rear brake components are correctly reassembled.

6   Remember, where necessary, to tighten the stub axle nut correctly and to stake it before refitting the hub dust cap (Sec 12).

---

**12   Rear hub and bearing – removal and refitting**

**Note:** The bearing is sealed, of the (non-adjustable) double-row ball journal type and is intended to last the vehicle's entire service life without maintenance or attention. **Do not** attempt to remove the bearing (or to remove the hub from the stub axle) unless absolutely necessary, as it will probably be damaged during the removal operation.
The bearing's outer race is an interference fit in the hub, so a press will be required to dismantle and rebuild the assembly. If a press is not available, a large bench vice and suitable spacers will serve as an adequate substitute.

1   Remove the roadwheel trim (where fitted) and prise off the hub dust

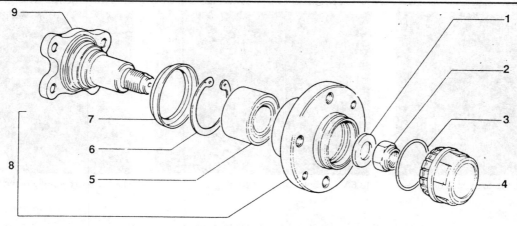

**Fig. 9.9 Exploded view of rear stub axle and bearing (Sec 12)**

| | | | |
|---|---|---|---|
| 1  *Washer* | 4  *Dust cap* | 6  *Retaining circlip* | 8  *Hub assembly* |
| 2  *Stub axle nut* | 5  *Bearing* | 7  *Dust shield* | 9  *Stub axle* |
| 3  *Sealing ring* | | | |

12.1 Hub dust cap can be prised off as shown

12.11A Tighten stub axle nut to specified torque setting ...

12.11B ... and stake into stub axle groove(s) to secure it

cap (photo). Relieve the staking of the stub axle nut using a hammer and punch or (if necessary) an electric drill, then use a suitable socket, a strong T- bar and a long extension tube to slacken the nut.

2    Remove the stub axle from the vehicle (Sec 11).

3    Unscrew the stub axle nut and withdraw the metal washer, then press the stub axle out of the hub. If the bearing's inboard inner race remains on the stub axle, use a proprietary general purpose bearing puller to remove it. Two special flats are provided on the axle for this purpose.

4    Extract the retaining circlip from the hub and press out the bearing.

5    Thoroughly clean the bearing, the stub axle and the hub. Check all components for signs of wear or damage and renew them if necessary. Check with particular care the roadwheel bolt threads. The bearing should be renewed as a matter of course whenever it is disturbed (see the note at the beginning of this Section), but if it appears fit for further service it can be examined as follows. Check that it rotates smoothly and easily, with no signs of noise or roughness. If the races and balls can be seen, check them, for signs of scoring, pitting or flaking.

6    Renew the dust shield if it is worn or damaged and check that the circlip is fit for re-use.

7    On reassembly, check (as far as possible) that the bearing is packed with grease, then press in the bearing until it seats against the hub shoulder. Ensure that pressure is applied only to the bearing's outer race or the bearing may be damaged.

8    Refit the circlip to the hub groove and, if necessary, refit the dust shield.

9    Ensuring that pressure is applied only to the bearing's inner race, press the hub on to the stub axle. Fit a new metal washer and stub axle nut. Owners are advised **always** to renew a stub axle nut whenever it is disturbed. Each nut is secured by being staked and the manufacturer specifies that it must be refitted so that the original staking point is **not**

re-used, even if this means fitting a new nut (which is good practice anyway, for such an important fastener) or one that has been used on another vehicle.

10    Refit the stub axle to the vehicle (Sec 11).

11    Refit the roadwheel, lower the vehicle to the ground and tighten the stub axle nut and roadwheel bolts to their specified torque settings. Using a hammer and punch, secure the stub axle by staking its collar into the stub axle groove(s) (photos). As noted above, ensure that the original staking point is **not** re-used (if the original nut is refitted).

12    Refit the hub dust cap and roadwheel trim (where fitted). Finally, check that the wheel rotates smoothly and easily, with no trace of free play.

---

**13    Rear suspension unit – removal and refitting**

**Warning:** *The rear suspension units consist of an hydraulic damper with a concentric coil spring. When the vehicle's weight is off the rear roadwheels the spring is secured only by the unit's top mounting nut. Once this is unscrewed, the spring could be released suddenly and cause serious damage or personal injury unless care is taken to follow precisely the instructions given below.*

1    Start with the vehicle parked on smooth, level ground, all its weight on its wheels. Select first or reverse gear and chock the front wheels.

13.2 Remove plastic cap to expose unit top mounting ...

13.6A ... unbolt bottom mounting ...

13.6B ... and carefully withdraw unit

2    Working inside the vehicle, remove the parcel shelf (where fitted) and prise up the plastic cap from the top of the suspension unit turret (photo).
3    Using Lada service tool A.57070 or a small open-ended spanner to prevent the piston rod from rotating (Churchill Tools numbers A-8335/1 and A-8335/2), unscrew only **one** suspension unit's top mounting nut. Withdraw the nut and its washer, followed by the larger dished washer and the rubber pad.
4    Jack up the rear of the vehicle evenly and support it securely on axle stands so that both roadwheels are clear of the ground (see *'Jacking, towing and wheel changing'*). Remove the roadwheel only if better access is required.
5    The rear suspension is now effectively 'hanging' on the remaining unfastened suspension unit, this being all that still restricts the coil spring. To avoid the risk of the suspension dropping suddenly and releasing the spring, **never** unscrew **both** rear suspension unit top mounting nuts at the same time. If both units are to be renewed, remove and refit them in succession, not at the same time.
6    Unbolt the suspension unit's bottom mounting and carefully withdraw the unit. The remaining spring pressure can be controlled by hand if a firm grip is applied (photos).
7    Refitting is the reverse of the removal procedure, noting the following points.
8    Pull out the piston rod to its fullest extent and ensure that all components are correctly installed on the unit before feeding the piston rod back into the top mounting. Rotate the unit until the highest point on the spring bottom seat is facing to the outside of the vehicle then refit the bottom mounting bolt and nut and lightly tighten them.
9    Lower the vehicle to the ground. When all the vehicle's weight is back on its wheels, refit the rubber pad, the dished washer and the top mounting nut and washer. Tighten the nut lightly. Rock the vehicle to settle the suspension and load it with four people (or the equivalent weight, 320 kg) plus 40 kg in the luggage compartment, then tighten the top and bottom mounting nuts to the specified torque setting.

### 14   Rear suspension unit – overhaul

1    Remove the suspension unit and spring from the vehicle (Sec 13) and thoroughly clean the assembly.
2    Remove the spring, the rubber pad, the rubber buffer and the dust cover. Withdraw the spring upper seat from under the wheel arch (photo).
3    Visually inspect all components and renew any that are showing obvious signs of wear or damage. Check particularly the top mounting components, looking for cracks, distortion or deterioration of the rubber itself.
4    Check the bottom mounting bush and renew it if it is cracked, worn, split or perished. It must be removed (and the new bush fitted) using a press, although it may be possible to achieve the required result using a strong bench vice and sockets or pieces of tubing. Soak the old bush in

14.2 Spring upper seat in place in wheel arch

penetrating fluid before attempting removal and use liquid soap or petroleum jelly as a lubricant on pressing in the new bush. Ensure that the new bush is located symmetrically and note that the manufacturer recommends that newly fitted bushes should be left to settle for 24 hours before being installed on the vehicle.
5    If the spring is obviously broken or damaged it must of course be renewed, but if it is thought to have sagged, seek the advice of a Lada dealer. Most UK-specification Samara models are fitted with shortened springs, so a suspect spring can be checked only (in the absence of sufficient accurate information) by direct comparison with a new spring of the correct type. Note that if either of the rear springs requires renewal, it is good practice to renew both together as a matched pair. Ensure that the spring colour code (painted on the outside of the middle coils) is the same on both rear units and matches that on the front suspension.
6    Check the unit's damping action by mounting it upright in a vice and moving the piston rod fully up and down. Firm, even resistance should be felt in both directions. If the damping is weak, if the unit shows signs of oil leaks at any point or if the piston rod is bent, scored or damaged the complete unit must be renewed as individual components are not available to permit repairs. Note that if either of the rear units requires renewal, it is good practice to renew both together as a matched pair.
7    Always store suspension units in an upright position. If a unit is to be fitted after a long period of storage, mount it upright in a vice and move the piston rod fully up and down several times to prime the damper passages and restore full damping action.
8    On reassembly, ensure that all components are correctly installed and that the piston rod is pulled out to its fullest extent.
9    Refit the suspension unit to the vehicle (Sec 13).

15.5 Move aside brake components to reach rear suspension mountings (arrowed)

15.14 Tightening torsion beam axle pivot bolt nut – see text

## 15  Rear suspension torsion beam axle – removal and refitting

1    With the vehicle parked on smooth, level ground, select first or reverse gear and chock the front wheels.
2    Jack up the rear of the vehicle evenly and support it securely on axle stands so that both roadwheels are clear of the ground (see 'Jacking, towing and wheel changing') then remove the roadwheels.
3    Working as described in the relevant Sections of Chapter 8, remove the brake drums, disconnect the handbrake cables from the brake backplates and disconnect the brake pressure regulator linkage from the torsion beam axle.
4    Either disconnect the brake pipes from the wheel cylinders (Chapter 8) so that the brake and hub assemblies can be removed with the torsion beam axle, or remove the rear stub axle (Sec 11) so that the brake backplate can be detached and moved out of the way, thus avoiding the need to disturb the brake hydraulic system.
5    Removing bolts where necessary, unclip the handbrake cables and brake pipes from the torsion beam axle and its pivots. Move them clear of the working area, taking care not to kink or damage them, and secure them safely (photo).
6    Remove the suspension unit bottom mounting bolts.
7    Unscrew the torsion beam axle pivot bolt nuts. With an assistant working on the opposite side, tap out the bolts and lower the axle assembly to the ground.
8    If required, the pivot brackets can be unbolted from the body; each is secured by three nuts.
9    Thoroughly clean the axle and the underbody areas around its mountings, removing all traces of dirt, and of underseal if necessary, then check it carefully for excessive corrosion, cracks, distortion or any other signs of wear or damage. Do not forget to check the pivot bolts and nuts. Renew any worn or damaged component.
10    If either the axle, its pivot brackets or the underbody show signs of rusting, the affected area must be cleaned back to bare metal and treated before being repainted. If the underbody is seriously rusted or if any of the pivot bracket studs is damaged, seek professional advice.
11    Check the pivot bushes and renew them if they are cracked, worn, split or perished. Both must be removed and refitted using a press, although it may be possible to achieve the required result using a strong bench vice and sockets or pieces of tubing. Soak the old bush in penetrating fluid before attempting removal and use liquid soap or petroleum jelly as a lubricant on pressing in the new bush. Ensure that new bushes are located symmetrically and note that the manufacturer recommends that newly fitted bushes should be left to settle for 24 hours before being installed on the vehicle.
12    Refitting is the reverse of the removal procedure, noting the following points.
13    Tighten the pivot bracket retaining nuts to the specified torque wrench setting.

14    All other fasteners should be tightened only lightly at first until the suspension is reassembled and the vehicle is lowered to the ground. When all the vehicle's weight is back on its wheels, rock it to settle the suspension and load it with four people (or the equivalent weight, 320 kg) plus 40 kg in the luggage compartment, then tighten all disturbed nuts and bolts to the specified torque settings (photo).
15    Refer to the relevant Sections of Chapter 8 to ensure that the brake components are correctly reassembled and adjusted.

## 16  Steering wheel – removal and refitting

1    Disconnect the battery negative terminal.
2    With the vehicle parked on level ground, check that the roadwheels are in the straight-ahead position. The steering wheel spokes should be horizontal and the projection on the steering gear pinion dust guard should be aligned with the raised mark on the steering gear housing, visible behind the steering column bottom joint.
3    Prise off the spoke cover/horn push.
4    If the steering wheel nut is heavily staked, use a drill to relieve the staking. Unscrew the nut.
5    Check for alignment marks between the steering wheel and the steering column. If none can be seen, make your own.
6    Grasp the steering wheel firmly and rock it to jar it free, then pull it off the steering column splines. It is permissible to thump the wheel from behind with the palms of the hands, but do not hammer the wheel or column, or use excessive force.
7    On refitting, check that the horn contact tracks are clean and polished and apply a thin smear of grease. Also check that the steering column splines are clean (photo).
8    Refit the wheel, aligning the marks made or noted on dismantling which should leave the wheel positioned as described in paragraph 2 above.
9    Tighten to the specified torque setting the steering wheel nut, then use a hammer and a suitable punch to stake the nut at two points (photos).
10    Refit the spoke cover/horn push and reconnect the battery.

## 17  Steering column – removal and refitting

**Note:** *The steering column is secured by two nuts and two shear-head bolts, which must be renewed. Ensure that new bolts are available before beginning work.*

16.7 Refitting steering wheel

16.9A Tighten steering wheel nut to specified torque setting ...

16.9B ... and stake it at two points (arrowed) to secure it

17.2A Unscrew four screws ...

17.2B ... to release steering column top cover ...

17.2C ... slacken screw nearest facia ...

17.2D ... and withdraw bottom covers, ...

17.2E ... followed by ignition switch surround

1    Check that the steering is unlocked and remove the steering wheel (Sec 16).

2    Remove the retaining screws and withdraw the steering column top and bottom covers and ignition switch surround (photos).

3    Either remove the multi-function switches (Chapter 11) or disconnect their wiring.

4    Disconnect the horn wiring from behind the multi-function switch holder (photo).

5    Disconnect the ignition switch wiring (Chapter 11).

6    Unscrew the pinch-bolt securing the steering column lower joint to the steering gear pinion shaft (photo).

7    Unscrew the two nuts (and remove their washers) that secure the steering column mounting bracket upper end.

8    Centre-punch the shear-head bolts that secure the steering column mounting bracket lower end, then drill off the bolt heads. New bolts will be required on refitting.

9    Withdraw the steering column through the facia, then unscrew the remains of the shear-head bolts using a self-locking wrench or similar on the exposed ends.

10    Refitting is the reverse of the removal procedure, noting the following points.

11    Loosely assemble the column mountings and lower joint ensuring that the joint is positioned on the steering gear pinion shaft so that the pinch-bolt bore is aligned exactly with the pinion shaft groove, then refit the pinch-bolt and tighten it to the specified torque wrench setting.

12    Check that the column is seated without stress on its mountings, then tighten the nuts to the specified torque wrench setting and tighten the new shear-head bolts until their heads shear off (photo).

13    Reconnect the switch and horn wiring, then refit the ignition switch surround and steering column top and bottom covers.

14    When refitting the steering wheel (Sec 16), ensure that the road-wheels are in the straight-ahead position and that the steering wheel and column are aligned as described in Section 16, paragraph 2.

15    When reassembly is complete, raise the front of the vehicle and turn the steering from lock to lock to ensure that it is functioning correctly.

17.4 Disconnecting horn wiring from switch holder

17.6 Unscrew steering column lower joint pinch-bolt

17.12 Steering column mountings seen through facia – nut and intact shear-head bolt (arrowed)

## 18  Steering column – dismantling and reassembly

1    Remove the steering column from the vehicle (Sec 17).
2    Mount the steering column jacket tube in a vice and withdraw the column itself. If the column has to be driven out, temporarily refit the steering wheel nut to protect it.
3    If it is worn, the ball-bearing at the tube's upper end can be removed using an internally-expanding bearing puller. Note the installed depth of the bearing before removing it. On refitting, use a hammer and a drift such as a socket which bears only on the bearing's outer race and tap the bearing in to the position recorded on removal.
4    Check the column lower joint carefully. If there are any signs of free play or of wear in the joint, or of perishing or other damage to the rubber element, the complete column must be renewed. The joint rivets are available separately but owners are advised to leave the removal and fitting of these to a Lada dealer, if they should be found to be worn.
5    Check the splines at the column's upper and lower ends. Renew the column if these are worn or damaged.
6    Refitting is the reverse of the removal procedure. Apply a thin coat of grease to the column before refitting it to the jacket tube.

## 19  Steering lock/ignition switch – removal and refitting

**Note:** *The steering lock/ignition switch is secured by two shear-head bolts which must be renewed. Ensure that new bolts are available before beginning work.*

1    Check that the steering is unlocked and remove the steering wheel (Sec 16).

2    Remove the retaining screws and withdraw the steering column top and bottom covers and ignition switch surround.
3    Either remove the multi-function switches (Chapter 11) or disconnect their wiring.
4    Disconnect the horn wiring from behind the multi-function switch holder. Remove the switch holder (Chapter 11).
5    Disconnect the ignition switch wiring.
6    Centre-punch the shear-head bolts, then drill off the bolt heads. New bolts will be required on refitting.
7    Withdraw the steering lock/ignition switch, then unscrew the remains of the shear-head bolts using a self-locking wrench or similar on the exposed ends.
8    On refitting, carefully align the assembly on the steering column (photo), lightly tighten the bolts and check that the steering lock works smoothly.
9    Tighten the shear-head bolts evenly until their heads shear off (photo).
10   The remainder of the reassembly procedure is a reversal of removal.

## 20  Steering gear – removal and refitting

1    Remove the steering column from the vehicle (Sec 17).
2    Working inside the engine compartment, unbolt the track rods from the steering gear (Sec 23). Remove the air cleaner assembly (Chapter 3) if better access is required.
3    Unscrew the four steering gear mounting nuts, collect the two clamps and manoeuvre the steering gear out of the vehicle (photo).
4    On refitting, first ensure that the steering gear rack is at the exact

19.8 Align steering lock on column before tightening bolts

19.9 Steering lock shear-head bolts – one sheared, one intact

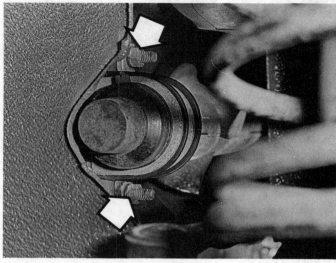

20.3 Steering gear mounting nuts (arrowed) – seen through wheel arch

mid-point of its travel (Sec 22, para 5). The projection on the pinion dust guard should be aligned with the raised mark on the steering gear housing at that point.

5    Use liquid soap or petroleum jelly as a lubricant to ensure that the mounting rubber bushes are correctly seated when the steering gear is refitted. Tighten the mounting nuts evenly to the specified torque wrench setting.

6    The remainder of the reassembly procedure is a reversal of removal. Tighten all disturbed nuts and bolts to the specified torque wrench settings.

7    Have the wheel alignment and steering angles checked as soon as possible (Sec 25).

## 21  Steering gear rubber gaiter – renewal

1    Remove the steering gear from the vehicle (Sec 20).
2    Cut or unfasten the clips securing the gaiter, remove the left-hand

mounting rubber bush and withdraw the gaiter from the steering gear housing.

3    Check the gaiter for any signs of splits, tears or perishing. Renew it if any such damage is found or if it is not a tight fit on the housing. The clips should be renewed as a matter of course whenever they are disturbed.

4    On refitting, check that the steering gear components are correctly greased, then slide on the gaiter, ensuring that its openings align with the housing track rod slot.

5    Position the gaiter's left-hand end at a distance of 28.5 ± 0.5 mm inboard of the housing's end face (see Fig. 9.10), then fasten the clip to secure it.

6    Settle the gaiter evenly on the housing and fasten the remaining clip.

7    Refit the left-hand mounting rubber bush, hard against the gaiter.

8    Refit the steering gear to the vehicle (Sec 20). When checking the steering's operation (Sec 17), ensure that the gaiter does not snag or bulge at any point in the steering gear travel. If necessary, unfasten the clip(s) and reposition the gaiter on the housing.

## 22  Steering gear – overhaul

**Note:** *Before attempting to overhaul the steering gear, check the price and availability of individual components and the price of a new or reconditioned unit, as gear overhaul may not be viable on economic grounds alone. Also, read through the procedure and check that the special tools and facilities required are available.*

1    Remove the steering gear from the vehicle (Sec 20).
2    Thoroughly clean the gear assembly, prepare a clean working area and observe scrupulous cleanliness throughout the overhaul.
3    Cutting or unfastening the clips as required, remove both housing end caps, the mounting rubber bushes and the gaiter.
4    First establish for future reference the exact mid-point of the steering gear rack travel, which will correspond to the roadwheel straight-ahead position when the gear is installed.
5    To find the mid-point, rotate the pinion until the rack is at full lock on one side and measure the distance between one end of the rack and a fixed point on the housing. Move the rack across to the full opposite lock and measure again the distance between the same two points. The difference between the two measurements is the total rack movement. Halve this distance and return the rack to that point. For ease of reference either use a straight-edge and a scriber to mark a line across the housing slot and the rack (between the track rod mounting points),

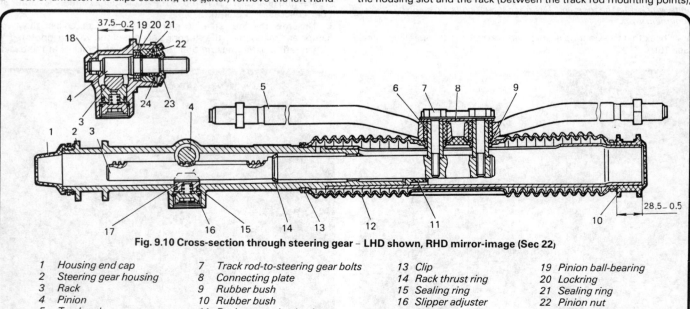

**Fig. 9.10 Cross-section through steering gear – LHD shown, RHD mirror-image (Sec 22)**

| | | | | |
|---|---|---|---|---|
| 1 | Housing end cap | 7 | Track rod-to-steering gear bolts | 13 | Clip | 19 | Pinion ball-bearing |
| 2 | Steering gear housing | 8 | Connecting plate | 14 | Rack thrust ring | 20 | Lockring |
| 3 | Rack | 9 | Rubber bush | 15 | Sealing ring | 21 | Sealing ring |
| 4 | Pinion | 10 | Rubber bush | 16 | Slipper adjuster | 22 | Pinion nut |
| 5 | Track rod | 11 | Rack supporting bush | 17 | Slipper | 23 | Pinion dust guard |
| 6 | Spacer | 12 | Rubber gaiter | 18 | Pinion roller bearing | 24 | Lockwasher |

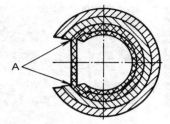

**Fig. 9.11 Details of rack supporting bush and rubber rings (Sec 22)**

or measure and record the depth from each housing end face to each end of the rack, so that the rack can be quickly and accurately positioned when required. Note that the projection on the pinion dust guard should be aligned with the raised mark on the steering gear housing at the mid-point of rack travel.

6   Unscrew the eight-sided female socket-headed slipper adjuster using Lada service tool 67.7812.9537 (Churchill Tools number A-677812-9537). If the adjuster is heavily staked, use a drill to relieve the staking. Withdraw the coil spring and lockring, dislodge the slipper and extract it using circlip pliers or similar which fit into the slipper's spring recess. Remove and discard the slipper's sealing ring.

7   With the rack at the mid-point of its travel (see para 5 above), remove the dust guard and the lockwasher beneath.

8   Unscrew the pinion nut using Lada service tool 67.7812.9536 (Churchill Tools number A-677812-9536). Remove and discard the nut's sealing ring.

9   Extract the pinion and ball-bearing from the steering gear housing. If the bearing is to be renewed, remove the protective washer and the lockring, then draw the bearing off the pinion shaft.

10   Withdraw the rack from the housing's right-hand end, then extract the rubber rings and withdraw the rack supporting bush, noting that it has locating lugs which engage in the gear housing.

11   If the pinion roller bearing is to be renewed, have the work carried out by a Lada dealer or similar expert. The worn bearing will be difficult to remove without special tools and its replacement must be pressed in to a precise depth (37.5 – 0.2 mm) from the ball-bearing's locating shoulder – see Fig. 9.10) or it may be damaged.

12   Thoroughly clean all components and renew any that show obvious signs of wear or damage. Roll the rack on a sheet of plate glass or similar flat surface to check that it is not bent or distorted, then check the teeth both of the rack and of the pinion. Check for wear all bearings, bushes and bearing surfaces. Whenever they are disturbed, renew as a matter of course all sealing rings and gaiter clips, the rack bush rubber rings and the pinion nut lockwasher.

13   On reassembly, thoroughly lubricate all components with the specified grease.

14   To refit the rack supporting bush, first fit the new rubber rings into their grooves so that the narrower part of each ring will be aligned with the bush slot. Press in the bush, ensuring that its lugs engage with the housing locating holes, then cut away the narrower part of each ring (at points 'A', Fig. 9.11).

15   Grease the rack and refit it, aligning the track rod threaded holes with the housing track rod slot. Position the rack at the mid-point of its travel (see para 5 above).

16   If a new pinion ball-bearing is to be fitted, press it on to the pinion shaft until it seats against the shoulder. Ensure that pressure is applied only to the bearing's inner race. Refit the lockring and protective washer.

17   Pack the pinion and both bearings with grease, then refit the assembly with the flat on the pinion's shaft pointing to the left. Using a hammer and a drift such as a piece of tubing which bears only on the ball-bearing's outer race, tap the assembly into the housing until it is correctly seated. Ensure that the rack and pinion teeth mesh properly and that the pinion shaft enters the roller bearing correctly.

18   Pack the remainder of the specified quantity of grease into the housing and move the rack from one lock to the other, checking that it moves smoothly and easily. Return it to the mid-point of its travel.

19   Fit a new sealing ring to the pinion nut, grease it and refit the nut, tightening it to the specified torque wrench setting. Fit a new lockwasher, pack the space above with grease and refit the dust guard, aligning its projection with the raised mark on the steering gear housing.

20   Fit a new sealing ring to the slipper, grease it and refit the slipper, pressing it firmly against the rack, noting that there must be **no** free play

between the rack and the slipper. Refit the coil spring and lockring, followed by the adjuster.

21   Tighten the adjuster to a torque wrench setting of 11 to 13 Nm (8 to 9.5 lbf ft), then slacken it through an angle of 24° (two flats) to achieve an initial setting. Again check that the rack moves smoothly and easily from one lock to the other, then return it to the mid-point of its travel.

22   Using a length of string and a spring balance, check that the rotating torque of the pinion is between 0.6 and 1.7 Nm (0.4 and 1.3 lbf ft). To do this accurately move the rack to one lock, then measure the torque while rotating the pinion all the way to the opposite lock. Return the rack to the mid-point of its travel.

23   If necessary, tighten or slacken the adjuster until the rotating torque is correct, then lock it by staking the housing at two points around the adjuster's perimeter and mark it with paint so that it can be easily checked in future.

24   Refit both housing end caps, the mounting rubber bushes and the gaiter (Sec 21), ensuring that the new gaiter clips are correctly fastened.

25   Refit the steering gear to the vehicle (Sec 20).

26   Note that the rack slipper setting should be checked as follows whenever it has been disturbed, or if a steering fault has arisen.

27   First check that the tyres are in good condition and inflated to the correct pressure, and that the brakes are not binding.

28   Drive the vehicle along a flat, level road and check that it continues to move in a straight line when the steering wheel is released from the straight-ahead position (spokes horizontal).

29   Carefully check that the steering wheel returns to the straight-ahead position when released from a slightly (approx 20°) rotated position on each side of straight-ahead.

30   If the self-centring action and response is slow or stiff, the slipper adjustment must be reset, as described above. Note however that this means removing the steering gear from the vehicle, as the adjuster is inaccessible when the gear is in place.

## 23   Track rod – removal and refitting

**Note:** *This Section refers to the removal and refitting of each track rod as an assembly, complete with its balljoint.*

1   Disconnect the balljoint from the suspension strut steering arm (Sec 24).

2   Flatten back the lockplate raised tabs and slacken **both** track rod-to-steering gear bolts (photo), then unscrew its bolt and withdraw the track rod required. Be prepared to collect the spacer which may drop clear from the track rod inboard end.

3   If the balljoint is to be renewed, refer to Section 24.

4   Check the bush for signs of wear or damage. If required it can be pressed out and a new bush can be pressed in, using liquid soap or petroleum jelly as a lubricant.

5   The lockplate must be renewed whenever all of its locking tabs have been used.

23.2 Track rod-to-steering gear bolts (arrowed)

24.3 Hold threaded sleeve whenever locknuts are slackened or tightened

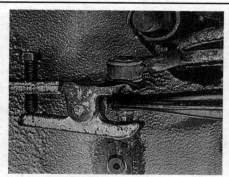

24.4 Using balljoint separator tool to remove track rod balljoint

24.8 Fit split pin as shown to secure balljoint retaining nut

6    Refitting is the reverse of the removal procedure, noting the following points.

7    Ensure that the track rod is seated securely against the steering gear rack without fouling or trapping the gaiter, then refit the connecting plate, the lockplate and the bolt.

8    Tighten the bolt to its specified torque wrench setting and bend up an unused lockplate tab against one of its flats. Check that there is no free play evident but that the track rod can pivot on its mounting to accommodate suspension movement (ie only in a vertical plane).

9    Reconnect the balljoint to the suspension strut steering arm (Sec 24).

10    Have the wheel alignment and steering angles checked as soon as possible (Sec 25).

## 24   Track rod balljoint – removal and refitting

**Note:** *To prevent damage to the balljoints, always use a suitable spanner to hold the threaded sleeve whenever the locknuts are slackened or tightened so that an excessive loading is not applied to the balljoints themselves. Whenever the balljoints or threaded sleeves are disturbed, always check that the ball is seated firmly in its socket on completion.*

1    If better access is required, raise the front of the vehicle and remove the roadwheel (see *'Jacking towing and wheel changing'*).

2    Open the bonnet. If the balljoint is to be re-used, use a straight-edge and a scriber or similar to mark its relationship to the track rod and the threaded sleeve.

3    Holding the threaded sleeve, unscrew by one-quarter of a turn the balljoint/threaded sleeve locknut (photo).

4    Working under the wing, extract the split pin and unscrew the balljoint retaining nut. Using a universal balljoint separator tool if necessary, separate the balljoint from the suspension strut steering arm (photo).

5    Counting the exact number of turns necessary to do so, unscrew the balljoint from the threaded sleeve.

6    Carefully clean the balljoint and the threads. Renew the balljoint if its movement is sloppy or if it is too stiff. No grease leakage should be visible. The dust cover can be renewed separately if it is split, perished, torn or damaged; it is retained by two rings. Renew the balljoint if it is excessively worn or if it is damaged in any way – check the stud taper and threads carefully. Renew as a matter of course the retaining nut split pin whenever it is disturbed.

7    On refitting, screw the balljoint into the threaded sleeve by the number of turns noted on removal. This should, of course, bring the balljoint to within a quarter of a turn from the locknut, with the alignment marks that were made on removal lined up (if applicable).

8    Degrease the tapers of the balljoint stud and of the strut steering arm, then press the balljoint firmly into the steering arm while the retaining nut is refitted and tightened to its specified torque wrench setting. Fit a new split pin and spread its ends securely (photo).

9    Note that if, when the nut has been tightened to the specified torque setting, the stud hole does not align with any pair of the nut's slots the nut can be tightened further (through no more than 60°) until the split pin can be inserted.

10    If the vehicle is to be driven to have the wheel alignment and steering angles checked professionally, hold the threaded sleeve and tighten the balljoint/threaded sleeve locknut securely. Otherwise, refer to Section 25.

11    Where applicable, refit the roadwheel and lower the vehicle to the ground.

## 25   Wheel alignment and steering angles – checking and adjusting

### Wheel alignment and steering angles – general

1    Wheel alignment consists of five elements. All angles are expressed in degrees and the steering axis is defined as an imaginary line drawn through the centres of the suspension strut top mounting and of the suspension lower arm balljoint, extended where necessary to contact the ground.

2    **Camber** is the angle between each roadwheel and a vertical line drawn through its centre and tyre contact patch when viewed from the front or rear of the vehicle. Positive camber is when the roadwheels are tilted outwards from the vertical at the top and negative camber is when they are tilted inwards.

3    Camber is adjusted by rotating the upper (eccentric) front suspension strut-to-hub carrier clamp bolt.

4    **Castor** is the angle between the steering axis and a vertical line drawn through each roadwheel's centre and tyre contact patch when viewed from the side of the vehicle. Positive castor is when the steering axis is tilted so that it contacts the ground ahead of the vertical and negative castor is when it contacts the ground behind the vertical.

5    Castor is adjusted by adding or removing shims to the front suspension tie-bar.

6    **Steering axis inclination/SAI** (also known as **kingpin inclination/KPI**) is the angle between the steering axis and a vertical line drawn through each roadwheel's centre and tyre contact patch when viewed from the front or rear of the vehicle.

7    SAI/KPI is not adjustable and is given for reference only.

8    **Toe** is the difference, viewed from above, between lines drawn through the roadwheel centres and the vehicle's centre-line (see Fig. 9.12). It is expressed as the amount by which the distance between the

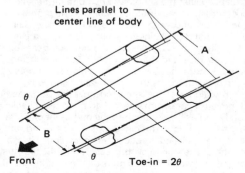

Lines parallel to
center line of body

$\theta$

A

B

$\theta$

Front        Toe-in = $2\theta$

**Fig. 9.12 Calculating toe setting (Sec 25)**

25.24 Adjusting camber angle

25.30 Castor adjusting shim on tie-bar front end – note chamfer on inner edge

front inside edges of the roadwheel rims differs from that between the rear inside edges, measured at hub centre height. If the distance at the front is less than at the rear, the roadwheels are said to 'toe-in'. If the distance at the front is greater than at the rear, the roadwheels 'toe-out'.
9     The toe setting is adjusted by using the threaded sleeves to alter the effective length of the track rods.
10    **Toe-out on turns** (also known as turning angles or Ackermann angles) is the difference, viewed from above, between the angles of rotation of the inside and outside front wheels when the outside roadwheel has been turned through an angle of 20°
11    Toe-out on turns is set in production and is not adjustable as such but can be upset by altering the length of the track rods unequally. It is essential, therefore, to ensure that the track rod lengths are exactly the same and that the threaded sleeves are turned by the same amount whenever the toe setting is altered.

### Checking – general
12    Due to the special measuring equipment necessary to check the wheel alignment and steering angles and the skill required to use it properly, the checking and adjustment of these settings is best left to a Lada dealer or similar expert. Note that most tyre-fitting shops now possess sophisticated checking equipment.
13    For accurate checking, the vehicle must be at kerb weight (see *'General dimensions, weights and capacities'*.
14    Before starting work, always check first the tyre size, type, pressures and tread wear (Sec 26), then check the roadwheel run-out, the condition of the hub bearings, the steering wheel free play and the condition of the front suspension components (Sec 2). Correct any faults found.
15    Park the vehicle on level ground, check that the front roadwheels are in the straight-ahead position, then rock the rear and front ends of the car to settle the suspension.
16    Working as described in the relevant sub-Section below, check in the following order:

   (a)   *Toe-out on turns*
   (b)   *Camber*
   (c)   *Castor*
   (d)   *Toe setting (and recheck toe-out on turns to ensure that track rods have been adjusted equally)*

### Toe-out on turns – checking and adjusting
17    This can be checked only using a pair of scuff plates.
18    Prepare the vehicle as described in paragraphs 13 to 15 above. Roll the vehicle backwards, check that the front roadwheels are in the straight-ahead position, then roll it forwards on to the scuff plates until each front roadwheel is seated squarely on the centre of each plate.
19    Turn the steering wheel first one way until the outside roadwheel is at an angle of 20° and record the angle of the inside roadwheel. Next turn the steering wheel back through the straight-ahead position and repeat the check on that side.

20    If, in either check, the inside roadwheel is not at the angle specified, check that both track rod assemblies are exactly the same length. If they are different this can be corrected by using the threaded sleeves, but this will affect the toe setting (see below) and the steering wheel position (Sec 16, para 2).
21    If the angles are incorrect but the track rods are the same length and the steering mechanism components are known from the preliminary checks to be unworn, then there is damage to, or distortion of, part of the steering mechanism, the front suspension or the body itself. This will require careful checking, preferably by an expert such as a Lada dealer, as soon as possible.

### Camber – checking and adjusting
22    This can only be checked using a camber checking gauge.
23    Prepare the vehicle as described in paragraphs 13 to 15 above. Attach the gauge and follow its manufacturer's instructions to check the camber angle.
24    If adjustment is required, slacken both nuts securing the front suspension strut-to-hub carrier clamp bolts and rotate the upper (eccentric) bolt until the setting is correct (photo).
25    Tighten the two nuts to the specified torque wrench setting, recheck the angle to ensure that it has not altered, then repeat the check on the remaining side.

### Castor – checking and adjusting
26    This can only be checked using a castor checking gauge.
27    Prepare the vehicle as described in paragraphs 13 to 15 above. Attach the gauge and follow its manufacturer's instructions to check the castor angle.
28    If adjustment is required, first note the number of shims at the front and rear ends of the front suspension tie-bar, between the bar's squared section and the large metal washer next to the rubber bush. There should be no more than two at the front and four at the rear.
29    Each shim is 3 mm thick and will alter the castor angle by 19°. Remove shims to increase the castor angle. If the angle is to be reduced, do not fit more than the maximum number of shims (see above), especially at the front where the length of thread available is less.
30    To alter the setting, remove the tie-bar (Sec 7, paragraphs 2 and 3) and remove or add shims as required. Each shim has a chamfer on one inner edge which must face away from the rubber bush, towards the tie-bar's centre section (photo). Refit the tie-bar (Sec 7, paragraphs 8 to 11).
31    Recheck the angle to ensure that it has not altered, then repeat the check on the remaining side.

### Toe setting – checking and adjusting
32    This can only be checked using a toe checking gauge (sometimes known as a tracking gauge) which can measure the distance between the front and rear inside edges of the roadwheels. While such gauges

are available in relatively inexpensive form from accessory outlets, a home-made version can be fabricated from a length of steel tubing, cranked to clear the engine/transmission or suspension components, with a long bolt and locknut at one end.

33    Prepare the vehicle as described in paragraphs 13 to 15 above. Roll the vehicle backwards for several feet, check that the front roadwheels are in the straight-ahead position, then roll it forwards again.

34    First measure the distance between the inside edges of the front roadwheel rims, at hub centre height at the rear of the roadwheels. Call this dimension 'A'.

35    Push the vehicle forwards so that the roadwheels rotate exactly 180° (half a turn) and measure the distance again, but now at hub centre height at the front of the roadwheels. Call this dimension 'B'.

36    To ensure absolute accuracy, repeat the measurements twice more, at points spaced 120° apart around the roadwheel rims and take the average of the three readings.

37    To calculate toe-in, subtract 'B' from 'A' (Fig. 9.12). The result should be within the specified tolerance.

38    If adjustment is required, refer first to the note at the beginning of Section 24. Clean the track rod threads, and if they are corroded, apply penetrating fluid before starting adjustment.

39    Holding each threaded sleeve in turn, unscrew both locknuts fully.

40    Alter the length of **both** track rods **by exactly the same amount** by rotating the threaded sleeves one-quarter of a turn at a time and rechecking the toe setting until it is correct. To ensure that the track rod lengths remain equal, always rotate the threaded sleeves in the same direction (viewed from the centre of the vehicle), shortening the track rods will reduce toe-in.

41    When the setting is correct, hold the threaded sleeves and tighten the locknuts securely. Check that the balljoints are seated correctly in their sockets and measure the length of both track rods. If they are not the same then the adjustment has not been made equally and problems will be encountered with tyre scrubbing in turns, while the steering wheel will no longer be in the straight-ahead position (Sec 16, para 2).

42    Note that it is recommended that the toe-out on turns is rechecked whenever the toe setting is altered, to ensure that the track rods have been adjusted equally.

---

## 26    Wheels and tyres – general care and maintenance

Wheels and tyres should give no real problems in use provided that a close eye is kept on them with regard to excessive wear or damage. To this end, the following points should be noted.

Ensure that tyre pressures are checked regularly and maintained correctly. Checking should be carried out with the tyres cold and not immediately after the vehicle has been in use. If the pressures are checked with the tyres hot, an apparently high reading will be obtained owing to heat expansion. Under no circumstances should an attempt be made to reduce the pressures to the quoted cold reading in this instance, or effective underinflation will result.

Underinflation will cause overheating of the tyre owing to excessive flexing of the casing, and the tread will not sit correctly on the road surface. This will cause a consequent loss of adhesion and excessive wear, not to mention the danger of sudden tyre failure due to heat build-up.

Overinflation will cause rapid wear of the centre part of the tyre tread coupled with reduced adhesion, harsher ride, and the danger of shock damage occurring in the tyre casing.

Regularly check the tyres for damage in the form of cuts or bulges, especially in the sidewalls. Remove any nails or stones embedded in the tread before they penetrate the tyre to cause deflation. If removal of a nail *does* reveal that the tyre has been punctured, refit the nail so that its point of penetration is marked. Then immediately change the wheel and have the tyre repaired by a tyre dealer. Do **not** drive on a tyre in such a condition. In many cases a puncture can be simply repaired by the use of an inner tube of the correct size and type. If in any doubt as to the possible consequences of any damage found, consult your local tyre dealer for advice.

Periodically remove the wheels and clean any dirt or mud from the inside and outside surfaces. Examine the wheel rims for signs of rusting, corrosion or other damage. Light alloy wheels are easily damaged by 'kerbing' whilst parking, and similarly steel wheels may become dented or buckled. Renewal of the wheel is very often the only course of remedial action possible.

The balance of each wheel and tyre assembly should be maintained to avoid excessive wear, not only to the tyres but also to the steering and suspension components. Wheel imbalance is normally signified by vibration through the vehicle's bodyshell, although in many cases it is particularly noticeable through the steering wheel. Conversely, it should be noted that wear or damage in suspension or steering components may cause excessive tyre wear. Out-of-round or out-of-true tyres, damaged wheels and wheel bearing wear/maladjustment also fall into this category. Balancing will not usually cure vibration caused by such wear.

Wheel balancing may be carried out with the wheel either on or off the vehicle. If balanced on the vehicle, ensure that the wheel-to-hub relationship is marked in some way prior to subsequent wheel removal so that it may be refitted in its original position.

General tyre wear is influenced to a large degree by driving style – harsh braking and acceleration or fast cornering will all produce more rapid tyre wear. Interchanging of tyres may result in more even wear, but this should only be carried out where there is no mix of tyre types on the vehicle. However, it is worth bearing in mind that if this is completely effective, the added expense is incurred of replacing simultaneously a complete set of tyres, which may prove financially restrictive for many owners.

Front tyres may wear unevenly as a result of wheel misalignment. The front wheels should always be correctly aligned according to the settings specified by the vehicle manufacturer.

Legal restrictions apply to the mixing of tyre types on a vehicle. Basically this means that a vehicle must not have tyres of differing construction on the same axle. Although it is not recommended to mix tyre types between front axle and rear axle, the only legally permissible combination is crossply at the front and radial at the rear. When mixing radial ply tyres, textile-braced radials must always go on the front axle, with steel-braced radials at the rear. An obvious disadvantage of such mixing is the necessity to carry two spare tyres to avoid contravening the law in the event of a puncture.

In the UK, the Motor Vehicle Construction and Use Regulations apply to many aspects of tyre fitting and usage. It is suggested that a copy of these regulations is obtained from your local police if in doubt as to current legal requirements with regard to tyre condition, minimum tread depth, etc.

---

## 27    Fault diagnosis – suspension and steering

**Note:** *Before diagnosing suspension or steering faults, ensure that the problem is not due to overloading (or uneven loading), to incorrect tyre pressures, a mixture of tyre types or binding brakes.*

---

| Symptom | Reason(s) |
|---|---|
| Vehicle wanders or pulls to one side | Incorrect wheel alignment<br>Wear in front suspension or steering components<br>Wear in rear suspension components<br>Weak suspension struts or units |

| Symptom | Reason(s) |
|---|---|
| | Faulty tyre or incorrect tyre pressures |
| | Accident damage to body, suspension or steering components |
| Steering stiff and heavy | Incorrect wheel alignment |
| | Steering column or rack bent or damaged |
| | Seized track rod or suspension lower arm balljoints |
| | Damaged suspension strut |
| | Faulty tyre or incorrect tyre pressures |
| Excessive play in steering | Worn steering or suspension joints |
| | Worn steering column lower joint |
| | Worn steering gear or slack gear mountings |
| Excessive pitching or rolling | Weak suspension struts or units |
| | Worn anti-roll bar mountings |
| Roadwheel wobble and vibration | Roadwheel bolts loose |
| | Roadwheels out of balance, damaged or distorted |
| | Tyres faulty, damaged or incorrectly fitted |
| | Worn steering or suspension joints |
| | Weak suspension struts or units |
| | Worn hub bearings |
| Excessive or uneven tyre wear | Incorrect tyre pressures |
| | Incorrect wheel alignment |
| | Roadwheels out of balance |
| | Driver abuse |
| | Wear in steering or suspension components |
| | Weak suspension struts or units |
| | Accident damage to body, suspension or steering components |

**Note:** *This Section is not intended to be an exhaustive guide to fault diagnosis but summarises the more common faults which may be encountered during a vehicle's life. Consult a dealer for more specific advice.*

# Chapter 10 Bodywork and fittings

## Contents

## 1 General description

The bodyshell is made of pressed-steel sections welded together, with front and rear crumple zones and bolt-on front wings, in three-door Hatchback, five-door Hatchback and Van configurations. The five-door body is identical to the three-door apart from the obvious extra doors. Childproof locks are fitted to the rear doors, and as one would expect of a USSR-built vehicle, all door locks are freeze-resistant. The Van body consists of the three-door Hatchback body with no rear quarter windows and the rear seat etc. stripped out.

Extensive use is made of plastic materials, mainly on the interior but also in exterior components such as the polycarbonate radiator grille, the grille/headlamp surround and the front and rear bumpers (or skirts, on SLX models). Both bumpers are fitted over a duraluminium reinforcing member. The interior trim has been improved progressively to approach Western standards, and in fact the SL and SLX trim and accessories are UK-built.

The heater has a three-speed fan housed in the engine compartment, face level vents in the centre and at each of the facia and air ducts to front and rear footwells. Illuminated sliding controls for air temperature, supply and distribution are housed in the facia centre console with the heater fan switch. The controls operate flap valves to deflect the air flowing through the heater. Cold air enters through the grille at the rear of the bonnet, is boosted when required by the radial fan, and flows through the ducts according to the control setting. If warm air is required, fresh air is passed over the heater matrix which is heated by the engine's coolant.

## 2 Routine maintenance – bodywork and underframe

The general condition of a vehicle's bodywork is the one thing that significantly affects its value. Maintenance is easy but needs to be regular. Neglect, particularly after minor damage, can lead quickly to further deterioration and costly repair bills. It is important also to keep watch on those parts of the vehicle not immediately visible, for instance the underside, inside all the wheel arches and the lower part of the engine compartment.

The basic maintenance routine for the bodywork is washing – preferably with a lot of water, from a hose. This will remove all the loose solids which may have stuck to the vehicle. It is important to flush these off in such a way as to prevent grit from scratching the finish. The wheel arches and underframe need washing in the same way to remove any accumulated mud which will retain moisture and tend to encourage rust. Paradoxically enough, the best time to clean the underframe and wheel arches is in wet weather when the mud is thoroughly wet and soft. In very wet weather the underframe is usually cleaned of large accumulations automatically and this is a good time for inspection.

Periodically, except on vehicles with a wax-based underbody protective coating, it is a good idea to have the whole of the underframe of the vehicle steam cleaned, engine compartment included, so that a thorough inspection can be carried out to see what minor repairs and renovations are necessary. Steam cleaning is available at many garages and is necessary for the removal of the accumulation of oily grime which sometimes is allowed to become thick in certain areas. If steam cleaning facilities are not available, there are one or two excellent grease solvents available, such as Holts Engine Cleaner or Holts Foambrite, which can be brush applied. The dirt can then simply be hosed off. Note that these methods should not be used on vehicles with wax-based underbody protective coating or the coating will be removed. Such vehicles should be inspected annually, preferably just prior to winter, when the underbody should be washed down and any damage to the wax coating repaired using Holts Undershield. Ideally, a completely fresh coat should be applied. It would also be worth considering the use of such wax-based protection for injection into door panels, sills, box sections, etc, as an additional safeguard against rust damage where such protection is not provided by the vehicle manufacturer.

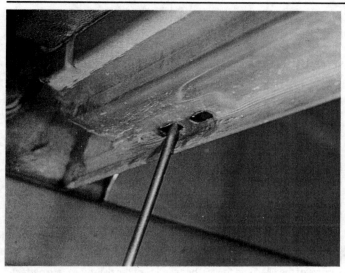

2.0 Clearing a door drain hole

After washing paintwork, wipe off with a chamois leather to give an unspotted clear finish. A coat of clear protective wax polish, like the many excellent Turtle Wax polishes, will give added protection against chemical pollutants in the air. If the paintwork sheen has dulled or oxidised, use a cleaner/polisher combination such as Turtle Extra to restore the brilliance of the shine. This requires a little effort, but such dulling is usually caused because regular washing has been neglected. Care needs to be taken with metallic paintwork, as special non-abrasive cleaner/polisher is required to avoid damage to the finish. Always check that the door and ventilator opening drain holes and pipes are completely clear so that water can be drained out (photo). Bright work should be treated in the same way as paint work. Windscreens and windows can be kept clear of the smeary film which often appears by the use of a proprietary glass cleaner like Holts Mixra. Never use any form of wax or other body or chromium polish on glass.

### 3  Routine maintenance – upholstery and carpets

Mats and carpets should be brushed or vacuum cleaned regularly to keep them free of grit. If they are badly stained remove them from the vehicle for scrubbing or sponging and make quite sure they are dry before refitting. Seats and interior trim panels can be kept clean by wiping with a damp cloth and Turtle Wax Carisma. If they do become stained (which can be more apparent on light coloured upholstery) use a little liquid detergent and a soft nail brush to scour the grime out of the grain of the material. Do not forget to keep the headlining clean in the same way as the upholstery. When using liquid cleaners inside the vehicle do not over-wet the surfaces being cleaned. Excessive damp could get into the seams and padded interior causing stains, offensive odours or even rot. If the inside of the vehicle gets wet accidentally it is worthwhile taking some trouble to dry it out properly, particularly where carpets are involved. *Do not leave oil or electric heaters inside the vehicle for this purpose.*

### 4  Routine maintenance – hinges, locks and door catches

1   At regular intervals oil the hinges of the bonnet, doors and tailgate with a light machine oil (Duckhams Home Oil).
2   At the same time lightly lubricate the bonnet release mechanism and cable and the door and tailgate catches, strikers and locks. Check carefully the security and operation of all these, adjusting them where required.
3   Check the condition and operation of the tailgate struts, renewing them if either is leaking or no longer able to support the tailgate securely when raised.

### 5  Routine maintenance – seat belts

1   All models are fitted with three-point lap and diagonal inertia reel seat belts at both front and (except Vans) the rear outer seats. The rear centre seat has a two-point lap-type belt which is fixed (ie not inertia reel).
2   Maintenance is limited to regular inspection of the belts for signs of fraying or other damage. Also check the operation of the buckles and retractor mechanisms and ensure that all mounting bolts are securely tightened. Note that the bolts are shouldered so that the belt anchor points are free to rotate.
3   If there is any sign of damage, or any doubt about a belt's condition, it must be renewed. If the vehicle has been involved in a collision any belts in use at the time must be renewed as a matter of course and all other belts should be checked carefully.
4   Use only warm water and non-detergent soap to clean the belts. Never use any chemical cleaners, strong detergents, dyes or bleaches. Keep the belts fully extended until they have dried naturally; do not apply heat to dry them.

### 6  Minor body damage – repair

*The colour bodywork repair photographic sequences between pages 32 and 33 illustrate the operations detailed in the following sub-sections.*

Note: For more detailed information about bodywork repair, the Haynes Publishing Group publish a book by Lindsay Porter called The Car Bodywork Repair Manual. This incorporates information on such aspects as rust treatment, painting and glass fibre repairs, as well as details on more ambitious repairs involving welding and panel beating.

#### Repair of minor scratches in bodywork

If the scratch is very superficial, and does not penetrate to the metal of the bodywork, repair is very simple. Lightly rub the area of the scratch with a paintwork renovator like Turtle Wax New Color Back, or a very fine cutting paste like Holts Body + Plus Rubbing Compound to remove loose paint from the scratch and to clear the surrounding bodywork of wax polish. Rinse the area with clean water.

Apply touch-up paint, such as Holts Dupli-Color Color Touch or a paint film like Holts Autofilm, to the scratch using a fine paint brush. Continue to apply fine layers of paint until the surface of the paint in the scratch is level with the surrounding paintwork. Allow the new paint at least two weeks to harden: then blend it into the surrounding paintwork by rubbing the scratch area with a paintwork renovator or a very fine cutting paste, such as Holts Body + Plus Rubbing Compound or Turtle Wax New Color Back. Finally, apply wax polish from one of the Turtle Wax range of wax polishes.

Where the scratch has penetrated right through to the metal of the bodywork, causing the metal to rust, a different repair technique is required. Remove any loose rust from the bottom of the scratch with a penknife, then apply rust inhibiting paint, such as Turtle Wax Rust Master, to prevent the formation of rust in the future. Using a rubber or nylon applicator, fill the scratch with bodystopper paste like Holts Body + Plus Knifing Putty. If required, this paste can be mixed with cellulose thinners, such as Holts Body + Plus Cellulose Thinners, to provide a very thin paste which is ideal for filling narrow scratches. Before the stopper-paste in the scratch hardens, wrap a piece of smooth cotton rag around the top of a finger. Dip the finger in cellulose thinners, such as Holts Body + Plus Cellulose Thinners, and then quickly sweep it across the surface of the stopper-paste in the scratch; this will ensure that the surface of the stopper-paste is slightly hollowed. The scratch can now be painted over as described earlier in this Section.

#### Repair of dents in bodywork

When deep denting of the vehicle's bodywork has taken place, the first task is to pull the dent out, until the affected bodywork almost attains its original shape. There is little point in trying to restore the original shape completely, as the metal in the damaged area will have stretched on impact and cannot be reshaped fully to its original contour. It is better to bring the level of the dent up to a point which is about 3 mm below the level of the surrounding bodywork. In cases where the dent is very shallow anyway, it is not worth trying to pull it out at all. If the underside of the dent is accessible, it can be hammered out gently from behind, using a mallet with a wooden or plastic head. Whilst doing this, hold a suitable block of wood firmly against the outside of the panel to absorb the impact from the hammer blows and thus prevent a large area of the bodywork from being 'belled-out'.

Should the dent be in a section of the bodywork which has a double skin or some other factor making it inaccessible from behind, a different technique is called for. Drill several small holes through the metal inside the area – particularly in the deeper section. Then screw long self-tapping screws into the holes just sufficiently for them to gain a good purchase in the metal. Now the dent can be pulled out by pulling on the protruding heads of the screws with a pair of pliers.

The next stage of the repair is the removal of the paint from the damaged area, and from an inch or so of the surrounding 'sound' bodywork. This is accomplished most easily by using a wire brush or abrasive pad on a power drill, although it can be done just as effectively by hand using sheets of abrasive paper. To complete the preparation for filling, score the surface of the bare metal with a screwdriver or the tang of a file, or alternatively, drill small holes in the affected area. This will provide a really good 'key' for the filler paste.

To complete the repair see the Section on filling and re-spraying.

### Repair of rust holes or gashes in bodywork

Remove all paint from the affected area and from an inch or so of the surrounding 'sound' bodywork, using an abrasive pad or a wire brush on a power drill. If these are not available a few sheets of abrasive paper will do the job just as effectively. With the paint removed you will be able to judge the severity of the corrosion and therefore decide whether to renew the whole panel (if this is possible) or to repair the affected area. New body panels are not as expensive as most people think and it is often quicker and more satisfactory to fit a new panel than to attempt to repair large areas of corrosion.

Remove all fittings from the affected area except those which will act as a guide to the original shape of the damaged bodywork (eg headlamp shells etc). Then, using tin snips or a hacksaw blade, remove all loose metal and any other metal badly affected by corrosion. Hammer the edges of the hole inwards in order to create a slight depression for the filler paste.

Wire brush the affected area to remove the powdery rust from the surface of the remaining metal. Paint the affected area with a rust inhibiting paint like Turtle Wax Rust Master. If the back of the rusted area is accessible, treat this as well.

Before filling can take place it will be necessary to block the hole in some way. This can be achieved by the use of aluminium or plastic mesh, or aluminium tape.

Aluminium or plastic mesh or glass fibre matting, such as the Holts Body + Plus Glass Fibre Matting, is probably the best material to use for a large hole. Cut a piece to the approximate size and shape of the hole to be filled, then position it in the hole so that its edges are below the level of the surrounding bodywork. It can be retained in position by several blobs of filler paste around its periphery.

Aluminium tape should be used for small or very narrow holes. Pull a piece off the roll and trim it to the approximate size and shape required, then pull off the backing paper (if used) and stick the tape over the hole. It can be overlapped if the thickness of one piece is insufficient. Burnish down the edges of the tape with the handle of a screwdriver or similar, to ensure that the tape is securely attached to the metal underneath.

### Bodywork repairs – filling and re-spraying

Before using this Section, see the Sections on dents, deep scratches, rust holes and gash repairs.

Many types of bodyfiller are available, but generally speaking those proprietary kits which contain a tin of filler paste and a tube of resin hardener are best for this type of repair, like Holts Body + Plus or Holts No Mix which can be used directly from the tube. A wide, flexible plastic or nylon applicator will be found invaluable for imparting a smooth and well contoured finish to the surface of the filler.

Mix up a little filler on a clean piece of card or board – measure the hardener carefully (follow the maker's instructions on the pack) otherwise the filler will set too rapidly or too slowly. Alternatively, Holts No Mix can be used straight from the tube without mixing, although daylight is required to cure it. Using the applicator, apply the filler paste to the prepared area; drawing the applicator across the surface of the filler to achieve the correct contour and to level the filler surface. As soon as a contour that approximates to the correct one is achieved, stop working the paste – if you carry on too long the paste will become sticky and begin to 'pick up' on the applicator. Continue to add thin layers of

filler paste at 20-minute intervals until the level of the filler is just proud of the surrounding bodywork.

Once the filler has hardened, excess can be removed using a metal plane or file. From then on, progressively finer grades of abrasive paper should be used, starting with a 40 grade production paper and finishing with a 400 grade wet-and-dry paper. Always wrap the abrasive paper around a flat rubber, cork, or wooden block, otherwise the surface of the filler will not be completely flat. During the smoothing of the filler surface the wet-and-dry paper should be periodically rinsed in water. This will ensure that a very smooth finish is imparted to the filler at the final stage.

At this stage the 'dent' should be surrounded by a ring of bare metal, which in turn should be encircled by the finely 'feathered' edge of the good paintwork. Rinse the repair area with clean water, until all of the dust produced by the rubbing-down operation has gone.

Spray the whole repair area with a light coat of primer, either Holts Body + Plus Grey or Red Oxide Primer, which will show up any imperfections in the surface of the filler. Repair these imperfections with fresh filler paste or bodystopper, and once more smooth the surface with abrasive paper. If bodystopper is used, it can be mixed with cellulose thinners to form a really thin paste which is ideal for filling small holes. Repeat this spray and repair procedure until you are satisfied that the surface of the filler, and the feathered edge of the paintwork, are perfect. Clean the repair area with clean water and allow to dry fully.

The repair area is now ready for final spraying. Paint spraying must be carried out in a warm, dry, windless and dust free atmosphere. This condition can be created artificially if you have access to a large indoor working area, but if you are forced to work in the open, you will have to pick your day very carefully. If you are working indoors, dousing the floor in the work area with water will help to settle the dust which would otherwise be in the atmosphere. If the repair area is confined to one body panel, mask off the surrounding panels, which will help to minimise the effects of a slight mis-match in paint colours. Bodywork fittings (eg chrome strips, door handles etc) will also need to be masked off. Use genuine masking tape and several thicknesses of newspaper for the masking operations.

Before commencing to spray, agitate the aerosol can thoroughly, then spray a test area (an old tin, or similar) until the technique is mastered. Cover the repair area with a thick coat of primer, but note that the thickness should be built up using several thin layers of paint rather than one thick one. Using 400 grade wet-and-dry paper, rub down the surface of the primer until it is really smooth. While doing this, the work area should be thoroughly doused with water, and the wet-and-dry paper periodically rinsed in water. Allow to dry before spraying on more paint.

Spray on the top coat using Holts Dupli-Color Autospray, again building up the thickness by using several thin layers of paint. Start spraying in the centre of the repair area and then, with a side-to-side motion, work outwards until the whole repair area and about 2 inches of the surrounding original paintwork is covered. Remove all masking material 10 to 15 minutes after spraying on the final coat of paint.

Allow the new paint at least two weeks to harden, then, using a paintwork renovator or a very fine cutting paste such as Turtle Wax New Color Back or Holts Body + Plus Rubbing Compound, blend the edges of the paint into the existing paintwork. Finally, apply wax polish.

### Plastic components

With the use of more and more plastic body components by the vehicle manufacturers (eg bumpers, spoilers, and in some cases major body panels), rectification of more serious damage to such items has become a matter of either entrusting repair work to a specialist in this field, or renewing complete components. Repair of such damage by the DIY owner is not really feasible owing to the cost of the equipment and materials required for effecting such repairs. The basic technique involves making a groove along the line of the crack in the plastic using a rotary burr in a power drill. The damaged part is then welded back together by using a hot air gun to heat up and fuse a plastic filler rod into the groove. Any excess plastic is then removed and the area rubbed down to a smooth finish. It is important that a filler rod of the correct plastic is used, as body components can be made of a variety of different types (eg polycarbonate, ABS, polypropylene).

Damage of a less serious nature (abrasions, minor cracks etc) can be repaired by the DIY owner using a two-part epoxy filler repair material like Holts Body + Plus or Holts No Mix which can be used directly from the tube. Once mixed in equal proportions (or applied direct from the tube in the case of Holts No Mix), this is used in similar fashion to the

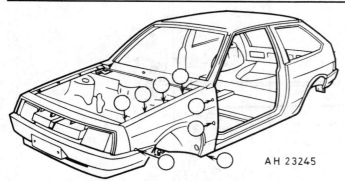

**Fig. 10.1 Front wing mounting points (Sec 8)**

bodywork filler used on metal panels. The filler is usually cured in 20 to 30 minutes, ready for sanding and painting.

If the owner is renewing a complete component himself, or if he has repaired it with epoxy filler, he will be left with the problem of finding a suitable paint for finishing which is compatible with the type of plastic used. At one time the use of a universal paint was not possible owing to the complex range of plastics encountered in body component applications. Standard paints, generally speaking, will not bond to plastic or rubber satisfactorily, but Holts Professional Spraymatch to match any plastic or rubber finish can be obtained from dealers. However, it is now possible to obtain a plastic body parts finishing kit which consists of a pre-primer treatment, a primer and coloured top coat. Full instructions are normally supplied with a kit, but basically the method of use is to first apply the pre-primer to the component concerned and allow it to dry for up to 30 minutes. Then the primer is applied and left to dry for about an hour before finally applying the special coloured top coat. The result is a correctly coloured component where the paint will flex with the plastic or rubber, a property that standard paint does not normally possess.

## 7 Major body damage – repair

Where serious damage has occurred, or large areas need renewal due to neglect, it means that complete new panels will need welding in, and this is best left to professionals. If the damage is due to impact, it will also be necessary to check completely the alignment of the bodyshell, and this can only be carried out accurately by a Lada dealer using special jigs. If the body is left misaligned, it is primarily dangerous as the car will not handle properly, and secondly, uneven stresses will be imposed on the steering, suspension and possibly transmission, causing abnormal wear, or complete failure, particularly to such items as the tyres.

## 8 Front wings – removal and refitting

1 Remove the direction indicator side repeater lamp (Chapter 11).
2 There is no need to remove the front bumper, but it may be necessary to slacken its mountings slightly (Sec 9) so that the cover moulding can be moved aside to reach the wing's front lower fastening screw.
3 Open the bonnet and remove the hexagon-headed screws securing the wing (Fig. 10.1).
4 Cut along the joints and remove the wing.
5 Before fitting the new wing, clean the body mating surfaces and apply new sealing strips.
6 Fit the wing and adjust its position, moving the screws in their slotted holes, then tighten them securely.
7 Apply protective coating under the wing and refinish the outer surface to match the body colour.
8 Refit all remaining components using the reverse of the removal procedure.

## 9 Bumpers – removal and refitting

1 Removing the retaining screws or nuts (whichever are easier to

9.1A Front bumper end mounting bracket nuts (arrowed) seen from below

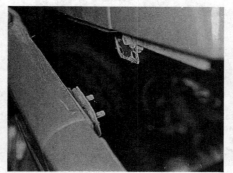

9.1B Pull bumper outwards to clear bracket

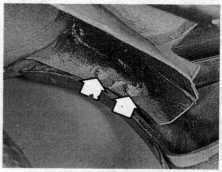

9.1C Rear bumper end mounting bracket nuts (arrowed) seen from below

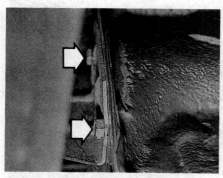

9.2A Unscrew main mounting bracket nuts (arrowed) – front bumper ...

9.2B ... and rear bumper (seen from below)

9.2C Front bumper main mountings (arrowed) – note elongated slots in bracket

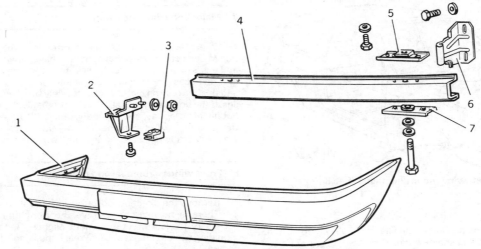

**Fig. 10.2 Bumper components (Sec 9)**

| | | |
|---|---|---|
| 1 Cover moulding | 3 Captive nut | 5 Upper fastening plate | 7 Lower fastening plate |
| 2 End mounting bracket | 4 Reinforcing member | 6 Main mounting bracket | |

10.1 Note location of metal plates under two of surround top screws

10.2 Unscrewing radiator grille-to-surround screws ...

10.3 ... and surround side end screws ...

reach), undo the bracket which secures each end of the bumper to the body (photos).

2   Reaching up underneath the bumper, unbolt its two main mounting brackets from the body (photos). Withdraw the bumper.

3   Unbolt the mounting bracket, if required, to separate the cover moulding from the duraluminium reinforcing member.

4   On SLX models, note that the front spoiler and rear skirt are riveted over the standard model cover mouldings.

5   Refitting is the reverse of the removal procedure. Note that the main mountings are slotted, to permit the bumper to be aligned with the surrounding bodywork.

## 10   Radiator grille/headlamp surround – removal and refitting

1   Open the bonnet and remove the screws securing the surround to the bonnet lock platform, noting the location of the metal plates under two of them (photo).

2   Prising up the surround if necessary, remove the screws securing it to the radiator grille's upper edge, noting the nylon bushes on the two end screws (photo).

3   Remove the screw securing each of the surround's side ends (photo). There is no need to remove the front bumper, but it may be necessary to slacken its mountings slightly (Sec 9) so that the cover moulding can be moved aside to reach the screw.

4   Unclip the surround from behind the front direction indicator lamps and the bumper (photo), then remove it.

5   The metal reinforcing plate under the surround is retained by nuts and washers.

6   Refitting is the reverse of the removal procedure. Do not over-tighten the retaining screws or the paint will crack, and ensure that the surround is aligned with the adjacent bodywork.

10.4 ... then unhook surround from behind lamp assemblies and bumper

## 11 Radiator grille – removal and refitting

1 Remove the radiator grille/headlamp surround (Sec 10).
2 Release the grille from the clips securing its lower edge (photo) and remove it.
3 Refitting is the reverse of the removal procedure.

## 12 Bonnet, removal, refitting and adjustment

1 The help of an assistant will be required for these operations. First, with the bonnet propped open, place a thick pad of cloth beneath each rear corner of the bonnet to protect the paintwork.
2 Disconnect the windscreen washer tubing.
3 Remove the under-bonnet lamp (Chapter 11), disconnecting its wiring and tie a length of string to the wire ends. Pull the wiring down through the bonnet channel, then untie the string, leaving it in the channel.
4 Mark with a pencil across the hinge arms where they enter the bonnet mountings, then slacken the bonnet-to-hinge arm bolts.
5 Working with one person at each side (photo), support the bonnet on the shoulders, lower the stay and unscrew the bolts. Remove the bonnet.
6 The hinge arms are each retained by a single, shouldered pivot bolt with a spring washer. Check that these are greased and securely fastened whenever the bonnet is removed.
7 The bonnet stay can be removed by working it out of its locating rubber bush in the bonnet lock platform.
8 Refitting is the reverse of the removal procedure, but align the marks made on removal and tighten only lightly at first the bonnet-to-hinge arm bolts, then gently close the bonnet and check that it aligns

11.2 Releasing one of radiator grille bottom mounting clips

evenly with the surrounding bodywork.
9 If adjustment is required, slacken the bonnet-to-hinge arm bolts and reposition the bonnet on the hinge arms until the fit is correct. In extreme cases it is permissible to bend the hinge arms. Refer to Section 13 for details of adjustments possible with the bonnet lock.
10 When the bonnet fit is correct, tighten the bolts securely. Use the string to pull the under-bonnet lamp wiring back throught the bonnet channel.

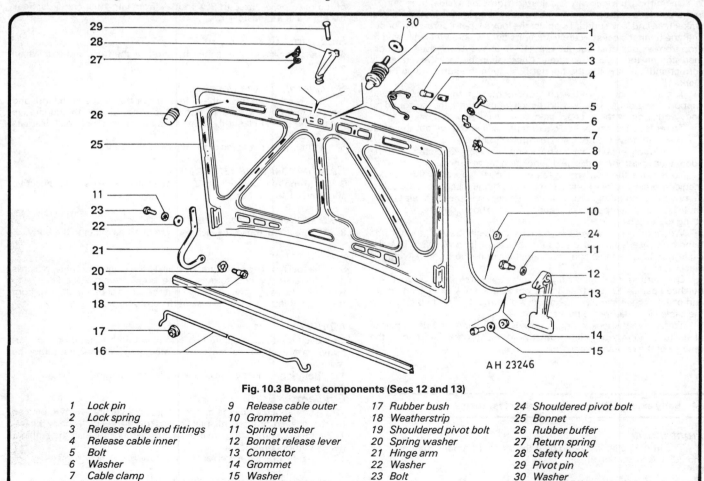

AH 23246

**Fig. 10.3 Bonnet components (Secs 12 and 13)**

| | | | |
|---|---|---|---|
| 1 Lock pin | 9 Release cable outer | 17 Rubber bush | 24 Shouldered pivot bolt |
| 2 Lock spring | 10 Grommet | 18 Weatherstrip | 25 Bonnet |
| 3 Release cable end fittings | 11 Spring washer | 19 Shouldered pivot bolt | 26 Rubber buffer |
| 4 Release cable inner | 12 Bonnet release lever | 20 Spring washer | 27 Return spring |
| 5 Bolt | 13 Connector | 21 Hinge arm | 28 Safety hook |
| 6 Washer | 14 Grommet | 22 Washer | 29 Pivot pin |
| 7 Cable clamp | 15 Washer | 23 Bolt | 30 Washer |
| 8 Cable tie | 16 Bonnet stay | | |

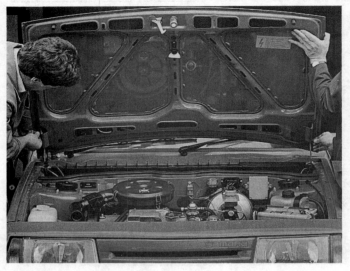

12.5 Always have an assistant to help with bonnet removal

13.7 Facia must be removed to reach bonnet release lever

---

### 13   Bonnet lock and release cable – removal and refitting

1    Open and prop the bonnet, then use a pencil to mark around the bonnet lock pin. Slacken the locknut and unscrew the lock. If it is worn or damaged, the lock must be renewed as a single unit.
2    On refitting, the lock can be adjusted (from side to side) by moving it in the bonnet's slotted mounting hole so that it aligns exactly with the striker hole and lock spring. To adjust the lock's length, screw it in or out until the bonnet closes securely under its own weight when allowed to drop from a point of about 300 mm (12 in) above its released position, then tighten the locknut securely. Check that the locks' operation is correct and that it holds the bonnet flush with the surrounding body-work.
3    The rubber buffers at each front corner of the bonnet should support the bonnet evenly and exactly flush with the surrounding bodywork. Renew them if necessary to achieve this.
4    To remove the safety hook, extract its clip and drive out the pivot pin, then withdraw the hook and its return spring.
5    On refitting, ensure that the hook engages securely on the lip of the bonnet lock platform and is held in position by its spring.
6    To remove the bonnet release cable, open and prop the bonnet, then compress the lock spring arm to the left and disconnect the cable. Remove the end fittings from the cable inner and outer and release the cable from any clamps or ties securing it to the body, then tie a length of string to the cable end.
7    Working inside the vehicle, remove the facia (Sec 33), unbolt the bonnet release lever and disconnect the lever (photo). Withdraw the cable into the passenger compartment, then untie the string, leaving it in place.
8    On refitting, use the string to draw the cable back through the bulkhead panels. Ensure the cable is not trapped or kinked at any point and check for satisfactory operation. Adjustment is made by bending the cable stops. Lubricate the cable (Sec 4).
9    To remove the lock spring, disconnect the cable and use a pair of pliers to unhook the spring from the lock platform. Refitting is the reverse of the removal procedure.

---

### 14   Body exterior fittings – removal and refitting

#### Front spoiler
1    The front spoiler is riveted over the standard model bumper cover moulding (see Section 9).

#### Rear spoiler (early type)
2    The spoiler is glued on to the tailgate, so seek the advice of a Lada

dealer as to the best solvent to use which will soften the adhesive without damaging the paintwork. On refitting, ensure that the mating surfaces are clean, smooth and grease-free and use only a recommended adhesive to attach the spoiler.

#### Rear spoiler (later type)
3    No information is available at the time of writing on the attachment of the rear spoiler fitted to SLX models from late 1990 onwards. Seek the advice of a Lada dealer.

#### Side skirts (SLX)
4    The side skirts are attached by rivets at the front and rear wheel arches.

#### B-pillar trim (three-door and Van)
5    Gently prise out the emblem from the bottom edge of the trim and remove the retaining screws, noting the supporting bush and captive nut behind each. Pull out the trim at the bottom and unhook it from its upper mounting.
6    Refitting is the reverse of the removal procedure.

#### Rear number plate reflective surround
7    With the rear number plate removed (two screws), the reflective surround can be withdrawn.

#### Rear wheel arch stoneguards
8    Where fitted, these are each secured by three rivets to the body.

#### Fuel filler flap
9    The fuel filler flap is secured by a pin to the hinge assembly, which is itself fastened by two screws to the body. Remove the screws to withdraw the assembly, then drive out the pin to separate the flap from the hinge. Refitting is the reverse of the removal procedure.

#### Mudflaps
10    Each mudflap is secured by two nuts to a bracket on the under-body. Unscrew the nuts, remove the mounting plate and withdraw the mudflap.
11    Refitting is the reverse of the removal procedure.

#### Emblems
12    The various emblems on the tailgate are secured by two pins on the rear of each, pressed into plastic clips that are set in the body panels. To remove the emblems, use a slim knife blade to prise off the emblem gently without breaking it.
13    To refit, press the emblem into its clips until it is firmly fixed.

#### Engine compartment undershields
14    The engine compartment left-hand undershield is retained by four

14.14 Engine compartment undershields

bolts to the body and inner wing panel, while the right-hand undershield is retained by five. In addition, the shields are joined to each other by two bolts in the middle (photo). Unscrew the bolts as required to release the shields.

### Roof drip channel

15 The drip channel along the roof edges is clipped in place and can be prised off if care is taken not to break it or to damage the paintwork. On refitting, ensure that the channel is pressed securely into place.

### 15 Winscreen, tailgate glass and quarterlight glass – removal and refitting

These areas of glass are secured by the tight fit of the weatherstrip in the body aperture. Although they are not fixed by the direct-bonding method used on many modern vehicles, the removal and refitting of these areas of fixed glass is still difficult, messy and time-consuming for the inexperienced. It is also difficult, unless one has plenty of practice, to obtain a secure, waterproof fit. Furthermore, the task carries a high risk of breakage, especially in the case of the laminated glass windscreen. In view of this, owners are strongly advised to have this sort of work carried out by one of the many specialist windscreen fitters.

### 16 Sunroof – general

1 The sunroof glass is removed by unfastening the rear catch and removing the screws securing the glass to the hinges. All screws are covered by small plastic caps.
2 The hinges can be unfastened from the roof and the weatherstrip peeled away if required.
3 If the sunroof leaks or is draughty, some adjustment is possible by slackening the screws and moving the glass as required, then retightening the screws.

### 17 Tailgate – removal, refitting and adjustment

1 The help of an assistant will be required for these operations. First, with the tailgate open, place a thick pad of cloth beneath each top corner of the tailgate to protect the paintwork.

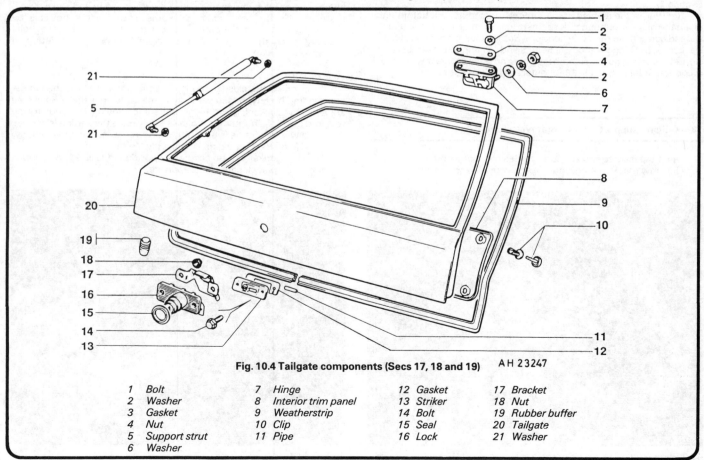

**Fig. 10.4 Tailgate components (Secs 17, 18 and 19)**        AH 23247

| | | | | | | | |
|---|---|---|---|---|---|---|---|
| 1 | Bolt | 7 | Hinge | 12 | Gasket | 17 | Bracket |
| 2 | Washer | 8 | Interior trim panel | 13 | Striker | 18 | Nut |
| 3 | Gasket | 9 | Weatherstrip | 14 | Bolt | 19 | Rubber buffer |
| 4 | Nut | 10 | Clip | 15 | Seal | 20 | Tailgate |
| 5 | Support strut | 11 | Pipe | 16 | Lock | 21 | Washer |
| 6 | Washer | | | | | | |

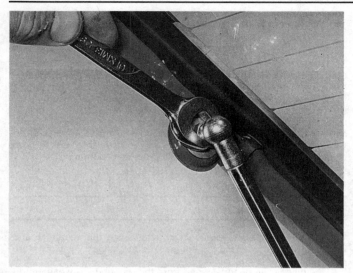

18.2 Unscrewing tailgate strut bottom mounting

2    Prise away the weatherstrip and detach the headlining rear edge so that the tailgate wiring connectors can be extracted and disconnected and the tailgate hinge mountings can be reached.
3    Support the tailgate and remove the struts (Sec 18).
4    Use a pencil to mark around the hinge mountings, then unscrew the hinge bolts or nuts (whichever are easier to reach) and remove the tailgate.
5    Note the earth connection on the left-hand hinge bolt, and ensure that there is clean, metal-to-metal contact at this point (Chapter 11, Section 1).
6    Refitting is the reverse of the removal procedure, but before tightening the hinge mountings, close the tailgate gently and check that it is aligned correctly in the body aperture. Some adjustment is possible by slackening the hinge-to-body fasteners and moving the assembly in the slotted mounting holes. Tighten the nuts and bolts securely when the fit is correct. Refer to Section 19 for details of lock adjustment.

---

### 18   Tailgate support struts – removal and refitting

1    Open the tailgate and support it with a piece of wood.
2    Unscrew the mountings (photo) and withdraw the strut(s).

19.2 Removing tailgate lock – note earth wire

3    The struts are sealed, containing gas under pressure. Do not attempt to dismantle them or apply any heat. Dispose of them safely.
4    Refitting is the reverse of the removal procedure.

---

### 19   Tailgate lock – removal and refitting

#### Lock
1    Remove the tailgate interior trim panel (Sec 26).
2    Unscrew the two retaining nuts, noting the earth wire terminals on one of them, then remove the lock (photo).
3    Refitting is the reverse of the removal procedure.

#### Striker
4    Open the tailgate and use a pencil to mark around the striker.
5    Unscrew the mounting bolts and withdraw the striker (photo).
6    Refitting is the reverse of the removal procedure, but before tightening the striker bolts, check that the tailgate lock catch and locating projection fit exactly into the striker. If adjustment is required, move the striker in its slotted mountings until the fit is correct, then tighten the bolts securely.

---

### 20   Doors – removal, refitting and adjustment

#### Removal and refitting
1    If necessary, remove the door interior trim panel (Sec 26) to disconnect any loudspeaker wiring.
2    Disconnect the check link, either by driving out the pin or by unbolting the link from the body (photo).
3    Support the door on blocks of wood, then unscrew the hinge bolts and remove the door.
4    Refitting is the reverse of the removal procedure, but lubricate the hinges and check components. Close the door gently and check that it fits closely in the body aperture. Some adjustment is possible by slackening the hinge bolts and moving the door. Tighten the bolts securely when the fit is correct. Refer to Section 21 for details of lock/striker adjustment.

#### Adjustment
5    If a door will not close properly, first check that it fits flush with the surrounding bodywork and centrally in the body aperture. This can be adjusted by slackening the hinge bolts and moving the door to the required position. Tighten the bolts securely once the setting is correct.
6    If the window frame is preventing closure, wind down the window glass and lever the frame gently until it fits.
7    The door striker can be accurately positioned (Sec 21) only when the door is properly located in its aperture.

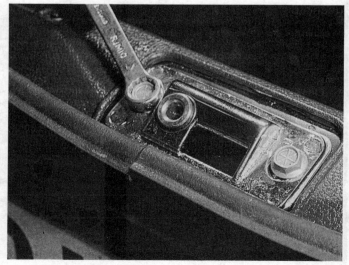

19.5 Tailgate striker

20.2 Rear door bottom hinge bolt 'A' and check link bolts 'B'

2   Wind the window glass fully up and, where necessary, pull off the inner weatherstrip and pull out the plastic water-deflecting sheet, carefully releasing the clips along its upper edge (photos).
3   Releasing the spring clips where necessary, disconnect the link rods from the handle assembly.
4   Unscrew the retaining nuts and remove the handle (photos).
5   Refitting is the reverse of the removal procedure.

### Interior handle

6   Remove the door interior trim panel (Sec 26).
7   Wind the window glass fully up and, where necessary, pull off the inner weatherstrip and pull out the plastic water-deflecting sheet, carefully releasing the clips along its upper edge.
8   Releasing the spring clips where necessary, disconnect the handle's link rod from the lock assembly.
9   Referring to Section 22, slacken the window regulator mounting nuts around the regulator handle, then press back the regulator to allow the door lock link rods to be moved.
10  Remove the retaining screws, then withdraw the handle (photos).
11  Refitting is the reverse of the removal procedure. Note that the handle's mounting holes are slotted to provide some means of adjustment.

## 21  Door lock and handle components – removal and refitting

### Exterior handle

1   Remove the door interior trim panel (Sec 26).

### Inside lock knob – front door

12  Remove the door interior trim panel (Sec 26).
13  Wind the window glass fully up and, where necessary, pull off the inner weatherstrip and pull out the plastic water-deflecting sheet, releasing carefully the clips along its upper edge.

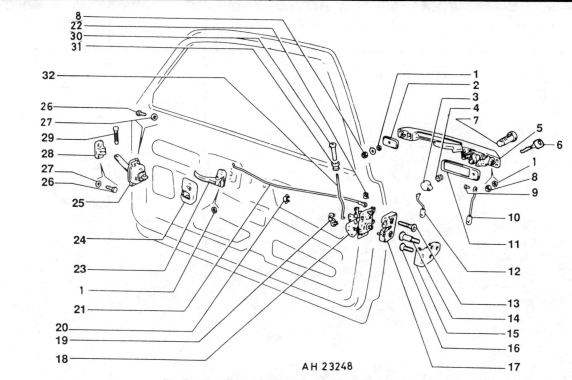

AH 23248

**Fig. 10.5 Front door lock components (Secs 20 and 21)**

| | | | |
|---|---|---|---|
| 1  Washer | 9  Screw | 17 Lock outer section | 24 Escutcheon |
| 2  Escutcheon | 10 Link rod (exterior handle-to-lock) | 18 Lock inner section | 25 Check link |
| 3  Lock driver | 11 Escutcheon | 19 Spring clip | 26 Bolt |
| 4  Spring | 12 Link rod (lock barrel-to-lock) | 20 Clip | 27 Washer |
| 5  Exterior handle | 13 Screw | 21 Link rod (interior handle-to-lock) | 28 Check link mounting |
| 6  Key | 14 Striker pin | | 29 Pin |
| 7  Lock barrel | 15 Striker | 22 Spring clip | 30 Inside lock knob |
| 8  Nut | 16 Screw | 23 Interior handle | 31 Grommet |

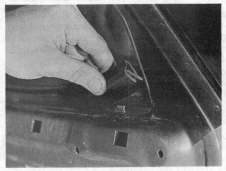

21.2A Pull off door window glass inner weatherstrip ...

21.2B ... and unclip plastic water-deflecting sheet

21.4A Unscrewing door exterior handle retaining nuts

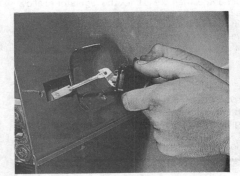

21.4B Removing door exterior handle

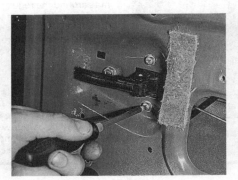

21.10A Remove retaining screws ...

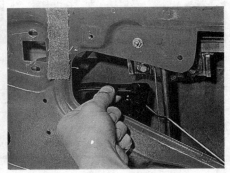

21.10B ... and manoeuvre interior handle, with link rod, out of door

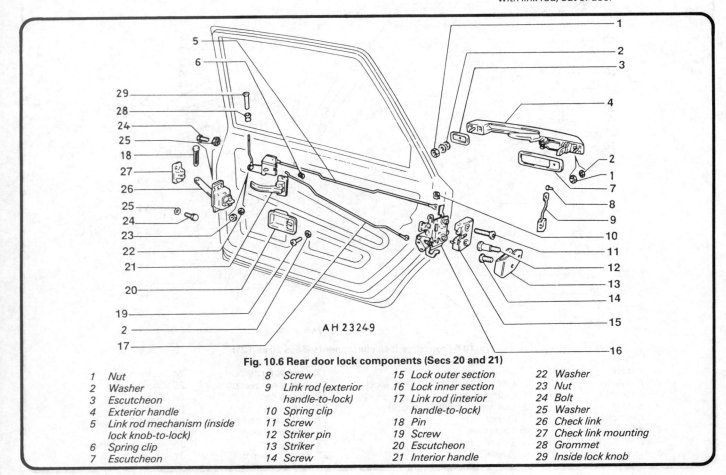

AH 23249

**Fig. 10.6 Rear door lock components (Secs 20 and 21)**

| | |
|---|---|
| 1   Nut | 8    Screw |
| 2   Washer | 9    Link rod (exterior handle-to-lock) |
| 3   Escutcheon | 10   Spring clip |
| 4   Exterior handle | 11   Screw |
| 5   Link rod mechanism (inside lock knob-to-lock) | 12   Striker pin |
| 6   Spring clip | 13   Striker |
| 7   Escutcheon | 14   Screw |

| | |
|---|---|
| 15   Lock outer section | 22   Washer |
| 16   Lock inner section | 23   Nut |
| 17   Link rod (interior handle-to-lock) | 24   Bolt |
| 18   Pin | 25   Washer |
| 19   Screw | 26   Check link |
| 20   Escutcheon | 27   Check link mounting |
| 21   Interior handle | 28   Grommet |
| | 29   Inside lock knob |

21.20 Rear door inside knob link rod mechanism is secured by the nut ...

21.21 ... showing arrangement of rear door inside knob link rod mechanism

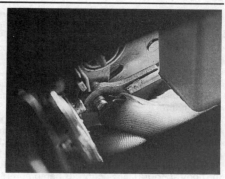

21.27A Refitting one of link rod spring clips to door lock inner section

21.27B Rear door lock inner section in place

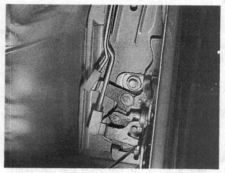

21.27C Front door lock inner section in place

14    Releasing the spring clips where necessary, disconnect the knob's link rod from the lock assembly. Withdraw the rod.
15    Refitting is the reverse of the removal procedure.

### Inside lock knob – rear door

16    Remove the door interior trim panel (Sec 26).
17    Wind the window glass fully up and, where necessary, pull off the inner weatherstrip and pull out the plastic water-deflecting sheet, carefully releasing the clips along its upper edge.
18    Releasing the spring clips where necessary, disconnect the knob's link rod from the lock assembly and from the door inner panel.
19    Referring to Section 27, slacken the window regulator mounting nuts around the regulator handle, then press back the regulator to allow the door lock link rods to be moved.
20    Unscrew the retaining nut from behind the interior handle (photo).

21    Withdraw the inside lock knob link rod mechanism (photo).
22    Refitting is the reverse of the removal procedure.

### Lock barrel

23    Remove the exterior handle (see paragraphs 1 to 4 above), then disengage the lock barrel from the handle.
24    Refitting is the reverse of the removal procedure.

### Lock mechanism

25    Remove the door interior trim panel (Sec 26).
26    Wind the window glass fully up and, where necessary, pull off the inner weatherstrip and pull out the plastic water-deflecting sheet, carefully releasing the clips along its upper edge.
27    Releasing the spring clips where necessary, disconnect the link rods from the lock assembly (photos).

21.28A Unscrewing rear door lock retaining screws

21.28B Note how lock outer and inner sections engage

21.32 Rear door striker

28    Remove the retaining screws, then withdraw the lock outer section, noting how it engages with the inner section (photos).
29    Withdraw the lock inner section.
30    Refitting is the reverse of the removal procedure.

### Striker

31    Open the door and mark around the striker with a pencil.
32    Unscrew the striker pin and retaining screws and withdraw the striker (photo).
33    On refitting, align the striker with the marks made on removal, tighten the screws and striker pin securely, then check that the door closes securely, flush with the surrounding bodywork and with no sign of rattles. If adjustment is required, proceed as follows.
34    To adjust the striker, check first that the door is properly located in the body aperture (see Section 20, paragraphs 5 and 6). When the door's fit is correct, slacken the striker screws and pin, then move the striker plate in or out until the door closes properly, or up or down until the lock engages squarely on the striker.
35    Tighten the striker screws and pin securely when adjustment is complete, then recheck the setting.

---

**22    Door window glass and regulator – removal and refitting**

### Window glass – removal and refitting

1    Open the door, wind the window glass fully up, then remove the interior trim panel (Sec 26).
2    Pull off the inner and outer weatherstrips (photo), then pull out the plastic water-deflecting sheet, carefully releasing the clips along its upper edge.
3    Lower the window glass halfway and mark the relationship of the regulator channel to the regulator before unscrewing the two bolts securing the glass to the regulator channel (photo).
4    Manoeuvre the window glass out of the door (photo). It may prove necessary to slacken the mounting bolts so that the vertical guide(s) can be moved aside, or even removed.

22.2 Removing door window glass outer weatherstrip

5    Refitting is the reverse of the removal procedure, but apply a little grease to the regulator mechanism and align the marks that were made on removal before tightening the two bolts. Check that the glass moves smoothly and easily through its full travel.

### Window glass – adjustment

6    If draughts etc show that the fit of the window in the door requires adjustment, remove the door interior trim panel and slacken the two bolts securing the glass to the regulator channel. Wind the window fully up and ensure that the glass is correctly positioned in the regulator channel, then tighten the two bolts. If the vertical guides need alteration, slacken their bolts and wind the window fully down, then position the guide(s) closely on the glass before tightening their bolts.

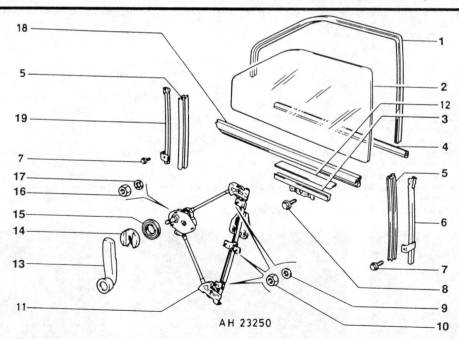

AH 23250

**Fig. 10.7 Door window glass and regulator components – front shown, rear similar (Sec 22)**

| | | | | | |
|---|---|---|---|---|---|
| 1 | Weatherstrip | 6 | Rear vertical guide | 11 | Regulator mechanism | 16 | 5 mm nut |
| 2 | Window glass | 7 | Screw | 12 | Packing | 17 | Washer |
| 3 | Regulator channel | 8 | Bolt | 13 | Regulator handle | 18 | Inner weatherstrip |
| 4 | Outer weatherstrip | 9 | Washer | 14 | Keeper | 19 | Front vertical guide |
| 5 | Guide channel | 10 | 6 mm nut | 15 | Collar | | |

22.3 Unbolting door window glass from regulator channel

22.4 Manoeuvring window glass from door

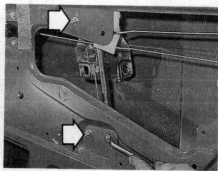

22.12A Rear door window glass regulator mounting nuts (arrowed) at rear ...

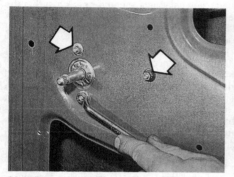

22.12B ... and around winder mechanism (arrowed)

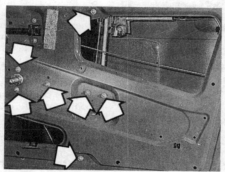

22.12C Front door window glass regulator mounting nuts (arrowed)

22.12D Removing window glass regulator mechanism from rear door

7 Check that the glass moves smoothly and easily through its full travel.

### Regulator

8 Open the door, wind the window glass fully up, then remove the interior trim panel (Sec 26).
9 Pull off the inner weatherstrip, then pull out the plastic water-deflecting sheet, releasing carefully the clips along its upper edge.
10 Lower the window glass halfway and mark the relationship of the regulator channel to the regulator before unscrewing the two bolts securing the glass to the regulator channel.
11 Wind the window glass fully up and secure it with adhesive tape, then wind the regulator halfway down again.
12 Unscrew the regulator retaining nuts (photos) and withdraw the regulator.

13 Refitting is the reverse of the removal procedure, but apply a little grease to the regulator mechanism and refit it, tightening the mounting bolts only loosely at first. Move the window glass several times through its full travel to check that the glass moves smoothly and easily. If necessary, slacken the mounting nuts and bolts to adjust the fit of those components that require it.

### 23 Exterior mirror glass – renewal

1 Prise the cover plug out of the mirror housing, then unscrew the retaining nut and remove the spring and dished washer beneath (photos).
2 Disengage the glass base from the adjustment lever and remove it (photo).
3 Refitting is the reverse of the removal procedure.

23.1A Prise cover plug out of exterior mirror housing ...

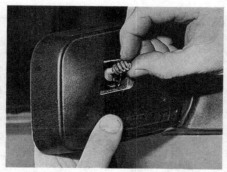

23.1B ... unscrew nut and remove spring ...

23.1C ... note which way round dished washer is fitted

23.2 Disengage glass base from adjustment lever

---

**24    Exterior mirror assembly – removal and refitting**

1    Pull off the mirror adjustment handle and prise off the trim panel. Note that on some vehicles the panel will also be secured by a single screw (photos).
2    Remove the retaining screws and withdraw the mirror assembly (photos).
3    Refitting is the reverse of the removal procedure.

---

**25    Interior rear view mirror – removal and refitting**

1    The mirror itself is secured by a single grub screw to a base that is

stuck to the windscreen. The base is mounted on the vehicle's centre-line, 105 mm below the windscreen's upper edge.
2    **Do not** disturb the base unless absolutely necessary, as it is very difficult to achieve a reliable bond. If the windscreen is to be renewed, this is a further argument for having the work carried out by a specialist windscreen fitter who will be well-versed in the removal and refitting of stick-on mirrors.
3    If the base is to be removed and is found to be glued in place, seek the advice of a Lada dealer. Find out how best to remove the base (without risking cracking the windscreen) and which commercially-available adhesive is suitable for use on reassembly.
4    On refitting, use a sharp knife or razor blade to clean off all traces of old adhesive and thoroughly degrease the base and windscreen mating surfaces using methylated spirit, isopropyl alcohol or ethyl alcohol. Apply the adhesive following its manufacturer's instructions and allow the adhesive to cure for the specified time. Note that with the standard Lada adhesive, the mirror must not be refitted for 24 hours after the base has been installed. A similar time limit may apply to the adhesive used.
5    If the base is attached using an adhesive patch, check first that the patch is available separately from Lada dealers. If not, try dealers in other makes (Ford and Rover, for example, supply patches separately), accessory shops or windscreen repair specialists.
6    Remove the base from the windscreen by 'sawing' through the adhesive bond using a length of nylon cord.
7    Remove all traces of the old patch, then degrease the base and windscreen mating surfaces with methylated spirit. Both areas must be perfectly clean. Generally speaking the windscreen must be at least at room temperature (20°C/68°F approx), but in some cases the instructions may call for it to be warmed as follows.
8    Warm the base, patch and windscreen to 50 to 70°C (122 to 158°F) using a heat gun, hair dryer or similar. Immediately remove the backing paper from the patch and press it on to the windscreen at the correct place, then refit the base, pressing it firmly for at least two minutes. The manufacturer's instructions may vary, but it is likely that the mirror cannot be refitted for at least an hour.
9    Beware of using proprietary adhesives (unless specifically recommended) to attach the mirror to the windscreen. Not all are suitable and some may leave residues which are difficult to remove, while others (such as the modern 'superglues') may actually cause the windscreen to crack.

24.1A Pull off exterior mirror adjustment handle ...

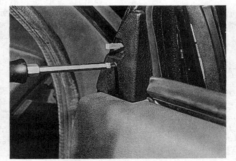

24.1B ... remove trim panel screw (where fitted) ...

24.1C ... and prise off trim panel

24.2A Remove retaining screws ...

24.2B ... and withdraw exterior mirror

26.2A Prise off door inside handle
escutcheon ...

26.2B ... and remove over handle

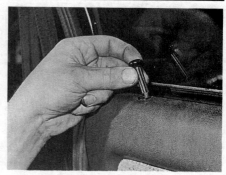

26.3 Unscrew inside lock knob

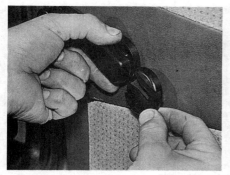

26.4A Press collar towards door and
withdraw keeper ...

26.4B ... pull handle off regulator ...

26.4C ... and withdraw collar, noting foam
seal

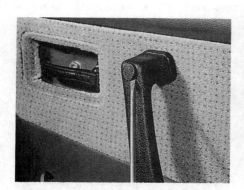

26.5A Prising cover plug out of grab handle ...

26.5B ... to remove handle retaining screws –
note handle escutcheon

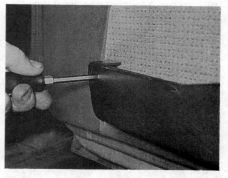

26.6 Door pocket screws must be removed –
front doors only

## 26 Interior trim panels – removal and refitting

### Door trim panel

1   On front doors, remove the trim panel surrounding the exterior
mirror adjustment handle (Sec 24).
2   Prise off the door inside handle escutcheon and withdraw it
(photos).
3   Unscrew the inside lock knob (photo).
4   Push its collar inwards (towards the door), slide out the keeper and
withdraw the window regulator handle, noting the foam washer behind
the collar (photos).
5   Prise out the cover plugs from the grab handle top and bottom ends
and remove the retaining screws. Withdraw the handle, noting the
escutcheon at its upper end (photos).
6   On front doors, remove the screws securing the door pocket
(photo).

7   Release the clips around its outer edge and carefully pull the trim
panel off the door (photo).
8   Refitting is the reverse of the removal procedure.

### Tailgate trim panel

9   Open the tailgate and carefully prise out the centre of each of the
two-piece clips securing the panel edge (photos). Withdraw the panel.
10   Refitting is the reverse of the removal procedure. Press each clip's
outer section into position, then secure it by pressing home the clip
centre.

### Door sill tread panels

11   Remove the retaining screws and lift away the panel. If they
overlap, it may also prove necessary to remove the adjoining trim
panels.

### A, B, and C-pillar trim

12   These panels are all retained by a number of screws. The correct

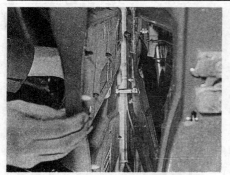

26.7 Removing door interior trim panel

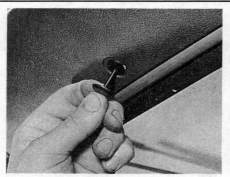

26.9A Tailgate trim panel clips are of two-piece type ...

26.9B ... and are released by prising out clip centre

removal procedure will be evident on inspection, but note that in some cases panels overlap and must therefore be removed in a certain sequence, and that the weatherstrip must be prised back to release some panels.

13    On three-door Hatchback models, the large trim panels at the bottom of each rear side window are secured by a number of clips, some of which are of the two-piece type described in paragraph 9 above.

### Luggage compartment trim panels

14    These panels are retained by a number of fasteners around their edges, either screws or clips being used. The basic removal procedure is as described in paragraph 12.

### Headlining

15    The moulded one-piece headlining is clipped to the roof and can be withdrawn once all fittings such as the grab handles, sunvisors and sunroof (if fitted) have been removed and the door, tailgate and sunroof aperture weatherstrips have been prised clear.

16    Note that headlining removal requires considerable skill and ex-

perience if it is to be carried out without damage and is therefore best entrusted to an expert.

### Carpets

17    The passenger compartment floor carpet is in one piece and is secured at its edges by screws or clips, usually the same fasteners used to secure the various adjoining trim panels.

18    Carpet removal and refitting is reasonably straightforward but very time-consuming due to the fact that all adjoining trim panels must be removed first, as must components such as the rear seat base cushion, the front seats, the centre console and some seat belt anchorages.

---

### 27    Seat belts – removal and refitting

---

### Front

1    Prise off the plastic cover and unbolt the belt top anchorage (photo).
2    Unbolt the belt bottom anchorage (photo).

27.1 Front seat belt top anchorage and cover

27.2 Unbolting front seat belt bottom anchorage

27.3 Release 'B' pillar trim panel to reach front seat belt retractor

27.4 Front seat belt buckle

27.7A Rear (side) seat belt bottom anchorage and cap

27.7B Rear (side) seat belt buckle and (centre) belt mountings

27.8 Rear (side) seat belt top anchorage and cover

27.10 Rear (side) seat belt retractor

3    Remove the 'B' pillar trim panel (Sec 26) and unbolt the retractor from the body (photo).
4    Peel back the rubber cover and unbolt the buckle from the floor (photo).
5    Refitting is the reverse of the removal procedure, but ensure that the anchorages are free to move when the bolts have been securely tightened.

### Rear

6    Lift the rear seat base cushion and remove the parcel shelf.
7    Unbolt the belt bottom anchorage and buckle from the floor (photos). Note that the centre two-point belt can be unbolted completely.
8    Prise off the plastic cover and unbolt the belt top anchorage (photo).
9    Fold forwards the rear seat back and remove its retaining screws as necessary to release the belt from the parcel shelf side section.
10   Unbolt the retractor from the body (photo).
11   Refitting is the reverse of the removal procedure, but ensure that

the anchorages are free to move when the bolts have been securely tightened.

## 28   Seats – removal and refitting

### Front

1    Operate the adjuster and move the seat fully forwards, then unhook the torsion bars.
2    Unscrew the front mounting rear nuts and rear mounting rear bolts (photo).
3    Move the seat fully backwards and unscrew the front mounting front nuts, then remove the front mounting clamps.
4    Tip the seat backwards and unscrew the rear mounting front bolts (photo). Remove the seat.

28.2 Unscrewing front seat rear mounting rear bolt ...

28.4 ... and rear mounting front bolt

28.5 Unscrewing front seat front mounting front nut – note arrangement of torsion bars

28.6 Unscrewing rear seat base cushion hinge mounting bolt

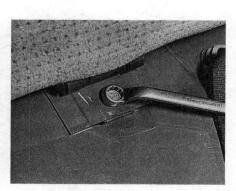

28.9 Unscrewing rear seat back hinge mounting bolt

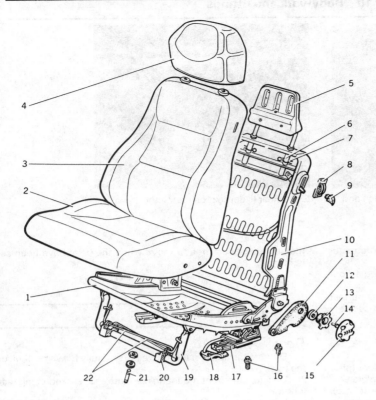

**Fig. 10.8 Front seat components – typical (Sec 28)**

1  Seat base frame
2  Base cushion
3  Backrest cushion
4  Head restraint cushion
5  Head restraint frame
6  Head restraint guide
7  Lockpin
8  Escutcheon
9  Backrest release handle
10 Backrest frame
11 Facing
12 Gasket
13 Holder
14 Bolt
15 Backrest adjustment handle
16 Bolts
17 Seat rail guide
18 Seat lock lever
19 Front support
20 Front mounting bracket
21 Stud
22 Torsion bars

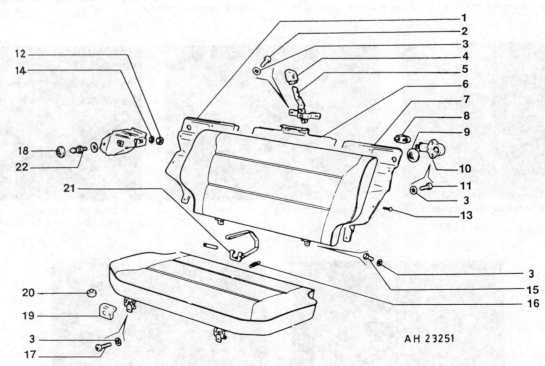

AH 23251

**Fig. 10.9 Rear seat components (Sec 28)**

| | | | |
|---|---|---|---|
| 1  Seat back right-hand panel | 7  Seat back left-hand panel | 13 Trim clip | 19 Hinge cover |
| 2  Screw | 8  Holder | 14 Washer | 20 Rubber buffer |
| 3  Washer | 9  Buffer | 15 Bolt | 21 Seat base cushion release tag |
| 4  Seat back lock knob | 10 Seat back lock | 16 Spring | 22 Locating stud |
| 5  Seat back lock catch | 11 Screw | 17 Bolt | |
| 6  Seat back centre panel | 12 Nut | 18 Facing | |

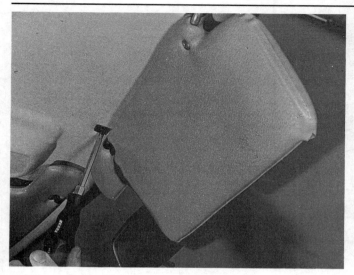

29.1 Unscrewing sunvisor clamp retaining screws

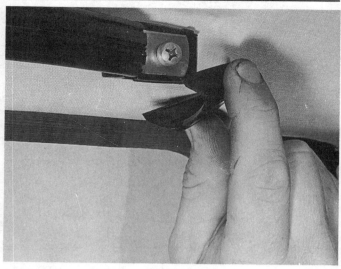

30.1 Grab handle end mounting and cover

5    Refitting is the reverse of the removal procedure. Ensure that the torsion bars are correctly arranged (photo).

*Rear*

6    Pull the seat base cushion release tag and lift the base cushion, then unscrew the single mounting bolt securing each hinge (photo).
7    Remove the seat base cushion.
8    Empty the luggage compartment and release the floor carpet.
9    Unscrew the single bolt securing each seat back hinge (photo) and release the seat back lock.
10    Remove the seat back, with the carpet.
11    Refitting is the reverse of the removal procedure.

### 29    Sunvisor – removal and refitting

1    Remove the retaining screws (photo) to release the pivot and clamp from the roof, then remove the assembly.
2    Refitting is the reverse of the removal procedure.

### 30    Grab handles – removal and refitting

1    Prise off the cover at each end and from the middle of the handle

and remove the retaining screws (photo). Withdraw the handle, noting the escutcheon at each mounting point.
2    Refitting is the reverse of the removal procedure.

### 31    Centre console – removal and refitting

1    Park the vehicle on level ground and chock the roadwheels so that it cannot move when the handbrake is released.
2    Release the gear lever gaiter and the seat belt buckle rubber cover from the centre console, then prise up the panel beneath the handbrake lever (photo).
3    Remove the retaining screws and withdraw the centre console, disengaging it from its front mounting clips (photos).
4    Refitting is the reverse of the removal procedure.

### 32    Glovebox – removal and refitting

1    The glovebox body is a moulded part of the facia, and its lid is retained by two pivot pins that can be withdrawn only when the facia is removed (Sec 33).
2    The lid catch is retained by a single pivot pin, which must be driven out to release the catch and its spring.

31.2 Remove panel from beneath handbrake lever and release gear lever gaiter

31.3A Unscrewing centre console rear mounting screws

31.3B Note centre console front mounting clips

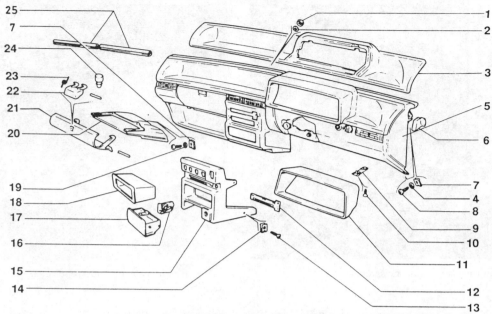

**Fig. 10.10 Facia components (Secs 32 and 33)**  A H 23252

| | | | |
|---|---|---|---|
| 1 | Nut | 8 | Screw |
| 2 | Washer | 9 | Clip |
| 3 | Facia cover | 10 | Screw |
| 4 | Washer | 11 | Instrument panel hood |
| 5 | Facia | 12 | Finisher |
| 6 | Stopper | 13 | Screw |
| 7 | Captive nut | | |

| | |
|---|---|
| 14 | Captive nut |
| 15 | Facia centre console |
| 16 | Ashtray guide |
| 17 | Ashtray |
| 18 | Ashtray surround |
| 19 | Washer |

| | |
|---|---|
| 20 | Glovebox body |
| 21 | Glovebox lid |
| 22 | Catch |
| 23 | Return spring |
| 24 | Rubber buffer |
| 25 | Seal |

33.8A Removing facia centre console retaining screws (one arrowed)

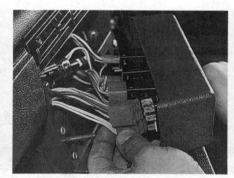

33.8B Disconnecting switch wiring from behind facia centre console

33.9A Removing heater control assembly retaining screws ...

## 33  Facia – removal and refitting

1   Disconnect the battery negative lead.
2   Disconnect the choke cable from the facia (Chapter 3).
3   Remove the steering lock/ignition switch (Chapter 9).
4   Remove the instrument panel (Chapter 11).
5   Remove the headlamp alignment control system control knob and unit (Chapter 11).
6   Remove the instrument panel rheostat (Chapter 11).
7   Remove the radio (Chapter 11).
8   Remove the four screws (two on each side) to release the facia centre console, pull off the heater fan and slider control knobs, disconnect the wiring from the cigarette lighter and the various switches and withdraw the console (photos).
9   Remove the four retaining screws and release the heater control assembly (photos).
10   Unscrew the two screws from inside the glovebox (photo).
11   Unscrew the four screws (two at each end) securing the facia. The upper pair are close to the door top hinge, while the lower pair are on a level with the check link (photos).
12   Carefully pull the facia away from the bulkhead, releasing it from the two clips (photo) along its upper edge. **Do not** use excessive force. This is not necessary and may damage the plastic components. If difficulty is encountered at any point check carefully that all fasteners, electrical connections and other components have been removed or disconnected as required.
13   The facia cover, the glovebox lid and the heater vents and ducts can be removed now if required, by unscrewing their mounting nuts or screws.
14   Refitting is the reverse of the removal procedure. Refer where necessary to the relevant Sections of Chapters 3, 9 and 11.

33.9B ... and releasing assembly from facia

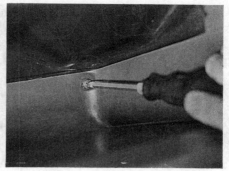

33.10 Removing facia retaining screw from inside glovebox

33.11A Removing facia securing screws at upper ...

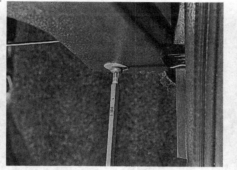

33.11B ... and lower mountings

33.12 Facia upper edge securing clip

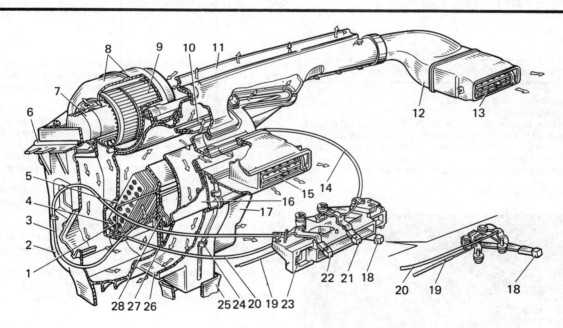

**Fig. 10.11 Heater system – LHD shown, RHD mirror image (Secs 34 to 39)**

1   Heater control shutter lever
2   Heater housing left-hand half
3   Feet-warming shutter control cable
4   Gasket
5   Heater matrix
6   Seal
7   Heater fan motor

8   Heater fan housing
9   Heater fan
10  Windscreen demisting shutter
11  Windscreen demisting duct
12  Connecting duct
13  Facia side vent
14  Windscreen demisting shutter control cable

15  Facia centre vent
16  Feet-warming shutter
17  Heater housing right-hand half
18  Heater control lever
19  Heater valve control cable
20  Heater control shutter control cable
21  Windscreen demisting shutter control lever

22  Feet-warming shutter control lever
23  Heater control assembly
24  Clamp
25  Rear footwell duct
26  Front footwell vent
27  Heater control shutter
28  Feet-warming shutter lever

34.3A Removing heater fan switch knob

34.3B Removing heater slider control knob

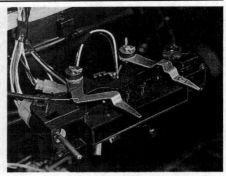

34.5A Heater control assembly (facia removed to show cable routing) ...

34.5B ... on heater right-hand side ...

34.5C ... and heater left-hand side

## 34   Heater controls – removal, refitting and adjustment

1   Disconnect the battery negative lead.
2   Remove the radio (Chapter 11).
3   Remove the four screws (two on each side) to release the facia centre console, pull off the heater fan and slider control knobs (photos), disconnect the wiring from the cigarette lighter and the various switches and withdraw the console.
4   Remove the four retaining screws and release the heater control assembly.
5   Working carefully through the facia apertures and making full notes as to how the individual components are connected, disconnect the heater fan switch and heater control panel illuminating lamp wiring, then prise off the cable retaining clips and disconnect the heater control cables (photos).
6   Withdraw the heater control assembly.
7   The heater fan switch can be removed from the control assembly by extracting its retainer. Do not attempt to dismantle the assembly any further as it is available only as a single unit.
8   The control cables can be disconnected from the heater levers once their retaining clips have been prised off. Renew any clip that is damaged or no longer effective.
9   Refitting is the reverse of the removal procedure. Ensure that all controls operate smoothly and easily through their full range before refitting the facia console.
10   To adjust any of the heater control cables, prise up the retaining clip (at either end) and pull back the cable outer to remove all traces of free play before refastening the clip. Check that the lever on the heater is able to move through its full travel.
11   Ensure that the control cables are routed in smooth loops and that the controls operate with ease. If any control is stiff or awkward in operation, check the cable and renew it if necessary.

## 35   Heater valve – removal and refitting

1   Drain the cooling system (Chapter 2).
2   Disconnect the heater feed and return hoses from their unions on the engine compartment bulkhead, catching the coolant that will be released.
3   When the cooling system is fully drained, disconnect the heater feed and return hoses from their unions on the passenger compartment bulkhead (photo). Use old towels or rag to soak up any remaining coolant that is released.
4   Prise off the cable retaining clip and disconnect the heater control cable from the valve lever.

35.3 Heater hose unions on valve (from passenger compartment side)

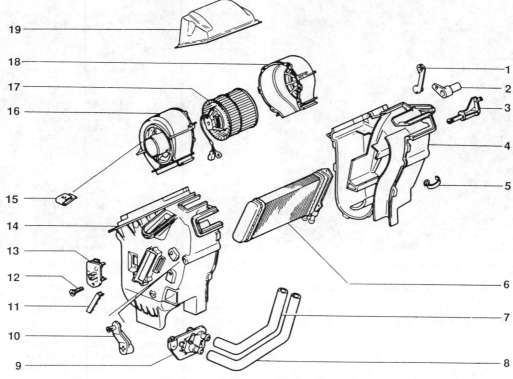

**Fig. 10.12 Heater components (Secs 35 to 38)**

| | | | | | |
|---|---|---|---|---|---|
| 1 | Rod | 6 | Heater matrix | 11 | Support |
| 2 | Lever | 7 | Heater return hose | 12 | Screw |
| 3 | Lever | 8 | Heater feed hose | 13 | Resistor |
| 4 | Heater housing right-hand half | 9 | Heater valve | 14 | Heater housing left-hand half |
| 5 | Clamp | 10 | Control lever | 15 | Captive nut |

16 Heater fan housing
   left-hand half
17 Heater fan and motor
18 Heater fan housing
   right-hand half
19 Top cover

5   Returning to the engine compartment, unscrew the two nuts securing the valve and withdraw the mounting plate.
6   Withdraw the valve itself into the passenger compartment.
7   Clean the mating surfaces of the valve, its mounting plate and both sides of the bulkhead. If required, use a suitable proprietary sealant to achieve a watertight seal on reassembly.
8   Renew the valve if it is leaking, if it is stiff in operation or jammed.
9   Refitting is the reverse of the removal procedure. Ensure that the hoses are correctly reconnected. The feed hose (from the coolant return hose union on the cylinder head) is connected to the valve left-hand unions.
10   Refill the cooling system (Chapter 2), and carefully check all disturbed unions for any signs of coolant leaks after the engine has been run.

## 36   Heater matrix – removal and refitting

1   Drain the cooling system (Chapter 2).
2   Disconnect the heater feed and return hoses from their unions on the engine compartment bulkhead, catching the coolant that will be released.
3   When the cooling system is fully drained, disconnect the heater feed and return hoses from their unions on the matrix. Use old towels or rag to soak up any remaining coolant that is released.
4   Check that the matrix retaining screws are accessible and that the matrix can be removed without disturbing the facia. It may be necessary to slacken the facia lower mounting so that it can be pulled far enough into the passenger compartment for the matrix to be withdrawn. If the matrix cannot be withdrawn with the facia in place (photo), the facia must be removed first (Sec 33).

5   Unscrew the three retaining screws and pull the matrix out of the heater, being careful not to damage it.
6   If the matrix is leaking it is best to obtain a new or reconditioned unit, as home repairs are seldom successful. If it is blocked it can sometimes be cleared by reverse flushing using a garden hose (Chapter 2, Section 4). If at all possible, avoid the use of searching chemical cleaners.

36.4 Heater matrix partially withdrawn (two mounting points arrowed)

37.8 Heater fan motor wiring connector and resistor (arrowed)

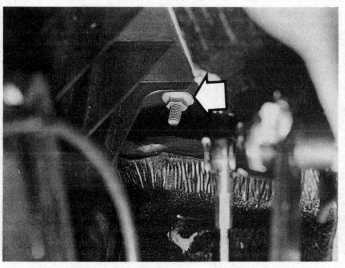

37.10 Heater right-hand front mounting nut (arrowed)

7   Refitting is the reverse of the removal procedure. Ensure that the hoses are correctly reconnected.
8   Refill the cooling system (Chapter 2), and carefully check all disturbed unions for any signs of coolant leaks after the engine has been run.

### 37  Heater – removal and refitting

1   Drain the cooling system (Chapter 2).
2   Disconnect the heater feed and return hoses from their unions on the engine compartment bulkhead, catching the coolant that will be released.
3   When the cooling system is fully drained, disconnect the heater feed and return hoses from their unions on the passenger compartment bulkhead. Use old towels or rag to soak up any remaining coolant that is released.
4   Prise off the cable retaining clip and disconnect the control cable from the heater valve lever.
5   Remove the facia (Sec 33).
6   Disconnect the heater fan switch and heater control panel illuminating lamp wiring from the heater control assembly (Sec 34). Either disconnect the cables and separate the control assembly from the heater, or release the cables from any clamps or ties securing them so that the heater and control assembly can be removed as a single unit.
7   Disconnect the rear footwell duct from the base of the heater.
8   Disconnect the heater fan motor and resistor wiring (photo).
9   Remove the heater fan motor cover from the fresh air intake (Sec 38).
10   Unscrew the four mounting nuts (photo), noting the heater fan motor earth wire under the left-hand front nut and withdraw the heater assembly, with the matrix and fan motor. If required the control cables can be disconnected (Sec 34) and the matrix (Sec 36) and fan motor (Sec 38) can be removed.
11   Remove its single retaining screw and withdraw the resistor.
12   To dismantle the heater assembly, disconnect the control cables from the levers (Sec 34), remove the matrix (Sec 36) and fan motor (Sec 38), then release the retaining clamps. Separate the housing halves, noting the seals at their mating faces.
13   Remove the support and withdraw the heater control shutter.
14   Compressing together the lugs of its fastener, remove the shutter control lever and withdraw the feet-warming shutter.
15   Disconnect the heater insert and withdraw the windscreen demisting shutter.

16   Clean all components thoroughly and check the shutter seals, using a suitable adhesive to stick down any seals that are loose. If any of the heater's internal components are worn or damaged, the complete assembly must be renewed.
17   On reassembly, reverse the dismantling procedure. Ensure that all mating surfaces are correctly fitted to give an airtight fit and check that the shutters and control levers operate correctly. Refit the resistor, the fan motor and the matrix, then if applicable reconnect the control cables.
18   Refitting is the reverse of the removal procedure. When refitting the heater, ensure that there is clean, metal-to-metal contact at the fan motor earth connection under the left-hand front mounting nut (Chapter 11, Section 1).
19   Use a suitable proprietary sealant to ensure that a waterproof seal is made between the heater top mounting flange and the underside of the bulkhead.
20   Ensure that the hoses are correctly reconnected. The feed hose (from the coolant return hose union on the cylinder head) is connected to the heater valve left-hand unions.
21   Refill the cooling system (Chapter 2) and carefully check all disturbed unions for any signs of coolant leaks which may subsequently appear.

### 38  Heater fan motor – removal and refitting

**Note:** *The heater fan motor can be removed either with the heater assembly (Sec 37) or on its own, as described below. The fan motor resistor is located in the heater assembly (see photo 37.8).*

1   Disconnect the battery negative lead.
2   Working in the passenger compartment, disconnect the heater fan motor wiring, including the earth connection under the heater left-hand front mounting nut. Tie a length of string to the wiring so that it can be drawn back into place on reassembly.
3   Returning to the engine compartment, remove its retaining screws and withdraw the grille at the rear of the bonnet.
4   Prise off the weatherstrip sealing the top of the engine compartment bulkhead.
5   Remove the four clamps and withdraw the water-deflecting shield.
6   Remove its retaining screws and withdraw the heater fan motor top cover.

38.7 Heater fan motor retaining screws (arrowed)

7   Remove the two retaining screws (photo) and withdraw the fan motor assembly. Untie the string as soon as the wiring connectors are accessible.

8   Release the retaining clips and separate the two halves of the housing, noting the seal at the mating faces.

9   Renew the fan and motor as a single unit if they are worn, damaged or faulty. Do not remove the fan from the motor.

10   On reassembly, ensure that the housing halves mate properly to achieve an airtight seal.

11   Refitting is the reverse of the removal procedure. Use the string to draw the wiring into the passenger compartment.

### 39   Heater ducts and vents – removal and refitting

1   To remove the ducts and vents mounted in the facia, the facia must be removed (Sec 33). Unscrew the retaining screws or nuts to release the various components (photos).

2   Remove the centre console (Sec 31) to release the rear footwell duct.

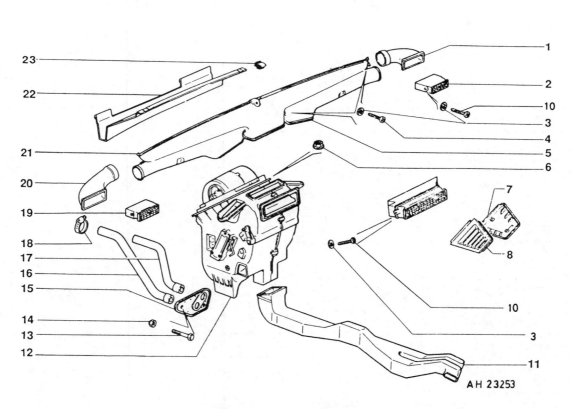

AH 23253

**Fig. 10.13 Heater ducts and vents (Sec 39)**

| | | | |
|---|---|---|---|
| 1  Connecting duct | 7  Right-hand vent | 13  Bolt | 18  Clip |
| 2  Facia side vent | 8  Left-hand vent | 14  Nut | 19  Facia side vent |
| 3  Washer | 9  Facia centre vent | 15  Heater valve mounting plate | 20  Connecting duct |
| 4  Screw | 10  Screw | 16  Heater feed hose | 21  Windscreen demisting duct |
| 5  Duct | 11  Rear footwell duct | 17  Heater return hose | 22  Water-deflecting shield |
| 6  Nut | 12  Heater assembly | | 23  Clamp |

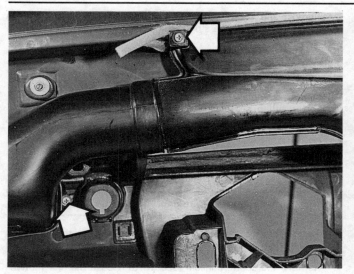

39.1A Heater duct mounting screws (arrowed) on facia forward side

39.1B Heater centre vent mounting screw (arrowed) on facia forward side

# Chapter 11 Electrical system

## Contents

## Specifications

### System type

12 volt, negative earth

### Battery

Type ....... Low-maintenance, heavy duty, lead-acid
Capacity ....... 55 Ah

### Alternator

Type ....... Three phase, self-excited, with integral voltage regulator
Identification:
  USSR-built unit ....... KAT3K (or r224) – 37.3701 – 14B/V 55A
  ISKRA unit ....... AAK 4127 14V 60A 11.201.293
Output (@ 13 volts and 5000 rotor rpm):
  USSR-built unit ....... 55 amps
  ISKRA unit ....... 60 amps
Regulated voltage (@ 15 amp load and 5000 rotor rpm) ....... $14.1 \pm 0.5$ volts
**Note:** *5000 rotor rpm = 245 crankshaft rpm*
Brush minimum protrusion ....... 5 mm
Drivebelt deflection ....... 10 to 15 mm @ 98 N pressure (0.4 to 0.6 in @ 22 lbf)

### Starter motor

Type ....... 29.3708 (Pre-engaged)
Rating ....... 1.3 kW
Armature maximum run-out ....... 0.08 mm
Armature endfloat ....... 0.07 to 0.70 mm
Brush minimum length ....... 12 mm
Brush spring tension ....... $10 \pm 1$ N

### Windscreen and tailgate glass washer/wiper system

Washer reservoir capacity ....... 4.5 litres (7.9 Imp pints)
Washer fluid ....... Water and screen wash additive (Duckhams All Seasons Screen-wash)

Wiper blades:
- Windscreen ......................................................................................... Champion LD51 (20 in)
- Tailgate ................................................................................................ Champion 33 (13 in)

## Fuses

| Fuse | Rating (amps) | Circuit(s) protected |
|------|---------------|----------------------|
| 1 | 8 | Unused |
| 2 | 8 | Unused |
| 3 | 8 | Unused |
| 4 | 16 | Heater fan motor, washer system pump, windscreen washer solenoid valve, tailgate glass wash/wipe system, heated tailgate glass warning lamp and relay, radiator cooling fan relay |
| 5 | 8* | Direction indicator system and warning lamp, windscreen wiper motor and delay relay, alternator exciter circuit (when engine is being started), reverse lamp, fuel gauge, coolant temperature gauge, voltmeter and warning lamps for fuel reserve, choke, brake fluid level, handbrake, low oil pressure and 'STOP' |
| 6 | 8 | Stop lamps, courtesy lamp |
| 7 | 8 | Under-bonnet lamp, number plate lamps, sidelamp warning lamp, instrument panel illuminating lamp rheostat switch and lamps, heater control panel and cigarette lighter illuminating lamps |
| 8 | 16 | Horn and horn relay, radiator cooling fan |
| 9 | 8 | Left-hand side and tail lamps |
| 10 | 8 | Right-hand side and tail lamps |
| 11 | 8 | Hazard warning system and warning lamp |
| 12 | 16 | Heated tailgate glass, inspection lamp socket, cigarette lighter |
| 13 | 8 | Right-hand headlamp main beam |
| 14 | 8 | Left-hand headlamp main beam, headlamp main beam warning lamp |
| 15 | 8 | Left-hand headlamp dip beam |
| 16 | 8 | Right-hand headlamp dip beam |
| – | 8 | Rear foglamp circuit (located in in-line fuse holder, behind switch) |

***Note:** If this fuse blows repeatedly, especially in severe weather conditions, it is permissible to replace it with a fuse of 16 amps rating.*

## Relays and control units

| Location | Circuit(s) |
|----------|------------|
| In fuse and relay unit: | |
| K1 (rear row, right-hand end) | Tailgate washer timer relay (if fitted) – if relay is not fitted, terminal sockets 1 and 2 are bridged |
| K2 | Direction indicators and hazard warning relay |
| K3 | Windscreen wiper delay relay |
| K4 | Unused – in some cases the following terminal sockets will be bridged: |
| | 1 – 7 – 8 |
| | 9 – 10 – 11 |
| | 4 – 5 |
| K5 (rear row, left-hand end) | Headlamp main beam relay |
| K6 (front row, right-hand end) | Unused |
| K7 | Unused |
| K8 | Horn relay |
| K9 | Radiator cooling fan relay |
| K10 | Heated tailgate glass relay |
| K11 (front row, left-hand end) | Headlamp dip beam relay |
| On engine compartment bulkhead: | |
| At centre | Starter motor auxiliary relay |
| Above vacuum servo unit | Fuel cut-off system control module (black) |
| At left-hand end | Ignition amplifier module |
| Behind facia lower edge, near steering column | Ignition switch relay (if fitted) |

## Bulbs

| | Fitting | Wattage |
|--|---------|---------|
| Headlamp | H4 | 60/55 |
| Sidelamps | Bayonet | 5 |
| Direction indicator lamps | Bayonet | 21 |
| Under-bonnet lamp | Bayonet | 21 |
| Inspection lamp (if fitted) | Bayonet | 21 |
| Direction indicator side repeater lamps | Capless or bayonet | 3 (capless), 5 (bayonet) |
| Courtesy lamp | Festoon | 5 |
| Instrument panel warning and illuminating lamps | Integral with holder | N/Av |
| Lighting switch lamp | N/Av | N/Av |
| Heater control panel lamp | Capless | N/Av |
| Cigarette lighter lamp | Bayonet | 3 |
| Number plate lamps | Festoon | 5 |
| Stop lamps | Bayonet | 21 |
| Tail lamps | Bayonet | 5 |
| Reversing lamps | Bayonet | 21 |
| Rear foglamps | Bayonet | 21 |

## Torque wrench settings

| | Nm | lbf ft |
|---|---|---|
| Alternator pulley nut.................................................................... | 38.5 to 88 | 28 to 65 |
| Alternator pivot bolt nut .............................................................. | 58.5 to 72 | 43 to 53 |
| Alternator adjuster nut.................................................................. | 28 to 45.5 | 20.5 to 33.5 |

### 1 General description

**Warning:** *Before carrying out any work on the electrical system, read through the precautions given in* Safety First! *at the beginning of this manual and in Section 2 of this Chapter.*

The electrical system is of the 12 volt negative earth type and consists of a 12 volt battery, an alternator with integral voltage regulator, a starter motor and related electrical accessories, components and wiring.

The battery is of the low-maintenance type and is charged by the alternator which is belt-driven from a crankshaft-mounted pulley. Two types of alternator have been fitted. Most vehicles will have a USSR-built unit but from mid-1990 onwards alternators built by ISKRA have appeared on new vehicles and have been supplied as replacement parts by Lada Cars. Apart from the information given in the Specifications Section of this Chapter, no information is available at the time of writing on the ISKRA unit, which can be identified by its black plastic end cover and carriers.

The starter motor is of the pre-engaged type, incorporating an integral solenoid. On starting, the solenoid moves the drive pinion into engagement with the flywheel ring gear before the starter motor is energised. Once the engine has started, a one-way clutch prevents the motor armature being driven by the engine until the pinion disengages from the flywheel.

Further details of the various systems are given in the relevant Sections of this Chapter. While some repair procedures are given, the usual course of action is to renew the component concerned. The owner whose interest extends beyond mere component renewal should obtain a copy of the '*Automobile Electrical Manual*', available from the publishers of this manual.

### 2 Electrical system – precautions

1 It is necessary to take extra care when working on the electrical system to avoid damage to semiconductor devices (diodes and transistors), and to avoid the risk of personal injury. In addition to the precautions given in *Safety First!* at the beginning of this manual, observe the following when working on the system.

2 *Always remove rings, watches, etc before working on the electrical system.* Even with the battery disconnected, capacitive discharge could occur if a component live terminal is earthed through a metal object. This could cause a shock or nasty burn.

3 **Do not** reverse the battery connections. Components such as the alternator, the fuel cut-off control and ignition amplifier modules or any other having semiconductor circuitry could be irreparably damaged.

4 If the engine is being started using jump leads and a slave battery, connect the batteries *positive-to-positive* and *negative-to-negative*. This also applies when connecting a battery charger.

5 Never disconnect the battery terminals, any electrical wiring or any test instruments, when the engine is running.

6 Never use an ohmmeter of the type incorporating a hand-cranked generator for circuit or continuity testing.

7 Always ensure that the battery negative lead is disconnected when working on the electrical system.

8 Before using electric-arc welding equipment on the car, disconnect the battery leads and the alternator leads.

### 3 Routine maintenance

**Note:** *Refer to the warnings given in* Safety First! *and in Section 2 of this Chapter before starting work.*

1 Carry out the following procedures at the intervals given in '*Routine maintenance*' at the beginning of this manual.

#### *Check the alternator drivebelt*
2 Refer to Section 7.

#### *Check the battery electrolyte level and terminals*
3 Refer to Section 4.

#### *Check for charging rate*
4 Refer to Section 8.

#### *Check the operation of all instruments, lights and controls*
5 Check the operation of all the electrical equipment, ie wipers, washers, lights, direction indicators, horn etc. Refer to the appropriate Sections of this Chapter for details if any of the circuits are found to be inoperative.

6 Note that the adjustment and testing of the stop lamp switch are described in Chapter 8.

7 Visually check all accessible wiring connectors, harnesses and retaining clips for security and for signs of chafing or damage. Rectify any faults found.

#### *Check the headlamp beam alignment*
8 Refer to Section 19.

#### *Check and lubricate the starter motor*
9 Refer to Section 13.

#### *Check the windscreen and tailgate glass washer/wiper system*
10 Check and if necessary top up the washer fluid level in the reservoir. If topping-up is required, it is permissible to use only clean water in summer, though this is best mixed with a screenwash additive. In winter mix the water either with methylated spirit or with a combined screenwash additive and antifreeze. Follow the manufacturer's instructions for the mixing ratio.

11 **Never** use strong detergents (washing-up liquids etc) or engine antifreeze in the washer fluid. Not only can they cause smearing of the glass, but they can also damage the vehicle's paintwork.

12 Check the security of the pump and solenoid valve wires and the washer tubing.

13 Check the condition of the wiper blades, and if they are cracked or show any signs of deterioration, renew them (Sec 29). For maximum clarity of vision the windscreen wiper blades should be renewed annually.

14 Check the operation of the windscreen and tailgate washers. Adjust the nozzles using a pin if necessary, aiming the spray to a point slightly above the centre of the windscreen.

### 4 Battery – maintenance

1 The battery fitted as original equipment is of the low-maintenance type, which requires regular inspections as follows.

2 Check the electrolyte level, which should be visible through the battery's translucent casing. On type 'A' batteries (Fig. 11.1) the level should be 6 mm ($\frac{1}{4}$ in) above the plates. On type 'B' batteries (Fig. 11.2) the level should be at the centre of the three lines on the battery casing.

3 If a conventional battery has been fitted as a replacement, the electrolyte level of each cell should be checked every month and, if necessary, topped up until the separators are just covered. On some batteries the case is translucent and incorporates minimum and maximum level marks. The check should be made more often if the car is operated in high ambient temperature conditions.

4 If necessary, top up the level with distilled or de-ionized water after

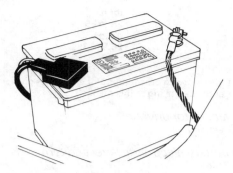

**Fig. 11.1 Battery casing electrolyte level markings – Type 'A' (Sec 4)**

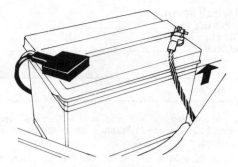

**Fig. 11.2 Battery casing electrolyte level markings – Type 'B' (Sec 4)**

removing the cell plug(s) or cover(s) from the top of the casing, although it should be noted that this should not be necessary often under normal operating conditions.

5    If a maintenance-free battery has been fitted as a replacement, it may not be possible to check the electrolyte level.

6    Check the battery terminals, and if there is any sign of corrosion, disconnect and clean them thoroughly. Smear the terminals and battery post with petroleum jelly before reconnection. If there is any corrosion on the metal battery carrier, remove the battery and its plastic tray, then clean the deposits away and treat the affected metal with an anti-rust preparation. Repaint the carrier in the original colour after treatment.

7    When the battery is removed for whatever reason, it is worthwhile checking it for cracks and leakage.

8    If frequent topping-up of the battery is required, and the battery case is not fractured, the battery is being over-charged, and the voltage regulator will have to be checked.

## 5  Battery – testing and charging

**Note:** *The procedures given apply to the original equipment battery. Follow the manufacturer's recommendations when working with replacement batteries of an alternative type. Refer to* Safety First! *as well as to Section 2 of this Chapter before proceeding.*

1    In normal use, the battery should not require charging from an external source unless very heavy use is made of electrical equipment over a series of short journeys. Otherwise, a need for regular recharging points to a fault either in the battery or in the charging system.

2    If, however, the vehicle is laid up for long periods (in excess of thirty days at a time) the battery will lose approximately 1% of its charge per week. Disconnect the battery negative lead to minimise this loss, and give the battery regular 'refresher' charges every six weeks or so.

3    If a discharged battery is suspected, leave it disconnected for at least two hours, then measure the (open circuit, or no-load) voltage using a sensitive voltmeter connected across the battery terminals. Compare the reading obtained with the following.

| Voltmeter reading | Charge condition |
|---|---|
| *10.50 volts* | *Fully discharged (renew battery)* |
| *12.30 volts* | *50% charged* |
| *12.48 volts* | *75% charged* |
| *12.66 volts or more* | *Fully charged* |

4    The only full test of a battery's stage of charge is to use an hydrometer to check the specific gravity of the electrolyte. Compare the results obtained with the following table.

| | Normal climates | Tropics |
|---|---|---|
| *Discharged* | *1.120* | *1.080* |
| *Half charged* | *1.200* | *1.150* |
| *Fully charged* | *1.280* | *1.230* |

5    If the battery condition is suspect, first check the specific gravity of electrolyte in each cell. A variation of 0.040 or more between any cells indicates loss of electrolyte or deterioration of the internal plates.

6    If the battery is to be charged, remove it from the vehicle (Sec 6), and refer to *Safety first!* before starting work.

7    The manufacturer recommends the use of a charger which charges at a low current (around 2.75 amps). For most owners the equipment available will be a trickle charger, which can be used safely overnight.

8    Specially rapid 'boost' charges which are claimed to restore the power of the battery in 1 to 2 hours are not recommended, as they can cause serious damage to the battery plates through overheating. Under no circumstances subject the battery to rapid boost charging at voltages higher than 15.5 volts, or to charging currents above the normal recommended rate of 10% of the battery capacity (ie 5.5 amp for a 55 Ah battery).

9    Before commencing charging, remove the cell plug(s) or cover(s) from the top of the battery casing to allow the escape of the gases which will be produced during charging. This will prevent the build-up of gas pressure inside the battery which may occur if the cell vent holes are blocked. Charging should be carried out in a well-ventilated area.

10    Connect the charger leads to the battery, ensuring that the leads are connected *positive-to-positive* and *negative-to-negative*, then switch on the charger.

11    Charge the battery until all cells are gassing vigorously and no further rise in specific gravity or increase in no-load voltage is noted over a four-hour period. When charging is complete, turn the charger off before disconnecting the leads from the battery.

## 6  Battery – removal and refitting

1    The battery is located at the front left-hand side of the engine compartment.

2    Loosen the clamp and disconnect the negative (earth) lead from the

6.2 Disconnecting the battery negative lead

7.2 Showing principle of checking alternator drivebelt tension

battery (photo). Lift the plastic cover and repeat the procedure for the positive lead.
3    Unscrew the clamp nut sufficiently to enable the battery to be lifted from its location. Keep the battery in an upright position to avoid spilling electrolyte on the bodywork.
4    Refitting is the reverse of the removal procedure, but clean the terminal posts and leads, then smear petroleum jelly on the terminals when reconnecting the leads. Always connect the positive lead first and the negative lead last.

## 7  Alternator drivebelt – removal, refitting and adjustment

### Adjustment

1    Check the alternator drivebelt for cracks, fraying or damage. Renew the belt if worn or damaged. If it is satisfactory, check and adjust the belt tension as follows.
2    To check the belt's tension, apply a force of 98 N (22 lbf) to the belt's top run, midway between the pulleys, and measure the deflection (photo).
3    If the deflection measured is outside the specified range (see Specifications), slacken the alternator pivot bolt nut and adjuster nut

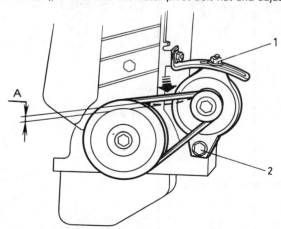

**Fig. 11.3 Alternator drivebelt adjustment (Sec 7)**

1    Adjuster nut          A    Drivebelt deflection
2    Alternator pivot bolt

and move the alternator·closer to the engine to slacken the belt or away from the engine to tighten it.
4    Tighten the nuts just enough to hold the alternator in place, then rotate the crankshaft through two revolutions to settle the belt and recheck the setting.
5    When the setting is correct tighten the nuts securely, to their specified torque wrench settings if possible.

### Removal and refitting

6    Although this is not strictly necessary, work would be easier if the engine compartment right-hand undershield were removed first (Chapter 10).
7    Slacken the alternator pivot bolt nut and adjuster nut and move the alternator closer to the engine until the belt can be removed from its pulleys.
8    Refitting is the reverse of the removal procedure. Adjust the belt as described above.

## 8  Alternator – fault tracing and rectification

**Note:** *Refer to the warnings given in* Safety First! *and in Section 2 of this Chapter before starting work.*

1    Should it appear that the alternator is not charging the battery, check first that the drivebelt is intact and in good condition and that its tension is correct (Sec 7). Also check the condition and security of the alternator electrical connections and the battery leads.
2    A rough idea of whether the alternator output is adequate can be gained by using a voltmeter (range 0 to 15 or 0 to 20 volts) as follows. Connect the voltmeter across the battery terminals, switch on the headlamps and check that the reading is between 12 and 13 volts. Start the engine and run it at a fast idle, then check that the voltmeter reads between 13 and 14 volts. With the engine still running at a fast idle, switch on as many electrical consumers as possible (heated tailgate glass, heater fan motor etc). The voltage at the battery should be maintained at between 13 and 14 volts, indicating that the alternator is functioning correctly.
3    For a comprehensive test of the alternator it will be necessary to take the vehicle to an electrical specialist who is equipped with an oscilloscope that can check the phased output of the unit and locate any fault in the rectifier diodes.
4    If the output is proved faulty from the check described in paragraph 2, remove the voltage regulator and brushes and check the brushes (Sec 10). Renew the brushes if necessary or if these are in good order, suspect the voltage regulator.

## 9  Alternator – removal and refitting

1    With the ignition switched off, disconnect the battery negative lead.
2    Disconnect the wires from the alternator left-hand end (photo). The main output (pink) wires are secured to the number 30 terminal by a nut under a rubber cover, while the two red/blue wires are connected by a Lucar-type fitting to the number 61 terminal.
3    Remove the drivebelt (Sec 7).
4    Unscrew and remove the pivot bolt and adjuster nut and withdraw the alternator from the engine.
5    The adjuster (photo) and alternator mounting brackets can be unbolted from the cylinder block/crankcase if required.
6    If the alternator is to be renewed and the pulley must be swapped over, clamp the pulley firmly in a vice with padded jaws and unscrew the pulley nut, taking care not to damage the pulley. Withdraw the pulley, noting its locating key. On reassembly, tighten the pulley nut to its specified torque wrench setting.
7    Refitting is the reverse of the removal procedure, but grease the pivot bolt (photos) and adjust the drivebelt (Sec 7).

## 10  Alternator brushes and regulator – renewal

**Note**: *The vast majority of actual alternator faults are due to the voltage regulator or to the brushes. If the renewal of these items does not cure the fault, the advice of an expert should be sought as to the best approach.*

9.2 Alternator wiring terminals (arrowed)

9.5 Alternator adjuster bracket installed

9.7A Grease alternator pivot bolt on refitting ...

9.7B ... refit spacer as shown ...

9.7C ... followed by spring washer and nut

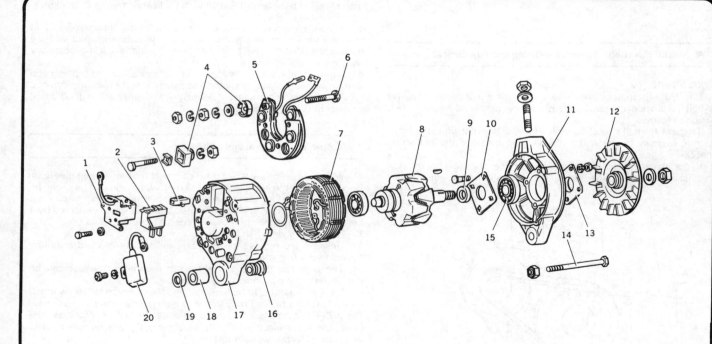

**Fig. 11.4 Exploded view of USSR-built alternator (Sec 10)**

| | | | |
|---|---|---|---|
| 1 Voltage regulator | 6 Bolt | 11 Drive-end housing | 16 Bush |
| 2 Brush holder | 7 Stator | 12 Pulley | 17 Slip ring-end housing |
| 3 Terminal | 8 Rotor | 13 Bearing retaining plate | 18 Centre spacer |
| 4 Insulating bushes | 9 Spacer | 14 Through-bolt | 19 Shouldered spacer |
| 5 Rectifier pack | 10 Bearing retaining plate | 15 Bearing | 20 Capacitor |

10.3 Disconnecting voltage regulator wire

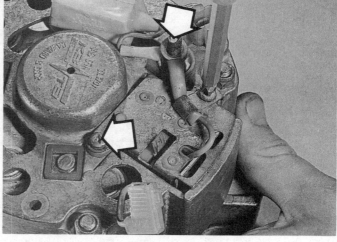

10.4 Disconnect wires from terminal arrowed, then unscrew regulator screws (arrowed)

*For most owners the best course of action will be to renew the alternator as a complete unit. In many cases overhaul will not be viable on economic grounds alone.*

1    The following procedure relates only to the USSR-built alternator (see Sec 1).
2    While it is physically possible to remove the voltage regulator and brushes with the alternator in place on the vehicle, owners are advised to remove the alternator (Sec 9) so that it can be serviced in clean working conditions.
3    Disconnect the wire from the voltage regulator 'B' terminal (photo).
4    Disconnect the voltage regulator and suppressor capacitor wires

from the alternator number 30 terminal and unscrew the voltage regulator retaining screws (photo).
5    Using a suitable screwdriver, gently prise the voltage regulator and brush holder apart until they can be withdrawn without damaging the brushes. Tilt the assembly as it leaves the alternator (photos).
6    To separate the brush holder from the regulator, press gently on the 'B' terminal blade (photo). Check carefully for signs of corrosion between the two and clean their mating surfaces if necessary.
7    Measure the amount by which each brush protrudes from the holder (photo), and if either brush is worn to the specified minimum or less, the brush holder assembly must be renewed.

10.5A Gently prise apart voltage regulator and brush holder ...

10.5B ... until assembly can be removed ...

10.5C ... without damaging brushes

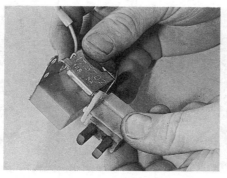

10.6 Separating voltage regulator from brush holder

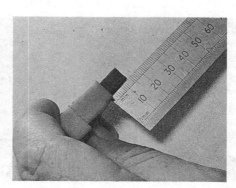

10.7 Measuring alternator brush protrusion

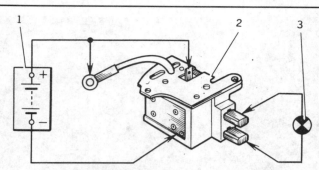

**Fig. 11.5 Testing the voltage regulator (Sec 10)**

1   *Test power source*
2   *Voltage regulator/brush holder assembly*

3   *Test lamp (12 volt, 1 to 3 watt bulb)*

8   To test the voltage regulator a 15 to 16 volt supply will be required. With the regulator and brush holder reassembled, connect a test lamp (12 volt, 1 to 3 watt bulb) across the brushes and connect first a 12 volt supply, then a 15 to 16 volt supply, between the regulator earth (its metal body) and the two terminals (see Fig. 11.5). If the voltage regulator is in good condition the bulb will light in the first test (12 volt), but not in the second (15 to 16 volt).

9   If the bulb lights in both tests the regulator is faulty and must be renewed. If the bulb does not light in either test, then either there is a fault in the regulator or there is no contact between the regulator and the brush holder terminals. Check the terminals before renewing the regulator.

10   While the voltage regulator and brushes are removed, check the condition of the slip rings after cleaning them with a fuel-moistened rag. If necessary polish the slip rings with fine glasspaper. If the rings are worn excessively they may be fine ground and polished by an auto electrician, though this will mean dismantling the alternator.

11   Refit the voltage regulator and brushes using a reversal of the removal procedure, then refit the alternator to the vehicle (Sec 9).

---

## 11   Starter motor – testing in the car

**Note:** *Refer to the warnings given in* Safety first! *and in Section 2 of this Chapter before starting work.*

1   If the starter motor fails to operate when the switch is operated, any of the following may be the cause:

(a)   *The battery is faulty*
(b)   *The electrical connections between the switch, solenoid, battery and starter motor are somewhere failing to pass the necessary current from the battery through the starter to earth*
(c)   *The solenoid is faulty*
(d)   *The starter motor is mechanically or electrically defective*

2   To check the battery, switch on the headlamps. If they dim after a few seconds the battery is discharged. If the lamps glow brightly, operate the ignition switch and see what happens to the lamps. If they dim then you know that power is reaching the starter motor, which is at fault. If the lamps stay bright (and no clicking sound can be heard from the solenoid) there is a fault in the circuit (see below). If the starter turns slowly when switched on, but the battery is in good condition, then either the starter must be faulty or there is considerable resistance in the circuit.

3   If the circuit is suspected, disconnect the battery terminals (including the earth connection to the inner wing panel), the starter/solenoid wiring and the engine/transmission earth lead, thoroughly clean their connections and refit them. Smear petroleum jelly around the battery terminals to prevent corrosion. Corroded connections are the most frequent cause of electric system malfunctions.

4   When the above checks and cleaning tasks have been carried out, but without success, you will possibly have heard a clicking noise each time the starter switch was operated. This was the solenoid contacts closing (if no clicking has been heard from the solenoid, it may be defective). The solenoid contacts can be checked by putting a voltmeter or bulb across the main cable connection on the starter side of the solenoid and earth. When the switch is operated, there should be a reading or lighted bulb. If there is no reading or lighted bulb, the solenoid is faulty and should be renewed.

5   If the battery and all connections are in good condition, check the circuit first by disconnecting the red wire from the solenoid blade terminal. Connect a meter or test lamp between the wire end and the terminal and check that the wire is live when the ignition switch is operated. If it is, then the circuit is sound and the fault probably lies in the starter; if not, proceed to the next check.

6   Disconnect the two red/blue wires from the alternator number 61 terminal and connect them to a good earth point and switch on the ignition. If the starter now operates, either the voltage regulator internal connections are loose or dirty, or the regulator is faulty. Check it and renew it if necessary (Sec 10). If the starter still does not operate, reconnect the wires and proceed to the next check.

7   Disconnect the connector plug from the bulkhead-mounted starter auxiliary relay and use a meter or test lamp to check that the heavy gauge red/blue wire is live when the ignition switch is operated. If it is not live, then the fault is either in the ignition switch or in the wiring between the switch and the relay. If it is live, proceed to the next check.

8   Check that the heavy gauge pink wire is permanently live (see above), then using a multimeter set to the resistance function or a battery and bulb test circuit, check that there is continuity between the red wire terminals on the relay connector and the solenoid. Renew or repair the wire if a fault is found. If the wiring is in good condition the fault must lie in the relay itself; check by substituting a new one.

---

## 12   Starter motor – removal and refitting

1   Disconnect the battery negative lead.
2   Disconnect the wiring from the starter motor solenoid (photo).
3   Unscrew the three retaining nuts and withdraw the starter motor (photos).
4   Refitting is the reverse of the removal procedure.

12.2 Starter motor wiring terminals (arrowed)

12.3A Two of the motor mounting nuts (arrowed)

12.3B Withdrawing starter motor from mounting studs

## 13  Starter motor – overhaul

**Note:** *Before commencing any repair work, always check the availability and cost of replacement parts and compare that with the cost of a new, reconditioned or exchange unit, which may in the long run be more viable.*

1    With the starter motor removed (Sec 12), clean its exterior surfaces.
2    Unscrew the nut and disconnect the motor cable from the solenoid lower terminal (photo).
3    Unscrew the three screws and withdraw the solenoid from the drive housing, noting the spring, then unhook the solenoid plunger from the lever (photos).
4    Unscrew the two screws and remove the end cap, noting the rubber seal (photos).

5    Extract the circlip from the armature end, followed by its washer (photo).
6    Mark the brush-end housing, yoke and drive-end housing in relation to each other.
7    Unscrew the through-bolts then pull off the brush-end housing and yoke (photos). Ensure that any shims remain in place on the armature.
8    Unscrew the retaining screws to disconnect the stator wires from the brush holders, then separate the brush-end housing from the yoke (photos).
9    Removing the screw securing the end of each brush's lead and using a suitable screwdriver to prise back the springs, remove the brushes (photo).
10    To release the armature, first use a metal tube to drive the holder back from the circlip at the armature drive end. Extract the circlip, then withdraw the armature (photos).
11    Extract the rubber pad from the drive-end housing (photo).

13.2 Disconnecting motor cable from solenoid

13.3A Remove retaining screws (arrowed) ...

13.3B ... and withdraw solenoid, noting spring ...

13.3C ... then unhook plunger from lever

13.4A End cap is secured by two screws

13.4B Remove end cap from starter motor ...

13.4C ... noting sealing ring

13.5 Prising off armature end circlip, noting washer

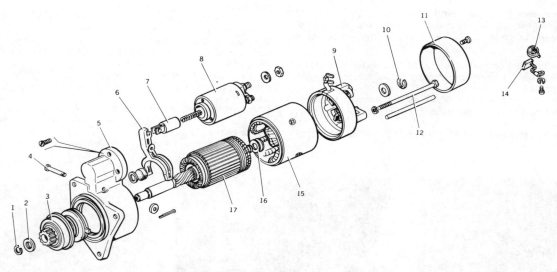

**Fig. 11.6 Exploded view of starter motor (Sec 13)**

| | | | |
|---|---|---|---|
| 1 Circlip | 6 Engagement lever | 10 Circlip | 14 Brush |
| 2 Holder | 7 Plunger | 11 End cap | 15 Yoke |
| 3 Pinion assembly | 8 Solenoid | 12 Through-bolt | 16 Shims |
| 4 Pivot pin | 9 Brush-end housing | 13 Brush spring | 17 Armature |
| 5 Drive-end housing | | | |

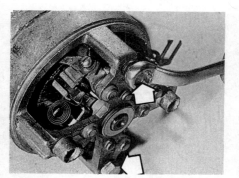

13.7A Unscrewing through-bolts (arrowed) ...

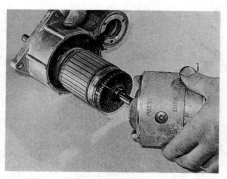

13.7B ... to separate brush-end housing and yoke from drive-end housing

13.8A Remove screws to disconnect wiring ...

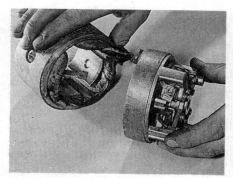

13.8B ... and separate brush-end housing from yoke

13.9 Press back springs as shown to release brushes

13.10A Drive back holder from circlip ...

13.10B ... then prise circlip out of armature groove ...

13.10C ... so that armature can be released from pinion

13.11 Extracting rubber pad from drive-end housing

13.12A Remove (and discard) split pin ...

13.12B ... to release engagement lever pivot pin

13.13A Prise engagement lever forks off drive carrier ring ears ...

13.13B ... and remove pinion assembly

13.14 Measuring starter motor brush length

13.19 Use puller as shown to draw holder fully over circlip

13.20 Armature endfloat is controlled by shims

13.21 Ensure that springs are correctly positioned on each brush

12    Remove and discard its securing split pin and drive out the engagement lever pivot pin (photos).
13    Gently prise the engagement lever forks off the pinion assembly's drive carrier ring ears, then withdraw the lever, followed by the pinion assembly (photos).
14    Clean all the components and check them for wear and damage. Measure the length of each brush (photo). Note that if any brush is worn to the specified minimum length or less, all four brushes should be renewed as a set. At the time of writing, this means that the complete brush-end housing assembly must be renewed, as the brushes are not available separately as Lada replacement parts. The same applies to the brush springs, if any should be found to be weak.
15    Clean the commutator with a fuel-moistened rag, or if it is very dirty use fine glasspaper.
16    Prise off the retaining circlip to dismantle the pinion assembly, and clean all components thoroughly. The complete assembly must be renewed if any part of it is worn or damaged. On reassembly, apply a smear of molybdenum disulphide grease to the drive carrier ring's bearing surfaces.
17    Reassembly is the reverse of the dismantling procedure, noting the following points.
18    Use engine oil to lubricate the armature helical splines, the pinion assembly, the pinion assembly's bore and armature bearing surface and the brush-end housing bearing bore and armature bearing surface. Apply a thin smear of grease to the engagement lever pivot pin.
19    When refitting the armature, fit the holder with its groove towards the end of the shaft, then press the circlip on to the shaft until it snaps into its groove. Use a puller to draw the holder fully over the circlip (photo).
20    Check that the armature endfloat is within the specified limits and if necessary alter the shims to bring it within that tolerance (photo).
21    Check that the brushes are free to move, against spring pressure, in their holders and ensure that the springs are correctly positioned on each brush (photo).

---

## 14  Fuses and relays – general

1    The fuse and relay unit is located in the engine compartment, on the left-hand side of the heater fresh air intake chamber (photo).

### Fuses

2    A blown fuse can be identified by the metal strip being melted. Switch off the circuit concerned (or the ignition), then pull out the old fuse and press in the new one, making sure that it is the same rating as the old one. Never use a fuse with a different rating from the original or substitute anything else. If the new fuse blows immediately, find the cause before renewing it again. A short to earth as a result of faulty insulation is most likely.
3    The clear plastic cover gives details of the principal circuits protected by each fuse (see Specifications). Where a fuse protects more than one circuit, try to isolate the defect by switching on each circuit in turn (if possible) until the fuse blows again. Note that the fuse protecting the rear foglamp circuit is fitted in an in-line fuse holder behind the switch (Sec 15).

4    If any of the spare fuses are used, always replace them immediately so that a spare of each rating is available.

### Relays

5    The relays fitted in the unit may correspond to the symbols on the unit cover, but care should be exercised as not all relay locations are used on UK models and even those that are appropriate are not always fitted (see Specifications).
6    Note that two relays are fitted elsewhere in the vehicle (photos).
7    If a circuit or system served by a relay develops a fault, always remember that the fault could be in the relay itself. Testing is by the substitution of a known good unit, but remember that some relays look similar but perform different functions.
8    To renew a relay, disconnect the battery, then simply pull direct from the socket and press in the new relay. Reconnect the battery on completion.

### Fuse and relay unit

9    To remove the fuse and relay unit, first disconnect the battery negative lead.
10    Remove the cover and pull out the relays and fuses as necessary to reach all the mounting screws. Unscrew the mounting screws and raise the unit until the wires can be disconnected.
11    The wiring is complex, so make careful notes as to the connections before disconnecting any of the wires. Remove the unit.
12    Refitting is the reverse of the removal procedure.

---

## 15  Switches – removal and refitting

**Note**: *Disconnect the battery negative lead before removing any switch, and reconnect the lead after refitting the switch.*

### Ignition switch

1    Refer to Chapter 9, Section 19 for details of the removal and refitting of the switch as an assembly with the steering lock.
2    To remove the ignition switch alone, first remove either the steering wheel (Chapter 9, Section 16) or the instrument panel (Sec 22), then remove the retaining screws and withdraw the steering column top and bottom covers and ignition switch surround.
3    Disconnect the switch wiring at the connector block just inside the facia (photo).
4    On USSR-made switches (stamped 2108-3704005), remove the single retaining screw to withdraw the switch body from the steering lock.
5    On Hungarian-made switches (stamped KZ 81 or KZ 813), remove the single retaining screw and press in the locking pin, then turn the key to the 'O' position and withdraw the switch body from the steering lock. To separate the switch from the steering lock, each wire must be released from the connector block by using a small screwdriver to press back the terminal's locking tab (photos).
6    Refitting is the reverse of the removal procedure.

14.1 Fuse and relay unit – see Specifications for details

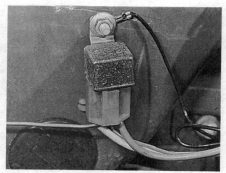

14.6A Starter motor auxiliary relay is mounted on bulkhead

14.6B Ignition switch relay (if fitted) is mounted behind facia lower edge

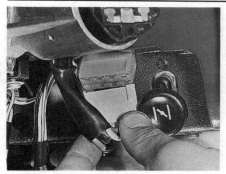

15.3 Disconnecting ignition switch wiring

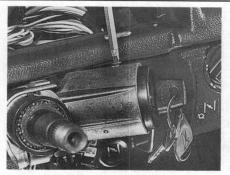

15.5A To remove Hungarian-built switch, remove screw ...

15.5B ... press in locking pin and turn key to extract switch ...

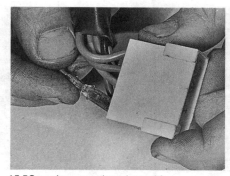

15.5C ... wires must be released from connector block to separate switch from steering lock

15.7 Remove steering wheel spoke cover/horn push to reach horn switch

## Horn switch

7    The horn push is formed by the steering wheel centre spoke cover, which can be prised off to reach the horn switch itself (photo). Remove the steering wheel (Chapter 9, Section 16) to check the horn switch contacts on the multi-function switch holder at the top of the steering column and the tracks on the steering wheel.

8    If the horn blows when the steering lock is activated, remove the steering wheel and the steering column top shroud (Chapter 9) and reverse the two wires connected to the horn switch contacts on the multi-function switch holder.

## Steering column multi-function switches

9    Remove the steering wheel (Chapter 9, Section 16), then remove the retaining screws and withdraw the steering column top and bottom covers.

10    To release either switch press together its retaining clips and slide the switch out of its holder (photo).

11    Disconnect the switch wiring at the connector block (photo).

12    If the switch holder is to be removed, **always** mark its height on the steering column before slackening the clamp screw (photo) and note that the holder is located by a notch on the top of the column. Also mark or note the horn switch wires so that they are connected the correct way round on refitting. Position the holder at its marked height before tightening the clamp screw.

## Facia switches

13    The lighting, hazard warning, rear foglamp and heated tailgate glass switches are all removed as follows.

14    Carefully prise the switch out of the facia and disconnect the wiring plug (photos).

15    Refitting is the reverse of the removal procedure.

## Instrument panel illuminating lamp rheostat switch

16    Pull off the rheostat knob and unscrew the retaining nut behind (photo).

17    Switch removal is easiest if the instrument panel is removed (Sec 22), but it is possible to get to the rear of the switch by reaching up

15.10 Press together retaining clips to remove multi-function switches from holder ...

15.11 ... then disconnect switch wiring

15.12 Mark height of holder on steering column before slackening clamp

15.14A To remove facia switches, prise up at lower edge ...

15.14B ... and disconnect wiring

15.16 Pull off knob and unscrew retaining nut ...

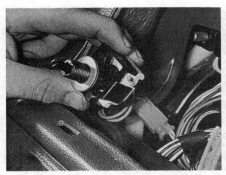

15.17 ... to remove instrument panel illuminating lamp rheostat switch

15.19 Door pillar courtesy lamp switches are secured by one screw

15.22 Under-bonnet lamp switch on bonnet lock platform

beside the steering column (photo). Disconnect the switch wiring and remove it.
18  Refitting is the reverse of the removal procedure.

### Courtesy lamp switches
19  Open the door, then unscrew the screw and ease the switch out from the door pillar (photo).
20  Disconnect the wire taking care not to allow it to drop back into the pillar.
21  Refitting is the reverse of the removal procedure.

### Under-bonnet lamp switch
22  This switch is of the same type as the courtesy lamp switches and is mounted on the bonnet lock platform (photo). Refer to paragraphs 19 to 21 above.

### Electric cooling fan thermostatic switch
23  Refer to Chapter 2, Section 11 for details of switch removal, refitting and testing.

### Choke warning lamp switch
24  Refer to Chapter 3, Section 13 for details of switch removal and refitting.

### Throttle switch
25  Refer to Chapter 3, Section 16 for details of switch removal and refitting.

### Reversing lamp switch
26  Refer to Chapter 6, Section 6 for details of switch removal, refitting and testing.

### Stop lamp switch
27  Refer to Chapter 8, Section 26 for details of switch removal, refitting and testing.

### Handbrake warning lamp switch
28  Refer to Chapter 8, Section 26 for details of switch removal, refitting and testing.

### Brake fluid level warning lamp switch
29  Refer to Chapter 8, Section 26 for details of switch removal, refitting and testing.

### Heater fan switch
30  Refer to Chapter 10, Section 34 for details of switch removal and refitting.

### Oil pressure switch
31  Refer to Chapter 1, Section 12 for details of switch removal and refitting.

### 16  Bulbs (exterior lamps) – renewal

### General
1  Whenever a bulb is renewed, note the following points.
2  Remember that if the lamp has just been in use the bulb may be extremely hot.
3  Disconnect the battery negative lead before starting work.
4  Always check the bulb contacts and holder, ensuring that there is clean metal-to-metal contact between the bulb and its live(s) and earth. Clean off any corrosion or dirt before fitting a new bulb.
5  Wherever bayonet-type bulbs are fitted (see Specifications) ensure that the live contact(s) bear firmly against the bulb contact.
6  Always ensure that the new bulb is of the correct rating and that it is completely clean before fitting it.

### Headlamp
7  Working in the engine compartment, rotate the black plastic cover anti-clockwise and unclip it from the rear of the lamp unit (photo).

16.7 Rotate anti-clockwise and unclip cover from rear of headlamp unit

16.8A Disconnecting headlamp wiring connector

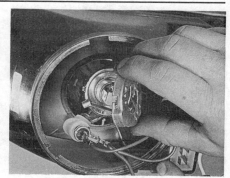

16.8B Press in and twist anti-clockwise to remove retainer

16.9 Removing headlamp bulb – do not touch glass

16.13 Front sidelamp is mounted in headlamp reflector

16.17 Removing front direction indicator bulb

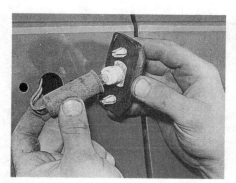

16.19 Unclipping direction indicator side repeater lamp bulbholder – lamp removed to show fixings

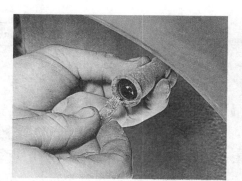

16.20 Removing a capless bulb

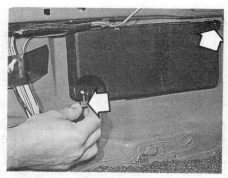

16.23 Rear lamp cluster cover is secured by two knurled plastic nuts (arrowed)

8    Unplug the wiring connector, then press in the retainer and twist it anti-clockwise (photos).
9    Withdraw the bulb (photo).
10    When handling the new bulb, use a tissue or clean cloth to avoid touching the glass with the fingers. Moisture and grease from the skin can cause blackening and rapid failure of this type of bulb. If the glass is accidentally touched, wipe it clean using methylated spirit.
11    Refitting is the reverse of the removal procedure. Ensure that the new bulb's locating tabs align with the reflector slots.

## Front sidelamp
12    Working in the engine compartment, rotate the black plastic cover anti-clockwise and unclip it from the rear of the headlamp unit.
13    Pull the bulbholder from the headlamp reflector (photo).
14    Press the bulb into the holder, twist anti-clockwise and remove.
15    Refitting is the reverse of the removal procedure.

## Front direction indicator
16    Working in the engine compartment, rotate the bulbholder anti-clockwise and unclip it from the rear of the headlamp unit. It may be necessary to unplug the wiring connector first.
17    Press the bulb into the holder, twist anti-clockwise and remove (photo).
18    Refitting is the reverse of the removal procedure.

## Direction indicator side repeater
19    Working behind the front wing, peel back the rubber cover and unclip the bulbholder from the lamp (photo).
20    If a capless (wedge-type) bulb is fitted, pull the bulb out of its socket (photo).
21    If a bayonet-fitting bulb is used, press the bulb into the holder, twist anti-clockwise and remove.
22    Refitting is the reverse of the removal procedure.

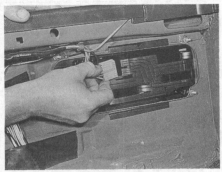

16.24A Disconnecting rear lamp cluster wiring

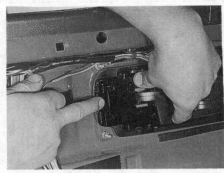

16.24B Unclipping bulbholder from lamp unit

16.24C All rear lamp cluster bulbs are bayonet-fitting

16.27 Removing number plate lamp

16.28 Number plate lamp bulb is a festoon type

## Rear lamp cluster

23   Open the tailgate and unscrew the two knurled plastic nuts securing the rear lamp cluster cover (photo), then remove the cover.

24   Unplug the wiring connector, then unclip the bulbholder from the lamp unit (photos).

25   All bulbs are a bayonet-fitting, so press the bulb into its holder, twist anti-clockwise and remove.

26   Refitting is the reverse of the removal procedure.

## Number plate lamp

27   Open the tailgate and use a suitable screwdriver to press the lamp unit towards the vehicle's centre-line, against spring pressure, then remove the lamp unit (photo).

28   The bulb is a festoon type which is prised out of its spring contacts once the lamp's rubber cover has been peeled back (photo).

29   Refitting is the reverse of the removal procedure, but ensure that the contacts are sufficiently tensioned to hold the bulb firmly.

## 17   Bulbs (interior lamps) – renewal

### General

1   Refer to Section 16, paragraphs 1 to 6.

### Courtesy lamp

2   Unclip the lens by pressing one side, then remove it (photo).

3   The bulb is a festoon type which is prised out of its spring contacts.

4   Refitting is the reverse of the removal procedure, but ensure that the contacts are sufficiently tensioned to hold the bulb firmly.

### Under-bonnet lamp

5   Open and prop the bonnet, press the bulb into its holder, twist anti-clockwise and remove (photo).

6   Refitting is the reverse of the removal procedure.

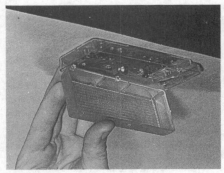

17.2 Removing courtesy lamp lens

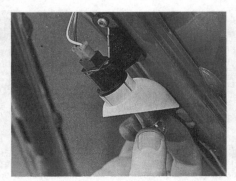

17.5 Removing under-bonnet lamp bulb

17.9 Removing bulbholder from rear of instrument panel

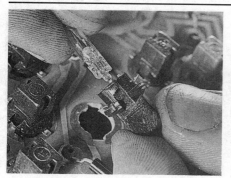

17.10 Some bulbs can be renewed separately from holders

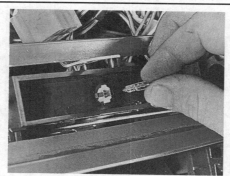

17.13 Removing heater control panel lamp bulb

17.15 Cigarette lighter illuminating lamp bulb is clipped to lighter assembly

### Inspection lamp

7 The inspection lamp (if fitted) is located next to the fuse and relay unit. Bulb removal and refitting is as described in paragraphs 5 to 6 above.

### Instrument illumination and warning lamps

8 Remove the instrument panel (Sec 22).
9 Twist the bulbholder anti-clockwise and withdraw from the rear of the panel (photo).
10 In some cases the bulbs are integral with their holders, but in others the bulbs can be renewed separately (photo). Seek the advice of a Lada dealer.
11 Refitting is the reverse of the removal procedure.

### Heater control panel lamp

12 Remove the facia centre console (Chapter 10, Section 34, paragraphs 1 to 3).
13 Pull the bulb out of its socket (photo).
14 Refitting is the reverse of the removal procedure.

### Cigarette lighter illuminating lamp

15 The bulb is secured in a container that is clipped to the side of the cigarette lighter assembly (photo).
16 If the container is not accessible from the ashtray aperture, the facia centre console must be removed (Chapter 10, Section 34, paragraphs 1 to 3) so that the container can be unclipped and the bulbholder extracted.
17 Press the bulb into its holder, twist anti-clockwise and remove.
18 Refitting is the reverse of the removal procedure.

### Lighting switch lamp

19 The switch itself is removed and refitted as described in Section 15 of this Chapter. No information is available at the time of writing as to whether the bulb can be renewed separately from the switch or not. Seek the advice of a Lada dealer.

### 18 Exterior lamp units – removal and refitting

### Headlamp unit

1 Disconnect the battery negative lead.
2 Unplug the wiring connector from the rear of the headlamp unit (photo).
3 Unclip the headlamp alignment control system actuator from the rear of the headlamp unit.
4 Unscrew the four retaining nuts, noting the earth connection on one of them, then remove the headlamp unit (photo).
5 Refitting is the reverse of the removal procedure. Ensure that the earth connection (photo) is cleaned back to bare metal.

### Front direction indicator

6 Remove the headlamp unit as described in paragraphs 1 to 4 above.
7 Remove the retaining screws and separate the direction indicator lamp from the headlamp unit (photo).
8 Refitting is the reverse of the removal procedure.

### Direction indicator side repeater

9 With the bulbholder removed (Sec 16), release the clips from behind the front wing and remove the lamp.
10 Refitting is the reverse of the removal procedure.

### Rear lamp cluster

11 Remove the rear lamp cluster cover and disconnect the wiring (Section 16, paragraphs 23 and 24).
12 Unscrew the four retaining nuts, noting the earth connection on one of them, then remove the assembly (photos).
13 Refitting is the reverse of the removal procedure, but ensure that the earth connection is cleaned back to bare metal.

### Number plate lamp

14 Refer to Section 16, paragraphs 27 to 29.

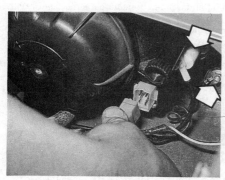

18.2 Disconnecting headlamp wiring – note alignment control system actuator and headlamp retaining nut (arrowed)

18.4 Removing a headlamp unit

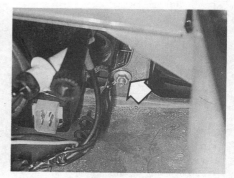

18.5 Headlamp unit earth connection (arrowed)

18.7 Front direction indicator lamps are secured to headlamp by two screws

18.12A Note earth connection on one of rear lamp cluster retaining nuts

18.12B Refitting rear lamp cluster

## 19  Headlamp beam alignment – general

1    It is advisable to have the headlamp beam alignment checked and if necessary adjusted by a Lada dealer using optical beam setting equipment. Correct alignment of the headlamp beams is most important, not only to ensure good vision for the driver but also to protect other drivers from being dazzled.

2    The headlamp alignment may be adjusted to compensate for the load being carried by turning a knob on the facia. The setting should be returned to the 'driver-only' position before any checks are made.

3    In an emergency, adjustment of the headlamps may be made by turning the adjustment knobs on the rear of the headlamps (photo). The upper knobs 'A' are for vertical adjustment and the lower knobs 'B' for lateral adjustment.

4    The vehicle should be at kerb weight (see *General dimensions, weights and capacities*), with the driver seated, the headlamp alignment knob correctly set (see above) and the tyres correctly inflated. Park the vehicle on level ground, approximately 5 metres (16 feet) in front of a flat wall or garage door and bounce it to settle the suspension.

5    Draw a vertical line on the wall or door corresponding to the centre-line of the vehicle. (This can be determined by marking the centres of the windscreen and tailgate glass with crayon, then viewing the wall or door from the rear of the vehicle).

6    With the centre-line established, construct the other lines shown in Fig. 11.7.

7    Switch the headlamps on to dipped beam. Cover one headlamp with cloth and use the two adjustment knobs to bring the centre of the other beam to the point 'C' on the appropriate side of the alignment chart.

8    Transfer the cloth to the adjusted headlamp and repeat the adjustment on the other.

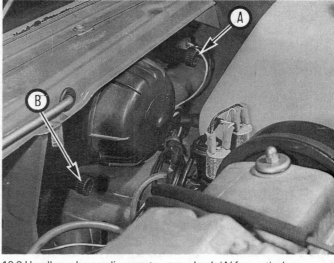

19.3 Headlamp beam alignment – upper knob 'A' for vertical adjustment and lower knob 'B' for lateral adjustment

9    While this will produce an acceptable setting, it is important to have accurate adjustments made at the earliest opportunity.

## 20  Headlamp alignment control system – general

1    The headlamp beam alignment may be adjusted to compensate for the load being carried by turning a knob on the facia.

2    The system is hydraulically-operated, using a special antifreezing solution and comprises the facia-mounted control unit, an actuator fitted to each headlamp unit and a pipe connecting each actuator with the control unit.

3    Note that the system is available only as a complete assembly. None of the component parts can be renewed separately.

4    The system can be checked by unclipping both actuators (see below) and comparing their range of movement. Each operating rod's projection should alter through a range of $7.0 \pm 0.5$ mm as the control knob is rotated. If either actuator's movement is incorrect, or if they do not work together as a pair, the system is faulty and must be renewed. Similarly, if signs of fluid leaks appear on any part of the system, it must be renewed.

5    To remove the system, unclip each actuator from the rear of the headlamp unit by pressing in its retaining tab and pulling it sharply to release the balljoint (photo), taking care not to damage the connecting pipe.

6    Releasing them from any clamps or ties, trace the pipes back to the bulkhead, press in the large sealing grommet and carefully pull the pipes and actuators into the passenger compartment.

7    Pull off the control knob (photo) and unscrew the retaining nut, then

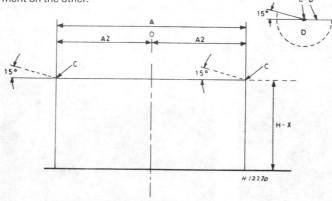

**Fig. 11.7 Headlamp beam alignment chart (Sec 19)**

A    *Distance between headlamp centres*
B    *Light/dark boundary*
C    *Dipped beam centre*
D    *Dipped beam pattern*

H    *Height from ground to headlamp centre*
O    *Vehicle's centre-line*
X  =  *65 mm (2.5 in)*

20.5 Removing headlamp alignment control system actuator

20.7 Pull off control knob and unscrew retaining nut to release control unit from facia

remove the unit from behind the facia. Withdraw the system.
8    Refitting is the reverse of the removal procedure.

## 21    Interior lamp units – removal and refitting

### Courtesy lamp
1    Remove the lamp bulb (Sec 17).
2    Unscrew the retaining screws and withdraw the lamp.
3    Refitting is the reverse of the removal procedure.

### Under-bonnet lamp
4    Remove the single retaining screw, disconnect the lamp's wiring and withdraw it (photo).
5    Refitting is the reverse of the removal procedure.

## 22    Instrument panel – removal and refitting

1    Disconnect the battery negative lead.
2    Disconnect the speedometer drive cable (Sec 24).
3    Disconnect the econometer hose from the inlet manifold (photo).
4    Unscrew its retaining knurled nut and disconnect the trip counter reset knob from the facia (photo). Ensure that the cable is free, behind the facia.
5    The instrument panel hood is secured by two clips at its upper corners (photo) and by two locating tabs at the lower corners.
6    Unscrew the two screws, one securing each clip at the hood's upper

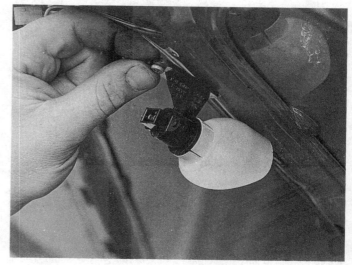

21.4 Under-bonnet lamp is secured by a single screw

corner, so that the hood could be withdrawn leaving the clips in place. The clips can then be removed without risk of damage (photos).
7    Squeezing together the two retaining tabs to release it (photo), withdraw the instrument panel while an assistant pushes the speedometer drive cable and econometer hose back through the bulkhead

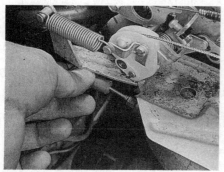

22.3 Disconnecting econometer hose from inlet manifold

22.4 Trip counter reset knob is secured by a knurled nut

22.5 Instrument panel hood top securing clips (arrowed)

22.6A Remove retaining screws and withdraw hood ...

22.6B ... leaving clips in place ...

22.6C ... to be withdrawn without risk of damage

22.7 Squeeze together retaining tabs to release instrument panel

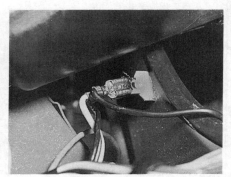

22.8 Note instrument panel earth connection on steering column support bracket

grommets. As soon as sufficient space is gained, disconnect the cable, the hose and the two wiring connector plugs, then remove the panel.

8    Note the earth connection for the panel wiring on the steering column support bracket, behind the panel right-hand end (photo), and ensure that it is cleaned back to bare metal.

9    Refitting is the reverse of the removal procedure, noting the following points.

10    When the wiring, econometer hose and speedometer drive cable are connected to the panel, grease the cable (Sec 24) and gently pull the hose and cable forwards through the bulkhead so that they do not foul

any other component or form kinks. Press the panel into place until its retaining tabs lock, then check that the econometer hose is still connected and that the econometer registers correctly when suction is applied to the hose end.

11    When refitting the hood, either secure the clips to the hood and refit the assembly, or fit the clips to the facia, engage the hood on them and then refit the screws.

12    Ensure that the trip counter reset cable is correctly routed, with no kinks.

23.2 Unplugging handbrake warning lamp circuit breaker from rear of instrument panel

## 23  Instrument panel components – testing

1    The instrument panel assembly is available only as a single unit.

2    The handbrake warning lamp circuit breaker (photo) can be unplugged from the rear of the panel. It must be renewed if the handbrake warning lamp ceases to flash.

3    If checking a warning lamp failure, note that the 'STOP' lamp operates on the handbrake, brake fluid level and low oil pressure lamps.

4    Refer to Chapter 2, Section 11 for details of tests of the coolant temperature gauge circuit.

5    Refer to Chapter 3, Section 9 for details of tests of the fuel gauge and fuel reserve warning lamp circuits.

6    If the voltmeter reading is suspect, compare it with the results of a charging system check (Sec 8). If the meter is faulty, the panel must be renewed.

7    If the econometer is faulty, first check the hose for damage such as cracks or splits or for kinks and blockages. If the hose appears to be sound, suck on its inlet manifold end and have an assistant note whether the gauge needle moves or not. If there is no movement, or if the needle's action is undamped, the gauge is faulty and the instrument panel must be renewed.

24.1 Unscrew knurled retaining ring (arrowed) to withdraw speedometer drive cable from transmission

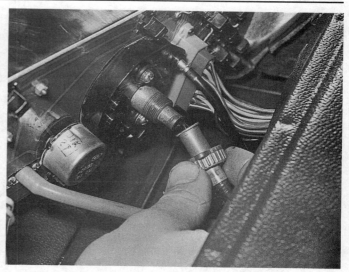

24.2 Disconnecting speedometer drive cable from instrument panel

## 24 Speedometer drive cable – removal and refitting

1   Unscrew the knurled retaining ring and withdraw the drive cable from the transmission (photo).
2   Remove the instrument panel (Sec 22) and unscrew the knurled retaining ring which secures the drive cable to the panel (photo).
3   Press the sealing grommet out of the bulkhead and pull the cable into the engine compartment. If faulty, it must be renewed as an assembly.
4   On refitting, smear grease over the cable outer around the grommet location and work the grommet up and down the cable to ensure that it slides easily, then route the cable as straight as possible between the bulkhead aperture and the instrument panel, through the steering column support bracket.
5   Connect the cable to the instrument panel and refit the panel (Sec 22).
6   Press the grommet into the bulkhead aperture, route the cable in a smooth loop over the brake pipes and clear of the steering gear and exhaust system, then connect it to the transmission.

## 25 Cigarette lighter – removal and refitting

1   Disconnect the battery negative lead.
2   The lighter assembly is secured by clips (see photo 17.15). If they cannot be released from the ashtray aperture, the facia centre console must be removed (Chapter 10, Section 34, paragraphs 1 to 3) so that the assembly can be unclipped.
3   Refitting is the reverse of the removal procedure.

## 26 Horn – removal and refitting

1   Disconnect the battery negative lead.
2   Remove the radiator grille (Chapter 10).
3   Unbolt the horn from the bracket and disconnect the earth wire, then remove the horn (photo).
4   Refitting is the reverse of the removal procedure. Check for satisfactory horn operation before refitting the grille.

## 27 Heater fan – general

1   The heating and ventilating system's fan motor is controlled by a switch mounted in the heater control panel assembly. The fan and its motor are mounted in the engine compartment, in the centre of the heater fresh air intake chamber.
2   The fan motor is regulated to any one of three speeds by switching in elements of a resistor unit which is mounted in the left-hand side of the heater itself.
3   Refer to the relevant Sections of Chapter 10 for details of removal and refitting of all of the above components.

## 28 Heated tailgate glass – general

1   The tailgate glass is heated by passing current through a resistive grid bonded to the inside of the glass.

26.3 Location of horn behind radiator grille

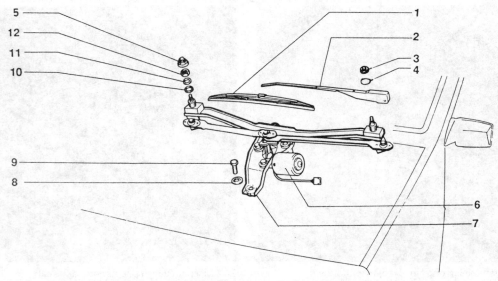

**Fig. 11.8 Windscreen wiper motor and linkage (Secs 29 and 30)**

| | | | |
|---|---|---|---|
| 1 | Wiper blade | 4 | Washer |
| 2 | Wiper arm | 5 | Rubber cover |
| 3 | Nut | 6 | Wiper motor |

| | | | |
|---|---|---|---|
| 7 | Wiper linkage | 10 | Seal |
| 8 | Washer | 11 | Washer |
| 9 | Bolt | 12 | Spindle housing nut |

2    The heater elements are fragile and so the following precautions should be observed.

   (a)  *Do not allow luggage or other items to rub against the inside surface of the glass*

   (b)  *Do not stick labels over the elements*

   (c)  *If you wear a ring, avoid scratching the elements when cleaning the glass*

   (d)  *Clean the glass with water and detergent only and rub in the direction of the elements using a soft cloth or chamois*

3    Should an element be damaged so that the current is interrupted, a repair can be made using one of the conductive paints available from motor accessory shops.

4    Note that the system draws a very high current and therefore has its own relay. It is protected by two fuses.

2    Swivel the blade through 90°, press the locking tab with the finger nail and slide the plastic block and blade out of the hooked end of the wiper arm.

3    Before removing a wiper arm, stick a piece of masking tape on the glass, along the blade. This will facilitate alignment of the arm when refitting.

4    To remove a windscreen wiper arm, pull the arm fully away from the glass until it locks.

5    To remove the tailgate glass wiper arm, flip up the cover.

6    Unscrew the nut and pull the arm from the splined drive spindle (photos). If necessary use a large screwdriver blade to prise off the arm.

7    Refitting of both blade and arm is the reverse of the removal procedure, but do not overtighten the arm retaining nut.

## 29   Wiper blades and arms – removal and refitting

1    To remove a wiper blade, pull the arm fully away from the glass until it locks.

## 30   Windscreen wiper motor and linkage – removal and refitting

1    Disconnect the battery negative lead.

2    Remove the wiper arms and blades (Sec 29).

29.6A To remove windscreen wiper blade and arm, unscrew nut ...

29.6B ... and pull arm from spindle

30.6 Windscreen wiper linkage is secured by spindle housing nut under rubber cover ...

3    Remove the fuse and relay unit cover and pull out the relays.
4    Remove the heater fan motor (Chapter 10).
5    Disconnect the windscreen wiper motor wiring.
6    Remove the rubber covers and unscrew the spindle housing nuts, then remove each washer and seal, noting their locations (photo).
7    Unscrew the bolt securing the motor to the bulkhead (photo), then remove the assembly.
8    The motor can be unbolted from the linkage and renewed separately. If either is worn or damaged in any way it must be renewed.
9    Note the wiper motor earth connection on its mounting bolt, and ensure that this is cleaned back to bare metal.
10    Refitting is the reverse of the removal procedure.
11    Note that if the wiper motor stops working, check that the thermal

30.7 ... and wiper motor mounting bolt (arrowed) – note earth connection

cut-out contacts (located on the motor mounting bracket) are properly closed before assuming that the motor or its wiring are faulty.

## 31    Tailgate glass wiper motor – removal and refitting

1    Remove the tailgate interior trim panel (Chapter 10).
2    Disconnect the battery negative lead.
3    Remove the wiper arm and blade (Sec 29).
4    Remove the rubber cover and unscrew the spindle housing nut, then remove each washer and seal, noting their locations.
5    Unbolt the motor and its mounting bracket (photo), then manoeuvre the motor out of the tailgate.

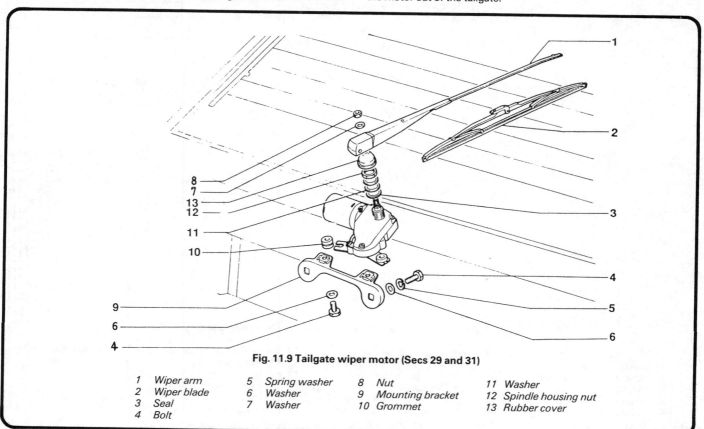

**Fig. 11.9 Tailgate wiper motor (Secs 29 and 31)**

| | | | | | |
|---|---|---|---|---|---|
| 1 | Wiper arm | 5 | Spring washer | 8 | Nut |
| 2 | Wiper blade | 6 | Washer | 9 | Mounting bracket |
| 3 | Seal | 7 | Washer | 10 | Grommet |
| 4 | Bolt | | | | |

| | |
|---|---|
| 11 | Washer |
| 12 | Spindle housing nut |
| 13 | Rubber cover |

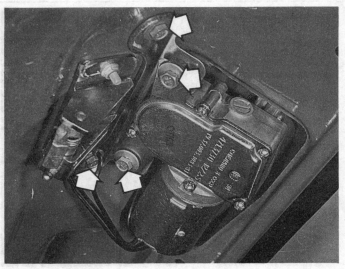

31.5 Tailgate glass wiper motor and mounting bracket bolts (arrowed)

6    Note the wiper motor earth connection on the mounting bolt, and ensure that this is cleaned back to bare metal.
7    Refitting is the reverse of the removal procedure.

## 32  Windscreen and tailgate glass washer system – removal, refitting and adjustment

1    Refer to Section 3 of this Chapter for details of maintenance requirements.
2    The system comprises the reservoir, a pump (mounted between the radiator and the right-hand headlamp unit) and two solenoid valves to direct flow either to the windscreen or to the tailgate glass, as required (photos).
3    The removal and refitting of all components is self-explanatory on examination. Make notes of the wiring connections so that all wires can be correctly refitted.

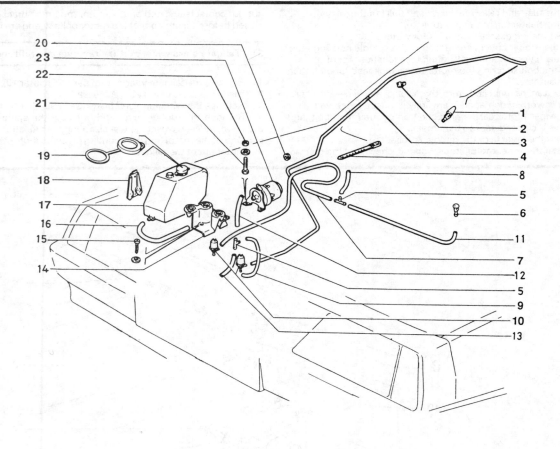

**Fig. 11.10 Windscreen and tailgate glass washer system components (Sec 32)**

| | | | | | |
|---|---|---|---|---|---|
| 1 | Tailgate washer jet | 7 | Windscreen washer tubing | 13 | Tube – T-piece to solenoid valve |
| 2 | Clamp | 8 | Tube – T-piece to washer jet | 14 | Mounting bracket |
| 3 | Tailgate washer tubing | 9 | Tube – T-piece to solenoid valve | 15 | Screw |
| 4 | Tie | 10 | Solenoid valve | 16 | Tube – reservoir to pump |
| 5 | T-piece | 11 | Tube – T-piece to washer jet | 17 | Reservoir |
| 6 | Windscreen washer jet – 2 off | 12 | Tube – pump to T-piece | 18 | Mounting bracket |

| | |
|---|---|
| 19 | Reservoir cap |
| 20 | Grommet |
| 21 | Bolt |
| 22 | Nut |
| 23 | Pump |

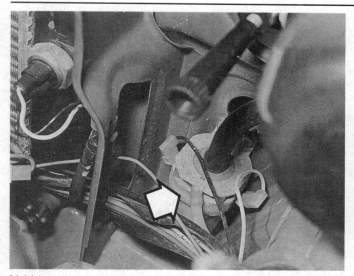

32.2A Location of windscreen and tailgate glass washer system pump (arrowed)

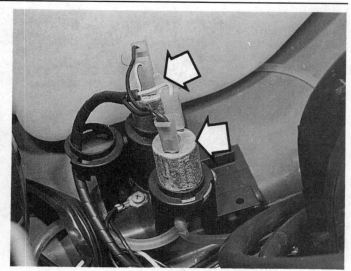

32.2B ... and solenoid valves (arrowed)

## 33  Radio/cassette player – removal and refitting

1  Actual removal and refitting procedures will vary according to the type of radio fitted, but the following is a reasonably representative procedure.
2  Two standard DIN extraction tools are required to unlock and remove the radio. The tools may possibly be obtained from a Lada dealer or any radio accessory outlet, or can be made out of 3 mm wire rod such as welding rod (photo).
3  Using the tools, push back the clamps on the left and right-hand sides.
4  Withdraw the radio and disconnect all the wiring plugs and aerial (photos).
5  Refitting is the reverse of the removal procedure.

## 34  Loudspeakers – removal and refitting

1  The front loudspeakers are mounted in the door interior trim panel (photo). Remove the trim panel (Chapter 10) if required to disconnect the wiring, then remove the retaining screws.
2  The rear loudspeakers (where fitted) are mounted in the luggage compartment parcel shelf side panels (photo). Prise up the speaker grille and remove the retaining screws to release the unit, then disconnect its wiring.
3  Refitting is the reverse of the removal procedure.

## 35  Radio aerial – removal and refitting

1  From the roof-mounted aerial, the aerial lead runs across to the left-hand 'A' (windscreen) pillar, down the pillar and under the facia to the radio unit.
2  If the aerial mounting screw(s) cannot be reached by prising out a small plug from the aerial base, the roof headlining must be unclipped at the front edge and peeled back until the aerial mountings can be reached.
3  Remove the radio (Sec 33), and disconnect the aerial lead.
4  To avoid having to remove the facia and 'A' pillar trim panel (Chapter 10), tie a long length of string to the aerial lead end, then pull the lead up through the bodywork. Untie the string when the end of the lead appears.
5  Refitting is the reverse of the removal procedure. Use the string to draw the lead down into place.

## 36  Wiring diagrams – explanatory notes

The wiring diagrams included at the end of this Chapter are of conventional type. While the colour code key has been translated into English and based on UK standards, note that the wire colour-coding itself obviously conforms to USSR standards.
The main diagram refers to a general-specification vehicle. Not all of the components shown will be found on UK models, as noted where possible. The individual circuit diagrams are correct for UK-specification models.

33.2 Using standard DIN extraction tools to remove radio

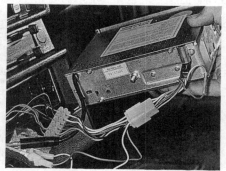

33.4A Disconnect aerial lead and wiring from rear of radio ...

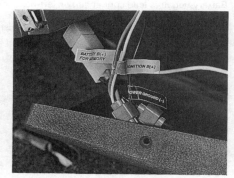

33.4B ... noting how it is connected to vehicle's electrical system

34.1 Front loudspeaker mountings on door interior trim panel

34.2 Rear loudspeaker is covered by a grille

While the numbering of terminals is based on the German DIN standard and should be matched by numbers marked on the components themselves, some markings remain in the original Cyrillic. In these cases, the markings given in the diagrams correspond as closely as possible. All terminal numbers prefixed with 'W' are the multi-plug connectors for the fuse and relay unit.

The wires can be identified by the colour(s) of their plastic insulating cover. For some wires this is one colour, but on many two colours are given. These show first the principal colour and second the colour of the thin spiral tracer. For example, wb would indicate a white wire with a black tracer.

## 37   Fault diagnosis – electrical system

**Note:** *If any fault is encountered in the electrical system, first check all relevant earth connections as detailed below. If this does not reveal the source of the fault, proceed to the main fault diagnosis table which follows*

### Fault diagnosis – earth connections

Many electrical system faults can be traced to poor earth connections. Dim lamps, motors (eg. windscreen wiper motor) running slowly, or apparently unrelated circuits (eg. fuel gauge and instrument panel lamps) affecting each other's operation, are examples. In the event of such a fault, ensure that the relevant earth connection is both clean and tight. If necessary, the suspect earth connection can be tested with a multimeter between the battery's negative terminal and the earth connection concerned. The combined resistance of the earth return should not exceed 0.5 ohms.

The locations of the earth connections on the vehicle are as follows:

| Earth connection | Circuit affected |
| --- | --- |
| Battery negative lead connection on left-hand inner wing panel | All (main earth connection), but especially the starter motor |
| Engine/transmission earth lead (rear of transmission-to-bulkhead) | All circuits, which incorporate sender units, switches or other components mounted on the engine/transmission, but especially the starter motor |
| Right-hand headlamp unit retaining nut | Right-hand headlamp, sidelamp and direction indicator lamp, electric cooling fan thermostatic switch |
| Left-hand headlamp unit retaining nut | Left-hand headlamp, sidelamp, direction indicator lamp, electric cooling fan motor |
| Starter relay mounting nut | Brake fluid level warning lamp |
| Ignition amplifier module mounting nut | Ignition system, diagnostic system, fuel cut-off system |
| Rear lamp cluster retaining nut | All lamp circuits on that side |
| Behind right-hand end of instrument panel | All panel components, second ignition relay (if fitted) |

| Earth connection | Circuit affected |
|---|---|
| Behind left-hand side of instrument panel | Relays located in fuse box |
| Washer system component mounting bracket retaining screw | Washer system |
| Windscreen wiper motor mounting bolt | Windscreen wiper motor |
| Heater left-hand front mounting nut | Heater fan motor |
| Tailgate frame | Heated tailgate glass |
| Tailgate lock mounting nut and/or tailgate wiper motor mounting bracket bolts | Tailgate wiper motor, number plate lamps |
| Tailgate left-hand hinge | All tailgate components |

## Fault diagnosis – electrical system

| Symptom | Reason(s) |
|---|---|
| Starter fails to turn engine | Battery discharged<br>Battery leads loose<br>Battery defective internally<br>Loose wiring connections at starter motor<br>Engine/transmission earth lead loose, broken or missing<br>Starter motor faulty or solenoid not functioning<br>Starter motor brushes worn<br>Starter motor armature faulty<br>Commutator dirty or worn<br>Field coils earthed<br>Auxiliary (bulkhead) relay not functioning |
| Starter turns engine very slowly | Battery discharged<br>Starter brushes badly worn, sticking<br>Loose wires in starter motor circuit or brush wires loose |
| Starter spins but does not turn engine | Pinion or flywheel gear teeth broken or worn<br>One-way clutch in pinion faulty |
| Starter motor noisy or excessively rough engagement | Pinion or flywheel gear teeth broken or worn<br>Starter motor retaining bolts loose |
| Battery will not hold charge for more than a few days electrolyte | Battery defective internally<br>Electrolyte level too low or too weak due to leakage<br>Alternator drivebelt slipping<br>Battery terminal connections loose or corroded<br>Alternator not charging<br>Short-circuit causing continual battery drain<br>Faulty voltage regulator |
| Charging warning lamp fails to go out, battery loses charge in a few days | Alternator drivebelt loose, slipping or broken<br>Alternator brushes worn, sticking, broken or dirty<br>Alternator brush springs weak or broken<br>Alternator defective internally |
| Charge warning lamp fails to light | Bulb blown<br>Fuse blown<br>Warning lamp open circuit<br>Alternator or voltage regulator faulty |

**Failure of individual electrical equipment to function correctly is dealt with under the headings listed below**

**Horn**

| Horn operates all the time | Horn push either earthed or stuck down<br>Horn cable to horn push earthed |
|---|---|
| Horn fails to operate | Blown fuse<br>Cable or connection loose, broken or disconnected<br>Horn defective internally |
| Horn emits intermittent or unsatisfactory noise | Cable connection loose |

| Symptom | Reason(s) |
| --- | --- |
| **Lamps** | |
| Lamps do not come on | Blown bulb |
| | Blown fuse |
| | If engine not running, battery discharged |
| | Wire connections loose, disconnected or broken |
| | Lamp switch shorting or otherwise faulty |
| Lamps give poor illumination | Lamp glasses dirty |
| | Lamps badly out of adjustment |
| Lamps work erratically, flashing on and off, especially over bumps | Battery or lamp connection loose |
| | Lamps not earthing properly |
| | Contacts in lamp switch faulty |
| **Wipers** | |
| Wiper motor fails to work | Blown fuse |
| | Wire connections loose, disconnected or broken |
| | Relay faulty |
| | Earth return faulty |
| | Brushes badly worn |
| | Armature worn or faulty |
| | Field coils faulty |
| Wiper motor works very slowly and takes excessive current | Commutator dirty, greasy or burnt |
| | Armature badly worn or faulty |
| | Armature bearings dirty or misaligned |
| Wiper motor works slowly and takes little current | Brushes badly worn |
| | Commutator dirty, greasy or burnt |
| | Armature badly worn or faulty |
| Wiper motor works but wiper blades remain static | Wiper motor gearbox parts badly worn |
| **Instruments** | |
| Fuel or temperature gauge gives no reading | Wiring open circuit |
| | Faulty sender unit |
| | Faulty gauge |
| Fuel or temperature gauge gives maximum reading all the time | Wiring short-circuit |
| | Faulty gauge |

**Note:** *This Section is not intended to be an exhaustive guide to fault diagnosis but summarises the more common faults which may be encountered during a vehicle's life. Consult a dealer for more specific advice.*

**Key to Fig. 11.11 (not all items fitted to all models)**

| No | Description | No | Description |
|---|---|---|---|
| 1 | Headlamp unit | 33 | Choke warning lamp switch |
| 2 | Headlamp wiper motor* | 34 | Heater control panel lamp |
| 3 | Under-bonnet lamp switch | 35 | Cigarette lighter |
| 4 | Horn | 36 | Glovebox lamp* |
| 5 | Electric cooling fan motor | 37 | Heater fan motor |
| 6 | Electric cooling fan thermostatic switch | 38 | Heater fan motor resistor unit |
| 7 | Reversing lamp switch | 39 | Heater fan switch |
| 8 | Coolant temperature gauge sender unit | 40 | Instrument panel illuminating lamp rheostat switch |
| 9 | Starter motor auxiliary relay | 41 | Steering column multi-function switch (direction indicators, sidelamp selector headlamp dipswitch) |
| 10 | Starter motor | | |
| 11 | Battery | 42 | Horn switch |
| 12 | Distributor | 43 | Steering column multi-function switch (windscreen and tailgate glass wash/wipe) |
| 13 | Spark plugs | | |
| 14 | Alternator | 44 | Ignition switch |
| 15 | Headlamp washer solenoid valve* | 45 | Lighting switch |
| 16 | Ignition HT coil | 46 | Hazard warning switch |
| 17 | TDC sensor | 47 | Rear foglamp switch |
| 18 | Fuel cut-off system solenoid valve | 48 | Heated tailgate glass switch |
| 19 | Fuel cut-off system throttle switch | 49 | Direction indicator side repeater |
| 20 | Oil pressure switch | 50 | Handbrake warning lamp switch |
| 21 | Washer system pump | 51 | Courtesy lamp switch (front door) |
| 22 | Windscreen washer solenoid valve | 52 | Courtesy lamp switch (rear door) |
| 23 | Tailgate glass washer solenoid valve | 53 | Instrument panel |
| 24 | Ignition amplifier module | 54 | Courtesy lamp |
| 25 | Brake fluid level warning lamp switch | 55 | Rear lamp cluster |
| 26 | Diagnostic socket | 56 | Fuel gauge sender unit |
| 27 | Fuel cut-off system control module | 57 | Tailgate glass heater element |
| 28 | Windscreen wiper motor | 58 | Number plate lamps |
| 29 | Inspection lamp socket | 59 | Tailgate glass wiper motor |
| 30 | Under-bonnet lamp | A | Connector for brake pad wear indicator transmitter* |
| 31 | Fuse and relay unit | B | Connector for individual courtesy lamp |
| 32 | Stop lamp switch | | *= *Not fitted to UK models* |

**Colour coding for all wiring diagrams**

| Code | Colour |
|---|---|
| w | White |
| u | Blue |
| y | Yellow |
| g | Green |
| n | Brown |
| o | Orange |
| r | Red |
| p | Pink |
| s | Grey |
| v | Violet |
| b | Black |

Fig. 11.11 Main wiring diagram

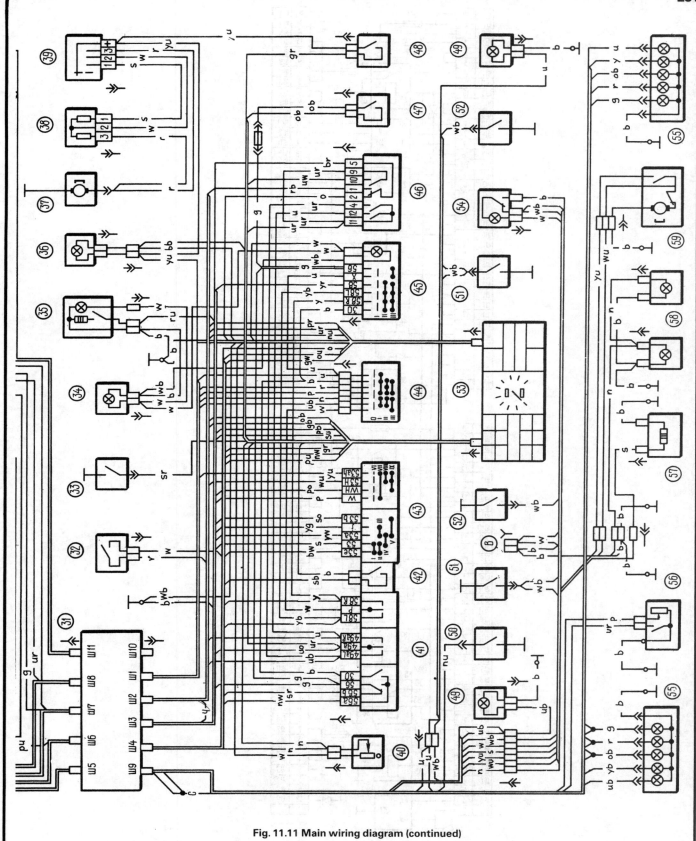

**Fig. 11.11 Main wiring diagram (continued)**

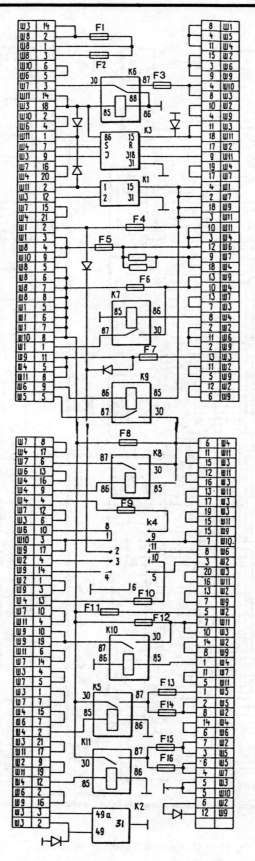

**Fig. 11.12 Fuse and relay unit internal connections**

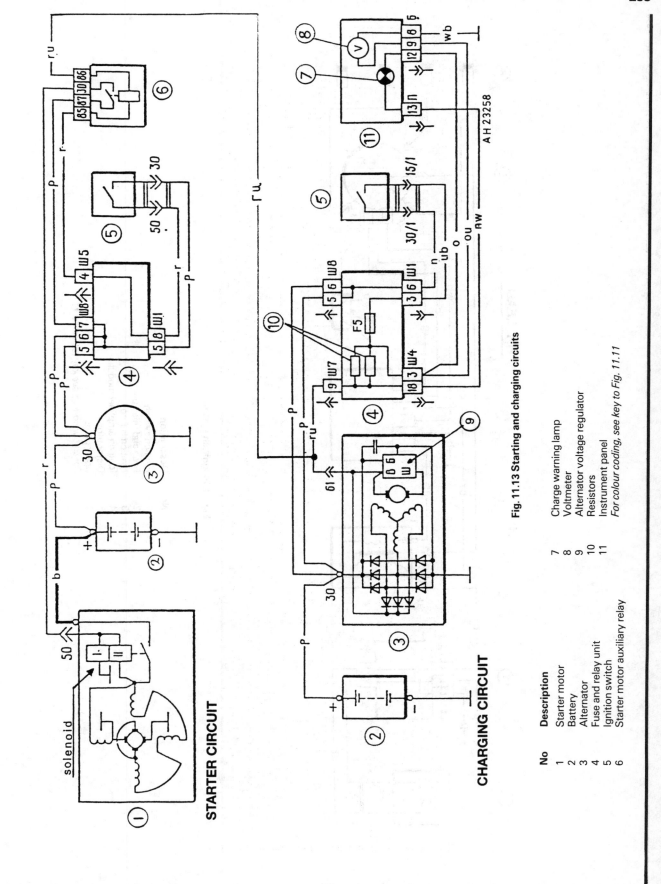

**STARTER CIRCUIT**

**CHARGING CIRCUIT**

**Fig. 11.13 Starting and charging circuits**

| No | Description | | |
|----|-------------|---|---|
| 1 | Starter motor | 7 | Charge warning lamp |
| 2 | Battery | 8 | Voltmeter |
| 3 | Alternator | 9 | Alternator voltage regulator |
| 4 | Fuse and relay unit | 10 | Resistors |
| 5 | Ignition switch | 11 | Instrument panel |
| 6 | Starter motor auxiliary relay | | *For colour coding, see key to Fig. 11.11* |

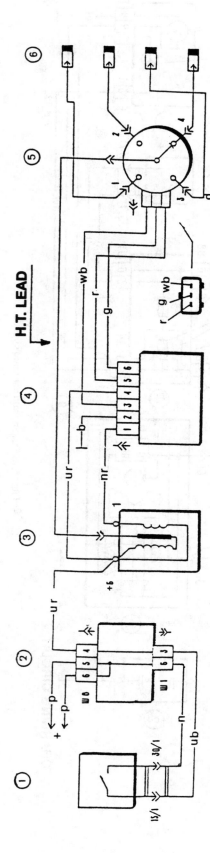

**H.T. LEAD**

**Fig. 11.14 Ignition system**

| No | Description |
|----|-------------|
| 1 | Ignition switch |
| 2 | Fuse and relay unit |
| 3 | Ignition HT coil |
| 4 | Ignition amplifier module |
| 5 | Distributor |
| 6 | Spark plugs |
| | *For colour coding, see key to Fig. 11.11* |

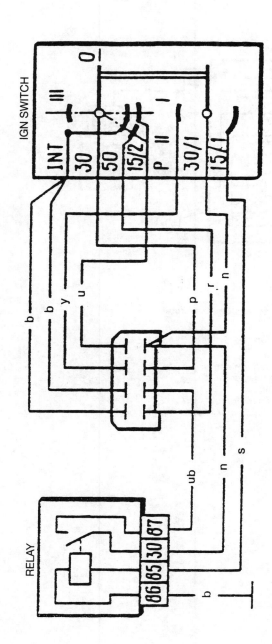

**Fig. 11.15 Ignition switch circuit, showing additional facia-mounted relay fitted to some models**
*For colour coding, see key to Fig. 11.11*

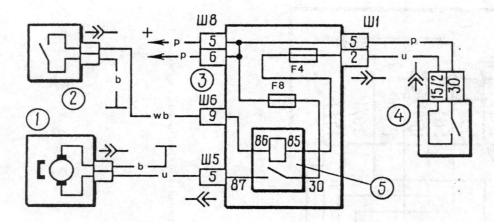

**Fig. 11.16 Electric cooling fan circuit**

| No | Description |
|----|-------------|
| 1 | Fan motor |
| 2 | Thermostatic switch |
| 3 | Fuse and relay unit |
| 4 | Ignition switch |
| 5 | Cooling fan motor relay |
|   | *For colour coding, see key to Fig. 11.11* |

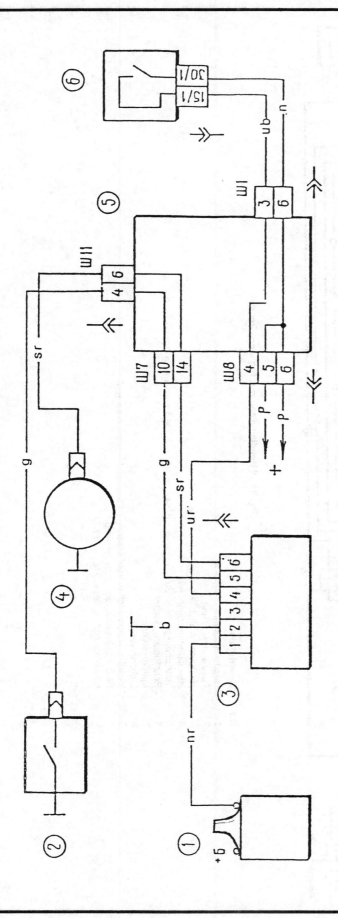

**Fig. 11.17 Fuel cut-off system**

| No | Description |
|----|-------------|
| 1 | Ignition HT coil |
| 2 | Throttle switch |
| 3 | Control module |
| 4 | Solenoid valve |
| 5 | Fuse and relay unit |
| 6 | Ignition switch |

*For colour coding, see key to Fig. 11.11*

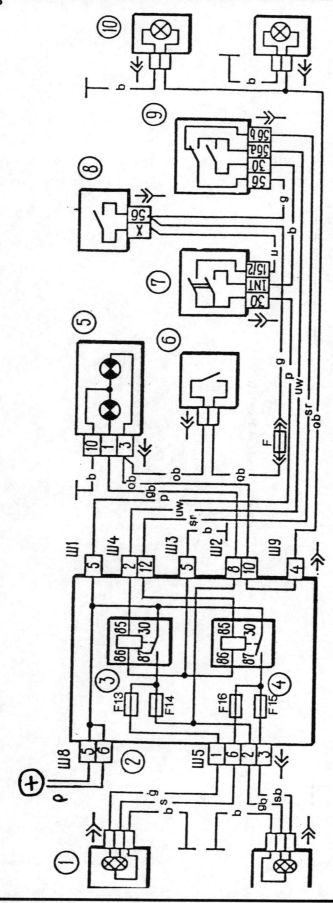

**Fig. 11.18 Headlamp and rear foglamp circuits**

**No   Description**
1     Headlamp units
2     Fuse and relay unit
3     Headlamp main beam relay
4     Headlamp dip beam relay
5     Instrument panel (main beam warning lamp on left, rear foglamp warning lamp on right)
6     Rear foglamp switch
7     Ignition switch
8     Lighting switch
9     Headlamp dipswitch (part of steering column multi-function switch)
10    Rear foglamps (in rear lamp clusters)
      *For colour coding, see key to Fig. 11.11*

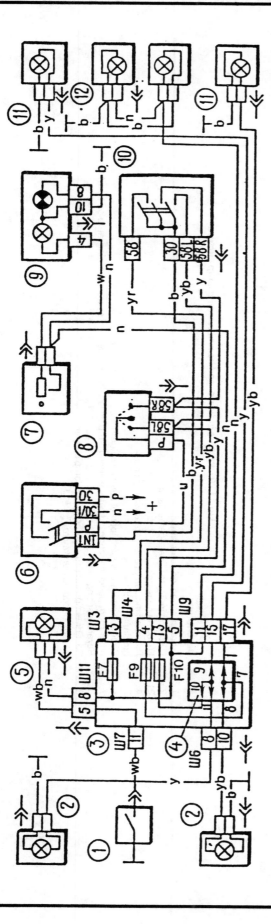

**Fig. 11.19 Sidelamp and tail lamp circuits**

| No | Description |
|----|-------------|
| 1 | Under-bonnet lamp switch |
| 2 | Sidelamp |
| 3 | Fuse and relay unit |
| 4 | K4 relay location (showing bridged terminal sockets) |
| 5 | Under-bonnet lamp |
| 6 | Ignition switch |
| 7 | Instrument panel illuminating lamp rheostat switch |
| 8 | Sidelamp selector (part of steering column multi-function switch) |
| 9 | Instrument panel (panel illuminating lamp on left, sidelamp warning lamp on right) |
| 10 | Lighting switch |
| 11 | Tail lamp (in rear lamp cluster) |
| 12 | Number plate lamp |

*For colour coding, see key to Fig. 11.11*

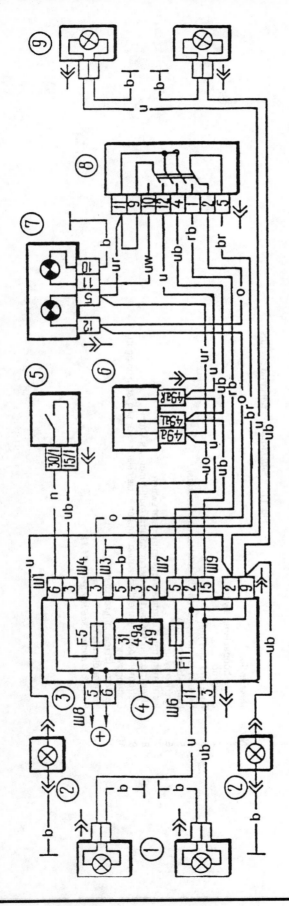

**Fig. 11.20 Direction indicator and hazard warning lamp circuits**

**No    Description**

1    Front direction indicator lamps
2    Direction indicator side repeater lamp
3    Fuse and relay unit
4    Direction indicators and hazard warning relay
5    Ignition switch
6    Direction indicator switch (part of steering column multi-function switch)
7    Instrument panel (direction indicator warning lamp on left, hazard warning system warning lamp on right)
8    Hazard warning switch
9    Rear direction indicator lamps (in rear lamp cluster)
*For colour coding, see key to Fig. 11.11*

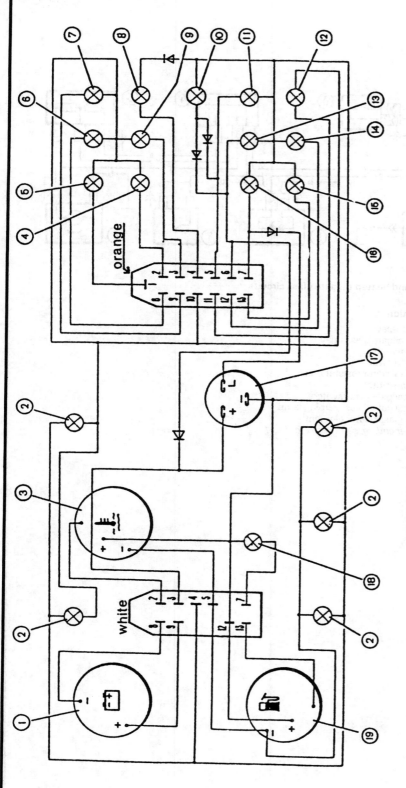

Fig. 11.21 Instrument panel connections (seen from rear of panel)

| No | Description |
|----|-------------|
| 1 | Voltmeter |
| 2 | Panel illuminating lamp |
| 3 | Coolant temperature gauge |
| 4 | Heated tailgate glass warning lamp |
| 5 | Headlamp main beam warning lamp |
| 6 | Rear foglamp warning lamp |
| 7 | Sidelamp warning lamp |
| 8 | Direction indicator warning lamp |
| 9 | Unused |
| 10 | 'STOP' warning lamp |
| 11 | Oil pressure warning lamp |
| 12 | Hazard warning system warning lamp |
| 13 | Brake fluid level warning lamp |
| 14 | Choke warning lamp |
| 15 | Charge warning lamp |
| 16 | Handbrake warning lamp |
| 17 | Handbrake warning lamp circuit breaker socket |
| 18 | Fuel reserve warning lamp |
| 19 | Fuel gauge |

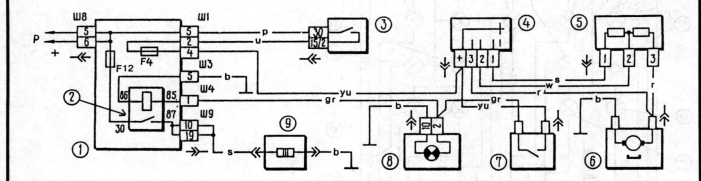

**Fig. 11.22 Heater and heated tailgate glass circuits**

| No | Description |
|----|-------------|
| 1 | Fuse and relay unit |
| 2 | Heated tailgate glass relay |
| 3 | Ignition switch |
| 4 | Heater fan switch |
| 5 | Heater fan motor resistor unit |
| 6 | Heater fan motor |
| 7 | Heated tailgate glass switch |
| 8 | Heated tailgate glass warning lamp |
| 9 | Tailgate glass heater element |

*For colour coding, see key to Fig. 11.11*

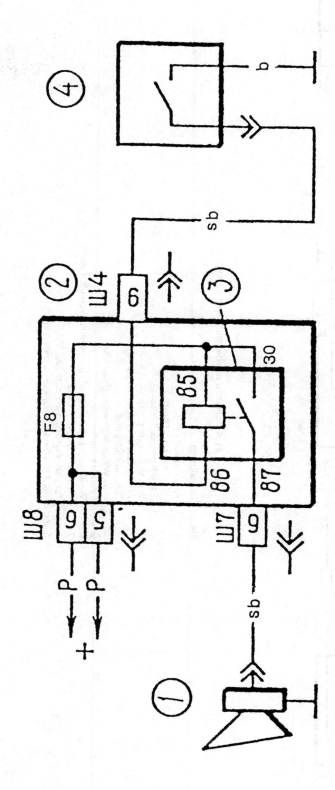

**Fig. 11.23 Horn circuit**

| No | Description |
|----|-------------|
| 1 | Horn |
| 2 | Fuse and relay unit |
| 3 | Horn relay |
| 4 | Horn switch |

*For colour coding, see key to Fig. 11.11*

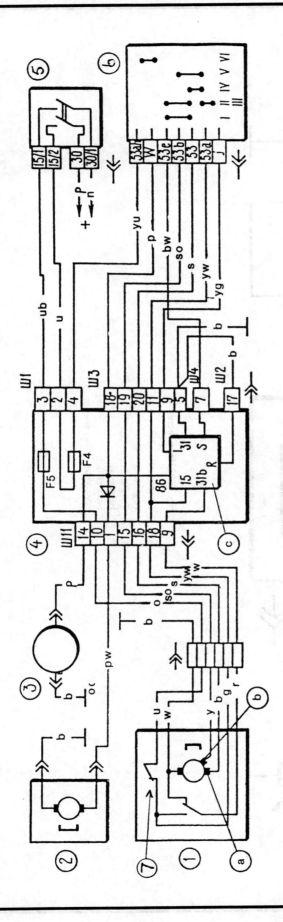

**Fig. 11.24 Windscreen washer and wiper circuits**

| No | Description |
|----|-------------|
| 1 | Wiper motor |
|   | (a) Low-speed brush |
|   | (b) High-speed brush |
| 2 | Washer system pump |
| 3 | Windscreen washer solenoid valve |
| 4 | Fuse and relay unit |
|   | (c) Windscreen wiper delay relay |
| 5 | Ignition switch |
| 6 | Wash/wipe switch (part of steering column multi-function switch) |
| 7 | Thermal cut-out contacts |

*For colour coding, see key to Fig. 11.11*

**Note:** *Items 2 and 6 are the same units shown in Fig. 11.25*

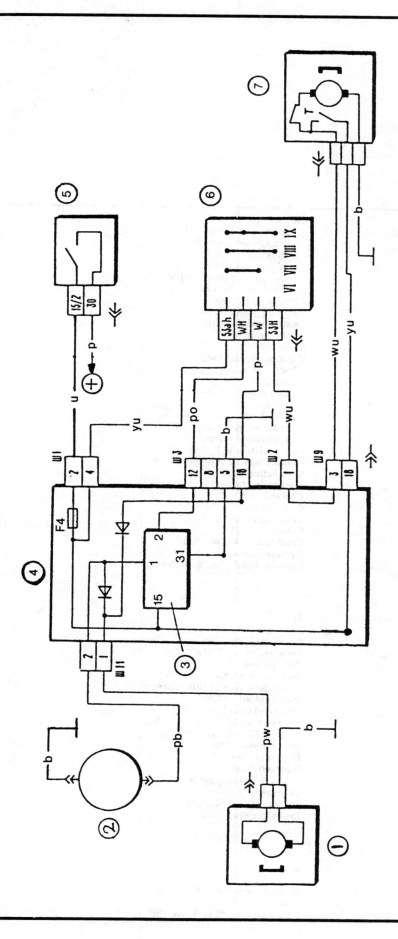

**Fig. 11.25 Tailgate glass washer and wiper circuits**

**No    Description**

1      Washer system pump
2      Tailgate glass washer solenoid valve
3      Tailgate washer timer relay
4      Fuse and relay unit
5      Ignition switch
6      Wash/wipe switch (part of steering column multi-function switch)
7      Wiper motor

For colour coding, see key to Fig. 11.11

**Note:** Items 1 and 6 are the same units shown in Fig. 11.24

# Index